Get the eBook FREE!

(PDF, ePub, Kindle, and liveBook all included)

We believe that once you buy a book from us, you should be able to read it in any format we have available. To get electronic versions of this book at no additional cost to you, purchase and then register this book at the Manning website.

Go to https://www.manning.com/freebook and follow the instructions to complete your pBook registration.

That's it!
Thanks from Manning!

Effective Data Analysis

HARD AND SOFT SKILLS TO
ACCELERATE YOUR CAREER

MONA KHALIL
FOREWORD BY BARRY MCCARDEL

MANNING
SHELTER ISLAND

For online information and ordering of this and other Manning books, please visit
www.manning.com. The publisher offers discounts on this book when ordered in quantity.
For more information, please contact

> Special Sales Department
> Manning Publications Co.
> 20 Baldwin Road
> PO Box 761
> Shelter Island, NY 11964
> Email: orders@manning.com

Manning Publications Co.	Development editor: Elesha Hyde
20 Baldwin Road	Technical editor: Ryan Folks
PO Box 761	Review editor: Radmila Ercegovac
Shelter Island, NY 11964	Production editor: Andy Marinkovich
	Copy editor: Andy Carroll
	Proofreader: Mike Beady
	Technical proofreader: Andrew Freed
	Typesetter and cover designer: Marija Tudor

ISBN 9781633438415
Printed in the United States of America

To my mother, who encouraged and inspired all of my ambitions.
Thank you for listening.
Andrea Khalil, 1958–2023

brief contents

contents

foreword

Early in my career, I was conducting a complex analysis as part of a consulting project. I spent weeks collecting and cleaning data and putting together a model that pointed to a clear recommendation. (True confession: if you were confused as to the seemingly random pricing of Wi-Fi on a major US airline in the early 2010s, I was partly to blame.)

As I walked my manager through it, however, his feedback was somewhat unexpected: he thought I did a great job on my analysis, but he wanted me to change my methodology, explaining that another angle would "better fit the story the client wants to hear."

What?! As a data analyst, I saw my job as a seeker of objective truth, out to understand the world through exacting measurement. Changing my approach because it fits a *story* someone *wanted* to hear felt . . . weird. But looking back, I'm not sure it was *wrong.* The alternative approach was completely valid—it's not like we were faking data. And just because it was what the client wanted to hear didn't make it inaccurate; it was just another way to look at the world.

Reading through this new book by Mona Khalil, I found myself reflecting on lessons from a career in data and finding a new appreciation for the science—and art!—of effective data analysis. I believe practitioners of any experience and technicality can benefit from this book and avoid common pitfalls so they can make new, unique mistakes of their own.

Situations like the one I described are incredibly common in the world of data analysis. There's rarely a straightforward "right" answer to the complex questions that arise in organizations. One often finds situations with incomplete data, varying assumptions, and unclear conclusions. Fusing objective measurement with subjective interpretation and thoughtful communication is a much larger part of the role of a data practitioner than most give credit for, and this took me years to fully understand.

That learning curve would have come much faster if I had access to this wonderful book. That's not just because it's full of helpful technical pointers, methodologies, and exercises (which it certainly is) but rather because it does such an effective job of breaking down *how to think* about the craft of data analysis, in all its nuance.

Mona takes the time to unpack topics like defining metrics and the theory of measurement. She breaks down how to think about results that don't support a hypothesis, and how to present findings to stakeholders (including how to debug the kind of situation I found myself in so many years ago).

This toolkit is especially important as we enter the exciting and exotic world of AI. It turns out that LLMs can write code pretty well; I certainly wouldn't recommend aspiring analysts to spend a lot of time memorizing arcane syntax, but I *would* encourage them to study how to properly interpret, contextualize, and communicate results—the kind of things that a model may never come to do as well as a human.

As a final note, I'll add that Mona shares the one lesson that *every* aspiring data scientist needs to learn: "simpler" is often "better."

—BARRY MCCARDEL, CEO, HEX TECHNOLOGIES

preface

I started my data analytics career in 2016 after leaving a PhD program in psychology. In my first role, I was the sole data analyst at a school, responsible for helping the administration make informed decisions and allocate resources effectively. I had to set my own priorities, identify high-value projects, and learn how to communicate effectively with various stakeholders. Needless to say, my work involved a lot of trial and error to align with the rest of the organization. To grow my career, I had to actively seek guidance outside of the workplace and learn many lessons on my own.

Among data professionals, I hear of similar experiences time and time again. We enter the workforce with a set of technical skills (e.g., statistics, programming) but struggle to apply them to complex real-world scenarios, such as managing stakeholders and prioritizing work on our own. We often report to managers who don't have data analytics experience, have few peers to collaborate with, and spend a large chunk of our time with data literacy education and advocating for the resources we need to perform our jobs effectively. It's not easy.

I wrote this book as a resource for early- to mid-career analysts. It's written with the type of guidance that a mentor might provide, structured in a way that I (and many colleagues I spoke to) would have considered a valuable reference in their day-to-day work. The world of data analytics can be overwhelming, and it can often seem like we need to figure things out on our own. This book is designed to go beyond the current resources on data analytics (e.g., Python, SQL, statistics) and guide you through the real-world application of these skills. It's intended to provide clear, actionable advice regardless of your industry or focus.

In today's world where organizations are inundated with data, the need for skilled analysts who can distill meaning from this data has never been greater. By mastering the comprehensive range of hard and soft skills covered in this book, you will be well-equipped to choose the right approach to solve complex problems, communicate your findings, and drive strategic decisions that add real value to your organization.

Writing this book has been an incredible journey. I had the opportunity to reflect on my career, learn from my past experiences, and reaffirm my belief in the value of learning and sharing knowledge. I hope this book inspires you to take your career to the next level, ask questions of your data, and become a leader at your organization who leaves a positive impact in their wake.

To the readers of this book, I wish you the best on your learning journey. While we're in a dynamic and ever-changing field, the core of our work remains the same. Ask questions, take on new challenges, and never stop learning. Remember that our goal is not just to *analyze* data, but to drive meaningful change and improvements with our analyses. Thank you for choosing this book as part of your learning journey. I hope it serves to empower you with knowledge and confidence in your career.

acknowledgments

I started writing this book at a crossroads in my life. I saw the opportunity to dive into a topic dear to my heart, hone my craft, and connect with so many professionals leveraging data in their day-to-day lives. There are so many people that I would like to thank for their support and contributions to this work.

First, I want to thank my dear friend Keshia, who spent countless hours with me on virtual writing sessions. I always appreciate how willing you were to set aside time to listen, share ideas, or simply work together on our respective goals. Thank you for being an amazing, supportive presence in my life.

Next, I'd like to thank my partner Srdjan. You've been my greatest advocate throughout the writing process. Thank you for watching our dogs so I can get work done, for setting aside time to write together, and for every ounce of encouragement you've given me during this process. I look forward to you completing your book as well!

Additionally, I want to extend all of my gratitude to my editor at Manning, Elesha. Thank you so much for working with me on this book. I deeply appreciate your guidance, your feedback, and your patience with each chapter, ensuring I covered each topic in an engaging and accessible manner. The final version of *Effective Data Analysis* is *so* much better thanks to your invaluable contributions.

A big thank you to my technical editor, Ryan Folks, whose feedback taught me so much. Ryan's experience as a data scientist specializing in healthcare analytics within the Department of Anesthesiology at the University of Virginia made him the perfect sounding board during the writing process. Thanks also to Jason Richter, for making sure all of the book's code was accurate and accessible to readers; Andrew Freed, for making sure every line of code ran perfectly and every detail was on point; and

Michael Stephens at Manning, who believed in me when I pitched a completely different topic for a book than we initially discussed. You're all incredible.

Finally, I want to thank everyone who took the time to review this book: to Alain Couniot, Andrej Abramušić, Ben McNamara, Cairo Cananéa, Carlos Pavia, David Shafer, Diogines Goldoni, Ed Lo, Helen Mary Labao-Barrameda, John Williams, Kristina Kasanicova, Laud Bentil, Maria Ana, Marlin Keys, Martin Czygan, Matthew Copple, Mattia Zoccarato, Murugan Lakshmanan, Nijil Chandran, Richard Vaughan, Sri Ram Macharla, Stefano Ongarello, Tony Dubitsky, Xiangbo Mao, Walter Alexander Mata López, Weronika Burman, and Werner Nindl, your suggestions helped make this a better book.

about this book

Effective Data Analysis was written to help you strategically apply the skills you've learned to the business problems you encounter in your work. It's designed to help you go beyond the technical and programming components of your work and understand the depth and value you can bring to the teams you collaborate with. This book can help you succeed in job interviews and become familiar with the day-to-day job of an analyst, and you can keep it on your desk as an ongoing reference throughout your career.

Who should read this book?

This book is primarily written for aspiring and early- or mid-career data professionals in analytics or data science and analytics engineers who answer questions for stakeholders and inform business decisions. We enter the field from a wide variety of backgrounds, giving each of us different strengths and opportunities to grow. There are many resources available on the specific technical aspects of our field (SQL, Python, R, statistics, machine learning), but few resources cover the skills you need to be a strategic partner to your colleagues. This book brings together the depth and nuance you'll need to know *how* and *where* to apply your skills to problems, creating a clear and efficient path to delivering value in your work.

How this book is organized: A roadmap

This book has 12 chapters organized into 3 parts.

Part 1 orients your analytical thinking around asking and answering powerful questions:

- Chapter 1 covers the areas of focus and specialization in analytics, as well as common tasks and responsibilities associated with each.

- Chapter 2 covers the process of crafting an analytical question, testing it, creating appropriate deliverables, and ensuring your work can be reproduced by other data professionals.
- Chapter 3 covers the construction of a hypothesis based on an analytical question and the process of gathering information and designing a research and analytical framework based on the hypothesis.

Part 2 covers the approaches in statistical testing and measurement that can be used to answer analytical questions:

- Chapter 4 breaks down the most common statistical tests used to answer questions. The underlying logic of each test and the limitations of their use are covered.
- Chapter 5 discusses aspects of statistics that aren't included in traditional curricula, including their historical development, non-parametric alternatives to common tests, and best practices for using statistics responsibly.
- Chapter 6 covers techniques used to appropriately translate abstract phenomena into measurable constructs.
- Chapter 7 breaks down the step-by-step strategies needed to design effective organizational metrics and KPIs based on available measures.

Part 3 encompasses a range of skills and strategies needed to take your analytics career to the next level:

- Chapter 8 covers the steps needed to responsibly handle and analyze sensitive and protected data.
- Chapter 9 describes the process of statistical modeling for different stakeholder deliverables.
- Chapter 10 discusses the value you can bring to your analyses by obtaining third-party data from APIs, web scraping, and public data sources.
- Chapter 11 teaches data management strategies, including data engineering stacks and the recently emerging practice of analytics engineering.
- Chapter 12 reviews modern data analytics tools and resources that can be used to enhance your deliverable's quality, speed of delivery, and capacity for enabling self-service.

About the code

This book contains many examples of source code in line with normal text. The source code is formatted in a `fixed-width font like this` to separate it from ordinary text. Code annotations accompany much of the source code, highlighting important concepts.

All of the code in this book is written in Python, and it assumes you have an intermediate working knowledge of Python for data analysis (e.g., the `numpy` and `pandas` libraries). The code and datasets from chapters 3 through 11 is available for download in an `ipynb` (Jupyter Notebook) format. Additional code for the chapter 4 and 5 exercises are available in separate Jupyter notebooks.

You can get executable snippets of code from the liveBook (online) version of this book at https://livebook.manning.com/book/effective-data-analysis. The complete code for the examples in the book is available for download from the Manning website at www.manning.com, and from GitHub at https://github.com/mona-kay/effective-data-analysis.

liveBook discussion forum

Purchase of *Effective Data Analysis* includes free access to liveBook, Manning's online reading platform. Using liveBook's exclusive discussion features, you can attach comments to the book globally or to specific sections or paragraphs. It's a snap to make notes for yourself, ask and answer technical questions, and receive help from the author and other users. To access the forum, go to https://livebook.manning.com/book/effective-data-analysis/discussion. You can also learn more about Manning's forums and the rules of conduct at https://livebook.manning.com/discussion.

Manning's commitment to our readers is to provide a venue where a meaningful dialogue between individual readers and between readers and the author can take place. It is not a commitment to any specific amount of participation on the part of the author, whose contribution to the forum remains voluntary (and unpaid). We suggest you try asking the author some challenging questions lest their interest stray! The forum and the archives of previous discussions will be accessible from the publisher's website for as long as the book is in print.

about the author

 **MONA KHALIL** is the senior manager of analytics engineering at Justworks, where she applies over ten years of experience in analytics and data science to data-informed decisions and strategies. She studied psychology at Fordham University and statistics at Baruch College, driving her passion for human-centered approaches to data analysis. Mona is passionate about making data and insights accessible to everyone. She and her partner live in New York City with their two dogs and two cats.

about the cover illustration

The figure on the cover of *Effective Data Analysis,* titled "Homme de Saint-Pierre," is taken from a book by Louis Curmer published in 1841. Each illustration is finely drawn and colored by hand.

In those days, it was easy to identify where people lived and what their trade or station in life was just by their dress. Manning celebrates the inventiveness and initiative of the computer business with book covers based on the rich diversity of regional culture centuries ago, brought back to life by pictures from collections such as this one.

Part 1

Asking questions

As an analyst, you'll wear many hats throughout your career. Depending on the project or request, you might shift between building dashboards, auditing data for quality, or calculating a key summary statistic. The variety in our work is vast.

At the core of all these tasks lies a guiding principle: a question. Every deliverable you create, whether explicitly stated or not, is an attempt to answer a question. This framework will accompany you throughout your career—whether you're directly answering questions (as an analyst, data scientist, or research scientist) or empowering others to do so (as a data or analytics engineer). We are, in essence, scientists—though often by another name.

This part explores how the scientific method underpins much of our work. You likely remember the steps from school: ask a question, develop a hypothesis, test it, and evaluate the results. In some cases, you'll have the luxury of following each step meticulously; in others, you'll be pressed to produce answers within hours. No matter the timeline, starting with a straightforward question and an open mind is crucial to setting yourself—and your stakeholders—up for success.

Sometimes, your stakeholders may have limited experience with this approach. They might assume that the organization's data holds the answers to all their problems, eliminating the need for strategic thinking or domain expertise. But that's rarely the case. In fact, one of the most effective things you can do is guide them through the process of asking the right questions. In this part, we'll cover everything you need to know to apply this essential skill across disciplines.

What does an analyst do? 1

This chapter covers

- Introducing analytics
- A review of common domains in analytics
- Using a data analyst's toolkit
- Preparing for your first role

So you're a newly minted data analyst—congratulations! Perhaps you just finished school and are looking for your first role, or maybe you just started your first job. It's possible you planned this career path, or perhaps you landed here without the preparation you would have liked. Maybe you're part of a large team or your organization's first and only analyst. All of that's okay! There are *so many* paths into the world of data, each bringing unique challenges. If you want to do your best work and become an expert in making data-informed decisions, this book is written for you.

Across the topics that we'll cover in this book, a combination of mathematics, programming, and business knowledge are necessary to derive value for your stakeholders. Throughout these twelve chapters, we will cover a range of topics and skills that can benefit *anyone* who uses data to inform decisions—analysts, data scientists, data engineers, operations specialists, and others can all gain a comprehensive skill set that many of us learn over time, through trial and error. My goal in the following chapters is to provide you with those skills up front, whether or not you have peers, a mentor, a large team, or are working independently. We will cover technical and soft skills that are less often covered in data analyst and data scientist curricula but are still vital to setting yourself up for career success.

1.1   What is analytics?

Analytics is an all-encompassing term for a broad domain with many definitions. For this book, we will define *analytics* as the *practice of using data to discover and communicate patterns, trends, and insights that inform decisions.* An analyst applies various methods to describe and infer information about a dataset. These can include descriptive statistics, inferential statistics, statistical models, financial models, and more. The specific methods used vary by field, with a set of core approaches and best practices being used by the majority of analysts.

As a data analyst, you'll likely play many roles in your career, and you may find that some suit you better than others. Each has a unique profile of skills and responsibilities. Let's look at some of the most common domains for data analytics, starting with business intelligence.

1.1.1   Business intelligence

Business intelligence or *business analytics* teams enable data tracking and the analysis of an organization's performance, using data to make informed and strategic recommendations for their stakeholders. This type of team can employ a wide variety of methods to synthesize data and communicate results, but it typically aims to present results in a clear and readable format for stakeholders less familiar with the interpretation of statistics and mathematics.

> ### Business intelligence vs. business analytics
>
> It's important to note that business *intelligence* and business *analytics* are not entirely interchangeable. Gartner defines business analytics as the specific application of analysis and statistical methods to inform a business. Some sources describe business intelligence as a more encompassing function that can include skills and tasks such as data mining, machine learning, data engineering, data governance, and more. In practice, the use of these terms may be interchangeable and continually evolve with the needs of an organization.
>
> Further, depending on the size and structure of an organization, a business intelligence function may include additional specializations such as marketing analytics, financial analytics, and human resources analytics. However, the primary distinguishing characteristic of business intelligence is that it supports the internal operational need for data within an organization.

The specific tasks and workflow owned by a business analytics team vary by organization but will typically involve the following:

- Developing metrics and key performance indicators (KPIs)
- Developing reports to generate business insights
- Developing dashboards for ease of information consumption
- Distilling and communicating results to business stakeholders

Let's look at these each in turn.

DEVELOPING METRICS AND KPIS

Metrics (standardized quantitative data tracked over time) and *key performance indicators* (KPIs; the most important indicators of business performance) aligned with an organization's objectives are key to its long-term success. Many business intelligence teams will track a combination of *standard metrics* (used across industries or fields) and *custom metrics* (unique to the organization) to provide a comprehensive picture of performance. These metrics are distilled into tools such as *dashboards* for ease of consumption, understanding, and decision-making. Figure 1.1 shows an example of how a monthly metric and its target value can be visualized.

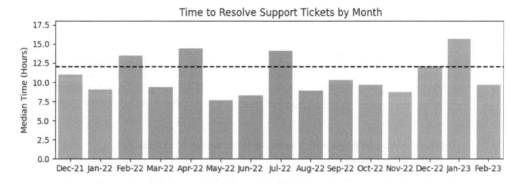

Figure 1.1 Line graph of a support team KPI with a threshold for the service level agreement (SLA) for resolving tickets in less than 12 hours. Metrics and KPIs generate value when tracked over time.

DEVELOPING REPORTS TO GENERATE BUSINESS INSIGHTS

In addition to developing and tracking metrics, a business intelligence team will often dedicate its time to generating novel insights about the function and operation of the business. They may identify areas of inefficiency and revenue-generating opportunities, and they may answer questions from stakeholders to enable them to make increasingly strategic decisions. These results are often shared as *reports* or *presentations.*

DEVELOPING DASHBOARDS FOR EASE OF INFORMATION CONSUMPTION

Nearly every type of analytics team produces *dashboards* as deliverables. Dashboards are highly curated visual representations of data, typically containing interactive charts and graphs that provide insight into a specific area of the organization. These deliverables typically use data sources that are automatically refreshed on a regular cadence, minimizing the time spent supporting routine updates for stakeholders.

Business intelligence teams will typically use a business intelligence tool (BI tool) purchased as software (e.g., Tableau, Power BI) or built and maintained by the organization. The team will often create dashboards to track metrics, KPIs, and trends that stakeholders monitor regularly. These tools are powerful assistants to the team, enabling much of the organization to become data-driven in their decision-making without needing direct support from the business intelligence analysts. Figure 1.2 shows a simple example of what a sales dashboard might contain.

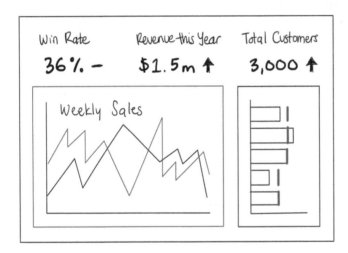

Figure 1.2   A dashboard typically contains summary information and the highest-value visualizations for quick interpretation.

DISTILLING AND COMMUNICATING RESULTS TO BUSINESS STAKEHOLDERS

A business intelligence team is highly flexible in delivering insights to the stakeholders they support. Depending on the purpose of the analysis and the data literacy of their stakeholders, the team will need to tailor their use of statistical and mathematical language, the depth of their analysis, and the formatting of the deliverable to maximize value. Deliverables may include dashboards, reports, summarized insights, or presentations.

1.1.2   *Marketing analytics*

Marketing analytics finds patterns in data related to an organization's marketing efforts. Evaluating and optimizing email campaigns, advertisements, conversion rates, and customer or prospective customer engagement are all common areas of focus within marketing analytics.

A marketing analytics team will often perform tasks similar to those of a business intelligence team. For example, a marketing analyst may track metrics and KPIs for a marketing team, create a dashboard, and develop an ad hoc attribution model to understand where visitors are converting to users in the pipeline.

EXPERIMENTATION

Experimentation refers to the process of testing a hypothesis in controlled conditions to discover cause-and-effect relationships. Many organizations use experimental procedures to guide the design and improvement of websites, applications, and products; without these approaches, teams may find themselves guessing which approaches would create a desired outcome for their users.

A/B testing is a common experimental procedure used by marketing analytics teams to understand how small iterations affect the engagement of prospective customers or users. These tests split a subset of users into one or more *experiment* and *control* groups, showing each group variations of an advertisement that invites them to ask for a product demonstration or convert to paid subscribers. One company tested engagement with a green versus red *"Sign up now!"* button on their website, finding that the red button led to a 21% higher click-through rate [1]!

By splitting your users into separate groups and testing simple variations of text, colors, images, calls to action, etc., you can build an understanding of their behaviors over time. Most A/B tests are shared as *reports* with stakeholders, often conducted using the same statistical tests covered in college statistics courses. Figure 1.3 shows two variations of a website layout that may be shown to users at random, evaluating whether one version has higher subscription rates.

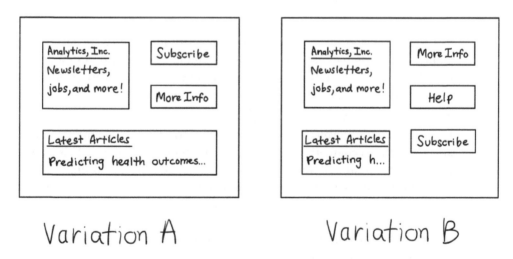

Figure 1.3 Example of two conditions in an A/B test, varying the location of the Subscribe button. Small iterative variations like this can significantly improve user engagement and revenue.

ATTRIBUTION MODELING

Attribution modeling is the analysis of each *touchpoint,* or step, prior to a purchase or subscription. For example, a prospective user may follow these steps in order: click on an advertisement, visit the marketing page, start a free trial, and subscribe. At each step, a percentage of users will complete the following step, with a very small number making it to the end of the purchasing process (as shown in figure 1.4).

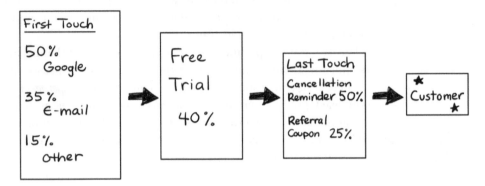

Figure 1.4 Attribution model showing first/last touch and example intermediary steps. Each model breaks down the sources at the touchpoint to understand which is most successful at generating new customers.

The task of the marketing analytics team is to determine what proportion of the success (subscription) can be *attributed* to each touchpoint and understand which are the most valuable in the customer acquisition process.

Some simple methods include first-touch attribution (attributing all credit to the first touchpoint) and last-touch attribution (attributing all credit to the final touchpoint). More complex approaches include multi-touch attribution and algorithmic techniques using statistical models. Each of these involves delivering an analysis breaking down the top sources of traffic or subscriptions at the selected touchpoint.

COMPETITIVE ANALYSIS

Competitive analysis involves various approaches to researching and obtaining publicly available data on competitor performance and business practices. This type of analysis helps an organization determine its market fit and ideal user profiles, and to understand specific areas where its competitors tend to win or lose. A marketing analytics team may be involved directly in the research and compiling of information for the competitive analysis, as well as in any comparisons of quantitative data discovered in the research process. This function is often performed collaboratively with a finance or financial analytics team.

1.1.3 *Financial analytics*

Financial analytics teams use payment and financial data about an organization to understand trends in its performance over time. Generating financial insights involves a range of tools and methods similar to business analysis, and it may involve some overlap with other teams (e.g., marketing analytics) where the performance of the business is concerned.

Depending on the business, a financial analytics team may include functions that require specialized coursework or skill sets (e.g., risk analysis). An investment firm will need a different set of deliverables from a financial analysis team than a software company, and jobs at these types of companies will have correspondingly different requirements. The following sections highlight financial analytics team approaches that are common to many types of businesses.

FINANCIAL METRICS

Financial analytics teams will monitor and report on a comprehensive set of standard *financial metrics* such as revenue, profitability, and customer lifetime value. Often, business metrics are monitored to understand the relationship between a team's work and the overall performance. These metrics often serve as *outcome measures* for other teams seeking to understand the effect of more specific actions on organizational performance.

RISK ANALYSIS

Risk analysis assesses the likelihood of different types of negative events affecting an organization, such as a reduction in revenue, an increase in customer churn, or an increase in operational costs. Financial analysts perform simulations and develop forecasting models and other approaches to quantify a business's numerous potential risks. The mathematical models a risk analysis includes can be complex but are ultimately limited by the number of factors that can be accounted for in a model.

BUSINESS FORECASTING

Forecasting models use historical data to provide insight into the expected financial performance of an organization. These can include projected growth based on seasonal and most recent trends, augmented by organizational factors and broader economic indicators. A range of statistical methods are used for this type of analysis, and organizations hiring to meet this need will often specify a requirement for skills in standard forecasting methods. Figure 1.5 shows a graph of a metric that includes a simple three-month forecast.

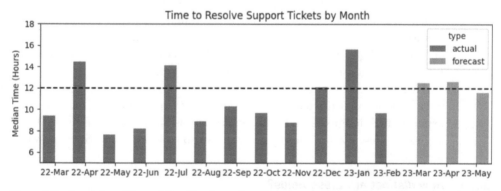

Figure 1.5   A revision of figure 1.2, with a 3-month rolling average forecast. Forecasting methods range from simple calculations such as this one to more complex time-series-modeling approaches. A simple forecast like this one will typically have less variability than the actual data.

1.1.4   *Product analytics*

Product analytics is the analysis of product usage and users to understand and continually improve users' experience with a product. Product analysis typically resides within a research and development (R&D) department supporting a product team in understanding users' needs, the value of investments, and more. This function is quite common at software companies. Product analytics can be *decentralized*, with product managers, software engineers, and other team members working together to answer questions leveraging data, or *centralized*, with product analysts answering questions using data to support the department's ability to make data-informed decisions.

OPPORTUNITY SIZING

An essential component of product development involves appropriately quantifying the value of pursuing a specific *opportunity (e.g., building a new feature in the software that solves a customer problem).* A product analytics team will try to answer questions about the expected effect on subscriptions, user engagement, productivity, or any metrics, and compare that to the amount of work involved.

For example, suppose a product team is considering redesigning parts of the website dedicated to a specific segment of users. The team discovers from available data that this segment of users has proportionally low engagement (website visits per week), tends to generate more support tickets than other segments, and tends to cancel their subscriptions more frequently. This new design addresses the most common sources of confusion mentioned in support tickets.

Overall, the examination of these data sources provides a comprehensive picture of the opportunity: the estimated loss to the business if they *don't* pursue it, the estimated labor costs, and potential increases in customer or user engagement. These analyses include a combination of gathering measurements (e.g., retrieving mean, median, or total values to answer *a lot* of questions) and developing metrics to measure the success of the opportunity.

EXPERIMENTATION

The experimental procedures that marketing analytics teams use are also frequently owned and performed by product analytics or *growth* teams. In addition to simple iterations on layouts, buttons, text, etc., product analytics teams will use a broad range of methods to design and evaluate more sophisticated experiments. These may include longer-running A/B tests on complex workflows with multiple outcome metrics and a more comprehensive range of statistical tests for evaluation.

In addition to evaluating metrics between two separate groups (e.g., in an A/B test), product analytics teams will use pre/post comparisons to measure effect, quasi-experimental designs when a true experiment is impossible, and more. The appropriate use of these methods and statistical tests to evaluate them will be covered in chapters 3 and 4.

1.1.5   *How distinct are these fields?*

Analytics functions and teams have a noticeable overlap in methods, tasks, approaches, and stakeholders. The lines between teams and functions may blur within an organization or for an individual role. The shape of an analytics practice within an organization constantly evolves, and you will readily discover opportunities for increased collaboration and division of labor. This will be especially true earlier in your career, when you may have a similar education and skill set to other analysts you meet. Over time, you will build a profile of specialized skills unique to the analytics function you work with and greater exposure to the needs and problems of that type of team. Figure 1.6 provides a visual of the tasks associated with each analytics team and where they tend to overlap.

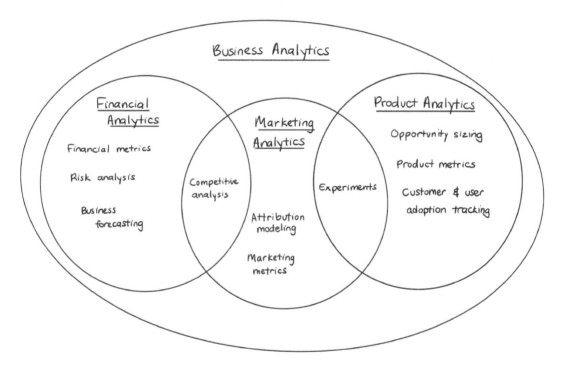

Figure 1.6   Concentric circles showing common areas of overlap for categories of deliverables provided by different analytics teams.

1.2   The data analyst's toolkit

A data analyst who has completed an education, training program, or coursework in this field will generally be exposed to various tools and languages necessary to complete their work. In the workplace, you may have access to a range of sophisticated proprietary tooling maintained by an engineering team, or you may only have access to the free versions of software you learned to use in a classroom.

Regardless of your organization's previous investment in data tooling, you will benefit from accessing the following categories of tools for your work.

1.2.1   Spreadsheet tools

In *all* titles and seniority levels, a data practitioner needs a readily available spreadsheet tool to directly manipulate, shape, present, and interact with data. Spreadsheets are often considered the *least common denominator* of the data world. Appropriately using a programming language and development environment can reduce the amount of manual and repetitive work when performing analysis in a spreadsheet. As the most widely used data manipulation and analysis software on the market, there's no avoiding the periodic need for a spreadsheet.

If you cannot access a proprietary spreadsheet tool, such as Microsoft Excel, the freely available Google Workspace and Google Sheets will meet most of your needs to manipulate data and add charts, formulas, and pivot tables. Google Workspace enables you to collaborate with teammates on projects and quickly support stakeholders with their analyses. In situations where a spreadsheet becomes challenging to use (e.g., complex statistics, large datasets), you can directly connect to and import data from an appropriately formatted sheet in a development environment of your choice using R or Python. You can easily develop dashboards for your stakeholders, such as the one shown in figure 1.7.

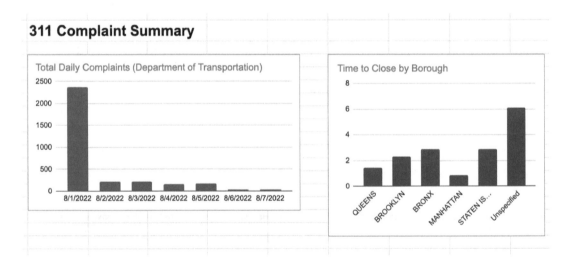

Figure 1.7   Don't underestimate the value of a spreadsheet for easy analysis and sharing!

1.2.2   Querying language

The majority of organizations store data in *tabular format* (in rows and columns, like you would see in a spreadsheet) across multiple sources. When working at organizations that collect and store large amounts of data from a website, application, or business process, you will typically have access to a *data warehouse* [2]. Data warehouses are large storage systems that synthesize the data an organization collects from multiple sources into *databases*, allowing teams to curate the structure of data into the following objects:

- *Tables*, which are sets of logically organized tabular data. Each row in a table is a record, and each column contains information about that record.
- *Views*, which are curated results of a query containing logically organized information that may come from multiple underlying tables. These are often constructed by data engineering or analytics engineering teams to better enable analysts to generate insights.
- *Schemas*, which are logically organized sets of tables.

In this situation, analysts usually need to draw from these data sources using a *query language*. This is almost always a dialect of *SQL* (structured query language) [3] similar to what is taught in classrooms, bootcamps, and online tutorials. Even if you are new to an organization and have never worked with their specific type of data warehouse, being familiar with SQL will give you the ability to quickly access, discover, and manipulate data in that warehouse. If the "dialect" of SQL differs from what you are used to, the data warehouse will typically have documentation on the functions that differ from one type to another (e.g., functions to manipulate dates often differ between warehouses).

Without a well-maintained data warehouse, a data analyst will still benefit from the knowledge and use of SQL. Manipulating data in programming languages such as R or Python involves the use of functions and methods with similar syntax to SQL statements. For example, the following example shows how the total population by state is calculated in SQL, R, and Python, respectively (note that this code will not run, as we don't have this table):

```
SELECT                                    ←┐  Group a dataset
    state,                                 │  using SQL.
    SUM(population) AS total_population
FROM city_populations
GROUP BY state
                            ┐  Group a dataframe
city_populations %>%     ←─┘  using dplyr in R.
    group_by(state) %>%
    summarise(total_population = sum(population))
                                                          │  Group a dataframe
city_populations.groupby('state')['population'].sum()  ←─┘  using pandas in Python.
```

The syntax is quite similar across each language—using `sum` and `group by` functions after selecting each column. In addition, both R and Python have functions that allow you to use SQL queries to manipulate data if you are more comfortable with that syntax.

If you have little to no opportunity to interact with a data warehouse, it may be a good idea to proactively identify opportunities to incorporate SQL in your data manipulation workflows. For example, you can write SQL or Python scripts that process data for you, saving time and reducing errors. Eventually, you will likely be required to use these tools more actively in your career, and keeping this skill fresh in your mind will benefit your long-term growth and opportunities.

1.2.3   *Programming languages for statistics*

A *statistical software* or *modeling language* is essential for any analytics job where you expect to evaluate data using descriptive or inferential statistics. Like the choice of data warehouse, the preferred software depends on the team and organization. SAS was a popular statistical software suite for decades and continues to be used in government agencies and some large corporations. Many smaller organizations, marketing agencies, and non-profits use SPSS for statistical analysis, especially when they primarily hire researchers and analysts with degrees in the social sciences (statistics courses in these programs frequently use SPSS).

If your team prefers proprietary software, it may still be beneficial to incorporate the use of a language such as R or Python into your workflow. In R, you can access, interact with, and save SPSS, SAS, and STATA files using the haven library or the upload tool available in the RStudio user interface. All of this can also be accomplished in Python using the pandas library.

USING R

R is a popular programming language for statistical computing in the data analytics, data science, and research space [4]. Its use compared to Python (discussed next) varies by industry, team area of expertise, seniority level, and type of project. R tends to be more widely used in the biological sciences, social sciences, and statistics. If you work with an organization or academic institution in these areas, you may be more likely to encounter R as the technology of choice in your work or coursework.

If you're experienced in using spreadsheets or proprietary statistical software such as SPSS, SAS, or STATA, the R community has a range of resources designed to ease the transition to your first programming language [5][6]. If you anticipate needing to develop explanatory statistical models as part of your work (discussed in chapter 9), R has easy-to-use native modeling capabilities and a wide ecosystem of packages for less commonly used statistical tests. It also has a well-structured collection of packages augmenting its base capabilities called the tidyverse [7]. For example, the `dplyr` package is used for data manipulation, `ggplot2` for data visualization, and `stringr` for string/ text manipulation.

USING PYTHON

Python quickly became the most popular programming language in the data world and is one of the top languages of choice for developers in general [8]. It tends to be most popular among data science teams, especially those working with larger data sources and those developing machine learning models as part of their workflow. Those with a math, engineering, or physics background may have been exposed to Python during their education.

If you expect your work as an analyst will grow to include predictive modeling (see chapter 9) or are interested in developing a career in data science, machine learning, or data engineering, Python may be an ideal choice of language for your work. There is a wide range of tutorials, online courses, books, and other resources to support learning Python.

CHOOSING A LANGUAGE

There is a long-standing debate about the benefits of R or Python for data practitioners. As you grow your career, I recommend learning to read and interface with both languages to enable you to work with a broader range of stakeholders and peers in an organization.

If your team has a preferred language and an established set of code, resources, and best practices in that language, it's most effective to adopt and contribute to the existing framework.

1.2.4   *Data visualization tools*

Your deliverables as an analyst will almost always include data visualizations to help stakeholders interpret your work. A dedicated data visualization and dashboard creation tool will support your productivity as an analyst.

STATIC VISUALIZATIONS

Reports and presentations that include charts, graphs, and other visuals require, at minimum, the ability to generate static (non-interactive) visualizations using your spreadsheet tool or programming language of choice. A written or oral presentation usually needs visuals for stakeholders to interpret your work appropriately.

As with other elements of the data analyst's toolkit, the choice of tool for creating data visualizations depends on the needs and practices of your stakeholders and team. If you expect teammates to collaborate with and interact with data in spreadsheets, using the charting capabilities in that tool will allow for greater interactivity and simplify updating it with new data. If you're generating reports or deliverables using R or Python, both have robust libraries allowing you to create sophisticated visualizations.

DYNAMIC VISUALIZATIONS AND DASHBOARDS

Unless your deliverables are in the form of presentations or static reports, your work as an analyst will benefit from creating reproducible tools for your stakeholders. A dynamic and interactive dashboard is the most common reproducible tool that allows others to explore insights without you needing to refresh and update documents.

There is a range of open source and proprietary dashboard and business intelligence solutions available on the market. For the moment, I recommend you consider making use of a dashboard tool (e.g., Tableau, Power BI) if you expect your stakeholders will need to do any of the following:

- Review the same analysis repeatedly over time with new data
- Drill down into an analysis to view subsets or subgroups of data in customizable ways beyond what fits into a report or presentation

- Answer predictable questions beyond what your team can support in an ad hoc capacity

1.2.5 Adding to your toolkit

Over time, augmenting your toolkit will enable you to continually increase the value of your work and reduce your time spent repeating routine work. You can employ various strategies to incrementally save time and effort, freeing up your capacity for further improvement. Regardless of the size or seniority of your team, or whether you're a solo analyst at an organization, or if the overall investment in the data practice at your organization is low, we will discuss strategic investments you can recommend to the organization to elevate the visibility and value of your efforts. We'll discuss the amazing range of available tools and strategies for investing in a data toolkit in chapter 12.

1.3 Preparing for your role

This book assumes you are in the early stages of your career, and each chapter aims to prepare you to solve common problems that an analyst faces in their work. An analyst's success in solving each of these problems is highly dependent on access to mentorship, guidance, and skills not taught in common technical resources. Your ability to choose the most appropriate statistical test, justify a hypothesis, or build a high-value dataset is as crucial as your ability to write performant SQL queries and efficient Python code. The former, however, is more challenging to prepare for and can slow down performance and career growth.

1.3.1 What to expect as an analyst

Your career can branch in numerous directions based on your interests, opportunities in an organization, and skill set (technical and non-technical skills). Knowing how to avoid common challenges and pitfalls will set the foundation for your career in analytics, data science, or other data practices and better enable you to excel as a professional.

CAREER TRAJECTORIES

Analytics careers typically offer opportunities to grow within your job function as a technical expert or people manager and branch out into other adjacent fields. Some examples of job functions include

- Data science
- Data engineering
- Research science
- Technical communication

Analytics in organizations have been around for decades, and their core functions will continue to exist as newer fields like data science mature and differentiate into specialized roles. Analytics is a valuable foundation for all data practitioners and is an inherently valuable field in itself. It's an excellent skill set that can enable you to grow your career into another domain, develop your expertise, and increase your leadership capabilities in and outside the data world.

DEMONSTRATING VALUE

Take a look at the following scenario:

> Clara is a data analyst at a startup in the education technology space. Her team of three analysts supports stakeholders in their marketing, fundraising, programs, and human resources decisions. They maintain a backlog and schedule of work deliverables and support ad hoc requests from team leads and executives. These ad hoc requests often have strict and limited turnaround times (two business days or less). In the past year, the team is finding it more challenging to meet the deadlines of routine requests due to the increase in requests from the growing leadership team.

> Clara's team lead has requested additional headcount to support the influx of requests. As part of the request process, the company has asked for a summary of the expected return on investment and value for the business associated with the increased headcount. The executive team reviewing the request has responded with questions about why their requests have a long turnaround and are causing disruption, since they are considered relatively straightforward.

If this scenario is familiar, you're not alone. Being an analyst requires more than a formulaic approach to processing datasets and generating findings. It includes managing stakeholder expectations, strong communication about expected timelines and processes associated with fulfilling requests, and more. It's easy for stakeholders to fall into an *analytics fallacy*, where the simplicity of the deliverable (e.g., a summary statistic, table, or chart) is perceived as indicative of the level of simplicity in producing that deliverable. This can contribute to misalignment in communication, investment decisions in the data practice, and rapid turnaround times for deliverables.

   Quantifying the return on investment (ROI) in data is not usually accomplished using straightforward calculations or metrics. It takes collaboration, qualitative insights, and a mature relationship with the people whose decisions you support. Throughout this book, we will review strategies for aligning with your organization on the value of an investment in analytics and minimizing miscommunications on deliverables.

1.3.2 *What you will learn in this book*

Analytics coursework, books, and other curricula teach comprehensive *direct technical skills*, such as the programming languages, software, and statistical tests you will use daily in your role. You may have spent time practicing SQL for retrieving data from relational databases, Python or R for processing and evaluating the data, a business intelligence tool for visualizing the data, and more. These topics are well covered in a range of great resources that you can access in ways that best fit your learning style.

   As you read this book, you'll work through many hands-on examples of problems faced by different types of analysts in different industries. I encourage you to roll up your sleeves and try each example as if you're in the role specified. By the end of this book, you'll have experience with the skills an analyst needs to succeed in their career—managing complex projects, communicating with non-technical stakeholders, understanding the limitations of measurement techniques, and much more.

Summary

- There is a wide range of analytics domains (such as marketing analytics and product analytics). Each has a standard set of workflows and deliverables and unique methods to solve problems for the team's stakeholders.
- Analysts typically use spreadsheet tools, querying languages, programming languages, and data visualization tools to complete their work and develop deliverables for stakeholders.
- Being successful as an analyst involves more than producing the output assigned to you; it involves strategic stakeholder communication and alignment to create value over time.

From question
to deliverable

This chapter covers

- Preparing an end-to-end analytics project
- Setting expectations with stakeholders
- Managing the interpretation of results
- Creating resources for reproducibility

Analytics projects begin with a question: How well is the business performing? Is the product easy for users to learn how to use? Did the marketing campaign produce a return on our investment? Questions such as these guide data analysis, statistical methods, and visualizations for communicating insights. The answer you provide to the question will ideally provide strategic information and direction to your stakeholders and their work.

While some analysts' work is guided by their own questions, most provide insights into the questions posed by their stakeholders. These are delivered in a variety of ways—quick summaries can enable decisions, whereas larger projects may require statistical analyses and the presentation of results.

2.1   The lifecycle of an analytics project

With a question in hand, your responsibility as an analyst is to distill the organizational process, the research idea, or your curiosity into something you can define, measure, and report on. While some routine questions and analyses have well-structured metrics and data sources, most novel questions your team addresses will not have an available data source, metric, or statistical analysis method to guide your approach.

Many businesses draw heavily from scientific methods in their approaches to deriving insights. The step-by-step process recommended here will give you the appropriate tools to make confident decisions, align and clarify areas of ambiguity with your stakeholders, and make concrete recommendations. For each stage of the project lifecycle (shown in figure 2.1), this book will provide you with a checklist to proactively identify the best path forward to the next stage.

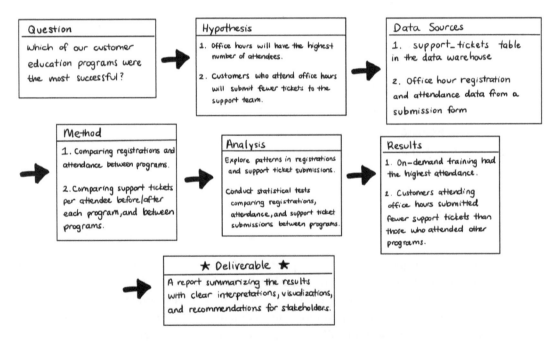

Figure 2.1 Flowchart of an analytics lifecycle, looking at the effect of a customer education and outreach program. Each step distills the question into measurable items that can be analyzed and used to produce actionable recommendations.

2.1.1   Questions and hypotheses

Questions you receive as an analyst are informed by your stakeholders' domain expertise, previous experience, and heuristics they're familiar with in their teams. These same heuristics rarely translate to a singular data source, metric, or method of operationalization in analysis and can lead to confusion about definitions. The first step of effectively working with a stakeholder is to agree on how to define their question.

Operationalization is the process of translating an abstract concept into a process you can measure. The term is commonly used in social sciences research methods and statistics courses to define the process of distilling complex behavioral and social phenomena. Operationalizing concepts is valuable as an analyst, since the business and organizational processes you interact with are complex and typically involve a dimension of human behavior and processes that don't exist in a vacuum. Many behavioral and cognitive processes can't be measured directly, so additional steps and diligence are necessary to develop assessments agreed upon within an academic discipline.

Operationalizing a process involves aligning on precise definitions of the concepts in your stakeholders' questions. We'll demonstrate this with a hypothetical product analytics team throughout this chapter.

Operationalizing customer behavior

Jane is a product manager at a software company. She has a question: "Is it easier to use the website's Help Center after updates to its search functionality?" Sam is a product analyst working with Jane's team, and he notices that *easier* is a heuristic that can have multiple definitions with the available data at their company: Do customers spend less time in the Help Center? Do they call the Customer Support Center less frequently? Do they respond positively to the feedback question that pops up on the Help Center screen?

Sam responded to Jane's request by proposing alternative, more specific, definitions of her identified outcome—an *easier* customer experience. Sam's proposed definitions are not the only methods of defining *easier* in this context—dozens of possible measures could indicate an easier customer experience. The questions Sam identified for the analysis in this context are based on the practical availability of data at the company. The list of questions being evaluated may be expanded or revised as operationalizing an easier customer experience becomes better understood at the company.

In academic settings, operationalizing behavioral and cognitive processes involves rigorous peer review, measurement development, and psychometric testing to ensure the reliability and validity of the developed metrics. In a business or organizational setting, the rigorous peer review process is rarely feasible for analytics teams to apply in daily work. Sometimes you'll have the opportunity to dig into this process to aid in the long-term understanding of a process, but other times you'll have to make rapid decisions to meet a deadline. I recommend considering the following questions as you operationalize concepts with your stakeholders:

- What terms in the question are vague or could have multiple meanings?
- What operationalized versions of the question are most practical to measure with the available data at your organization? (This will be discussed in more detail in the next section.)

- What specific, operationalized versions of the question can have multiple viable competing definitions (e.g., are there arguments that both "more time" and "less time" can be considered desirable, positive outcomes)?
- Are there industry standard, peer-reviewed, or otherwise widely agreed-upon measurable definitions of the concepts in the original question?

2.1.2   Data sources

The data you can access is often the primary driver of how questions are ultimately operationalized. Data is typically available to analytics teams in various *tabular* formats (e.g., CSVs and relational databases) as well as in unstructured formats that require additional processing time. Each type of source has its strengths and limitations for how you approach your work. We will discuss these in greater depth in chapter 10.

We'll focus on three types of data sources that product analytics teams can use to answer their questions:

- Clickstream and behavioral data
- Customer support records
- Survey responses

These are great examples of data available at many organizations, but this is by no means an exhaustive list. We will discuss *a great many* data sources in chapters 5 and 10, as well as the strengths and limitations of each.

CLICKSTREAM AND BEHAVIORAL DATA

Clickstream and *behavioral data* are high-value sources of information for analytics teams whose organizations primarily operate in the digital world. *Clickstream data* refers to the record of a user's activity and navigation on a website or application. It allows you to track the sequence of *clicks* a user makes and often includes the following information:

- The order in which the events happened within a single session on the website or application, allowing you to generate the full sequence of steps performed.
- The time spent on each page, which can be used to understand large-scale usage patterns on your website or application.
- Individual elements or links clicked on a page, showing granular information on how users interact with your website or application.

Clickstream data is frequently used by product and marketing analytics teams in A/B testing, attribution modeling, website analytics, and more. It's often one of the *largest* datasets collected by an organization.

Behavioral data is a broader term that encompasses data related to a user's or customer's actions, behaviors, and decisions. Clickstream data is a *type* of behavioral data, which can also include a wide variety of other data sources (e.g., purchases, email opens, survey responses). These data sources are integral to the purpose of product and marketing analytics: understanding the behavior of users, customers, and prospects to create a better product or service.

Figure 2.2 shows an example of a curated table that records page views of the website. The types of metadata in each column are common to this type of data source, allowing you to understand which pages are most frequently visited or revisited and the length of time spent on the page. Many comprehensive sources of page view data will also enable you to track users' journeys across a website.

event_time	visit_id	session_id	user_id	page
2022-10-24 22:18:23.751292	11680601	1446638	915441	Settings
2022-10-24 23:22:23.751292	10088479	1088166	18840	What's New
2022-10-24 23:56:23.751292	11935535	1791443	736562	What's New
2022-10-25 01:57:23.751292	6617370	1571759	254287	What's New
2022-10-25 02:15:23.751292	3944598	1876849	182038	Help Center

Figure 2.2 A sample of data from a table on page view events

Taking a look at the characteristics of this table, we can see the following:

- A unique visitor ID (`user_id`) allows you to track customer page views over time.
- A unique session ID (`session_id`) for each time a customer visits the website tracks all pages they visit during that time.
- The Help Center is available as a page, with no further detail on where a customer navigated (e.g., articles read or searches performed).
- The amount of time spent on the page isn't directly available, limiting your ability to assess trends or changes in time spent at the Help Center.

While sources of clickstream and behavioral data can be some of the most valuable for an organization wanting to understand its users, it does have limitations worth noting. This data is typically collected using a third-party software, which can be expensive. It also requires manual effort by technical teams to proactively define the events they want to track (e.g., clicks on the Add to Cart button). Data can also be missing if users have ad-blockers installed, which can prevent browser tracking from third-party sources.

CUSTOMER SUPPORT RECORDS

Organizations with a support team or function will often keep records of calls, chats, and other customer communications for analysis. Business analytics teams will use this data to track metrics on the volume of communications, time to resolve customer problems, and customer satisfaction as indicators of the team's performance.

This type of data can also be used as a measure for analytics projects looking to improve the customer's experience. In our example, Jane's product team was looking to implement changes that would improve the experience of customers and the website's ease of use. If these changes are successful, it's reasonable to develop a hypothesis about changes in the volume of communications the support team receives.

Exploring chat support data

The following figure shows a sample of the dataset on chat support available at Sam's organization.

contact_id	chat_id	support_rep_id	chat_start	visited_help_ctr
u1v2b3	10550	139	2022-10-24 22:18:23.751292	True
d5t4e6	5180	451	2022-10-24 23:22:23.751292	True
g9h7i8	3270	357	2022-10-24 23:56:23.751292	False
w3g1l2	7431	58	2022-10-25 01:57:23.751292	True
c6p4o5	13558	258	2022-10-25 02:15:23.751292	True

A sample of data from a table on chat support requests

The dataset contains the following characteristics we can consider in the analysis:

- The `contact_id` is not in the same format as the `user_id` field on the page views table (figure 2.2), which means you may not be able to connect users between data sources.
- The `visited_help_ctr` column is a Boolean value (`True`/`False`) indicating whether or not the customer visited the Help Center before starting the chat support conversation. This may be a helpful *proxy* metric for Help Center visitor volume.
- The dataset contains columns allowing for multiple methods of measuring chat volume: total chat requests, chat requests per support rep, and queue time.

Data from support calls, chats, and tickets are a great source of information on the areas where your customers and users struggle with the product or service provided. However, the software and systems used to manage customer support can vary widely in the data they capture, how they're set up, and how easily they can be incorporated into a data warehouse.

SURVEY RESPONSES

The vast majority of organizations conduct surveys of their users, customers, population of interest, and employees. This data is collected from questionnaires or interviews, and it can be administered in a variety of ways. Survey data is used to discover insights, opinions, perceptions, and self-reported behaviors on a set of topics flexibly defined by the organization.

Simple one-question surveys are often capable of being built into websites and applications to gather large volumes of data on very specific topics. However, when those questions are asked using third-party software, additional work may be required to collect, download, and connect that data to other information about your users and customers.

Leveraging survey questions

Sam's team discovered some potential survey data for their project.

The product and marketing teams recently added a pop-up at the bottom of Help Center articles asking customers, "Did this article answer your question?" Customers can select "Yes" or "No" in response to the question. Unfortunately, Sam's team has discovered that this dataset is unavailable for analysis in their data warehouse. The team has access to the following information via a vendor's website:

- An aggregate Customer Satisfaction score is computed in a dashboard as a percentage of customers that responded "Yes" over time.
- No information about the users or which Help Center articles they visited is provided.
- No information is provided on the response rate to the question.

Sam's team has requested that the data engineering team ingest the data from the Help Center survey in the data warehouse. They anticipate the effort will take 4–6 weeks, at which point Sam will conduct a follow-up analysis.

While it's easily available and widely used, survey data does have significant limitations in terms of quality and accuracy. Small differences in questions and response scales can have drastic effects on the responses you receive. We'll discuss this in depth in chapter 6, where you'll learn how to design effective measures.

IDENTIFYING CHARACTERISTICS OF YOUR DATASET

What does that timestamp mean? You may be surprised to learn that a specific piece of data doesn't always mean what you think it does. Analysts will benefit from an initial effort to challenge their assumptions about the characteristics of a dataset *before* conducting an analysis—this will reduce the likelihood of inaccurate conclusions and misinterpretations of results.

As you've seen in the previous three sections, many data sources have limitations that determine their usability:

- Clickstream data can contain missing or inaccurate data from users with ad-blockers, making it difficult to use when precise measurements are necessary. For example, if you need a list of *every* user who visited a page, you may find that the list is incomplete.
- Data collected about business processes using third-party software (e.g., customer support data) can vary widely in its ease of access and available data about the support interaction.

- Data collected from surveys can be low in quality and accuracy when best practices in the science of measurement are not used.

As you build domain expertise at your organization, you will develop an understanding of the types of research questions you need to ask to thoroughly examine your data. The following are examples of questions you can ask:

- Is the data raw, *event-level* information (e.g., one row per page view, click, or call)? Or is it partially aggregated at some level (e.g., per user per day)?
- Are you able to connect different datasets to the same user or customer using a shared primary key?
- What timestamps are available on each row? Are they captured by the server or entered by users? Do they capture the time *between* actions, the time to *complete* an action, or the volume of actions over time?
- What percentage of rows have missing data in a field you're considering using for your analysis?
- What fields are *missing* from your dataset that might be valuable if you had them? How are your questions or hypotheses affected by not having those fields available?

After answering these questions and determining the scope of analysis possible with the available data, you can move on to the appropriate measurement and method selection.

What's in the dataset?

Sam's team has determined that some of the fields of interest are not available in the data sources he's been looking at. There is no measure of the time spent on a page, and the survey question on the support page asking whether an article was helpful is only available in aggregate form. Thus, the original research questions need to be revised.

With an understanding of the characteristics and limitations of each dataset, Sam's team can narrow down and revise the precise research questions agreed upon with Jane's product team:

- Do customers spend less time on the Help Center?
- Do they call the customer support center less frequently?
- Do they respond positively to the feedback question on the Help Center screen?

The first two questions can be answered without the ability to join users between the two datasets. The third question can only be partially answered using the vendor's aggregate summary and is limited in its ability to understand the nuances of *why* a customer may respond "Yes," or "No," or choose not to respond at all.

Sam has aligned with Jane on the data available to their team, which questions are possible to answer, and at what depth. Jane agrees that the analysis results will be valuable to the team, even with limited access to granular data.

2.1.3 Measures and methods of analysis

Research methods, study designs, and the statistical tests to evaluate them are essential tools in your analyst's toolkit. There are countless ways to ask and answer questions, and study designs are intended to provide structure and guidance to your work. In this section, we'll primarily focus on the role, value, and procedures used in designing a study or research project: diving into the data, choosing a statistical test, and preparing your results. We will cover the types of methods available in depth in chapters 3, 4, 5, 6, and 8.

EXPLORING DATASET CHARACTERISTICS

Analysts will almost always engage in the crucial process of *exploratory data analysis* (EDA). This is a series of steps in which the main focus is on understanding the characteristics and patterns within the data, often beyond the hypotheses being investigated. Nearly every analytics project should include a detailed EDA to understand the overall trends, patterns, and limitations of the data you are working with.

EDA often includes steps such as the following:

- When the data is plotted on a histogram or boxplot, what does the *shape of the distribution* look like?
- Are there records with extremely high or low values for a given measure? Is there a legitimate reason for those values? Are they *outliers* that should be removed from your dataset, and why?
- What number or percentage of records have *missing or duplicate data?* Is this data missing for legitimate reasons, or is there a problem with how the information is being saved? How should these missing values be handled? Should the entire row be removed from the dataset, should an appropriate value be imputed into the row (e.g., the overall average), or should the missing value be left alone? Conversely, are there duplicate rows for information that's supposed to be unique?
- What do you find when *summarizing the data?* What are the mean, median, standard deviation, minimum, maximum, number of values, and number of unique values?

This is not an exhaustive list; we will be discussing EDA throughout this book as it applies to different types of projects. We will also cover each of the statistical concepts and summary statistics mentioned in this section in chapters 4 and 5.

CHOOSING METHODS AND STATISTICAL TESTS

If you take care to operationalize and structure your questions and hypotheses, choosing a research method and statistical tests will be clear and easy decisions. There are dozens of research and study designs available, but the majority of questions can be answered with only a handful of approaches. We will discuss this process in depth in chapter 3.

After selecting an approach, it's valuable to touch base with your stakeholders to set expectations on the type of information you will show them: Will there be charts comparing average values between groups? Will you show a series of boxplots for each of the groups included in your statistical test? Setting expectations early will save you time in the development of your report; we will discuss strategies for tailoring the results of your methods and analysis to the data proficiency level of your stakeholders.

Developing a plan of analysis

Sam communicates the data discovered and the proposed analysis plan to the rest of the team:

- Descriptive statistics showing the total Help Center visits and chat support requests over time, the average Help Center and chat support requests *per unique user* over time, and the average customer satisfaction scores over time.
- A *between-subjects study design* (discussed in chapter 3) comparing daily Help Center visits and chat support requests in the 90 days *before* the search functionality change was deployed and 90 days *after*. Additional follow-up comparisons will be completed 90 days after the first comparison.
- An *independent samples t-test* (discussed in chapter 4) to assess the statistical significance of any differences in daily Help Center visits and chat support requests before and after the changes.

Sam receives positive feedback from the team on the analysis plan and recommends an additional *non-parametric* statistical test to add to the final step. With their support, Sam can begin preparing the data for analysis.

APPLYING BEST PRACTICES

I recommend the following considerations when preparing your dataset for analysis and statistical comparison:

- *Budget time appropriately*—Running statistical tests usually takes the *least* time compared to every other step discussed in this chapter. You can expect planning, data preparation, EDA, and interpretation to require a far more significant time investment. Make sure you consider this when communicating expected deliverable deadlines to stakeholders.
- *Lead with your question*—The questions you ask should guide the methods and statistical tests you choose—not the other way around. If you try to fit a question into a specific type of statistical model, you risk confusing stakeholders and misinterpreting trends in your data.
- *Simpler is often better*—It can be tempting to start your analysis with complex statistical modeling to grow your skill set and derive better insights—I highly recommend you exercise caution with this! Start with a more straightforward test where possible, and look for examples that use the same tests to ensure you're using the right approach, that your data is in the right shape, and that you thoroughly understand the results.

2.1.4   Interpreting results

Interpreting and distilling the results of statistical tests for stakeholder communication is the final component of an analytics project, and it's arguably the most essential step. Tailoring results communication for the intended audience is crucial to creating value with your work.

When scoping a project, aligning with your stakeholders on their experience and their understanding of basic statistical concepts is often valuable: Do they understand correlations? Statistical significance? Means comparisons (e.g., *t*-tests)? Each piece of information tells you how much detail you should provide about the statistical results in your final deliverable.

If you learned statistics and research methods in an academic setting, you likely learned to share your findings in a standardized results section of a paper. These are often written as rote recitations of statistical test coefficients and values, making for easy reproducibility by other academic professionals. But unless you are preparing a publication for peer review, this format is *not* ideal for communication outside of academia and the classroom. Instead, I recommend aiding interpretation with clear summary statements and visuals.

Final report

Sam has finished all the steps in the analytical plan: the descriptive statistics have been calculated, the statistical tests show significant decreases in daily chat support volume after the search functionality changed, and the team is excited to share their findings. What exactly should they communicate to Jane and the product team?

Sam's final report includes a summary of findings with statements describing the methods used and the significance of the statistical tests for Jane's team. Sam confirmed with Jane that she's familiar with statistical significance and that knowing the coefficient values returned by the statistical tests would be helpful. The following is an excerpt from the results section of the report, which also includes bar graphs comparing the values for each measure in the 90 days before and after the search bar changed:

> Daily Help Center page visits and daily volume of chat support requests were compared in the 90 days before and after deploying search functionality changes. The daily chat support requests decreased significantly ($p<.01$) in the 90 days after changes were made. Daily Help Center visits did not change significantly ($p=.42$) in this time period. Additionally, customer satisfaction scores increased by 5%.

The choice, application, and interpretation of statistical tests can frequently confuse your stakeholders (especially those in non-technical roles). Statistics education in most undergraduate and graduate curricula is pretty limited, and opportunities to advance data literacy in day-to-day work are highly asymmetrical across functions, domains, and organizations. While Jane understood Sam's summary, it's feasible that other stakeholders in the same organization will gloss over the details of the statistical tests and limitations if they are unfamiliar with their meaning. Choose your level of detail carefully!

2.1.5   Exercises

Imagine you are part of a business analytics team at a high-end fitness company. The marketing team has reached out to your team for help answering a question: "What effect has the recent promotion at the gym (one month free for new members) had on the business?"

1   What *operational concepts* and *heuristics* are referenced in the preceding question? How might you translate the heuristics into measurable concepts?
2   Which datasets may be valuable to investigate when answering the stakeholder question? What columns or fields might you look for in each?
    –   Customer gym check-ins
    –   Customer payment records
    –   Company payroll records
    –   Customer experience survey feedback

3   What methods or statistical tests might you use to measure the effect of the promotion? (If you're unfamiliar with the appropriate choices, you can return to this question after reading chapters 3 and 4.)
4   The director of marketing has informed you that most team members are unfamiliar with statistics. How might you tailor your presentation to their experience?

Use the lists, recommendations, and example scenarios in each section as a guide for operationalizing each question, suggesting appropriate datasets and metrics, choosing statistical tests, and identifying appropriate levels of detail for the stakeholders in marketing.

2.2   Communicating with stakeholders

You have aligned with stakeholders, operationalized their questions, identified appropriate data sources, performed an analysis, and written a well-structured report with proper visuals and summary statements that are aligned with the expertise of your stakeholders. Is your job done?

Not quite—an analyst's role includes creating resources to aid stakeholder interpretations and next steps and communicating results to *their* stakeholders to ensure all parties receive the appropriate message about your work. *Analytics telephone* (illustrated in figure 2.3) is a situation that occurs when results from peer-reviewed articles, internal analyses, statistical modeling, or any other synthesis of quantitative or qualitative information is distilled and summarized from one source to another, ultimately losing their meaning.

Figure 2.3 Analytics telephone can diffuse the quality of your insights.

Analytics telephone is commonly seen in the communication of scientific findings in news media. For example, an article is published detailing a study showing a positive association between a behavior and a health outcome in a small sample of adults. A press release summary is produced, excluding the details about the sample and limits of the association. A local news channel reviews the press release and reports that engaging in the behavior causes the health outcome, without mentioning the limitations. The public then assumes that engaging in the behavior will cause the health outcome, and when it does not, it can ultimately lead to distrust in future findings presented to them.

As an analyst, it's valuable to be mindful that the findings and results from your project can generate excitement among your teammates, who are eager to read and share with others. In that process, it's easy for your findings to be diluted into colloquial language that lacks the precise wording used by professionals in the data world. Analysts should be cautious when telling stakeholders that their findings indicate *causation* or *proof*. It's challenging to walk back from those claims at a later date if new data surfaces with contradictory findings, and this can result in a lack of trust in the analytics function of the organization.

2.2.1   *Guiding the interpretation of results*

Language and words matter in analytics. The terms used to describe findings carry tremendous weight in how consumers of your work interpret—or misinterpret—the results. Words such as *cause, prove, associate, predict, suggest, difference,* and *findings* may have distinct definitions in research and analytics, but they are often conflated in conversational speech.

THE SCOPE OF INTERPRETATION

Analysts benefit from the strategic communication of two concepts in their findings:

- *The scope of interpretation* is the acceptable degree to which your results can be generalized beyond the specific findings communicated. This includes generalizability to a broader population beyond what was included in your work and the interpretation of null or alternative hypotheses (e.g., does a non-significant result mean there is no relationship between two variables?).
- *Precision of language* is the responsible and intentional use of keywords that aid stakeholders in interpreting correlation, causation, statistical significance, and other concepts. This strategy minimizes conflation with colloquial terminology and provides a roadmap to your stakeholders on the appropriate interpretation of your research design, methodology, and findings.

Carefully considering these concepts in your deliverables will help stakeholders understand the information you provide them. It can also guide appropriate follow-up questions that strengthen your partnership with the stakeholder team. Over time, both strategies will be valuable for managing expectations, taking effective action, and building a data-informed and data-literate culture within your organization.

> #### Summarizing results
> Let's return to Sam and Jane's customer Help Center visit and chat volume analysis. The scenario in the following figure shows what's possible when *analytics telephone* occurs—a situation where your results are shared between teams and the eventual conclusions drawn are beyond the scope of your work.

Summary

- Chat support requests decreased in the 90 days after the Help Center changes.
  - This indicates initial evidence of the impact of these changes.
  - We recommend re-evaluating this measure after an additional 90 days to assess the scope of the impact.

- Daily Help Center visits did not change in the 90 days after the changes.
  - This likely indicates that Help Center visits were *not* the correct behavior to measure for this outcome.

- While customer satisfaction scores increased slightly in the same time period, we do not recommend using this metric as an indication of success.

A slide such as this delineates the scope of interpretation and helps ensure the long-term success of your work.

In the course of Sam's colleagues sharing the team's results, the scope of interpretation became diluted until the executive team was making broad inferences about the value of future efforts to optimize search functionality on the Help Center and suggesting that those changes would *cause* further reductions in chat support volume. Suppose these inferences become recommendations for additional optimization work before due diligence on this inference was completed. In that case, multiple teams' time and effort could be dedicated to work whose justification is based on a faulty premise.

At the team's recommendation, Sam made the following changes:

- He added the following details on the methodology:
  - The number of users visiting the Help Center and contacting chat support in the 90 days before/after the search changes.
  - The number of users doing each of the above in the last year, as a benchmark.
- He added the following details on the results:
  - Updated the language on the lack of association between search functionality changes and Help Center visits to indicate that no relationship was *detected* and there was insufficient information to show whether there was an effect on Help Center experience.
- He added clear hypotheses for each of the operationalized questions, indicating the expected *association* between search functionality changes and outcomes rather than an expected *causal* relationship.

ENUMERATE LIMITATIONS AND NEXT STEPS

Mitigating the likelihood of analytics telephone scenarios can be done with a few intentional steps and information communicated as part of your lifecycle report. I recommend considering the following steps, especially when you expect your results will be shared with a wide audience:

- *Include a limitations section in your report or presentation.* This is a standard section in peer-reviewed papers that is valuable in your reports as a slide or page for stakeholders to read. Include a list of bullet points of data unavailable for in-depth analysis, the scope of interpretation, and any interpretations you *cannot* make with your findings.
- *Include a section with suggestions for further research.* This is standard in peer-reviewed papers, helping provide a strategic lens into future research. Enumerating recommendations for further research and evaluation steps is an easy way to provide a roadmap for stakeholders looking for the strategic investment of time and resources.
- *Create a guide to statistical interpretation to share with stakeholders.* If you don't already have this as a resource, find or develop an appropriate guide to understanding correlation, causation, statistical significance, and to generalizing findings. We will discuss creating this resource in depth in chapter 11.

Documenting limitations

Sam's team was informed of the executive team's discussion about recommending continued work on optimizing the search functionality of the Help Center. They decide to augment the report and presentation initially delivered to Jane's team with some simple information that clarifies the project and its scope. A slide incorporating the first two bullet points can be added to the presentation:

Limitations

- The full dataset for customer satisfaction scores was not available.
- Chat support request volume should be re-evaluated at +90 and +180 days to assess continued reduction.
- Chat support reduction was assessed after this specific search change. Hypotheses on further search optimization should be evaluated in follow-up tests before generalizing.
- The original goal of reducing Help Center page views should be examined in greater depth before drawing conclusions.

Addendum slide to Sam's original presentation

This addendum provides direct clarification to the leadership teams planning strategic efforts. In response to this information, the executive team recommends further research into the efficacy of two modular changes to the search functionality before proposing a much more extensive overhaul to the feature. Thus, the additional information provided Sam's team with two new clear deliverables that add information to the decisions made by the product and customer teams.

2.2.2 *Results that don't support hypotheses*

As an analyst, you will *regularly* and *frequently* discover findings that do not support your hypotheses or those of your stakeholders. This happens to every analyst and is *not* an inherent reflection of your capability of working with your stakeholders. If you went for long periods in your career without findings that contradict hypotheses, I *would* be concerned with the accuracy of your results and methodological approaches to your work. I repeat: this is a part of the job.

Hypotheses aren't developed in a vacuum; they're usually tied to strongly held beliefs, domain knowledge, and heuristics about an organizational process or behavior. You can expect to experience resistance, skepticism, or pushback on these findings at multiple points throughout your career. Nonetheless, the frequency with which findings don't support hypotheses does not make it easy to communicate this to stakeholders.

FINDINGS MISALIGNED WITH HYPOTHESES

Even when a hypothesis is not enumerated as part of the analytics lifecycle, stakeholders will frequently have expectations about the analysis outcome based on preconceived notions of patterns or behaviors in the domain area. They may plan to take actions aligned with one or more of these expectations, and results that don't match those findings can create frustration and delay work if it's started ahead of the analysis.

When this misalignment occurs frequently, it often indicates that a more significant culture shift is necessary within the organization to derive value from quantitative insights. However, even in organizations with a mature approach to analysis, this can *still* happen. High-quality research takes time and questions free of bias, and not everyone you work with will have the time or ability to approach your work the way you expect.

I recommend handling each of the following misalignments in structured ways:

- *Results that oppose the hypothesis*—When you have statistically significant results that directly contradict stakeholders' hypotheses, it's beneficial to discuss the contextual background that informed the hypothesis in the first place. What guided them to develop the hypothesis? Can you break down the hypothesis into granular behaviors that can be measured and examined in more depth?
- *Results that show no significant relationship*—The lack of statistically significant results can be interpreted by stakeholders as the absence of a relationship or can be conflated with an *opposite* relationship. These results can also be interpreted as their work being ineffective toward achieving a desired outcome. In this case, a

detailed discussion about the behaviors and outcomes chosen for comparison is beneficial. Were they the proper measures to assess the behavior or outcome of interest? Are there more appropriate measures that can be considered for future analyses?

- *Non-significant differences supporting the hypothesis*—Statistical significance can be challenging to explain to stakeholders unfamiliar with the concept and its application. When reporting this type of result to stakeholders, it can be valuable to communicate that those initial findings are promising and that additional time, users, or data is necessary to report on the findings confidently.

FINDINGS MISALIGNED WITH COMMUNAL KNOWLEDGE

Over time, organizations build up collective knowledge from various sources: customer interviews, free-text surveys, competitive research, peer-reviewed articles, product feedback, and more. As time goes by, this knowledge guides the strategy and direction of the organization. However, that knowledge can become outdated and misaligned with current customers or stakeholders.

There are two common types of misalignments in this area:

- *Quantitative findings contradict qualitative findings*—Organizations commonly augment quantitative findings with qualitative data, such as free-text survey comments, product feedback, customer interviews, and focus groups. Smaller organizations with fewer customers, clients, or external stakeholders often lean heavily on the latter instead of investing in an analytics function. Figure 2.4

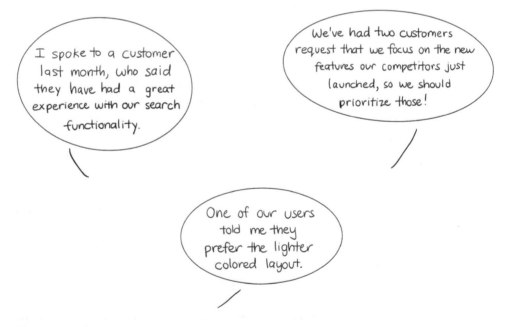

Figure 2.4   Example quotes referencing qualitative findings

shows some stakeholder responses to your results that indicate a reliance on qualitative information.

When recent quantitative findings do not align with qualitative findings, I recommend the following:

- Check for overlap in users or customers between quantitative and qualitative findings. You will likely find that qualitative insights were generated using a small subset of highly engaged people who are not representative of the broader base of users.
- Check the recency of references to qualitative insights compared to quantitative insights. In most cases, it's easier to refresh data from a statistical analysis than to redo a set of interviews, focus groups, or other qualitative method. Raise questions about the applicability of findings that may be outdated and not representative of the current base of users.

- *Quantitative findings contradict common organizational beliefs*—Good ideas and rapid feedback loops help small organizations get off the ground and scale rapidly. The information gained in the early days of developing a product or service is necessary to understand the need being met and the likelihood of success. These early insights become foundational to the mission and goals of the organization, and they can be difficult to challenge as the organization matures and quantitative insights demonstrate a different picture from what was previously believed. Figure 2.5 shows some responses that point to strong beliefs at an organization.

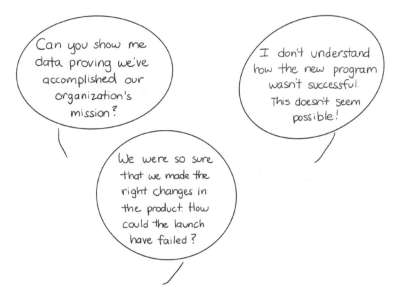

Figure 2.5 Example quotes referencing common organizational beliefs.

When quantitative findings do not align with strongly held beliefs, I recommend the following steps as a long-term strategy for your team. This will *not* be quickly resolved within the scope of a single project:

- Work with core stakeholders to understand the source of the organizational belief—was early research done to inform these beliefs? Can the research be updated with a larger, currently representative group of customers? Can you develop a strategy to highlight any gaps in the sources of information being used?

- Scope out a project roadmap to understand how and where the user base has grown and changed. This will help mature commonly held beliefs at the organization and demonstrate where customers' profiles, needs, or behaviors have changed from previous years.

Providing updated results to stakeholders

Let's return to Sam's analytics team. During the presentation of the proposed project follow-up plan, a marketing team leader expressed concern with the product team's goal to reduce chat support volume. "I thought customers who engage with chat support are less likely to cancel their subscriptions with us. Why would we want to reduce it?"

The marketing team leader referenced an analysis performed several years prior, showing that customers who contacted the support team at least once were less likely to cancel subscriptions after one year. Sam's team shared an updated version of the analysis to answer the question posed during the presentation, showing that the conclusions from five years ago were no longer accurate for the current customer base.

FINAL NOTE ON RESULTS

Aligning with stakeholders is an expected part of the job of an analyst. The data literacy of your stakeholders will vary widely, based on their domain expertise, previous experience, and the expectations of your current organization. We don't yet have widespread data literacy or competency education in schools, nor is it necessary to be effective in many roles.

It's generally helpful for your team to understand your stakeholders' degree of comfort working with data so you can tailor messages to them and their teams. Taking the time to align to stakeholders' communication preferences will enable better understanding and increase their comfort with data over time.

Until a comprehensive data literacy curriculum is part of early education, the role of an analyst will include communication and *data translation* at multiple levels. I will continue incorporating communication strategies throughout this book to build your confidence in this fundamental skill.

2.2.3 Exercises

Let's return to your analysis plan for the business analytics team of the high-end fitness company. Your goal is to complete a report and presentation for the marketing team, detailing the effect of the current member promotion on the number of paying customers, gym check-ins, and customer satisfaction:

1 The number of new paying customers increased significantly in the 30 days after the promotion launched, compared to the previous month. Write a one or two sentence summary of these findings, guiding stakeholders through the interpretation.

2 The marketing team is excited to hear the results you shared and recommends a strategy of making the one-month-free promotion permanent at the next executive team meeting. Can you identify or explore any limitations with this strategy, based on the available data?

3 The customer satisfaction score decreased slightly in the 30 days after the promotion launched. Did the promotion cause this? How can you communicate the *scope of interpretation* for this finding?

4 The number of check-ins at the gym did not change in the 30 days before and after the promotion launched. A marketing team member informs you that they had previously learned from gym owners that new members tend to check in at much higher rates in the first 90 days of their gym membership. How can you reconcile your findings with the qualitative information shared with you?

As with the previous exercises, it's important to note that there is no *single* correct answer to each question. It's valuable to document and be prepared to explain your rationale for any interpretation of the results.

2.3 *Reproducibility*

The technical steps of an analytics project are designed to be repeated: identifying, retrieving, cleaning, processing, and analyzing data should ideally be possible for others to *reproduce* using the report you publish as a source of documentation on the steps taken. Additionally, many of these steps are repetitive should you wish to redo or duplicate the analysis later, making an eye toward *reproducibility* beneficial to your peers and a significant time-saver for you.

2.3.1 What reproducibility is

Reproducibility is the capacity for a scientific study, analysis, or project to be replicated by your peers. A project is considered *reproducible* if the steps to re-create the methods, datasets, measures, and statistical tests are documented with the necessary detail for others to understand the steps taken and redo the same project. Figure 2.6 shows a recommended set of steps for enabling others to reproduce your research. In academic sciences, reproducibility is usually an essential condition for the publication of findings in peer-reviewed journals. Outside of a research institution, providing documentation for a project to enable reproducibility depends on the time and resources available within the organization.

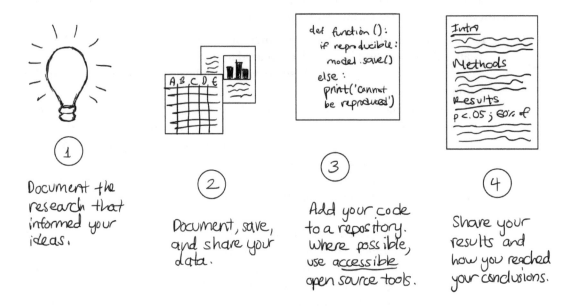

Figure 2.6 Recommended steps involved in reproducing a project

Regardless of the implementation of reproducible practices in the broader analytics team, it's beneficial to keep this detailed documentation for your work wherever possible. Ensuring that others can retest your findings with new or similar datasets or *build upon* your findings and create additional insights based on your work can have widespread benefits on the data-driven capacity of your team and organization.

2.3.2 *Documenting work*

In analytics projects, *documentation* is defined as a record of relevant detail so that the work can be reproduced or augmented by your peers at a later date. These records are rarely surfaced in detail as part of your stakeholder deliverables. Still, they are crucial, should your stakeholders request detailed follow-ups or want to dig deeper into your work.

Depending on the available tools and software, analytics teams may keep a separate internal record system or have reporting software that enables more granular viewing and editing permissions for the underlying queries and code. Regardless of the system or level of diligence of your specific team, there are some goals worth striving for in your work that will improve its accuracy and save you time in the long run:

- If you leave the team or organization for another role, the rest of the team should be able to understand the steps you took in a project and replicate them.
- At a high level, your stakeholders should understand the purpose of the steps you took in your projects.
- You should be able to redo a project without having to rewrite your queries or code.
- You should draw from previous projects' queries and code where applicable to save time and improve consistency across your work.
- You should be able to revisit a project two years later and understand the rationale and context for the work, based on the records kept.

With these principles in mind, let's discuss strategies for keeping high-quality records for each step in your analytics with minimal additional effort.

QUESTIONS AND HYPOTHESES

The questions and hypotheses developed as part of a project are presented in most final deliverables. Beyond restating them for your audience, it's valuable to share a summary of the rationale and context and any background research motivating the project. Questions asked of you by stakeholders do not exist in a vacuum, nor are they developed at random. Enumerating the sources of information that guided the questions helps get everyone on the same page. It allows others to build the knowledge base you and your stakeholders have developed as part of the project.

If you're familiar with the format of peer-reviewed papers, you'll know that a lengthy introduction or background section on all relevant background research precedes the statement of hypotheses and methods. Ideally, the reader is guided to the question and hypothesis based on the information provided.

A comprehensive introduction (often 10 or more pages) is rarely necessary outside of academia. Instead, the principles of structuring this section can be applied to the documentation you create for your questions and hypotheses. The level of detail included in each of the following can be tailored to the deliverable (e.g., a report or presentation):

- Begin the introduction or background section with the most *general* background information. This may include the organization's motivation for solving a problem, a component of a company's values, or other broad goals.
- Summarize any research conducted or previous work informing decisions on the organizational problem over time. Each example discussed should be increasingly narrower in scope, bringing increased focus to the current questions and problems the team is attempting to solve.
- By the end of the introductory section, it should be relatively clear to your audience why the question is being asked and why resources are dedicated to answering it instead of other questions.

Background

Sam's team writes a Background section for the detailed report deliverable.

> Creating a seamless customer experience is one of the company's core values. For years, we have sought to provide insights into the customer experience and understand what behaviors indicate a positive experience or friction when using the product.
>
> Visits to the Help Center, conversations with our support team, and customer satisfaction are key progress indicators measured across the company. Our research shows that high customer satisfaction consistently predicts customers renewing their subscriptions. Previous research (4 years ago) had identified increased visits to the Help Center and outreach to the support team as predictors of customer renewal. However, these trends have shifted with the growth of our customer base. The more customers visit the Help Center and contact Support, the *less* likely they are to renew their subscription.
>
> In the past two years, we've seen a substantial increase in the percentage of customers who visit the Help Center and contact Support. This has placed a strain on the Support staff and created concern, as our renewal rates have decreased in that period. We're also aware that in any month, at least 50% of customers contacting Support had first visited the Help Center and could not find the resources they needed. To that end, the product team aims to improve the experience and functionality of the Help Center to reduce the volume of requests to Support and mitigate customer cancellation risk.

Each statistic referenced in the Background section includes a link to another report or a reference for further information. The full report containing the summary is referenced in the appendix of the slideshow to share across the organization. An abbreviated Background section was developed for the slideshow presentation.

Background

- Recent research shows that higher frequency of visiting the Help Center and contacting Support is associated with decreased likelihood of customer subscription renewal.
- The percent of customers visiting the Help Center and contacting Support has been increasing for 2 years.
- Over 50% of customers contacting support first visited the Help Center and were unable to find the resources they needed.

Background slide in Sam's presentation summarizing information in the long-form report.

When working on ad hoc deliverables with a tight deadline, it's still valuable to provide brief documentation on the relevant context of the question. With just a few sentences, you can create reusable resources to share with your stakeholders and expand on them over time as follow-up questions are asked. We'll cover these types of deliverables in more depth throughout this book.

DATA SOURCES

Keeping a record of data sources used, and the methods for retrieving them, is crucial to reproducible work. This is the *most* important record to keep in developing your work. A complete history of all queries run to retrieve data from your database, datasets from third parties, or other information is necessary to rerun your analysis later and debug or correct any problems you identify as part of your work.

Imagine that a stakeholder identifies an error in your summary results, but you do not recall the exact steps you took to generate that summary in the first place! I recommend avoiding this scenario by keeping a *comprehensive history* of how you retrieved, shaped, and processed your data.

The record of data sources is usually quite simple compared to writing a background summary, and it's easily done as you perform the analysis. I recommend including the following steps in this process:

- Keep a record of all queries used in the final analysis. Depending on your organization's reporting or business intelligence software, this may be a built-in capability that requires no additional work.

- Keep an additional record of queries in exploratory steps that you chose *not* to include in the final report. These are useful if your stakeholders ask why you chose or chose not to take your work in a specific direction.

- Keep a record of all links to third-party data (e.g., a dataset from a government database) and the code used to retrieve that data.

- Add comments to your queries and your code to document their specific purpose and how to use them.

- When communicating with stakeholders in the final report and presentation, share the high-level data sources rather than the specific queries and code. Link to them or provide information on how to access them in your report.

Retaining a well-documented record of queries, code (including appropriate docstrings for your code), and data sources ensures you can edit or update your findings at a later date. This record can also be a starting place for future analyses, metrics, or data warehouse tables, saving your team effort over time.

Datasets

Sam's team uses reporting software that allows readers to view the report's underlying queries powering the charts and summaries. Thus, a single summary is written for both the report and slideshow:

> The following data sources were used in this analysis: (1) Page View events, which include visits to the Help Center, (2) Support ticket data, which includes chat support requests, and (3) aggregate customer satisfaction scores available in our *Customer Experience Pro* account. Average scores were compared between July to September and October to December, representing 90 days before and after changes were made.

(continued)

In addition to the summary, Sam included comments in each query underlying the report, indicating its purpose, the date range for which data is intended to be retrieved, and a brief rationale for any records filtered out of the final dataset. Since all datasets will likely be included in follow-up projects making changes to the Help Center, evaluating those changes will take a fraction of the time.

MEASURES AND METHODS

Nearly all consumers of your work will require sufficient context to understand how you chose to summarize and present quantitative results. This includes aggregating, tracking, and summarizing data, sharing the statistical techniques used, and explaining the steps taken to evaluate your results. Though we use summary tables, charts, and graphs to aid in the visual interpretation of the data, it's not always immediately apparent *why* you chose to measure and display something in a specific manner.

Documenting your methods involves creating a section on the methodological steps you take and interspersing relevant context throughout the presentation of results. This information is geared toward answering *why* you chose the steps you did to make sense of the data. This documentation strategy includes the following:

- Write a Methods section in all forms of deliverables (reports, presentations, etc.). This should include a list of *exploratory data analysis* steps taken to produce charts and summary tables, a list of statistical tests used, and any special considerations for how the data was evaluated.
- Include clear titles, labels, and brief descriptions of all charts and summary tables in your deliverables.
- Include a brief explanation of why the data is summarized in a specific way, especially when it differs from methods stakeholders are used to viewing (e.g., weekly totals instead of monthly).

Methods

Sam's team included the following Methods summary in their long-form report, which was then rewritten and abbreviated in a bullet-point format for the presentation.

Descriptive statistics were shown for the 90 days before and 90 days after the changes to the Help Center. Each measure where granular data was available (Help Center page views, chat support requests) had a daily total calculated, and a mean/median was calculated based on those totals. This aligns with the team's established daily volume metric for both measures. The overall average customer satisfaction score for the 90 days before/after the change was included. No other customer satisfaction aggregations were shown for this analysis due to the lack of availability of granular data.

A repeated measures *t*-test was used to compare the mean (average) daily volume of Help Center views and chat support requests in the 90 days before and after the changes were made. The results were evaluated with a 95% confidence interval.

In addition, Sam included the following notes in the presentation, where aggregate information on each metric was shown in a chart:

- A description of why the weekly volume was shown in the chart instead of daily volume (aggregating by week accounted for a drop in page views over the weekend, making it easier to see the increase over time).
- A reminder that the bar graph showing before/after customer satisfaction scores did not include row-level granular data.

Each strategy supports Sam's team in being proactive about expected questions from stakeholders and consumers of the report. This documentation saves time and effort for the team, builds stronger relationships with stakeholders, and aids stakeholders in developing a skill set in analytical methods.

2.3.3 *Exercises*

Now that you have a comprehensive example of the documentation included in a report for reproducibility, let's add relevant documentation to your analysis plan for the business analytics team of the high-end fitness company:

1. Since it opened its first gym seven years ago, the company has seen an average monthly membership increase of 5%, opening 18 locations across 3 cities. Write a background summary for your stakeholder presentation slideshow that highlights the relevant information motivating the analysis of the current promotion.
2. Provide a summary slide of the data sources used to analyze the promotion. In this summary, share the datasets that were *not* included and why.
3. Each data source is available in the company's data warehouse with the granular detail of each record. What type of documentation might you include about the queries used to retrieve that data?
4. Provide a summary slide of the methods used to analyze the data.

Keep returning to this example project as we discuss specific technical skills throughout this book. You'll have an opportunity to review and evaluate the appropriate level of detail for different stakeholders with each new topic discussed.

Summary

- The lifecycle of an analytics project starts with a *question*. Previous knowledge motivating the question guides the development of hypotheses, which inform the datasets and methods used to evaluate the question.
- *Operationalization* involves translating a concept into something *measurable*. This usually involves working with your stakeholders to take a heuristic (e.g., customer satisfaction) and creating a technical definition that can be directly assessed using data.

- Organizations have many different *data sources* that can be used for analysis. Some examples include clickstream data (tracking clicks, page views, and other individual events on a website or application), customer support data, and survey data. Each data source has strengths and limitations that you will need to consider when determining if the information you have can be used to answer your question.
- *The scope of interpretation* is the degree to which you can reasonably generalize your findings beyond the people included in your analysis. Your assessment of the appropriate scope of your findings will help guide your strategic recommendations to stakeholders.
- *Communicating results* to stakeholders involves tailoring final deliverables to their understanding of analytics, statistics, and previous information about the topic. There are many areas where you can expect follow-up questions and strategies you can apply for responding to common types of follow-ups.
- Documenting your background research, context, datasets, measures, and methods ensures that your work is appropriately *reproducible,* and it saves time, improves accuracy, and optimizes your team's ability to take on new projects.
- Managing the steps we learned requires developing an improved understanding of your stakeholders and their needs over time. However, you can apply many great strategies in your work today to better set yourself up for success.

Testing and
evaluating hypotheses

This chapter covers

- Conducting appropriate research to inform your hypothesis
- Choosing and implementing methods for gathering information
- Choosing and implementing a research design for your analysis
- Using testing and evaluation methods in different research programs

Now that you know what to expect at each step of an end-to-end analytics project, let's zoom in on the process of operationalizing questions, developing hypotheses, and choosing an appropriate method for evaluating your hypothesis.

The overarching topics in this chapter are usually covered in undergraduate and graduate courses in the sciences, with titles such as Research Methods or Experimental Design. The methods we will cover primarily draw from these curricula, but we will take a less traditional approach in covering each topic—we'll focus on *probabilistic* methods of thinking about our hypotheses and how to evaluate them. As in previous chapters, we will focus on a range of applied examples in a business or organization outside of those typically covered in academic coursework.

At this point, you may wonder why this book contains lengthy instructions for what will amount to a small portion of your deliverable—especially since we aren't covering the statistical tests used in the evaluation process until chapters 4 and 5. You're right to be skeptical, but hear me out! Regardless of whether you've practiced these skills in a formal capacity, I argue that this is *the most crucial chapter* to follow in depth. Here's why:

- *Your hypothesis is your foundation.* How you structure your hypothesis will help guide your audience through the methods of analysis you are using. Documenting your background evidence and informed guesses sets a clear standard for your organization and how they should do the same in their work.
- *Investigating a question and hypothesis is the core of data analytics.* An analyst asks and answers questions, choosing from various methods to evaluate data. Whether comparing groups, tracking a metric, or training a machine learning model, you are drawing on this skill set to decide how to reach your goal.
- *Mastering this skill set can determine the success of your career.* This applies to most professionals in the world of data (data analyst, data scientist, etc.). If you can demonstrate rigor in asking and answering questions, you will find it easier to succeed in your work and career.

3.1 *Informing a hypothesis*

Let's start off with a personal anecdote: during the first semester of my PhD program, my advisor sent me a public dataset to evaluate for potential analysis and publication. The dataset contained survey responses on adolescent behaviors and opinions across the United States. I was instructed to explore the available measures for interesting research questions and return with a hypothesis. After weeks of poring through the data catalog, published papers about the dataset, and some theoretical frameworks in our field, I came up empty. No amount of research got me closer to the right question, hypothesis, and methods.

It took discontinuing the degree and working as an analyst for several years to understand what led to that project's failure. As a new student and junior researcher, I approached the project with a naive understanding of the analytic constraints I was operating within. I did not understand the limitations of available data, how to navigate those gaps, and where I should exercise my agency as a researcher and make a decision with the best information available. I didn't know what the output of my project would even look like (which can lead to even more confusion, as depicted in figure 3.1). I was under the impression that if I consumed as much information as possible, a straightforward question and hypothesis would emerge, representing the next sensible direction for the field.

Figure 3.1   When you and your stakeholders agree on the question, hypothesis, and methods, you'll be able to better focus on delivering concrete recommendations.

Chapter 2 emphasized that research is not conducted in a vacuum. We seek information to inform our hypothesis and make an informed decision about how to structure a project. Conversely, there is rarely a complete and ideal set of information to guide our processes. You will often use your best judgment and acknowledge the information you have and don't have and the rationale for your decisions, so others can contribute over time.

For most of your projects, you will synthesize information from a handful of sources to set the context for your stakeholders. We'll discuss strategies you can use to gather information, even when you may lack sufficient context and information.

3.1.1   Collecting background information

Starting a new project can be daunting. Where do you begin to understand what's already been studied or researched? How do you know you're on the right track? Will your analysis and findings make sense to stakeholders who know the domain better than you?

If you've ever asked yourself the preceding questions, you're far from alone. Many analysts are brought into projects because of their experience working with *data* but not in the domain area. In these cases, accumulating background knowledge is necessary to understand the context of the project.

> **Starting an analytics project**
>
> Jay is an analyst on the insights team at a nonprofit raising money for cancer research. His typical tasks involve analyzing the success of fundraising campaigns and donor and volunteer engagement efforts, and creating reports for the board of directors. The

(continued)

team received a request for a new effort to bring in adolescent volunteers. The orga-nization wants to know what factors contribute to adolescent interest in volunteering, and what positive outcomes can adolescents expect when they do volunteer?

Jay has been designated the project lead for the effort to conduct research. Since this is a new area of focus for the insights team, they will have to synthesize a large body of work to understand the topic better.

I recommend taking a strategic approach to collecting information about a topic: research, interviews, and exploration.

RESEARCH

Research has a couple of definitions:

- The investigation and synthesis of available information to establish a baseline understanding of a topic
- The process of investigating a topic as a study or experiment to gain *new* information

The first definition of research enables the effective execution of the second defini-tion. In an ideal situation, a feedback loop can develop, leading to continued informa-tion gain on a topic.

Outside of an academic setting and specialized roles, few analysts are involved in publishing peer-reviewed papers. However, the principles of information synthesis remain the same: you compile an understanding of existing research and use it in your decisions about how to approach your investigations.

When researching a topic, I recommend the following steps:

1. *Identify academic domains that research your topic.* You can often draw a wealth of knowledge from academic and public sources. Does your project require an understanding of human behavior? Take a look at domains of study within psy-chology and sociology. Economic or job trends? Look for topics within macro and labor economics.

2. *Search for peer-reviewed papers about your topic.* If you're unfamiliar with your research topic, some trial and error may be necessary to identify the terminol-ogy used in a specific field. Once you've identified search terms that return appropriate results, look for 3 to 10 papers to inform your topic, prioritizing recent papers published by different authors.

3. *Evaluate the papers you've selected.* The introductions in recent papers from top journals in a field can provide a lens into cutting-edge questions about a domain area and an existing synthesis of the field. In addition to high-profile and recent research, look for papers with methods and samples closest to the population you will be working with (e.g., people in similar demographic groups and regions).

4   *Search for synthesized information outside of peer review.* Many resources draw from peer review outside the academic system. Government agencies publish datasets and reports regularly, providing insights into a topic over time. Many fields have journalists or industry experts publishing work on a topic—these can be followed for a layperson's evaluation of cutting-edge findings.

Synthesizing background information

Let's return to the insights team at the nonprofit to understand how they can strategically synthesize research. Jay's first step is to understand where the organization has gaps in its knowledge. The team understands the success of adult volunteering efforts but has no experience working with *adolescents*. They know adolescents may have different motivations, availability, and financial resources, and they will need guardian permission to participate. The team starts with a search for papers on adolescent volunteering behaviors. They guess that these are likely covered in the field of *developmental psychology*.

Next, Jay searches Google Scholar and an open-access journal called *PLOS ONE* for papers on *adolescent volunteering*. He narrows the search to papers published in the last 20 years, saving eight papers he believes are most relevant.

Jay's third step is to read the papers in depth to understand their methods and findings. One paper looks at outcomes associated with adolescent volunteering, finding that adolescents who volunteer are more likely to *continue* volunteering in adulthood. The study took place in Australia, which he notes may have economic and social conditions different from the United States, where he is located. However, the sample is quite large ($n > 2000$), and the study controls for socioeconomic status, indicating that the effect of volunteering was seen regardless of income. He saves this paper for the team to review.

Finally, Jay searches for information on the benefits of adolescent volunteering outside of peer-reviewed papers. He discovers informational pages on several nonprofit websites summarizing the benefits of volunteering. They cite additional studies that were not discovered in his initial search. They also give his team a concrete example of how their organization can communicate the benefits of volunteering for adolescents.

In applying these steps, Jay identifies information to guide questions and hypotheses while providing summary information that can be shared with other teams to drive their decisions.

STAKEHOLDER INTERVIEWS

Your stakeholders can be a wealth of information on the domain-specific context and rationale of the work they request from you. Domain experts likely have access to information about resources in their field (e.g., publications, conferences, industry experts) and lessons learned from their hands-on experience. As you build relationships with those you support, you will find opportunities for a *bidirectional flow of information* that enables you and your teams to better make decisions in your roles.

If you're unsure where to start with appropriate questions, I recommend building and iterating on a list of standard information you find helpful in your work. This will change over time, become more comprehensive, and better reflect the needs of your projects.

Here are some examples to get you started:

- *General context*—This is especially important when working with a new team or one that has shifted focus. Why is the project important, and why now?
- *Background information*—Ask your stakeholders what sources of information (colleagues, peer-reviewed papers, podcasts, talks, etc.) informed the decision to pursue a project.
- *Expected outcomes*—As discussed in chapter 2, ask your stakeholders what they expect (or *hypothesize*) will happen due to pursuing the project or initiative. What is the value of the project succeeding or failing?

A simple conversation asking your stakeholders the proper contextual questions can go a long way in a new project. You'll likely learn the information you need to close the gap between your deliverable and their *expectations* for the deliverable.

Clarifying open questions with stakeholders

Jay sets up a meeting with the project lead for the volunteer initiative on the program management team. He has prepared questions for the project lead, Emma, to fill gaps in his knowledge and share the results of his research.

Jay: Can you tell me about the motivation for reaching out to adolescents as potential volunteers? This is a new direction for us, and I want to understand why this is valuable.

Emma: The number of volunteer registrations is far lower than last year. My team manager spoke to the program management team at another nonprofit, and they've successfully increased registration by engaging adolescents.

Jay: What helped you decide this was the right initiative to pursue?

Emma: We did some research to see if other volunteer programs existed for adolescents at high schools or local community centers. We saw a few events at community centers, but none had a consistent presence or advertisements discussing the benefits of volunteering.

Jay: We found a good amount of information about that from peer-reviewed literature. In addition, the websites of many nonprofits have well-designed pages summarizing the benefits to volunteers, the community, and more.

Emma: Thanks for the information. A page on our website summarizing what we've learned about the benefits of volunteering may be a great addition to this project plan.

Jay: What are the specific outcomes you're hoping for by reaching out to potential adolescent volunteers?

Emma: We hope to increase the volunteer registration rate and tenure—the time a person continues to volunteer with us. It's also important to know what benefits might exist for adolescents who volunteer, since that's likely different from adults. We hope they do better in school, have fewer disciplinary problems, and improve their well-being. We want to report on each benefit to the board and in future grant applications.

EXPLORING AVAILABLE DATA

The third step is to explore the available data at your organization. This is done before the *exploratory data analysis* of the data collected as part of your project, and it serves to help operationalize your concepts (as discussed in chapter 2) and determine the size of the opportunity your organization is pursuing.

Opportunity sizing is a term commonly used in product management, and it refers to the process associated with estimating the potential quantitative effect of a project or course of action. The process involves the synthesis of external research and context with additional exploration and evidence gathered from data at the organization (sound familiar?). The outcome of an opportunity sizing effort is typically an estimated range of users, customers, or behaviors expected to be affected by the project or action. When multiple potential projects have quantitative measures that can be directly compared, opportunity sizing can be an excellent tool for prioritizing work within an organization.

Opportunity sizing

Jay needs to estimate the size of the opportunity to engage adolescent volunteers. He searches the organization's shared drive for information that can help estimate the potential effect of an adolescent volunteering initiative. The drive contains a historical record of presentations, whitepapers, program evaluations, and submitted grants for multiple efforts across five years. He also searches their city's database of grants to determine how many opportunities may be available to their organization by pursuing this effort.

Jay discovers the most recent performance report, which shows that the number of active volunteers has decreased for six months and is 20% lower than last year. New registrations are down, and volunteer tenure has slightly decreased in the same period.

In the donor database, Jay finds several previous donors have asked when the organization will directly engage younger volunteers. He also finds several available grants for organizations engaging youth in their community, totaling an opportunity of more than $200,000.

3.1.2 *Constructing your hypothesis*

With your background research complete, you're ready to construct an informed hypothesis. In a research methods class, students learn a formalized method of stating a *null hypothesis* (H_0) and an *alternative hypothesis* (H_1).

A study is conducted to determine if sufficient evidence exists to *reject* the null hypothesis and *accept* the alternative hypothesis. Here's an example of a hypothesis represented in this standardized format:

- H_0: The test scores in the treatment group (individual tutoring) are equal to or less than in the control group (no tutoring).
- H_1: There are significantly higher test scores in the treatment group (individual tutoring) compared to the control group (no tutoring).

This demonstrates a hypothesis with a *directional prediction*, indicating a desired *direction* of differences for the test group (higher scores). Specifying a direction in an alternative hypothesis is not required, though most studies have an inherent "desired" direction for the outcome. If the results support the statistical criteria you set for your evaluation, you *reject* the null hypothesis. You fail to reject the null hypothesis if your results do not meet the directional and statistical criteria.

A strong hypothesis adheres to the following criteria:

- It identifies the *independent variables* (predictors) and *dependent variables* (outcomes).
- It is a declarative statement about the expected outcomes.
- It is a clear, concise statement easily interpretable by your stakeholders and audience.

You may notice that the criteria for an alternative hypothesis include a specified *direction*, not a specific, *quantifiable estimate* of the expected change. In most studies and analyses, this is acceptable and well-understood by your audiences. Where possible, I recommend taking additional steps to estimate the *quantifiable difference* expected as part of your study, program, or experiment. This can be well-received by your stakeholders and provides you with additional numerical criteria to evaluate against your expectations.

3.1.3 *Quantifying your hypothesis*

The methods of defining a hypothesis that we've discussed so far are most closely aligned with the school of *frequentist hypothesis testing*. Frequentist testing is a specific interpretation of probability that aims to make inferences about the broader population based on samples of data from that population. As part of that school of research and statistics, hypotheses are typically structured as an educated guess about the presence of group differences, and sometimes about the direction of those differences. However, you may notice that we have stopped short of making specific, numerical estimates of the magnitude of those differences.

Quantifying a hypothesis is a process more aligned with the *Bayesian* approach to hypothesis testing, which interprets probabilities as a number representing the degree of belief about an event, based on the evidence available. This is not often taught in introductory statistics courses, but it can be a valuable approach that encourages you to think strategically about the actual differences and changes that you hypothesize will occur.

Quantifying a hypothesis is simple—estimate the size of the difference between groups, and state it as part of your hypothesis. Now, I'm not suggesting you make something up! As part of this process, you will have an opportunity to learn about existing information on your topic of interest through peer-reviewed research, existing data at your organization, or domain knowledge from your stakeholders.

Beyond quantifying a hypothesis, we won't go into depth on probability and Bayesian statistics—there are already fantastic resources out there on those topics. However, this is a great first step toward *thinking probabilistically* as an analyst.

Let's look at an example using Python. We will generate two overlapping distributions to simulate a hypothetical *treatment* and *control* group for the hypothesis in section 3.1.2. The distribution for the treatment group is shifted two standard deviations to the right to demonstrate what a highly effective treatment with a statistically significant difference will look like:

```python
import numpy as np                              ◁── Import
import matplotlib.pyplot as plt                      libraries.

c = np.random.normal(0, 1, size=500)            ◁── Create two distributions two
t = np.random.normal(2, 1, size=500)                 standard deviations apart.

plt.hist(c, alpha=0.5, bins=25, color="black")      ◁── Visualize the
plt.hist(t, alpha=0.5, bins=25, color="lightgray")      distributions.
plt.legend(["Control", "Treatment"])
```

If the two distributions shown in figure 3.2 accurately represent the population we are studying, we can estimate that any sample from the population of interest would have scores *two standard deviations higher* if placed in the experimental group. Since we can't study the entirety of most populations, we will use our sample data to estimate the *magnitude* of change we might see in the whole population.

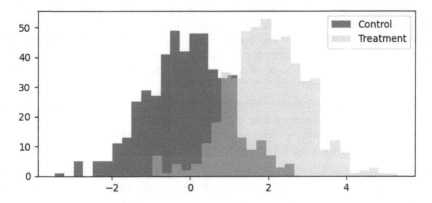

Figure 3.2 Distributions showing a hypothetical group difference between the treatment and control groups

However, if you were conducting a study on test scores in a school district of 100,000 students, you might be able to estimate the population's distribution of by looking at every student's grades. The existing data about their performance could be used to quantify your hypothesis and understand the true shape of the underlying distribution. You probably *wouldn't* have time to put all 100,000 into experiment and control groups, but you could randomly sample a subset of students and make several assumptions about their information:

- The control group will have a distribution roughly identical to the student population.
- The treatment group will have a distribution representing a positive shift in the number of standard deviations (or a specific point increase in raw test scores) in line with those found in previous studies.

Where comprehensive research is not available to estimate change, you can quantify expected change using the best available information from qualitative sources and the goals of the program or study.

Quantifying hypothesized changes

Jay constructs the following hypotheses for his report on the upcoming evaluation of the new volunteer engagement:

- H_0: There is no significant difference in the registration rate between adult and adolescent volunteering events.
- H_1: There is a significant difference in the registration rate between adult and adolescent volunteering events.

In addition to null and alternative hypotheses with an expected direction, Jay attempts to estimate the quantifiable change in registrations for the program team. He recalls that one peer-reviewed paper found that more than 50% of adolescents participate in volunteering activities, compared to less than 30% of adults. This aligns with the organization's knowledge of volunteer registration rates at engagement activities for adults: about 25% of event attendees will register to volunteer. The organization estimates 5,000 adolescents from local, middle, and high schools will attend the volunteer fairs at schools and community centers. If 50% of them register across the six months when the events are scheduled, the number of weekly volunteer registrations for the organization will increase by 60% overall. Jay *quantifies* his hypotheses with this estimation:

- H_0: The is no significant difference in the registration rate between adult and adolescent volunteering events.
- H_1: The registration rate for adolescent volunteering events will be 50%, compared to 25% for adult volunteering events.

Jay can comprehensively evaluate the program outcomes with a quantified hypothesis. He can compare the actual versus hypothesized changes and monitor how closely their performance aligns with reported trends on volunteering behavior and nonprofit success.

3.1.4 *Exercises*

You are part of a product analytics team at an e-commerce company that designs A/B test experiments to increase subscriptions and improve users' experience with the software. You are designing a series of experiments to answer the question, "What page layouts, tooltips, and recommendations decrease the rate of abandoned shopping carts without a purchase?":

1 What sources of information can you use to collect background information on the expected outcomes of the software changes? What questions will you ask your stakeholders to gain the appropriate context for the experiment?

2 Design an experiment that compares three experiment groups with different layouts and one control group. Write null and alternative hypotheses based on the research question.

3 Update your null and alternative hypotheses to *quantify* the expected outcome for the experimental and control groups.

When completing this exercise, you can define the expected outcomes (hypothesized group differences, direction, and quantified values) using an appropriate example. You can also suggest data sources internal to an organization that would be valuable to have access to (e.g., database tables and reports).

3.2 Methods of gathering evidence

With a defined hypothesis, the next step is to collect and report on data to test and evaluate that hypothesis. But what shape should the data be in? How exactly is everything structured? There are *a lot* of methods to choose from, guided by your question. We'll cover three methods under which most research can be classified: descriptions, correlations, and experiments. The use of each method differs by the discipline of study and type of data usually collected, but these approaches are common to work in product analytics, marketing analytics, business analytics, and more.

3.2.1 *Descriptions*

The simplest data analysis is a presentation of *descriptive information.* As the name suggests, this method *describes* a phenomenon without manipulating a test variable or condition. This approach to analysis is ideal for understanding new data sources, developing metrics, and opportunity sizing.

Descriptive methods can involve existing data analysis or active data collection and can be performed on quantitative and qualitative information. Data is often presented using measures of central tendency, trends over time, or group differences.

DESCRIPTIVE STATISTICS

The term *descriptive statistics* refers to methods used to summarize insights from a quantitative dataset. An analyst determines which descriptive measures are most appropriate for the dataset and what information they want stakeholders to glean from the data. The descriptive measures can include measures of central tendency (e.g., mean, median, mode) and measures of the distribution (such as standard deviation) for continuous data, and counts or proportions for categorical data.

Reporting on descriptive statistics can be part of an inferential statistical workflow or exist as a standalone deliverable if it meets the stakeholder's needs. Many reports and dashboards rely entirely on descriptive statistics to deliver value. While the actual analysis is straightforward, descriptive statistics can be the most useful routine insights used within an organization.

When conducting *observational research,* descriptive statistics are often the *only* quantitative information shared with your stakeholders. Instead of using them as context in experiments to guide your use of statistical tests, they often need to be shared quickly in order to enable decision-making. In these situations, I recommend the following points to ensure you're sharing the most valuable information:

- *Select your statistics carefully.* Choosing appropriate descriptive statistics requires you to thoroughly explore the dataset, including the shape of its distribution, and to understand what you *cannot* interpret if you exclude a statistic from your final deliverable. Graphs with the mean may lead your readers to very different conclusions than they would draw about the same information if presented with the median, sum, or percentage of the total.
- *Guide your stakeholders through interpreting results.* Deliverables relying on descriptive statistics are often designed to be straightforward self-service tools (e.g., a dashboard). However, stakeholders have a broad range of analytic proficiency and may draw different conclusions from the same information set. Include strong guidance for what you can and cannot conclude from a specific tool.
- *Take care not to conflate explanations with causation.* Descriptive data points tracked over time are common within organizations. If their presentation is not paired with a strong understanding of what *affects* the tracked data points, stakeholders may be left with poor estimations of what causes the changes and trends.

Let's look at an example of how different descriptive statistic presentations can affect interpretation. We'll use a dataset called `rat_sightings.csv`, a subset of the NYC Open Data 311 dataset. Each row is the number of calls to the 311 hotline about public rat sightings per day between January 1, 2018, and June 30, 2022 (the entire 311 hotline dataset contains billions of rows about thousands of call types).

How might we answer the question, "Have the number of rat sightings changed over time?" Our independent variable is the *number of rat sightings*, and our dependent variable is *time*; no group differences or pre/post comparisons are necessary for this question.

We can import the dataset in Python and generate a line plot as follows:

```
import pandas as pd                              Import
import matplotlib.pyplot as plt                  libraries.

rats = pd.read_csv("rat_sightings.csv", index_col=0)    Import the csv as a
                                                        pandas dataframe.
```

```
plt.plot(rats["rat_sightings"])                    Plot the
plt.xlabel("Day (Starting 1/1/2018)")              line graph.
plt.ylabel("# of Rat Sightings")
```

From the resulting graph in figure 3.3, we can see the following:

- The number of daily rat sightings has been trending upward in recent years.
- There are consistent weekly and monthly seasonal trends in the number of rat sightings.

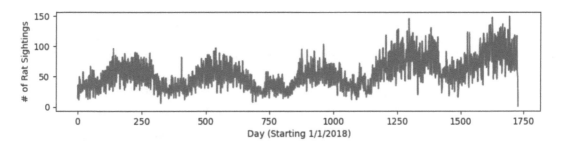

Figure 3.3   Time series plot of daily reports of rat sightings in NYC

The daily plot makes it challenging to estimate the true *volume* of rat sightings in larger time periods (e.g., a week or a month). If this were a final deliverable, you could expect to receive follow-up questions to create views at different granularities (e.g., week versus month). This can be achieved through aggregations, such as a mean, median, or sum:

```
                                                   Convert the
                                                   column to a
rats = rats.reset_index()                          date format.
rats["day"] = pd.to_datetime(rats["day"], format="%m/%d/%y")

rats_group = rats.groupby(pd.Grouper(key="day", axis=0, freq="ME")).agg(
    ["sum", "mean", "median"]
)                                    Aggregate the dataset by month.

rats_group.columns = rats_group.columns.get_level_values(1)    Reset the
                                                                column names.
plt.plot(rats_group["sum"])                        Plot the
plt.xlabel("Month (Starting 1/1/2018)")            line graph.
plt.ylabel("# of Rat Sightings")
```

The resulting visual in figure 3.4 makes it easier for stakeholders to understand the *volume* of rat sightings over time. The weekly seasonality causing the dense spikes has been removed, highlighting the monthly seasonality associated with colder months (approx. November through March) and warmer months (April through October) in New York City.

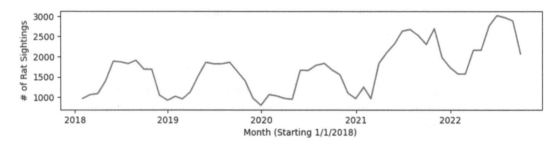

Figure 3.4   Time series plot of total monthly rat sightings in NYC

Finally, we will compare the mean and median values. This will help us determine if there are properties of the underlying distribution we should highlight in a deliverable:

```
plt.plot(rats_group["mean"], marker="o")        ←┐ Plot the mean
                                                   as a line graph.

plt.plot(rats_group["median"], marker="x")      ←┐ Plot the median as an
                                                   overlapping line graph.
plt.legend(["Mean", "Median"])   ←┐ Add a legend
                                    and labels.
```

There's minimal difference in figure 3.5 between the mean and median values over time, indicating that there is likely a consistent normal distribution underlying the dataset. We can also see that the shape of the data over time is identical to the graph showing the *sum* of rat sightings. Given that this second graph adds little new information, we can leave it out of our final deliverable. Instead, we can include a table or sentence describing the mean and median values and how they have changed over time.

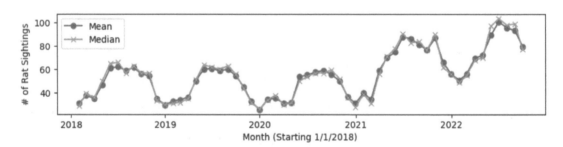

Figure 3.5   Time series plot of mean and median monthly rat sightings in NYC

Describing a dataset

Let's return to Jay's insights team and review the statistics he includes in his report. Three months have passed, and 20 of the planned 40 volunteering events have concluded.

For those 20 events, the registration rate was an average of 36%. This is lower than the anticipated rate (50%); however, this is higher than the rate for the 22 adult volunteering events (21%), and the overall number of registrations is the highest in the organization's history. The average volunteer tenure has not changed; however, we do not expect to determine if there are changes for at least another 3 to 6 months.

This descriptive information highlights the percentage change (a *relative* value) and a rolling average value of weekly registrations (an *absolute* value). Including both together is more valuable than each measure on its own and sets the context for statistical tests performed in the evaluation.

QUALITATIVE RESEARCH

Qualitative analysis involves the synthesis, analysis, and interpretation of non-numerical data. This often requires deriving insights from unstructured or free-form language data recorded as text. As an analyst, you may be asked to employ methods used in humanities and social sciences (e.g., one-to-one interviews, focus groups) or to derive insights from much larger samples of text data using *natural language processing.*

We will discuss each of these approaches in more detail throughout this book. For now, I recommend the following takeaways when deriving insights from qualitative data:

- Quotes and themes from interviews, focus groups, or free text survey responses are excellent *aids* to bring quantitative insights to life. A slide or section with anecdotes that support your interpretation can help ground your analysis in the experience of the people you collect data from.
- Small-sample qualitative methods (e.g., one-to-one interviews, focus groups) can be an appropriate starting point for research but struggle with *generalizability* when performed independently. You will likely need to complement qualitative with quantitative methods.
- Natural language processing approaches (e.g., sentiment analysis, topic modeling) can support generating insights for larger samples of text data but can be confusing for someone unfamiliar with the methods. Set strong expectations with stakeholders on what the deliverable will look like and how it is derived.

WORDS OF WARNING: DESCRIPTION VS. INFERENCE

Descriptive methods are intended to summarize the characteristics of *a specific set of data.* But how do you know if any group differences are statistically meaningful or if you can *infer* that your measures exist in the broader population?

If you are presenting descriptive information in a deliverable, consider the following limitations and communicate them to your intended audience:

- A trend, mean, or median value is *not* sufficient to infer that your findings exist beyond the dataset you are working with.
- A mean or median value between groups is *not* sufficient to determine if differences are large enough to be meaningful.

- A current trend is not guaranteed to *continue*—especially if you don't yet understand the factors influencing the trend.

3.2.2 *Correlations*

One of the most common approaches to comparing continuous data is to look for
associations between variables. These associations usually take the form of a measure of
covariance (an unstandardized measure of how two variables *vary together*) or *correlation*,
which is a standardized covariance measure. The term *correlation* is well understood
outside of data practitioners and can be explained to your stakeholders using plain
language terminology and mathematical concepts from high school algebra.

Pearson's correlation is the best-known method of identifying linear associations
between variables. It can be used with any continuous data, does not require you to
standardize your units, and the direction of the relationship is easy to interpret and
explain (e.g., a negative correlation coefficient indicates a negative relationship). You
can also expect that most stakeholders and partners outside a data team have encountered Pearson's correlations in their careers.

Let's build on our example `rat_sightings.csv` data. We saw in the previous section that there is a seasonality to the number of rat sightings in New York City, with
more being reported during warmer months and fewer during winter months. We
can explore whether there are associations between rat sightings and weather parameters (temperature, humidity, wind speed, or precipitation) on a given day by combining these two data sources. A new file, `weather.csv`, contains daily weather
parameters from January 1, 2018, to December 31, 2020 (three out of the five years
included in the rat dataset). We'll join the dataset and generate a matrix of Pearson's
correlations as follows:

```
weather = pd.read_csv("weather.csv", index_col=0)        ◁—┐ Import the dataset and
weather = weather.reset_index()                               convert the day column
weather["day"] = pd.to_datetime(weather["day"], format="%m/%d/%y")    to a datetime.

rats_weather = pd.merge(
    weather, rats, how="left", on="day"        | Join the weather
).fillna(0)                                     ◁—┘ and rat datasets.

corrs = rats_weather.corr()                                      ◁—┐ Generate a correlation
corrs.style.background_gradient(cmap="RdBu", vmin=-1)               | matrix and add color.
```

The daily sightings of rats (shown in figure 3.6) have a strong positive linear correlation with high and low temperatures on the same day. We can see that the high and
low temperatures are correlated at nearly $r = 1$, indicating they are likely not independent, and we should select *one* of the variables to highlight the relationship. We can
also see a weak to moderate *negative* correlation with wind speed and little to no association with humidity or precipitation.

	rat_sightings	high_temp	low_temp	humidity	wind_speed	precip
rat_sightings	1.000000	0.600707	0.615463	0.153749	-0.242205	-0.029722
high_temp	0.600707	1.000000	0.962917	0.151777	-0.231311	-0.036839
low_temp	0.615463	0.962917	1.000000	0.177102	-0.260153	-0.026765
humidity	0.153749	0.151777	0.177102	1.000000	0.029353	0.233285
wind_speed	-0.242205	-0.231311	-0.260153	0.029353	1.000000	0.212698
precip	-0.029722	-0.036839	-0.026765	0.233285	0.212698	1.000000

Figure 3.6 Pearson's correlations between the number of daily rat sightings and weather parameters

An association with a strong Pearson's correlation coefficient is often easy to visualize and share as a scatterplot in reports or dashboards. If the trend is unclear, add a regression line to the plot to demonstrate the linear relationship better.

```
import seaborn as sns                          ◁─┐  Import seaborn for more
                                                  │  advanced visualizations.

sns.regplot(               ◁─┐  Generate a scatterplot
    x="low_temp",             │  with a regression line.
    y="rat_sightings",
    data=rats_weather,
    marker="+",
)                                    ┐  Add x- and
plt.xlabel("Daily Low Temp")    ◁──┘  y-axis labels.
plt.ylabel("Daily Rat Sightings")
```

As we saw in the correlation matrix, figure 3.7 depicts a clear positive correlation between the daily low temperature and the number of rat sightings. The warmer the temperature, the more rat sightings people report to the city's 311 hotline.

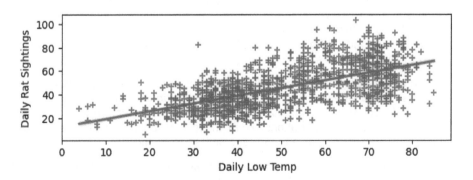

Figure 3.7 Scatterplot of daily low temperatures versus daily rat sightings

DELIVERABLES USING CORRELATIONS

The previous correlational relationship is an example of an association that is valuable to deliver in advance of a complete statistical analysis with predictors of change. A simple deliverable communicating the expected increase in rat sightings associated with warmer months or a heat wave will allow interested parties (e.g., a government agency or a restaurant) to make preparations based on the information. It won't be sufficient information to comprehensively *reduce* rat populations—that requires more sophisticated methods we will cover in later sections. However, this is an example of knowledge that generates value by sharing in advance of more complex analyses.

When sharing deliverables based on correlations, I recommend the following steps to ensure the accuracy of the results you share:

- If you're using Pearson's correlation, explore and visualize all correlations for the *linearity* of the trend. The scatterplot in figure 3.7 shows that the trend is approximately linear; in many cases, the relationship may be better fit by a *curvilinear* trend line. We'll discuss methods for achieving this in chapter 4.
- Ensure that the default Pearson's correlation is appropriate for your analysis when generating correlations. If you are generating correlations between ordinal data points or are more interested in the *relative* scores of your variables, Spearman's correlation is a more appropriate choice for your analysis.
- As shown in this section, correlations can provide a great starting point for planning and decision-making. However, they are rarely sufficient if the goal is to move the needle on one of the measures. Work with your stakeholders to determine if the correlations you report on are appropriate for their needs or if an experimental method is necessary.

Discovering correlations

Let's return to Jay and the insights team at the nonprofit to see the associations they discovered in their evaluation and how they report on them.

Jay has shared the initial descriptive summary with Emma, the program manager in charge of the youth volunteering events. The initial findings seem promising; however, she notes that the number and percentage of event attendees registering to volunteer varies widely. She asks Jay if he can identify some factors correlated with event registration rates.

Since only 20 events have occurred by this point, Jay decides to retrieve data from the last 100 adult events and select information about them: the number of staff, the number of event attendees, the amount of money spent on food and catering, and the number of registrations. From these data points, he derives the ratio of attendees to registrations and the ratio of staff to attendees.

Jay discovers the strongest correlation ($r = 0.65$) is between the ratio of attendees to registrations and the ratio of staff to attendees. When he creates a scatterplot of these two variables, he sees a clear linear trend between the variables; when he generates separate trend lines for adult versus youth events, they appear to be nearly identical.

Jay incorporates his findings into the draft report he prepares for the program team. He recognizes that communicating the insight to the team *now* can potentially benefit the volunteer events scheduled in the coming weeks. He informs Emma of the relationship he discovers and recommends increasing the total number of staff scheduled to support larger events. He stresses that the relationship he discovered is only an association and that he will follow up with a more in-depth analysis after the scheduled volunteer events have passed.

Correlations can be inherently valuable insights to share as part of your deliverables. Sometimes, they may even derive value if shared before the final deliverable. When doing so, manage stakeholder expectations about the validity and noncausal nature of the relationship you are communicating.

WORDS OF WARNING: CORRELATION VS. CAUSATION

You may have heard the phrase, *correlation does not equal causation.* This is emphasized in statistics and research methods curricula. It's a phrase associated with analytics humor—for example, Tyler Vigen has a web page dedicated to spurious correlations (https://tylervigen.com/spurious-correlations).

Conflating correlation with causation can pose challenges for an analytics team. In addition to stakeholder misalignment, conflating correlational with causal relationships can detract from efforts to effect change on an outcome, leading to poor-quality recommendations and inefficient resource use. The examples of strong correlational relationships shown in figures 3.6 and 3.7 are valuable to share on their own, with an emphasis that no requisite work was done to establish cause and effect.

In the case of associating rat sightings with warmer temperatures, we can look at the following information to dissect the limitations of this relationship:

- Does warmer weather *cause* more rat sightings? If we attribute a causal relationship to this question, can we manipulate our independent variable (temperature) to change the dependent variable (the number of rat sightings)?
- Are rat sightings representative of the rat *population* or the *visibility* of the rat population?
- Is the goal to reduce the rat *population* or the *visibility* of the rat population? (We will expand more on this in chapters 6 and 7.)

Investigating these questions will guide your messaging to stakeholders, help you focus on what you can and cannot manipulate in your evaluations, and set you up for an *experimental design* to more appropriately attribute cause and effect to a phenomenon you are analyzing.

3.2.3   Experiments

An *experiment* is an investigation where an independent variable is directly manipulated and the dependent variable is observed and measured. A researcher will seek to control as many conditions of the experiment as possible so that changes in the dependent variable can be confidently attributed to the manipulation of the independent variable. Simply put, the goal is to determine to the best of one's ability whether A *causes* B. A simple example is depicted in figure 3.8.

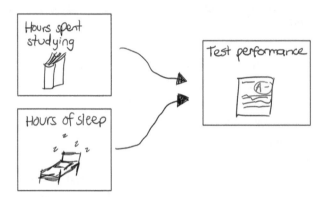

Figure 3.8   A hypothesized causal relationship between two independent and one dependent variables

In an ideal situation, an experiment meets the following conditions:

- *Random selection*—Participants or subjects in an experiment should be randomly selected from the population. Selection can be purely random, *stratified* (participants chosen in proportion to relevant subgroups), or *clustered* (participants divided into groups, and randomly selected at the group level).
- *Random group assignment*—Selected participants should be randomly assigned to one of the groups in the experiment (e.g., treatment versus control). Just as with random selection, assignment can be purely random or stratified.
- *Controlled environment*—The experiment should occur in highly controlled conditions, where as many variables as possible are managed or removed from the environment to better attribute cause to the independent variable. For example, an A/B test might *only* change the color of a button on a website and track differences in newsletter subscription rates between groups. Since only the color differed between the three groups (red, blue, green), the team can confidently say that the red button *caused* or *influenced* more people to subscribe to the newsletter.
- *Manipulating independent variables*—The independent variable should be a condition that you can directly *manipulate* and change to confidently attribute cause to the changes you control for as the researcher.

In an academic or clinical setting, you may be familiar with a *randomized controlled trial* as the ideal standard of experiment used to attribute cause. This includes trials for new medication, medical treatment, psychological studies, and more. Experimentation is also commonly used in other industries, absent the laboratory settings associated with the practice. Experiments are used in nonprofits to evaluate the effectiveness of programs. Businesses can use experiments to assess the efficacy of iterative changes on a website or product.

QUASI-EXPERIMENTS

In many cases, you will want to design experiments where the independent variable is a characteristic inherent to your participants and not something you can directly manipulate and assign. Statistically significant differences will often exist between participant demographic groups or inherent characteristics. Depending on the questions you are answering, you will likely either be looking to control for these variables or to measure them inherently as part of your core evaluation. The latter study design is known as a *quasi-experiment*.

For example, a study comparing the efficacy of a blood pressure medication between men and women has a valid body of research suggesting there will be differences in blood pressure decreases between those groups. However, the researcher cannot randomize participants into the Male/Female categories—they can only work with the characteristics of the participants selected for the study. Figure 3.9 shows a simple comparison of blood pressure records between participants after receiving medication for four weeks.

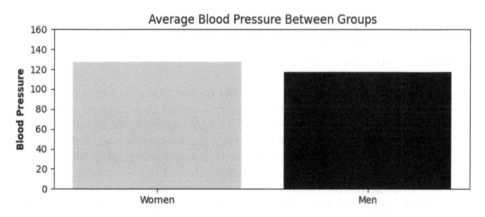

Figure 3.9   Quasi-experiments have a similar design to controlled experiments without random group assignment.

Quasi-experiments comparing participant demographics are common in academic research, clinical trials, and nonprofits, where differences between groups are often expected and meaningful phenomena to report on. In a business setting, participant demographic groups are frequently used as the basis for *segmenting* users into cohorts based on observed or expected behaviors.

Here are some example quasi-experimental research questions across industries:

- Do male/female and elementary/middle school students see improved math scores when participating in an individualized tutoring program?
- Do customers renew their subscriptions for longer in rural, urban, or suburban areas?
- How do youth from different family income brackets benefit from extra tutoring?
- How often do users at different career stages visit and engage with our website and product?

Quasi-experimental studies can be incorporated into a randomized controlled trial or exist as a standalone evaluation. In both cases, researchers will typically compare multiple participant characteristic groups to ensure appropriate documentation of all subgroup trends. A combination of subgroups is often compared for *interaction effects*. This view of participants is more prone to Type 1 (false-positive) errors but can also lead to more granular insights.

WORDS OF WARNING: EVIDENCE VS. PROOF

Evidence and proof are not the same thing. *Evidence* is information supporting a hypothesis or theory; *proof* is a claim treated as a rule and not designed to be refuted. Even if someone references data or evidence supporting a "proven" statement, that does not make their conclusions data-informed. A "proven" statement or belief is remarkably impervious to change or new information that contradicts previous information. As analysts and researchers, we collect *evidence* with the understanding that future information can counter previous information and be accepted if the methods used to collect and analyze it are sound.

> **NOTE** Using the word "proof" is a pet peeve of mine as a data professional. I have stakeholders who jokingly share that they know not to use that word around me, as if it were a generally inappropriate term to use in the workplace. While I may be considered on the lookout for attempts to "prove" something with data, this is evidence of a strong relationship with the teams I collaborate with. My colleagues will catch and correct themselves mid-sentence as we discuss projects. Over time, I have found that they are far more prepared for the times we find evidence contradicting previous knowledge within the organization.

It may seem like I am making a trivial distinction over two words. Still, I emphasize this because how the language is used within an organization is reflective of its data-informed culture. Organizations and teams that frequently assume information is *proof* of a phenomenon are often resistant to change and new information, even when ignoring that information could have a negative effect on the organization. In fact, many such organizations tend to approach data in a backward capacity—they look for information that *proves* a strongly held belief.

Managing the misuse and misinterpretation of findings can be challenging for an analyst; you may functionally take on an entire organization's culture without sufficient resources. At a *minimum,* I recommend sticking to a script around the interpretation of findings in your deliverables and communications:

- *Use your language carefully*—Phrases like "we discovered evidence in support of the hypothesis" can go a long way when re-emphasized across deliverables.
- *Guide stakeholder interpretations*—As we discussed in chapter 2, a slide or section with recommended statements of interpretation can be *very* helpful to your stakeholders if they are less experienced in leveraging data and evidence in their work.
- *Provide context for why findings change*—If you present findings that contradict previous findings or strongly held beliefs, include context for why the findings or trends may have changed. Has your user base transformed since the analysis was last performed? Was your study conducted on a different sample than usual? Did you approach your work in a novel way?

Standardizing your communication with stakeholders can go a *long way* toward building a data-informed relationship with your stakeholders, even when you lack the resources to create an organizational culture shift around using data.

3.2.4   *Types of study design*

When researchers choose to conduct an experiment, they have to select an appropriate *study design* in order to identify how to best evaluate their participants. The study design refers to the method of assigning participants into *comparison groups*, which serve as the independent variable of the study. The study design informs what statistical tests should be used to determine if group differences are statistically meaningful.

When evaluating multiple hypotheses, a study can feasibly include more than one study design. However, a single hypothesis is usually evaluated with one study design and one type of statistical test.

We'll be discussing some of the most common study designs used in academia, businesses, and other types of organizations. This list is *far* from exhaustive; there are dozens of study designs used to answer specialized questions in specific domain areas beyond the scope of this book. However, the study designs we'll cover here will likely apply to 90% or more of the use cases you will encounter in the first few years of your analytics career.

BETWEEN-SUBJECTS

A *between-subjects design* compares your dependent variable between *separate groups of participants*, which is your *independent variable* (e.g., total purchases made on a website compared between geographic locations). This method is used in the majority of experiment and study examples we've discussed so far.

In this design, participants belong to *mutually exclusive groups* either based on an inherent characteristic (e.g., age) or random assignment to a group (e.g., treatment versus control). Statistical tests for *independent samples* (referring to different, independent groups, which will be covered in chapter 4) are then used to compare values on the dependent variable between each group in the study. Figure 3.10 shows a bar graph comparing blood pressure *between* two treatment groups and a control group.

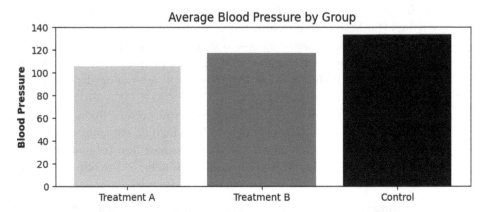

Figure 3.10   Between-subjects comparisons evaluate differences between mutually exclusive characteristics or assignments.

WITHIN-SUBJECTS

A *within-subjects design* (also known as a *repeated measures design*) involves exposing *every participant* to *every independent* variable condition in an experiment. Participants are repeatedly measured on the dependent variable before and after exposure to the independent variable condition. The study design may include a two-group pre/post comparison or repeated assessment across multiple time points. Experiments with a repeated measures design will use different variations of statistical tests than those used to evaluate a between-subjects design. Figure 3.11 shows one group's recorded blood pressure before and after a treatment was administered.

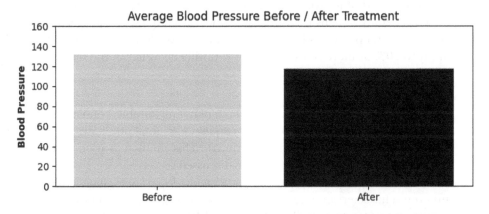

Figure 3.11   Within-subjects comparisons evaluate differences before and after treatment.

COHORT COMPARISONS

A *cohort study* is a type of study that groups participants into meaningful cohorts to be evaluated on a selected measure over extended periods of time. Participants can be assigned to cohorts based on characteristics that change over time (e.g., age or the year they subscribed to a service) or on static characteristics (e.g., school attended, subscription tier).

Cohort study designs combine within-subjects and between-subjects approaches in order to track meaningful changes over time that would otherwise be missed with a simple before versus after comparison. These studies also exclude random assignment and instead seek to identify whether measurable differences in trends occur over time between mutually exclusive groups. Figure 3.12 shows the blood pressure of three *age cohort* groups each week over a period of twelve weeks.

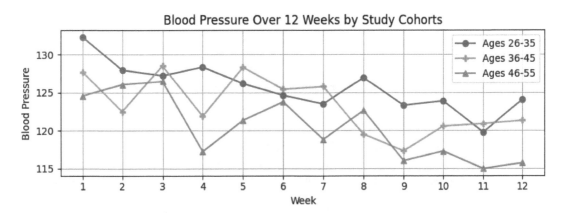

Figure 3.12 Cohort comparisons evaluate *meaningful* cohort groups over time.

LONGITUDINAL COMPARISONS

Both within-subjects and cohort designs are types of *longitudinal comparisons*. A longitudinal study design assesses participants *repeatedly* at *multiple points over time*, many collecting data repeatedly over weeks, months, or even years. These study designs look for discernable changes and trends in a dependent variable over the desired time period, and they are often used to study health outcomes that would be challenging to detect in shorter clinical trials.

Longitudinal studies can also incorporate both between-subjects and within-subjects comparisons in order to assess differences between randomly assigned groups or cohorts over time. Participants may be assigned to one of multiple treatment groups for a multi-year pharmaceutical trial, or different geographical cohorts might be monitored to understand their spending patterns over a calendar year.

Longitudinal tests with a limited number of time periods are often assessed using repeated measures univariate tests (e.g., *t*-tests, ANOVAs). Those who follow participants for longer periods of time may require more specialized statistical methods tailored to the question (e.g., survival analysis, growth curve analysis). Figure 3.13 shows a longitudinal study measuring blood pressure each year over the course of twelve years for two treatment groups and a control group.

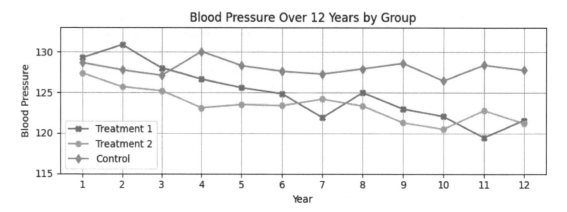

Figure 3.13   **Longitudinal comparisons evaluate participants over months, years, or even lifetimes.**

Evaluating the efficacy of a program

Our analyst Jay is ready for the final step of his evaluation. The program team has completed all of its 40 youth volunteering events. Jay has retrieved and prepared the data for analysis, recalculated his descriptive statistics, and updated correlations on the relationship between staff-to-attendee ratios and the registration rate (percentage of attendees who register to volunteer).

He also performs an *independent samples* t-test to assess his *between-subjects design* comparing the registration rate of the 40 youth volunteering events to the 38 adult volunteering events held in the previous six months—the same duration of time in which the youth events were held. He finds that the youth events had significantly higher registration rates than the adult volunteering events. There was *no* difference in the staff-to-attendee ratio that might account for this finding, so Jay concludes that the youth volunteering events were more effective at registering new volunteers than adult events.

In 3, 6, and 9 months, he intends to follow up on his analysis to compare the *tenure* of the new adolescent and adult cohorts that registered and the percentage that are still active. He plans to perform a repeated measures ANOVA to assess the differences in tenure and a survival regression analysis to assess trends in continued volunteering activity.

Jay's complete analysis plan includes a range of valuable descriptive methods (weekly trends), correlations (between staff-to-attendee ratio and registration rates), and experiments using a between-subjects and within-subjects comparison. Along with the results from each method, he provides the program team with recommendations on how to register new volunteers and continue to engage them over time.

3.2.5 Exercises

Your product analytics team at the e-commerce company has completed the A/B test comparing three different website layouts implemented with the goal of *decreasing the rate of abandoned shopping carts without a purchase*:

1 What type of experiment and study design was used?
2 As part of your analysis, you can access the following demographic information about users on their website: geographic region, web browser type, time of visit, and number of previous visits. Which comparisons or cohorts might you include as part of your final deliverable?
3 One of the three new website layouts performed better than the other test groups (3% fewer abandoned shopping carts than the original), but it performed *worse* than the original layout (2% higher abandoned carts). What conclusions might you draw about this finding, and what action would you recommend?
4 The product management team is concerned that the website layout will perform better only for a short period of time before returning to the original value when customers get used to the layout. How might you recommend adjusting your experiment to account for this phenomenon?

You can build on the decisions made in your previous activities, writing recommended study designs and follow-ups that align with your original examples.

3.3 Types of research programs

We've covered a comprehensive range of methods for gathering evidence (descriptions, correlations, experiments) and types of study designs (between-subjects, within-subjects, cohorts, longitudinal). Combining these two types, you can appropriately design a study to answer almost any measurable research question.

As an analyst, you will likely evaluate successive or concurrent studies requiring more in-depth strategies to ensure success. A single team or organization will typically specialize in one or two types of *research programs*. We will discuss some of the most common programs in academic institutions and organizations: basic and applied research, A/B testing, and program evaluation.

3.3.1 Basic and applied research

Basic research refers to a program whose primary goal is to contribute to the overall available knowledge base in a specialized field. Studies are usually designed and conducted in succession, accumulating and advancing knowledge on the research area over a long period of time. This is a common approach in academic and other laboratory research, where a team sometimes dedicates their careers to the topic of interest.

The value of a basic research program is usually measured by the effect of the accumulation of findings over time rather than that of an individual study. After a series of studies are published, the research team will use them to form the basis of a larger theory (e.g., the theory of evolution). Research teams will contribute findings that support, refute, and augment the theory. Over time, a more sophisticated view of the research topic is developed and disseminated for a broader audience.

An *applied research program* seeks to collect and analyze data about a specific, targeted population to build direct knowledge about that population and influence how practitioners engage with them. Studies are designed to generate direct, actionable insights that translate to programs, products, and services tailored to the population from which the sample was drawn. This method is standard in community and psychological research, organizational settings, and nonprofits.

While applied research programs don't have a primary goal of contributing to basic theories within the field of study, they will usually add to knowledge about distinct subsets of a population (e.g., children in a geographic area, second-generation immigrant youth, persons with a specific disability).

3.3.2   *A/B testing*

In business settings, experiments are often designed as between-subjects tests, also known as *A/B tests*. An A/B test is a type of experiment comparing two variations of a variable against each other to determine which performs better on key business metrics. Users are randomly assigned to a variant (e.g., group A, B, or C) for a duration. At the conclusion of the experiment, one or more statistical tests are used to compare the performance of the groups.

A successful A/B test typically examines the effect of small, modular changes to a website on conversions, visits, subscriptions, or time to complete a workflow (such as the one shown in figure 3.14). Each test is expected to have a limited scope of influence—a small increase in the critical business metrics or information gained

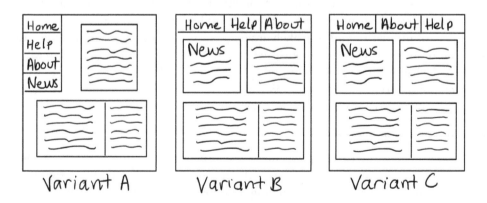

Figure 3.14   Example of an A/B/C group comparison with minor changes to a website

about what types of changes *don't* have an effect. The actual value is in building and scaling an *A/B testing experimentation program* within an organization. When this type of program is mature, dozens to hundreds of experiments are run concurrently or in rapid succession to accumulate knowledge about how users interact with the product or service (basic research) while having a direct, measurable effect on how they use the product with each change (applied research).

A/B testing uses the same principles we have discussed in this chapter and the statistical tests and metrics we will discuss in depth later in the book. The laboratory of an A/B testing program is essentially a website or application, and the population of the testing program is the base of current and potential users.

3.3.3 Program evaluation

Program evaluation is the most common strategy for assessing the efficacy of nonprofit, government, and academic programs that liaise directly with institutions. These institutions design *programs* intending to meet a need or provide a service within a specific population. Participants are assessed on outcome measures before, throughout, and several times after the program. Over time, data collected can enable an organization to systematically enhance its programs and their effect on the target population.

The goals of such an evaluation are typically narrower than the previous two types of research programs discussed. A basic or applied research or A/B testing program will continually expand its areas of study as it generates findings about a topic. Program evaluation will often retain a specific focus over time (e.g., reducing the prevalence of a disease) as it improves its ability to achieve a goal cost-efficiently.

Incorporating the evaluation into the broader research program

The research Jay conducted to evaluate the efficacy of adolescent volunteering events is part of a larger series of *programs* at the nonprofit. The organization's overarching goal is to raise money for cancer research and increase public awareness about new scientific discoveries and challenges associated with different forms of cancer. Multiple initiatives are run within the organization—volunteer engagement, fundraising, awareness campaigns, and more. The new adolescent program provides an additional component to evaluate, report on, and continually improve the efficacy of volunteer engagement.

In addition, the new adolescent volunteering initiative is beginning a new *program* for the organization—engaging adolescents in volunteering with the organization at fundraisers, charity events, walk/run events, and more. As part of this program, the organization will conduct evaluations of volunteers 3, 6, 12, and 24 months after their first volunteer engagement. The evaluations will include school performance, well-being, peer connections, family relationships, and more. This information can be used for grant opportunities, peer-reviewed research, and more. The organization hypothesizes that adolescents volunteering with the organization will see improvement in school performance, well-being measures, and increased peer connections with other volunteers.

Summary

- Developing a data-informed and quantifiable hypothesis involves synthesizing peer-reviewed and public research, gathering stakeholder information, and conducting foundational analyses of available data at your organization.

- *Research* is the process of investigating a topic as a study or experiment to gain *new* information about that topic. The goal is to accumulate information over time, enabling you to build expertise and better inform decisions, practice, and policy.

- Data can be evaluated as one of the following:

  - *Descriptive information,* which seeks to describe *only* existing information in a dataset without making inferences, predictions, or quantifying the relationships between variables.

  - *Correlations,* which measure a noncausal linear association between two variables. Correlations range from −1 to 1, with values further from 0 indicating a stronger relationship.

  - *Experiments* aim to determine if one phenomenon (your independent variable) causes something else to happen (your dependent variable). This is usually tested as an *experiment* under controlled settings to be able to confidently isolate an independent variable as the cause of the dependent variable.

- *Experimental designs* comparing differences between groups are often set up as *between-subjects comparisons* (e.g., random assignment between an experiment and control group) or *within-subjects designs* (e.g., a single experiment group compared before and after treatment). These standard designs allow for comparison across vast arrays of research.

- *Cohort comparisons* (e.g., participants grouped by age and tracked for the duration of an experiment) and *longitudinal studies* (tracking participants over long periods) are less common but highly valuable in many domains of study, research, and work.

- Individual study designs usually become part of more extensive research programs within an organization:

  - *Basic and applied research programs* seek to contribute to the overall knowledge base about a specific topic. These are common in academic settings.

  - *A/B testing programs* seek to continually improve on a product or business outcome through a continuous program of concurrent or successive experiments run on large numbers of users for short periods of time. These programs are common in marketing and product analytics, and they are primarily run in business settings.

  - *Program evaluations* are typical in nonprofit and government environments. These seek to evaluate the efficacy of new and ongoing programs for the populations they serve, continually improving their ability to achieve a specific goal (e.g., reducing rates of cancer).

Part 2

Measurement

The majority of analysis involves transforming information into something measurable. Once you can quantify something, you can more easily explore it, making comparisons, identifying relationships, and drawing inferences about the broader population. These insights form the basis for setting goals, tracking progress, and making informed decisions that drive organizational strategy.

However, measurement is rarely straightforward. As analysts, much of our work involves examining interconnected processes—many of which revolve around human behavior. People, of course, are complex. How do you measure something as subjective as happiness or satisfaction with a product? Can you take self-reported data at face value? What does it truly mean when someone clicks a button on your website? Are they engaging with the content, or are they simply navigating? And, ultimately, what can you infer from these actions?

In this section, we'll explore measurement strategies from multiple angles. First, we'll examine the logic behind common statistical tests, helping you determine the best methods for your data. We'll cover widely used *parametric* statistical tests, along with *non-parametric* alternatives when your data doesn't fit traditional models. Next, we'll dive into the data collection process—how to distill abstract concepts into measurable outcomes, whether through direct observation or self-reported data. With this foundation in place, we'll conclude with a chapter on designing metrics, empowering you and your organization to use metrics effectively to drive success.

Statistics you (probably) learned: T-tests, ANOVAs, and correlations

This chapter covers

- Breaking down summary statistics and their underlying logic
- Using parametric statistical tests appropriately
- Understanding and managing the limitations of parametric statistical tests

Statistical tests can create rigor and alignment in the interpretation of numerical differences. There are common sets of methods used by most statisticians, social scientists, and analysts. Across a wide variety of domains of study and types of questions, practitioners use similar criteria to evaluate the coefficients of statistical tests to conclude whether or not they achieve statistical significance.

Despite these benefits, there are assumptions and limitations associated with common statistical tests, and there is a troublesome history associated with their development and widespread use. We will cover the context and development of common statistical tests, coefficients, and evaluation criteria, and we'll break down the mathematical logic behind each approach. These skills will enable you to share highly accurate and actionable results with your stakeholders.

4.1   *The logic of summary statistics*

Take a look at the line graph in figure 4.1, comparing the daily high temperatures, over a month, in New York City and Boston. Can you determine which city is warmer in July? You can see that there's likely a relationship between the weather patterns in the two cities, which is a sensible hypothesis given the geographical proximity of New York City and Boston. However, there are clear day-to-day deviations in how the daily temperatures fluctuate, making it challenging to visually discern if one city has a higher temperature.

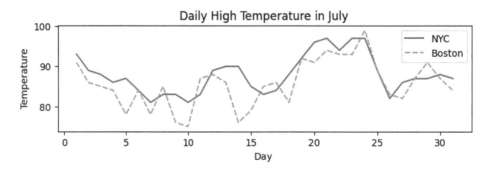

Figure 4.1   Comparison of temperatures in July between New York City and Boston

Figure 4.2 shows an alternative view of the same data, which takes the mean of each daily high temperature per city and plots it on a bar graph. You can see that the average temperature for New York City is slightly higher than for Boston, but is the difference in temperatures meaningful? How do you know? How much of a difference indicates

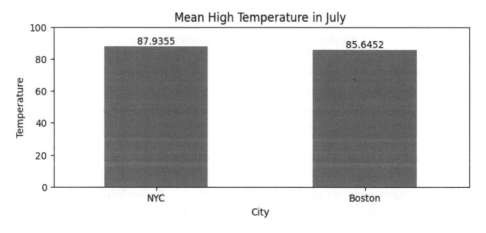

Figure 4.2   Comparison of the mean daily temperatures between New York City and Boston

that one city is *meaningfully* warmer than the other? In all likelihood, if these questions were asked of multiple people, you would get a range of answers. This indicates that there is no agreed-upon threshold at which the *numerical* difference becomes meaningful.

If you want to truly understand the data and answer these questions, you'll need to look at the data from a number of different angles. This will include several ways of summarizing it, as well as comparing it using statistical tests. Let's import the dataset now and take a look at the full set of available values for New York City:

```
import pandas as pd                                            Import the
                                                               pandas library.
weather = pd.read_csv("nyc_boston_weather.csv", index_col=0)   Import the
                                                                weather
                                                                dataset.
print(list(weather.nyc))
[93, 89, 88, 86, 87, 84, 81, 83, 83, 81, 83, 89, 90, 90, 85, 83, 84, 88,
92, 96, 97, 94, 97, 97, 89, 82, 86, 87, 87, 88, 87]
```

Print the NYC
daily temperatures.

List of daily temperature
values in New York City

From the full list of printed values, you can start to glean more information about the data. The temperatures ranged from 81 degrees to 97 degrees, and there was a 6-day period in which the temperature was 90 degrees or higher. If you *only* had access to figure 4.2, you wouldn't have been able to see any of these patterns.

However, you can't simply show your stakeholders a raw set of data and have them draw their own conclusions. We're only working with 30 days of weather data, but imagine having 100, 500, or 1,000 rows in your dataset. You wouldn't be able to just look at the raw data for trends—you'd *have* to summarize it. Every method of summarizing your data comes with trade-offs. We'll discuss several common ways of summarizing data and the information you highlight, or lose, with each calculation.

4.1.1 Summarizing properties of your data

Summary statistics are single-value measures that describe a property of the *distribution* of a dataset. Some of the measures covered in introductory statistics courses (e.g., mean and median) are easy for stakeholders to understand, given their prevalence in society. However, they are by no means the only important properties of a dataset, and looking at only one of them can provide a limited or even misleading view into the underlying data. For example, the distributions shown in figure 4.3 all have similar medians, but *very* different shapes.

I recommend breaking down summary statistics into three categories in your evaluation and reporting:

- Measures of *central tendency* (e.g., the mean, median, and mode)
- Measures of *variability* (e.g., standard deviation)
- Measures of the normality of a distribution (e.g., skewness, kurtosis)

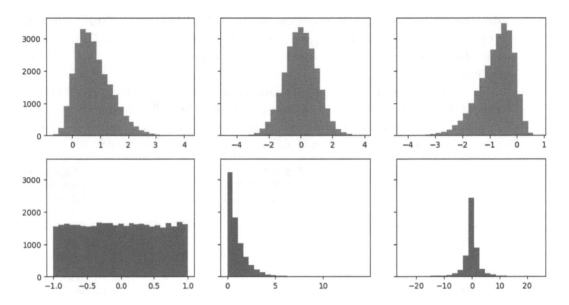

Figure 4.3   The shape of a distribution can vary widely, and different summary statistics will give you clues about those shapes.

In this chapter, we will focus on the first two categories of statistics from the perspective of best use, logic, and limitations. Evaluating each of these measures is *very important* before using inferential statistical tests. We will discuss the pros and cons of using measures as part of the *metrics* you report in chapter 6.

ASSUMPTIONS

Before we break down summary statistics, let's discuss the assumptions each category of summary statistics makes about the shape of your data. When your data does not meet the assumptions, your measures may not provide an accurate picture to your stakeholders. These are some of these assumptions:

- *Normality*—The assumption that your data roughly fits the shape of a bell curve (normal distribution).
- *Centrality*—The data has a meaningful midpoint representing a "typical" data point.
- *Symmetry*—The distribution has a similar number of data points to the left and right of the mean.

Centrality and *symmetry* are included in the *normality* assumption and exist as standalone assumptions for different measures. The distribution shown in figure 4.4, for example, adheres to each assumption: it's normally distributed, has a meaningful midpoint, and is roughly symmetrical. In the real world, data rarely looks this perfect: each summary statistic you might use will have benefits and limitations based on the shape of your data.

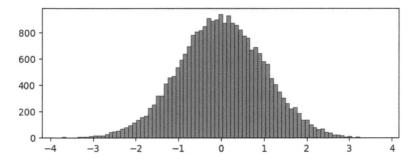

Figure 4.4 A standard normal distribution with a mean of 0 and standard deviation of 1

MEASURES OF CENTRAL TENDENCY

Measures of central tendency are single-point measures of the "typical" records in your dataset. As the name suggests, these measures assume your data is clustered at a meaningful *center*. We will focus on the appropriate use of the most widely used measures: the mean, median, and mode.

The *arithmetic mean* is the most common and widely used statistic for summarizing numerical data. Analysts will often start their work by taking means of their data. Using this measure has a lot of benefits:

- The majority of stakeholders you collaborate with will be familiar with the mean.
- The mean calculation is relatively easy to explain to stakeholders unfamiliar with the metric.
- The use of the mean is widespread, so you will likely have benchmark comparisons available at your organization, in peer-reviewed literature, and in public data sources.

The arithmetic mean also has key assumptions and limitations:

- Outliers, and the *skew* (the degree to which your data violates the assumption of centrality) of your distribution, heavily affect the mean calculation (see figure 4.5).

$$\{83,\ 97,\ 78,\ 81,\ 77\} = \frac{416}{5} = 83.2$$

$$\{83,\ 82,\ 78,\ 81,\ 77\} = \frac{401}{5} = 80.2 \quad \text{Mean}$$

Figure 4.5 A mean calculation is highly sensitive to skewed data and outliers. The mean noticeably decreases when the highest outlier value of 97 is replaced with a value closer to the rest of the set.

- An appropriately representative mean calculation assumes that your data has a meaningful midpoint or *center*. The mean can mask differences in the shape of your distribution and interpretation of the *center*.
- In practice, the mean is often interpreted as your dataset's "typical" value. If your dataset is non-normal, skewed, or otherwise asymmetrical, the mean might not be the best representation of a "typical" record in the dataset. When your distribution has a complex shape, be prepared to explain further details about this shape to your stakeholders.

The *median* is simply the *midpoint* of a sorted series of data points. The median has several advantages over the mean:

- By definition, it represents the *midpoint* rather than a weighted calculation. The median may be more appropriate to report for distributions without a meaningful center or symmetry (e.g., the second distribution in figure 4.6).

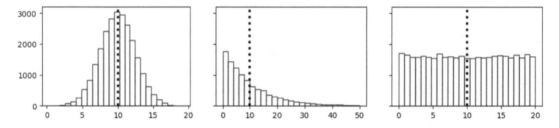

Figure 4.6   Three distinct distributions with an identical mean of 10. The interpretation of the mean or "average" is very different for each distribution.

- The median will be relatively well understood by many of your stakeholders.
- The median is more robust to skew and outliers than the mean (see figure 4.7). It can be a more appropriate representation of a "typical" record when a distribution is not symmetrical.

$$\{83,\ 97,\ 78,\ 81,\ 77\} \rightarrow \{77,\ 78,\ \underline{81},\ 83,\ 97\} = 81$$
$$\updownarrow \qquad\qquad\qquad\qquad\qquad\qquad\qquad\qquad\qquad Median$$
$$\{83,\ 82,\ 78,\ 81,\ 77\} \rightarrow \{77,\ 78,\ \underline{81},\ 82,\ 83\} = 81$$

Figure 4.7   The median is robust to skewed data and outliers. When the highest outlier value of 97 is replaced with a value closer to the rest of the set, the median remains the same.

As with the mean, there are key limitations to note about the median:

- The median can be more robust to change than the mean. If you compare changes in a median over time or between groups, you may be less likely to detect differences.
- Reporting both the median and mean values may require additional context for how stakeholders should interpret each measure.

When preparing a report, you will most often choose between the mean and median to share with stakeholders based on the measure that provides the greatest clarity and value. Outside of direct stakeholder reporting, the differences between the mean and median indicates that your dataset is likely skewed or otherwise non-normal (such as those shown in figure 4.8). You may want to note or correct the non-normality as part of your statistical analysis (see section 4.3).

3000
2000
1000
0
0
5
10
15
20
0
10
20
30
40
50
0
5
10
15
20

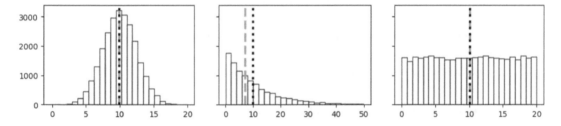

Figure 4.8 The mean (black dotted line) and median (gray dashed line) are approximately identical in the first and third distributions. The measures noticeably deviate in the second skewed distribution.

The *mode* is the most frequent value that occurs in your dataset (see figure 4.9). It's generally used to point out values that are disproportionally represented among your sample.

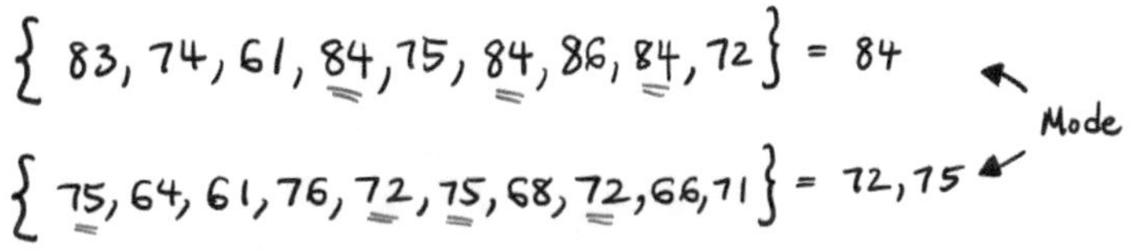

{ 83, 74, 61, 84, 75, 84, 86, 84, 72 } = 84
Mode
{ 75, 64, 61, 76, 72, 75, 68, 72, 66, 71 } = 72, 75

Figure 4.9 The mode is the most frequently occurring value in a dataset.

You may sometimes need to round or bin values to derive a meaningful mode, as shown in figure 4.10. When testing a rounding calculation on a series with a large range or floating-point continuous data, your choice of bins or decimal point to round to can drastically change your outcome.

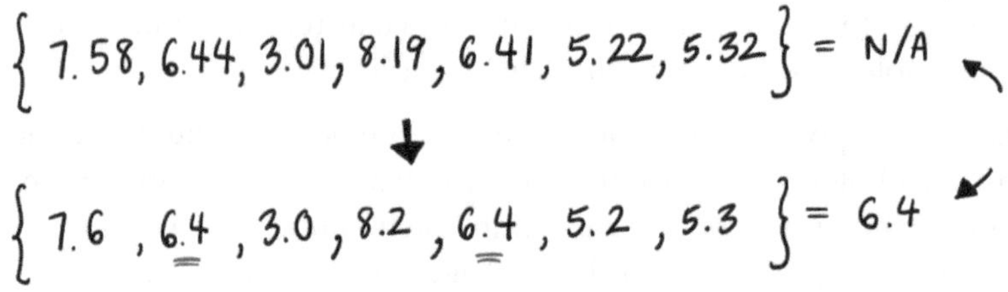

{ 7.58, 6.44, 3.01, 8.19, 6.41, 5.22, 5.32 } = N/A
{ 7.6 , 6.4 , 3.0 , 8.2 , 6.4 , 5.2 , 5.3 } = 6.4
Mode

Figure 4.10 Rounding floating-point values can better showcase the mode.

Additionally, the mode is often helpful as a relative calculation to describe the shape of a distribution. A dataset may have many relative modes best discovered by observing the distribution. Taking counts to find the most frequent value gives you the *absolute* mode.

Though the mode is used less often, highlighting the mode is important in situations such as the following:

- If a single value occurs disproportionately in a dataset.
- If rounding continuous or floating-point values yields a meaningful set of bins for representing the data, or a mode with a substantial frequency.
- If a distribution has multiple peaks with relative modes (*multimodal distribution*; see figure 4.11). These are often best discovered through visual observation of the distribution.

1400
1200
1000
800
600
400
200
0
60
80
100
120
140
160

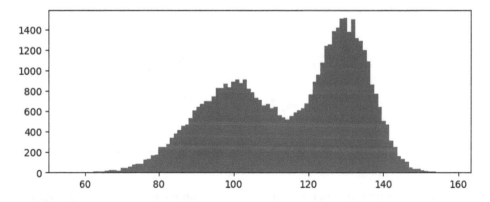

Figure 4.11 A bimodal distribution with two modes around 100 and 130 that are best discovered by visual observation

It's worth noting that when summarizing categorical data (e.g., counts of users in each city reported as a bar graph), you are reporting the dataset's *mode* (the most frequent category). Representing this data type as a percentage or relative proportion of the categories instead of a count by group will be far more understandable for your stakeholders. I will expand on representing this type of data in chapter 7.

Our case study for the chapter

Naomi is a research scientist at a pharmaceutical company. Her job includes data collection, analysis, and reporting for clinical trials of new experimental medications. The company regularly publishes its findings to government agencies, in public reports, and in peer-reviewed papers in collaboration with academic teams.

Naomi is tasked with preparing an analysis that evaluates the efficacy of a new drug for treating insomnia in a randomized controlled trial that compared the new drug to a placebo. Participants were brought into the lab to monitor their sleep quality on three separate occasions throughout the trial. In total, 473 participants were in the experimental group (received the experimental drug), and 455 were in the control group (received the placebo). Participants did not know which group they were assigned to. The participants were monitored for their total sleep hours each night and the number of sleep interruptions.

For the first part of her analysis, Naomi will evaluate whether there are statistically significant differences on the *final* day of the sleep quality evaluation. She begins by calculating measures of central tendency for the dataset and generates histogram plots of each outcome measure broken out by the study group. She first creates the following summary table for participants in the experimental group:

	Hours of Sleep	Interruptions
Mean	6.33	2.4
Median	7	2
Mode	7	2

The mean hours of sleep is lower than the median, whereas the reverse is true for the number of sleep interruptions. When Naomi creates a chart showing the distribution of both metrics, she discovers that Hours of Sleep is *negatively* skewed, with most participants reporting approximately 7–9 hours of sleep. She also finds that the number of sleep interruptions only ranges from 0 to 7, with most participants (52%) reporting one interruption.

Naomi begins the summary of her descriptive statistics with the mean and median for both measures and the mode for the number of sleep interruptions.

MEASURES OF VARIABILITY

Variability is the degree to which your data diverges from the mean or median value. Measures of variability give you an estimate of the width of your dataset and insight into the representativeness of the mean or median. We will focus on measures in increasing order of complexity: range and interquartile range, standard deviation, and standard error.

The *range* is the difference between a dataset's highest and lowest values. It's shared with stakeholders either as the difference between the two values or a single value that subtracts the highest and lowest values. In practice, it's often valuable to report both values together, as in figure 4.12.

$$\{83, 92, 78, 81, 67\} \rightarrow \{67, 78, 81, 83, 92\}$$

$$67 \text{ to } 92 \quad \text{OR} \quad 92 - 67 = 25$$

Temperatures ranged from 67 to 92, a difference of 25 degrees.

Figure 4.12   The range depicts the entire width of the dataset.

In addition to the full range, the *interquartile range* (IQR) shows the spread of the middle 50% of your data points from the 25th to the 75th percentile. This can be compared to the overall range to better describe the spread of your dataset between percentiles. With the median, range, and interquartile range, you can calculate the distance between any set of quartiles in your distribution.

In most cases, you will visually observe these ranges rather than just calculate and interpret the values. This is often done using a *boxplot* or *box and whisker plot*, as shown in figure 4.13.

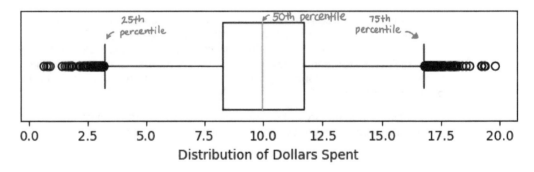

Figure 4.13   A boxplot shows the median and interquartile ranges in the box and the 25th and 75th percentiles in the whiskers by default. Values outside of the whiskers are typically treated as outliers.

Effectively communicating the results of a range calculation requires appropriate context to clarify its importance to your stakeholders in addition to or in place of other measures. If you decide the range is valuable to include in your findings, you can consider contextualizing it with statements such as the following:

- The middle 50% of participants finished the 10k race between 43 and 67 minutes.
- Test scores ranged between 42% and 93%, with the median student receiving 74%.
- 62% of website visitors stay on the home page between 8 and 17 seconds.

The second measure of variation we will discuss is the *standard deviation*. This measures the dispersal of your data from the mean, often defined as the *average distance from the mean*. The standard deviation is derived from the *variance* of a dataset by taking the square root (see figure 4.14). These two calculations serve a similar purpose for reporting purposes, so we'll discuss them together.

$$\sigma = \sqrt{\frac{\sum (x - \mu)^2}{N}}$$

Data	Mean	Difference	Squared
83	83.2	-0.2	.04
97		13.8	190.44
78		-5.2	27.04
81		-2.2	4.84
77		-6.2	38.44

$$\text{sum} = 260.8 \rightarrow \sqrt{\frac{260.8}{5}} = 7.22$$

Figure 4.14 The standard deviation essentially takes an average of the differences from the mean.

If you have a mean and standard deviation, and you assume your data is normally distributed, you can easily approximate the shape of the dataset. Similar to the range and IQR, the standard deviation can be used as a coordinate system to estimate the proportions of data points between two values.

To demonstrate, let's generate a *normal curve* representing the approximate distribution of heights (in inches) of men in the United States. The result is shown in figure 4.15:

```
import numpy as np              ⟵— Import the libraries.
import matplotlib.pyplot as plt
import seaborn as sns
                                    Generate a normal distribution
m, sd = 63.5, 2.5              ⟵— with 25,000 data points.
dist = np.random.normal(loc=m, scale=sd, size=25000)
                                    Plot the distribution with a
sns.histplot(dist, bins = 100, color = "white")   ⟵— vertical line for the mean.
plt.axvline(np.mean(dist), color = "black", linestyle = "dotted")
plt.title(f"Normal Distribution with Mean {m} and Standard Deviation {sd}")
```

In peer-reviewed papers and technical reports, the standard deviation and the mean are almost always included in the summary statistics. If you include the standard deviation in your reporting to less-technical stakeholders, you will likely need to provide a layperson's explanation to minimize confusion.

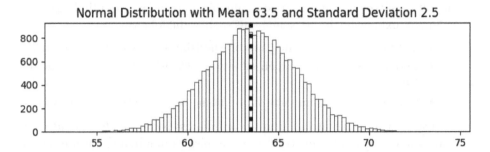

Figure 4.15 A normal distribution of heights (in inches) for men in the United States is easily generated if the mean and standard deviation are known.

Throughout my career, I have found the following explanations valuable in teaching statistics to undergraduate students and communicating with stakeholders:

- The standard deviation shows how much, on *average*, participants differ from the mean.
- The standard deviation estimates the most common range of data points you can expect to encounter above and below the mean.
- The standard deviation can be a reference point for how close the majority of the data is to your mean: approximately 68% of data points are within one standard deviation from the mean, and 95% are within two standard deviations.

The final variance measure we'll discuss in this section is the *standard error of the mean* (SEM or SE). The standard error estimates the distance between the sample mean and the overall population mean. It's calculated by dividing the standard deviation by the square root of the total sample size (see figure 4.16). In this way, it differs from the previous measures by *inferring* a property about the broader population rather than just describing the sample.

$$\underset{\text{Variance}}{\sigma^2 = \frac{\sum (x - \mu)^2}{N}} \rightarrow \underset{\substack{\text{Standard} \\ \text{deviation}}}{\sigma = \sqrt{\sigma^2}} \rightarrow \underset{\substack{\text{Standard} \\ \text{error}}}{SE = \frac{\sigma}{\sqrt{n}}}$$

Figure 4.16 Deriving the standard deviation and standard error from the initial variance calculation.

The standard error is a common choice for augmenting visualizations such as bar graphs to add context on variability within or between groups. It's an option in the seaborn `barplot` function in Python, and it's an easy addition in data visualization tools like Tableau.

You can often assume your audience will readily identify the error bars as a measure of variability (e.g., in figure 4.17). However, they may not be familiar with the underlying measures generating the error bars. Your deliverables should specify *which* of the error bars you're using and provide a brief reference or definition so your stakeholders understand why you chose it.

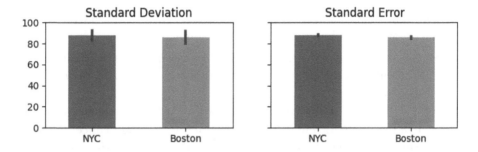

Figure 4.17   Bar graphs with error bars are very common visualizations, but they run the risk of misrepresenting the underlying data and creating confusion with stakeholders regarding the type and purpose of the error bars.

I strongly caution against using this common type of visualization without first ensuring the following assumptions and conditions are met:

- Your dataset is a *sample* from a larger population with a roughly *symmetrical* distribution. A bar graph with error bars will not depict a skewed distribution and may ultimately misrepresent the underlying shape of your data.
- The population that your dataset is drawing from is not measurable or measured in its entirety for your analysis (e.g., the population of interest is all adults in the United States).
- The representativeness of your sample mean to the theoretical population mean is of value to your stakeholders in understanding the deliverables you are creating.

If these conditions are satisfied, the standard error of the mean is a great first indication of potentially detectable *statistically significant differences* between groups using an appropriate inferential statistical test.

4.1.2   Recap

If we synthesize the measures we have covered, we can answer questions about the characteristics of our dataset, such as the following:

- What does the most typical data point look like (mean, median, mode)?
- How close to that "typical" data point are most of the records in the dataset (variance, standard deviation, interquartile range)?

- How wide is the entire or majority of the dataset (range, interquartile range)?
- How close to the true population mean is your sample mean (standard error)?

Each descriptive statistic you report has a trade-off: some dataset properties are prioritized, and others are masked. Many descriptive (and inferential) statistics also have underlying assumptions about the shape and properties of your dataset that *must* be checked and met before reporting on their values!

I emphasize this as an analyst who understands that many of us don't have the structures to enable us to apply statistical rigor to our work. I will leave you with some key takeaways about when to report on each summary statistic:

- Use the median to report on skewed or asymmetrical distributions. This measure will mask the effect of extreme outliers by prioritizing the *relative position* of data points.
- Use the mean or median with symmetrical data that has a meaningful center.
- Use the mode to report on a distribution with a high concentration of values within a bin that the mode can represent. Include another measure of central tendency, such as the mean or median, in this reporting.
- Use the standard deviation when a dataset is relatively symmetrical.
- If a dataset has no meaningful center (such as the third graph in figure 4.8), you may want to describe the range, median, and interquartile range *and* include a visualization of the distribution for your stakeholders.
- Check and report on each summary statistic before running statistical tests.

4.1.3   Exercises

Run the following code in the Python environment of your choice (e.g., Jupyter Notebook). You will need to have `numpy`, `matplotlib`, and `pandas` installed:

```
import numpy as np
import matplotlib.pyplot as plt
import pandas as pd

dist = pd.Series(np.sqrt(np.random.exponential(1,75000)))
plt.hist(dist, bins = 100)
```

1. How would you describe the shape of this distribution?
2. What is the mean and median of the distribution? Which of these measures would you use to share with a stakeholder?
3. What is the mode of the distribution? How does it change when you round values to different numbers of decimal points? Is there a meaningful value you would consider reporting to stakeholders?
4. What is the standard deviation of the distribution? What does it tell you about how much it deviates from the mean? Can you determine if the distribution is symmetrical from this value?
5. Write a summary of the statistics values you have discovered so far. Based on the examples provided, you will refine the summary in the following sections.

4.2 Making inferences: Group comparisons

Each approach and equation we covered in the previous section is used to describe and answer questions about a dataset (e.g., is Boston or New York City warmer in July 2024?). Often, the questions you want to answer with your data extend beyond its limitations (e.g., a limited time range or only two locations). Instead, what if you want to know if Boston or New York is warmer on average *every* July? Or even *every month*? How would you go about doing that?

To answer broader questions, analysts will use *inferential statistical tests* to draw conclusions about the *population* (all possible values or people of interest) using only the available sample. Most introductory statistics courses in a university setting cover a set of common inferential statistical tests. These tests are typically *univariate* (having one outcome variable) and *parametric* (assuming that your data conforms to a specific distribution). Consequently, these tests (e.g., *t*-tests, correlations, ANOVAs) are widely used in academic and professional settings. Analysts in almost *any* department or specialization benefit from knowing how to use parametric statistics at any stage of their career—figure 4.18 shows a correlation matrix that I delivered to a nonprofit as part of an internship early in my own career.

Correlation matrix for demographic questions.

	1	2	3	4	5	6	7	8	9	10
1	1									
2	-0.08	1								
3	0.62**	-0.21	1							
4	-0.46**	0.11	-0.72**	1						
5	0.19	-0.04	0.45**	-0.41**	1					
6	0.15	0.25	-0.02	-0.08	-0.04	1				
7	0.32*	0.02	0.21	-0.18	-0.01	0.28*	1			
8	0.58**	-0.38*	0.54**	-0.52**	0.39*	0.17	0.24	1		
9	0.14	0.28*	-0.18	0.11	-0.11	0.38**	0.06	-0.10	1	
10	0.11	0.16	0.12	0.04	-0.09	0.18	0.13	0.11	0.30*	1

* $p<.05$
** $p<.01$

Figure 4.18 **Statistical comparisons like correlations, *t*-tests, ANOVAs, and others are used *everywhere*. This example is a correlation matrix from a program evaluation I delivered to a non-profit in 2015.**

While these tests aim to have a broad application, data professionals will frequently apply them without exploring alternative (non-parametric) statistical tests that may be a better fit for the data they work with. This section will discuss parametric tests, their limitations, and how to maximize the value of your inferences and conclusions. I recommend reading carefully if you're new to these sorts of tests. The improper use of parametric statistics can lead to patently wrong conclusions (e.g., identifying a group difference where there is none), spending countless hours and resources at an organization, and risking the reputation of the analytics team.

4.2.1   Parametric tests

The term *parametric* refers to inferring a value about a parameter (a measurable value) of the population. From that definition stems *parametric statistics,* the branch of statistics inferring fixed parameters about a population. In other words, these statistical tests assume that true population data fits the specific shape of a probability distribution, can be modeled as such, and can be estimated based on a *representative sample* of data from that population. This is depicted in figure 4.19.

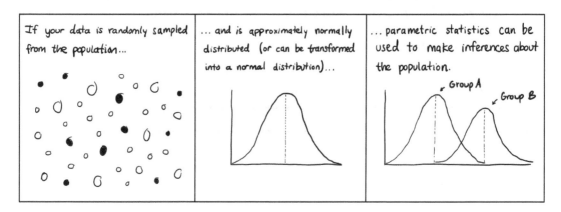

Figure 4.19   Parametric statistics assume that the population data follows a specific probability distribution and that you can make inferences about the parameters of that distribution based on your sample data.

Parametric statistical tests are ever-present in analytics. If you took an introductory statistics course in an undergraduate or graduate program, you likely covered a range of *univariate* approaches designed to evaluate one dependent variable per test. Many of the following tests may be familiar to you:

- *t-test*—The *t*-test is used to identify differences between the means of two groups. Comparisons can be between groups (independent samples) or within groups, typically comparing values before and after a change or intervention (paired samples).
- *ANOVA*—The ANOVA (analysis of variance) is used to identify differences between the means of two or more groups. Unlike a *t*-test, an ANOVA can include multiple groups per independent variable *and* multiple factors (e.g., a two-way ANOVA has two factors).

- *Pearson's correlation*—Pearson's correlation is used to identify linear relationships between two continuous variables. Unlike the previous methods, the coefficient (*r*-value) is standardized and can be directly interpreted for the strength and direction of the relationship.
- *Linear and logistic regression*—Linear and logistic regression are predictive models used to measure the relationship between a dependent variable (continuous and categorical, respectively) and one or more independent variables.

I will elaborate more on correlation and regression methods in section 4.3. However, this section's assumptions and interpretation of parametric statistics apply to these methods and should be considered foundational to the next topic.

ASSUMPTIONS

In addition to the assumptions of the measures of central tendency and variation discussed in section 4.1.1, parametric statistics have strict assumptions about the shape of the data within and between groups. Meeting these assumptions is *necessary* for making accurate inferences about your data.

The first assumption of parametric statistics is that the data is shaped according to a distribution the underlying population is believed to follow. In the majority of tests that we'll cover in this chapter, the underlying population is believed to follow a *normal distribution* (the assumption of *normality*). To meet this assumption, your data either needs to be *approximately normally distributed* or *capable of being transformed into a normal distribution*. This process is also called *normalizing* your data. It can be done via a number of mathematical transformations to the entire dataset, resulting in a reshaping of the distribution. For example, we can transform a positively skewed distribution by taking the *square root* of all of the data series' values, and we can transform a negatively skewed distribution by *squaring* the data. Figure 4.20 depicts the results of these transformations:

```
from scipy.stats import skewnorm              Import
import matplotlib.pyplot as plt               the libraries.

positive_skew = skewnorm.rvs(4, size = 25000)      Generate positively and
negative_skew = skewnorm.rvs(-3, size = 25000)     negatively skewed distributions.

fig, ax = plt.subplots(2, 2, sharey = True)        Plot the original and
ax[0][0].hist(positive_skew, bins = 25)            transformed distributions.
ax[0][1].hist(np.sqrt(positive_skew+1), bins = 25)
ax[1][0].hist(negative_skew, bins = 25)
ax[1][1].hist((negative_skew+5)**2, bins = 25)
```

Not every distribution can be effectively normalized for analysis with parametric statistical tests. Many data types, such as categorical and discrete count data, are not appropriate for numerical transformation. Some distributions won't transform into the desired shape if manipulated, even when suitable data types are used. When your data is uniformly distributed, extremely skewed with significant outliers, or is multimodal

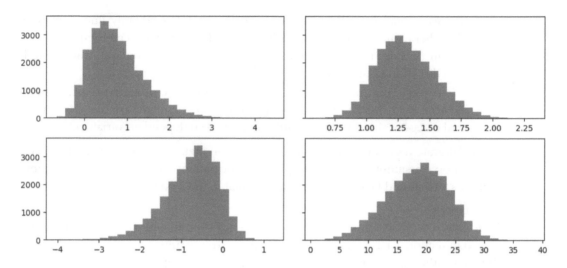

Figure 4.20   The two plots on the left show the original positively and negatively skewed data, respectively. The plots on the right show the transformation of each distribution (using square root and squared values, respectively), allowing you to approximate a normal distribution.

(has more than one mode), you will likely need to use a non-parametric statistical test to evaluate it.

The second assumption of parametric statistics is the *independence* of data points in your dataset. Unless otherwise indicated with the statistical test you use (e.g., a repeated measures *t*-test or ANOVA), the probability of events in your dataset is assumed *not* to affect the probability of other events. In practice, a lack of independence of data points might look like one of the following situations:

- Participants in a laboratory changed their answers on a survey after learning how their peers answered the same questions.
- Participants in an A/B test are randomized, but users within the same company compare and notice their user interfaces look different.
- Participants in the control group of an intervention notice that experimental group participants are experiencing more positive outcomes.

The third related assumption is the *equality of variances between groups* (also known as *homoscedasticity*). Parametric tests assume that the population(s) your samples are drawn from vary equally on your outcome measure of interest (figure 4.21 shows an example where two groups do *not* meet the equal variance assumption). Tests such as the *t*-test and ANOVA include the standard deviation (square root of the variance) in the denominator of the calculation; if one of the groups has a much higher variance, the calculation will be skewed, and results will be unreliable.

If you determine that your samples have unequal variances, you can use adjusted versions of *t*-tests and ANOVAs (Welch's tests) that are more robust to violations of this

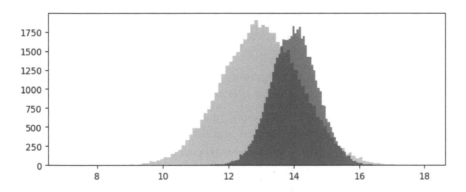

Figure 4.21 **Parametric statistics generally assume that your samples have equal variances. In this example, the unequal variance leads to greater overlap between the two distributions.**

assumption. Non-parametric tests for group comparisons may also be better choices for your work.

The fourth explicit assumption is the absence of *numerical outliers*. Parametric tests assume that your dataset lacks extreme outliers, and failing to correct them can significantly affect the accuracy of your results. In most cases, numerical outliers can be easily identified through visual dataset observation (see figure 4.22).

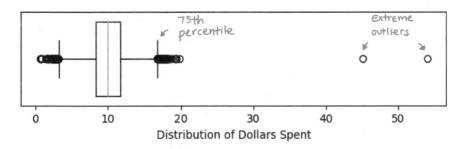

Figure 4.22 **Extreme outliers are often easily detected by generating a boxplot or a histogram of your data.**

It's recommended that you take one of the following steps to handle outliers in your dataset:

- *Systematically removing the values*—This can be accomplished by taking only a limited range of data around the median (e.g., the interquartile range). Dropping an individual value is not recommended—that can quickly turn into *p*-hacking, which we will discuss in section 4.3!

- *Transforming your data*—If your dataset is skewed and contains outliers, you can attempt one of the transformation methods shown in figure 4.20 to correct for the extreme values.

To put all of these assumptions together, parametric statistics require the use of sample data with the following characteristics:

- The data fits the shape of a specific mathematical distribution (e.g., normal distribution) or can be transformed into the distribution assumed by the test.
- The data has measures where events/participants do not affect each other's results.
- The data distributions are of the same or similar width and shape.
- The data does not have individual or small clusters of data points that have an extreme numerical deviation from the mean and median.

If you have taken a statistics course in an undergraduate or graduate curriculum, you likely covered these topics as part of your education. So why are we spending so much time covering things you may already know?

In my analytics career, I've seen that these steps are often neglected in the application of parametric statistical tests. It's common for people to apply a *t*-test or ANOVA to their data without first making the necessary checks and quickly drawing conclusions about the significance or non-significance of the results. In practice, we are often limited in time and capacity and have stakeholders who don't have the statistical knowledge to inspect our work in detail.

For the sake of the accuracy of your results and the long-term accrual of accurate information at your organization, please do not neglect these steps. You run a genuine risk of your results and conclusions being completely wrong. If the time and diligence to appropriately apply parametric statistics is not feasible in your workflow, I strongly recommend using non-parametric statistics instead.

COEFFICIENTS AND STATISTICAL SIGNIFICANCE

Statistical test calculations provide a *coefficient* or a numerical value for interpreting the strength and direction of the relationship between your groups or variables. Coefficients differ based on the statistical test used, but they are generally standardized values that can be used to evaluate your results against each other and a contingency table.

Let's use the *t*-value from a *t*-test as an example. The *t*-value represents the difference between the means of two samples (independent or repeated measures) or between a sample mean and a hypothesized value (one-sample *t*-test). A larger *t*-value indicates a larger difference between groups.

In most cases, a coefficient's numerical value is insufficient to determine if your results support your hypothesis. Coefficients can be compared *against* each other within the same test (e.g., multiple *t*-values from different *t*-tests). However, they cannot be compared against other coefficients (e.g., a *t*-value versus an *F*-value in an ANOVA) and, on their own, provide limited information about whether the differences between your groups are statistically meaningful.

⸳Appropriate interpretation of coefficients requires two additional pieces of information:

- The *degrees of freedom* and *p*-value threshold, which is one less than your sample size (e.g., if you have 200 data points, your degrees of freedom is 199).
- An appropriate *p*-value as a critical threshold. This is also known as the *alpha level.*

With this information, you can evaluate whether your results are statistically significant. Likely, you are already familiar with this process if you are an analyst—the *t*-test evaluation is covered fairly early in undergraduate statistics coursework, and the degrees of freedom and the *p*-value are ubiquitous in our work. However, there are clear limitations with these approaches and situations where the validity of parametric tests falls apart.

Yes, even if you check and meet all of your assumptions for using a parametric test, you can *still* generate superfluous results if your sample size is inappropriate for the test being used. Let's demonstrate these limitations with a *t*-distribution table for a two-tailed *t*-test.

Table 4.1 shows a *t*-distribution table that allows you to find the critical *t*-value to use for your statistical test, where the value is selected by comparing the degrees of freedom (values displayed vertically in column 1) and the alpha level (shown in the other columns). To use this table, select the approximate *degrees of freedom* that represent your sample sizes ($n_1 + n_2 - 2$) and an alpha level that you intend to use as the threshold for your *p*-value. If you have two groups with 31 records each, you get a degree of freedom (df) value of 60; you then choose an alpha level (0.05 is common) and identify the value in the same row as df=60 and alpha = 0.05, giving you a critical value of 2.00. If your *t*-statistic from your statistical test exceeds this value, you can generally conclude that your results are statistically significant.

Table 4.1 Abbreviated *t*-distribution table showing that increasing the degrees of freedom has diminishing returns on the *t*-critical values at each alpha level (*p*-value threshold).

degrees of freedom	alpha level				
	0.1	0.05	0.01	0.005	0.001
10	1.81	2.23	3.17	3.58	4.59
20	1.72	2.09	2.85	3.15	3.85
30	1.70	2.04	2.75	3.03	3.65
40	1.68	2.02	2.70	2.97	3.55
50	1.68	2.01	2.68	2.94	3.50
60	1.67	2.00	2.66	2.91	3.46
70	1.67	1.99	2.65	2.90	3.44
80	1.66	1.99	2.64	2.89	3.42

Table 4.1 Abbreviated *t*-distribution table showing that increasing the degrees of freedom has diminishing returns on the *t*-critical values at each alpha level (*p*-value threshold). *(continued)*

degrees of freedom	alpha level				
	0.1	0.05	0.01	0.005	0.001
90	1.66	1.99	2.63	2.88	3.40
100	1.66	1.98	2.63	2.87	3.39
150	1.66	1.98	2.61	2.85	3.36
200	1.65	1.97	2.60	2.84	3.34

You'll notice that the decrease in *t*-values is exponential, reaching a point of diminishing returns after a degree of freedom value around 50 to 100 total records in your dataset. This means that around this point, additional data does little to make your test more robust. However, the *t*-value formula does *not* follow this same exponential decrease—it will continue to increase with your sample size due to the way its formula is structured. This is shown in figure 4.23.

$$t = \frac{\overset{\text{sample means}}{X_1 - X_2}}{\sqrt{\dfrac{S_1^2}{n_1} + \dfrac{S_2^2}{n_2}}}$$

sample standard deviations, squared

sample sizes

Figure 4.23 Formula for an independent samples *t*-test

When the sample sizes n_1 and n_2 increase, the size of the overall *t*-value increases with no other changes to the mean or standard deviations. Let's take two samples with the summary information shown in table 4.2. If you calculate the *t*-value for these two groups, as shown in figure 4.24, your *t*-value is far below the critical threshold at the current sample size.

Table 4.2 Sample test score data for two groups of students

	Group 1	Group 2
Mean	80.4	79.9
Standard deviation	4	3.8
Sample size	45	44

$$t = \frac{80.4 - 79.9}{\sqrt{\dfrac{4^2}{45} + \dfrac{3.8^2}{44}}} = 0.6047$$

✗ not significant

Figure 4.24 The two groups have a non-significant difference.

If you double the sample size for each group to 90 and 88, respectively, you get the result shown in figure 4.25.

$$t = \frac{80.4 - 79.9}{\sqrt{\dfrac{4^2}{90} + \dfrac{3.8^2}{88}}} = 0.8551$$

✗ not significant

Figure 4.25 The two groups still have a non-significant difference, but the *t*-value is larger.

If you increase the sample size again by ten times the original number of participants, as shown in figure 4.26, the *t*-value increases considerably and far exceeds the critical *t*-value.

$$t = \frac{80.4 - 79.9}{\sqrt{\dfrac{4^2}{900} + \dfrac{3.8^2}{880}}} = 2.7042$$

✓ statistically significant

Figure 4.26 Increasing the sample size by a factor of 10 yields a statistically significant result.

As analysts in the age of big data, we frequently work with datasets substantially larger than in previous decades. Collecting data from participants in academic settings is time-consuming and costly, which leads the majority of researchers to moderately constrain their sample sizes (e.g., 100–200 participants). In contrast, data is often highly available and extremely cheap to capture in fields such as marketing or product analytics. It's increasingly common to access large data samples over extended periods and compute statistics on thousands or millions of records. When running parametric statistical tests, such large sample sizes can yield significant differences even when the group means that are being compared are nearly identical. The recommendations made from these results are unlikely to be valuable or actionable.

There are some steps you can take to correct for problems with datasets whose magnitudes exceed a few hundred records:

- Increase your significance threshold from .05 to .01 or .001.
- Use effect size measures such as Cohen's *d* to measure the magnitude of differences between your group means. These calculations are not affected by sample size.
- Set a minimum threshold of difference between group means that is meaningful based on your domain knowledge (e.g., student test scores with an average difference of 0.5% is likely not meaningful) and the implications of the differences (e.g., how much revenue does a 0.2% increase in conversion rate mean for your organization). The easiest way to do this is to use the confidence interval to compare the true difference between means to the desired value.

Comparing experimental and control groups with a *t*-test

Naomi is preparing her results for analysis. She has the following summary information about her primary measure of interest in the drug trial:

Hours of Sleep	Experimental	Control
Mean	6.54	6.11
Std. Deviation	1.7	1.8
Sample Size	473	455

The distribution of *hours of sleep* is normally distributed, with no extreme outliers. The two groups also have approximately equal variances. Since this dataset meets all of the assumptions of parametric statistical tests, Naomi elects to use an independent samples *t*-test to determine whether the differences between the two groups are statistically meaningful. She sets an alpha-level threshold of .001 because of her large sample size. Her criteria for statistical significance must be appropriate due to the implications of reporting inaccurate results on a trial for a new medication.

The results yield a *t*-value of 3.738. With 926 degrees of freedom, she concludes that her results are statistically significant.

In this book, we've discussed the concept of statistical significance, alpha levels, and *p*-values at length. The *p*-value is a universal tool in applying inferential statistics, and you're likely familiar with interpreting *p*-values of your statistical tests. However, providing a layperson's explanation of the value and its application can be challenging. It's not particularly intuitive. The first introduction to the *p*-value and its meaning in nearly every undergraduate statistics course I taught led to a classroom of confused faces.

The *p*-value is a *value between 0 and 1* representing the probability of returning your test coefficient or a higher value (e.g., *t*-value, *F*-value), assuming that your null hypothesis is true. The smaller the *p*-value, the more substantial the evidence that your null hypothesis is false. In less technical jargon, assuming there is *no true difference between the experiment and control group in the population,* a *p*-value of .05 indicates a 5%

probability you would see the observed magnitude of differences between your sample means. The smaller the *p*-value, the less likely your null hypothesis is to be true.

The *p*-value is *not* defined as any of the following, though you may frequently encounter these interpretations:

- The probability that your results occurred due to chance
- The probability that your alternative hypothesis is true
- A static, universal threshold where all values above .05 are not significant, and all values below .05 are significant

Like some statistical tests and concepts discussed in this section, the *p*-value's development and widespread application have a rocky history. Pearson developed the concept in the early 20th century to mitigate the need to manually compare your test statistic to a critical value (see table 4.1). The test was popularized in the 1950s by Fisher with the recommended .05 threshold commonly used today.

Using the *p*-value as an immutable threshold constrains the quality of an analyst's work (see figure 4.27). There's rarely a meaningful difference between a *p*-value slightly above or below your chosen alpha level. It's often easier to use a rigid interpretation of findings with a less restricted alpha level and present potentially erroneous results. Regardless, it can sometimes be challenging to present findings in some contexts with a flexible interpretation of the *p*-value (e.g., peer-reviewed articles, program evaluations) and have them perceived as legitimate.

Figure 4.27 The p-value is often treated as a magical boundary that unlocks findings considered worthy of peer-reviewed publication.

If you find yourself in a situation where you are expected to use the broadly accepted interpretation of a *p*-value, I recommend the following steps to maximize the quality of your deliverable:

- Set your alpha level intentionally at the start of any experiment, alongside your hypothesis generation, based on the following:
  - Your field of study or work (an experiment on user behavior on a website will usually have less restrictive criteria than a medical trial)
  - The number of groups and interaction effects in your study design (more groups and interactions produce a higher likelihood of false-positive results)
  - The implications of getting it wrong and reporting false-positive results (recommending a website design versus recommending a new type of therapy or educational intervention)
  - The degree of control you have over your experiment (a highly controlled laboratory setting can potentially limit the number of confounding effects, allowing you to set more conservative thresholds than studies in real-world settings)
- Check or recheck all the assumptions of your test. If you are unclear whether certain assumptions have been met, consider running tests (e.g., Welch's test for equality of variance) to validate your visual observations.
- Determine the appropriate *minimum* sample size to detect an effect using an *a priori power analysis*. Many free sample-size calculators are available online, and it's also possible to calculate this in most statistical software. With the limitations of sample-size sensitive parametric tests in mind, set a goal of collecting more than the minimum. For example, the following code determines the minimum sample size necessary to detect a small effect size of 0.3 at 80% power (the most commonly used threshold), with an alpha level of .05, and with four groups being compared:

```
from statsmodels.stats.power import FTestAnovaPower        ⊲⌐ Import the
                                                             │ libraries.
pwr = FTestAnovaPower()
sample = pwr.solve_power(effect_size = 0.3,
    power = 0.8,
    alpha = 0.05,
    k_groups = 4)              ⊲⌐ Calculate and print the
print(sample)                    │ recommended sample size.
```

This code produces the following result:

```
125.11669926824126
```

- If your *p*-value is slightly above the alpha level, consider collecting additional data with a *fixed sample size* to determine if the gap between your test coefficient and the critical value can be reduced or eliminated. Do not just collect data until you reach your desired threshold. That's one method of *p*-hacking, which we will discuss later in this chapter.
- Use and report on effect size measures such as Cohen's *d* alongside your measure of statistical significance to provide a robust picture of the magnitude of your results.

In general, marketing and product analytics units in business have opportunities to be flexible with their interpretations of statistical significance. If you can set a margin of error and apply qualitative judgments to results, I recommend many of the same steps: set your margin of error intentionally alongside your alpha level, collect an appropriately sized sample, and report on effect sizes.

4.2.2 Exercises

The following code performs an a priori power analysis to determine the minimum sample size necessary to detect a medium-sized effect (`effect_size = 0.5`) in a *t*-test at 80% power (`power = 0.8`). These two parameters are common defaults in an a priori test.

Run the code in the Python environment of your choice (terminal, Jupyter Notebook, etc.). You will need `statsmodels` installed for this step and `numpy` and `scipy` for the rest of this activity:

```
from statsmodels.stats.power import TTestIndPower      ⟵─┤  Import the libraries.

pwr = TTestIndPower()                                   ⟵┐  Calculate and print
sample = pwr.solve_power(effect_size = 0.5,               │  the recommended
    power = 0.8,                                           │  sample size.
    alpha = 0.05)
print(sample)
```

1 What is the minimum recommended sample size for a *t*-test? How does the value change when you adjust the alpha level to `.01` and then `.001`?

2 Run an independent samples *t*-test using the two normally distributed samples of data generated with the following code. Replace the value of `0` for n with the recommended sample size you just calculated for `alpha = 0.05` (divide the value by 2, because the test recommends a *total* sample size). Are the results statistically significant at the p = .05 threshold?

```
import numpy as np
from scipy import stats as st          ⟵─┤  Import the libraries.

n = 0                                  ⟵┐  Replace the n value with the
mu, sigma = 75.5, 6.2                    │  recommended sample size.
mu2, sigma2 = 77.9, 6.5
X1 = np.random.normal(mu, sigma, n)
X2 = np.random.normal(mu2, sigma2, n)  ⟵┐  Generate two normal
                                         │  distributions.
result = st.ttest_ind(X1, X2)
print(result)          ⟵┐  Conduct an independent
                         │  samples t-test.
```

3 Replace the value of n with the recommended sample size at `alpha = 0.01` (don't forget to divide the value by 2). Is the result statistically significant at the p = .01 threshold?

4 Summarize the changes you saw between each *t*-test conducted with different sample sizes. Why did the *t*-value and *p*-value change the way they did?

5 Note how the *t*-test results change with each alpha and sample size adjustment.

4.3 Making inferences: Correlation and regression

A *correlation* is a measure of the relationship between two variables. It's often one of the first steps taken to identify patterns in a dataset and establish an association between variables later examined for potential causal relationships in a regression model. A thorough understanding of correlation and regression is foundational to advanced statistics, predictive modeling, and machine learning.

4.3.1 Correlation coefficients

There are several types of correlation coefficients you can use to evaluate relationships between two variables:

- *Pearson's correlation* measures linear relationships between two continuous variables. It's the most commonly used of the correlational methods. To effectively use this coefficient, your data must meet the assumptions of other parametric statistics and represent a *linear* trend. If data is not checked for linearity (see figure 4.28), your coefficient can indicate a far weaker relationship than actually exists.

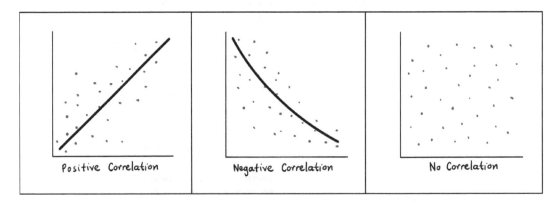

Figure 4.28   Linear and some non-linear correlations can be easily visualized.

- *Spearman's correlation* is a non-parametric statistic that compares the *ranked position* of each data point between two variables. It's often used for ordinal data and variables with non-linear relationships. We will discuss this method in chapter 5.

- *Kendall's rank correlation* or *Kendall's tau* is a measure of ordinal association between data points calculated by measuring the number of pairs with identical and disparate ranks. It's used less often than Spearman's correlation but can better identify some ordinal relationships. We will discuss this method in chapter 5.

- *Point-biserial correlation* is a special type of Pearson's correlation used to measure associations between one binary variable and one continuous variable. It's calculated by measuring the difference between the two group means for the continuous variable. It is one of several available coefficients for measuring associations between a binary and continuous variable.

All of these coefficients benefit from using the same standardized scale; values range from –1 to 1, with values closer to 1 or –1 indicating a *stronger* relationship, the +/– sign indicating the *direction* of the relationship, and with values closer to 0 indicating a weak or no relationship.

The choice of correlation coefficient is often dictated by the type of data you are working with (e.g., when relationships are not linear or if one variable is not continuous). When measuring associations between two continuous variables, you will generally benefit from visually observing a scatterplot of the relationship and determining if it can be *transformed* into a linear relationship.

For example, the negative correlation shown in figure 4.29 depicts two variables with a *curvilinear* relationship. The best-fit curve is easy to visualize, but one or more variables will need to be transformed to create a linear variable for Pearson's *r* coefficient to represent the strength of the relationship accurately. The *circle of transformations* is a common diagnostic tool for identifying appropriate transformations to your variables. Often, you will benefit from testing more than one of the transformations to determine if one method yields a higher correlation coefficient that better fits the data.

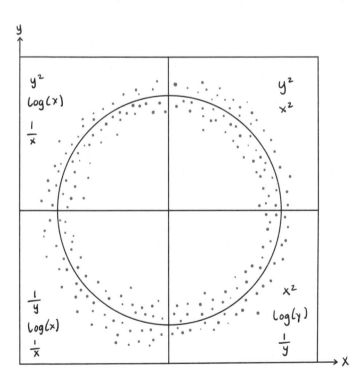

Figure 4.29 The circle of transformations recommends possible transformations to test, based on the shape of the two variables you are comparing, shown in a scatterplot.

4.3.2   *Regression modeling*

Like correlation, *regression* is a method for investigating the strength and direction of a relationship between two variables. Rather than providing a single coefficient to describe the relationship, a regression is used to model the relationship between a *dependent* variable and one or more *independent* variables. Regression modeling is used extensively in *predictive* and *causal* modeling, which we will discuss at length in chapter 9.

A *linear regression* models a line of best fit to describe the relationship between the dependent variable and one or more independent variables. The equation for a simple linear regression (one independent variable) is provided in one of the following forms:

$$y = mx + b$$

Linear regression formula with one independent variable

This is recognizable as the formula for the *slope of a line*, where b is the y-intercept (x-value where $y = 0$) and m is the slope (the change in y for a one-unit change in x). A *multiple linear regression* equation (more than one independent variable) will often be presented in the following format:

$$y = \beta_0 + \beta_1 X_1 + \beta_2 X_2$$

Alternative linear regression formula with two independent variables

In this version of the formula, β_0 is the y-intercept, and β_1 and β_2 are the respective slopes for each predictor. Both methods of representing a regression equation are appropriate for simple and multiple regression models. However, the latter is sometimes more prevalent in academic settings and for models with multiple predictors.

Linear regression is a *parametric* statistic that makes similar assumptions to the previous tests we've discussed. It assumes that your data represents a set of independent events and that a *linear relationship* exists between your dependent variable and its independent variables. Any data not meeting these assumptions should be appropriately transformed (see figures 4.20 and 4.29). Linear regressions also make the following assumptions:

- *The variables in your dataset are multivariate normal*—This means that across the variables in your model, their *combined* distribution follows what's known as a multivariate normal distribution. This is often assessed by generating a Q-Q plot to compare the *quantiles* of each variable to those of a normal distribution.
- *The independent variables are not highly correlated with each other, which is typically referred to as multicollinearity*—This is generally evaluated by reviewing correlation values between the independent variables and selecting between variables when there are strong correlations.

- *The spread of errors (residuals) is consistent for all values of the independent variables, known as homoscedasticity*—This is typically evaluated by plotting residuals against predicted values (a residual plot). When this assumption is violated, it's recommended that you use a *weighted least-squares regression* that weights observations based on the size of their errors or that you transform the dependent variable using a square root or logarithm, similar to how you might in the case of non-linear relationships.

We will discuss the statistical modeling in depth in chapter 9, including Python implementations of regression models for different types of deliverables.

4.3.3 Reporting on correlations and regressions

Correlations are one of the most widely known and understood statistical concepts. Many stakeholders can quickly gain value from visualizations, coefficients, and summaries with minimal additional context. By extension, many of the interpretations of correlations can be applied to regression modeling in the presentation of your final deliverable. In practice, how your stakeholders interpret correlation results can be an early diagnostic for the general comfort level with data and statistics across your organizations (see figure 4.30).

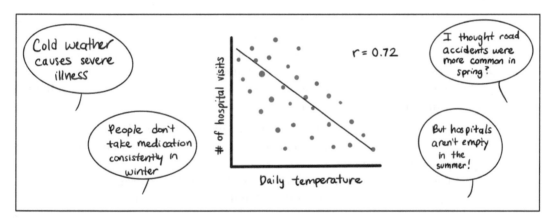

Figure 4.30   Interpretations of correlational results can provide insight into the misconceptions about their purpose and limitations.

In one of my roles in data science, our team identified some patterns of misinterpretation when reporting on correlations to various stakeholders:

- Attributing a direct causal relationship between the two variables
- Adding interpretation based on previously held beliefs
- Disputing the relationship based on partial information or previously held beliefs

To better assist interpretations, we developed a guide to evaluating correlations (see figure 4.31) and specific recommendations for interpreting results. The recommendations were delivered in presentations to large audiences that were recorded, disseminated, and archived for a large portion of the organization to refer to over time.

Interpretation of Results

✓ There is a negative correlation between the variables – the lower the temperature, the more hospital visits tend to occur.

✗ A lower daily temperature causes more hospital visits.

✓ We have several hypotheses about the underlying causes of this relationship that require investigation.

✗ We think that certain diseases spread more often in winter, causing the surge in hospital visits.

Figure 4.31   Example of a slide created to guide statistical interpretations of correlations

When reporting regression results, it may be necessary to distinguish between *predictive* relationships and *causal* relationships for your stakeholders (these are not the same, and we will discuss this at length in chapter 9). The predictive nature of a regression model is implied in its selection of independent and dependent variables, and its results are even more easily interpreted as causation.

In your deliverables and presentations, you may want to consider the following strategies for mitigating misinterpretations:

- Isolate and present the strongest independent variable relationships with your dependent variables. These may be best communicated as univariate correlations with scatterplots.
- Include clear, consistent language on what conclusions your stakeholders *can* draw and limitations highlighting what they *cannot* reasonably conclude.

4.3.4   *Exercises*

We haven't yet answered the first question of this chapter—is Boston or New York City warmer in July?

1. Import the `nyc_boston_weather.csv` dataset associated with this book. Generate distributions to visualize the data.
2. Check all of the assumptions of the *t*-test. Make any necessary transformations to normalize the data.
3. Determine if you have a sufficient sample size by running an a priori power analysis with an alpha level of .05, a medium effect of 0.5, and 80% power.

4 Run an independent samples *t*-test to determine if there is a significant difference between Boston and New York City's weather in July of 2022. Which city is warmer, if either?

5 Prepare a summary of your findings for a stakeholder who does not have direct experience with inferential statistics. Include statements on how you *can* and *cannot* interpret the results.

Summary

- *Measures of central tendency,* such as the mean, median, and mode, are used to quickly assess the characteristics of a dataset. Each can be used in reporting to stakeholders; however, valuable information about outliers, skew, and shape can be lost if only one measure is reported.

- *Measures of variability* tell you how much your dataset deviates from the mean or median. These measures give you an estimate of the spread of your dataset and a first point of comparison between two or more distributions.

- *Parametric statistical tests* are widespread across nearly every domain of analytics. These tests make explicit *assumptions* about the parameters and characteristics of the underlying population distribution.

- Many parametric tests assume that your population is *normally distributed.* These tests require that your data can be represented as a normal distribution through trimming, transformation, or other appropriate steps.

- The majority of statistical tests use the *p*-value in the interpretation of the test coefficient. This value estimates the probability that you would observe the magnitude of group differences if there were no actual differences in the population. This value is often used as a threshold to determine *statistical significance.*

- Each statistical test has a *minimum recommended sample size* to detect an effect between groups or variables. Many tests (e.g., *t*-tests) also have a theoretical upper limit on your sample size before you risk generating false-positive results.

- Making inferences using regression modeling requires that you meet many of the same assumptions as tests comparing two or more groups (e.g., *t*-tests, ANOVAs). In addition, Pearson's correlation and linear regression require that your variables have a linear relationship or can be transformed into a linear relationship.

- Reporting the results of inferential statistical tests to non-technical stakeholders requires precise language to guide teams through the appropriate interpretation and the limitations of your findings.

Statistics you (probably) missed: Non-parametrics and interpretation

This chapter covers

- The history and purpose of statistical tests
- Evaluating and using non-parametric alternatives to common parametric tests
- Using the chi-square test for categorical comparisons
- Mitigating the likelihood of false-positive and false-negative results
- Using statistics to ensure accurate findings

The number of ways you can misunderstand statistics is infinite. The number of ways you can understand it is finite.

—Dr. Lawrence Tatum

Parametric tests cannot be used in every situation. Despite statistics coursework covering the same limited topics, the tests we covered in chapter 4 are *not* the only options available to you as an analyst. When you cannot expect to produce reliable results with a *t*-test, ANOVA, or any other method we have covered so far, you have a wide range of *non-parametric* tests available for evaluating your data and making inferences about the broader population.

To provide some context for the underlying logic of parametric statistical tests, we will first briefly cover the development of these tests. Once you understand their intended purpose, you will be prepared to answer challenging stakeholder questions, communicate the limitations of a test, and think critically about an extensive range of questions you could answer in your organization and interviews as you seek to grow your career.

5.1 The landscape of statistics

Suppose you are an analyst on a product analytics team at a software company. The product team is evaluating whether one of the new page versions on the app leads to customers completing a workflow faster. You were asked to conduct a between-subjects ANOVA to assess the results of an A/B/C test. In your diligence as an analyst, you explore the distributions of the data to check the assumption of normality, which look like those in figure 5.1.

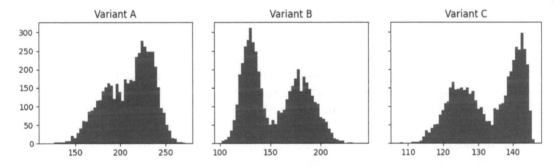

Figure 5.1 Each distribution is bimodal, which traditional measures of central tendency can't detect.

You try transforming each distribution with a few of the approaches we covered in chapter 4, but you cannot change the shape of the bimodal distributions. Figure 5.2 shows how your data changes when you apply square and square-root transformations to the data in figure 5.1.

Unfortunately, the transformations are no closer to a normal distribution. What do you do? Do you give up and *not* conduct your analysis? Based on the assumptions discussed in the previous chapter, you are unlikely to yield accurate results with a one-way ANOVA. If you provide recommendations that don't accurately reflect your users, you

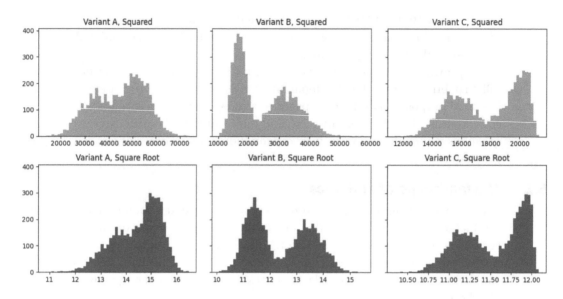

Figure 5.2   Square and square-root transformations of the original bimodal distributions in figure 5.1

could decrease their quality of experience in the app if those recommendations are implemented.

You've now reached one of the limits of parametric statistical tests—if you cannot meet their assumptions, you cannot reliably use them. Thankfully, these are *far* from the only options you have available to you. There are a wide range of statistical tests that have different, fewer, or no assumptions about the underlying data. If you want to use them effectively, it's first important to understand the historical context behind the popularity and widespread use of parametric statistics so you can responsibly choose the best option for your work.

5.1.1   *The evolution of statistical methods*

In some form, statistics have been actively used for centuries. Probability theory dates back to the 17th century when it was used to predict uncertain events (e.g., the number of annual births and deaths in a town). The theory was expanded over the following centuries, with methods and approaches (e.g., Bayes' theorem) still widely used today.

Most *parametric* statistical tests we're familiar with in analytics were developed in the last 100 to 120 years. Since their development, they have grown in influence and often dominate the methodological choices of fields in the social sciences, humanities, and others. But their rise to prominence does not necessarily reflect their efficacy across possible research questions.

The historical development of parametric statistics is usually left out of statistics education. If you sat through courses as I did, you might have been taught formulas for each test, as a rule of law or formulas you need to memorize, the same way you do in a calculus class. Statistics, however, is *not* the same as mathematics, and none of the formulas you learned were discovered—they were developed with a purpose in mind.

TESTS DEVELOPED FOR A PURPOSE

The story of how parametric statistics rose to prominence lies with the eugenics movement. From the turn of the 20th century to the 1930s, many statistical tests we know were developed by well-known eugenicists (Francis Galton, Karl Pearson, Ronald Fisher) as part of their efforts to operationalize the concept of *intelligence.*

In the view of this movement, intelligence was treated as a universal concept in which someone's intellectual capabilities were considered biologically determined. The IQ test was developed as a measure by which people could be "ranked" and differentiated by race or ethnicity. The ideas and philosophies of eugenics and its focus on differentiating groups of people as superior or inferior were cited by Nazi Germany as a key guiding factor in its atrocities.

While this type of explicit thought is less prevalent in today's academic world, many of the methods and tests developed as part of efforts to define and measure intelligence are still used today. The ideas and concepts of eugenics guided the development of statistical significance thresholds, the bell curve (the scaled shape of the distribution of intelligence scores), and correlations that still dominate academic and statistical thinking. We're taught to frame questions as looking for *differences* between groups or *correlations* between variables. We're taught that the normal distribution (figure 5.3) is ever-present in measures of behavioral and cognitive phenomena. We *still* use the IQ test to measure intellectual capabilities and discuss a general intelligence capable of being reduced to a single number. We *still* teach these topics in social sciences as if they're truth rather than hypotheses.

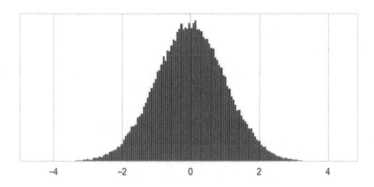

Figure 5.3 The bell curve (normal curve) is ever-present in statistics and *does* occur naturally for a handful of phenomena, such as the distribution of human heights.

THE DEVELOPMENT OF NON-PARAMETRIC STATISTICAL TESTS

In the decades after developing parametric methods, statisticians responded to the limitations of parametric methods and their assumptions about the underlying distribution of the population data. These assumptions (e.g., normality) were often unrealistic to meet, and they limited the practical applications of statistical tests and the ability to approach research questions as group differences or correlation/regression problems.

Statisticians developed non-parametric methods in the mid-20th century—methods that do not make assumptions about the distribution or shape of the data. A range of tests were created, and the approach grew in popularity over the decades. We continue to see advancements in new model development and model refinement today, with many new classes of non-parametric methods being developed with machine learning advancements.

FURTHER READING

Regardless of your research questions, beliefs about this topic, or the type of analytics work you do, it's essential to understand the context of the tools we use as analysts. In aggregate, the methods we regularly used were developed to compare, differentiate, and rank people. The way we think about the questions we ask is still a part of statistics and social sciences education a century later.

We won't go into detail about the history and development of statistics in this book; this topic can easily span multiple books and has been well-documented by amazing authors in the past decades. If you're interested in learning more, I recommend reading the following books:

- *The Theory that Would Not Die* by Sharon McGrayne [1]—This book is centered around the history and application of Bayesian statistical methods, which the purveyors of frequentist statistics heavily criticized.
- *The Mismeasure of Man* by Stephen J. Gould [2]—This book comprehensively criticizes eugenicist beliefs and applications of statistics. It is an excellent source for explaining statistical methods, such as factor analyses.

5.1.2 Choosing your approaches responsibly

To succeed as analysts, we still need to use parametric statistics appropriately. Despite their limitations and history, I recommend the following takeaways when choosing a research method and statistical test:

- We're trained as researchers and analysts to frame our questions as looking for group differences, correlations, or causal relationships. That is the primary focus of this book. Previous chapters covered research questions and hypotheses with this structure due to the prevalence and high availability of training material on these topics. However, looking for differences and correlations is not the only method you can use. You can use dozens of quantitative, qualitative, and mixed-method approaches, such as the following:
  - *Observational research* aims to observe and record data about behavior and events without manipulation or intervention. The overall goal of this method is to *describe* (see chapter 2 for more detail on descriptive methods) and understand a phenomenon. This is often the best method to use in analytics when first evaluating a new dataset.

- *Observation-oriented modeling* focuses on relationships and patterns in the data and how they relate to observed phenomena being studied. This approach uses graphical representations, statistical models, and machine learning algorithms to build models based on observations (see figure 5.4). You can read more about this method in the paper, "Observation Oriented Modeling" [3].

① Observation: Users struggle to set up and use your software

② Action: Do they visit your support site?

③ Question: Are users who visit your support site more likely to complete the setup process?

Figure 5.4   Visual representation of a causal phenomenon with observation-oriented modeling

- For each research method we covered in chapter 4 (group differences, correlations, and predictive/causal relationships), you can use numerous non-parametric and semi-parametric statistical tests to test your hypotheses. Many tests are available in Python, R, SPSS, SAS, or STATA.
- The near-ubiquitous parametric statistical tests taught in an introductory statistics course (e.g., *t*-test, ANOVA, Pearson's correlation) are not necessarily *better* than tests used less frequently. There were aggressive efforts within academic statistics to popularize parametric methods and discredit probabilistic methods. *The Theory that Would Not Die* [1] discusses this history in detail.
- Statistical tests were designed assuming you are leveraging a finite sample representing a relatively small proportion of the broader population. For example, many psychological studies and clinical trials recruit participants in the hundreds or thousands. In today's world, an analyst can easily work with datasets containing millions of records. If your statistical test assumes a smaller sample size, you will not yield meaningful or accurate results (as discussed in chapter 4).

5.2   *Non-parametric statistics*

We spent chapter 4 discussing tests that make rigid assumptions about the shape of your data. In many cases, those assumptions cannot be met, or the underlying distribution of the data is unknown. *Non-parametric statistics* is a class of methods that doesn't make assumptions about the underlying distribution of the data. They're commonly used instead of parametric statistics when assumptions cannot be met. Many tests offer additional flexibility on data types, enabling you to compare categorical and ordinal data.

As an analyst, you can apply a non-parametric alternative for each parametric test we covered. Each of the methods we will cover is available in Python or R, and most are also easily applied in SPSS, SAS, and STATA.

5.2.1   *Comparisons between groups on continuous or ordinal data*

The most prevalent parametric statistical tests assume that you use *continuous data* captured about a phenomenon of interest between or within groups. When your data is *not* normal, you have several possible options for evaluating your results.

COMPARISONS BETWEEN TWO GROUPS

The first test we will cover is the Mann-Whitney *U* test. This compares the *medians* of two *independent samples* and is performed by taking the *sum of ranks* between groups and calculating a *U* statistic from the group sums. The sum of ranks is calculated by adding the ranked values for each group; each sum is used to calculate a *U* value for each group, and the lowest among them is selected as the *U* statistic. The *U* statistic is compared to a critical value using a *U* table, just as we did with parametric tests in chapter 4. If the *U* statistic is *lower* (not higher) than the critical threshold, it's considered statistically significant.

Figure 5.5 shows an example of a hand-calculated *U* statistic comparing daily weather data from New York City and Boston. The *U* statistic is calculated using six values per city for a total sample size of 12. The *U* statistic for the city with the *lower* value (New York City) is compared to the appropriate critical value in a *U* table. In the same manner as the tests we discussed in chapter 4, we can conclude that the temperature difference between New York City and Boston is highly significant.

The Mann-Whitney *U* test is robust to violations of the assumptions of a *t*-test, which means that you can use this test in most cases where you cannot rely on a parametric test. The test compares the *relative position* of each data point to the rest of the dataset rather than being affected by the numerical value of that data point. Your data can be non-normal or have unequal variances with no effect on the validity of your results.

To summarize the value and advantages of this approach:

- It's agnostic to the shape of your distribution, producing reliable results when parametric test assumptions are violated. Any of the distributions shown in figure 5.6 can use the Mann-Whitney *U* test to compare the underlying data.
- It's more robust than a *t*-test to moderate differences in the sample sizes of each group.
- In addition to continuous data, the Mann-Whitney *U* test (and all non-parametric tests we will cover in this section) can be conducted with *ordinal* data, making statistical inference possible on far more data types than parametric tests alone.

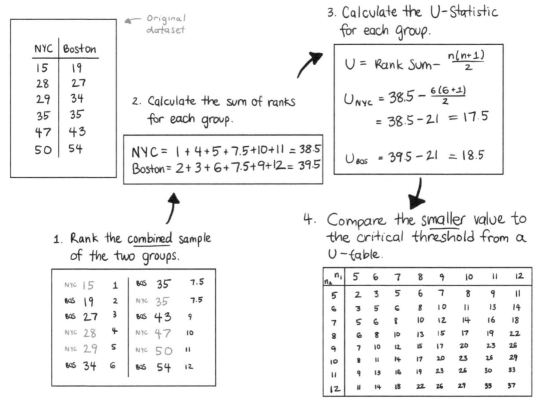

Figure 5.5 Steps for calculating the *U* statistic

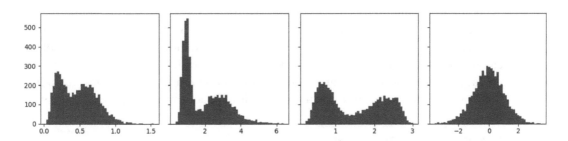

Figure 5.6 The Mann-Whitney *U* test can be used for any of the distribution shapes displayed, whereas the *t*-test is only appropriate for the rightmost (normal) distribution shape.

As with every statistical test we've covered thus far, the Mann-Whitney *U* test is not a silver bullet free of limitations. As an analyst, you will need to evaluate the properties of your data to determine if this non-parametric test is appropriate and take additional steps to interpret the results:

- When your sample is too small, you will likely generate results with false-positive errors. You can see this in the preceding example, where a minimal temperature difference was highly statistically significant with a sample size of 12 across groups.
- The test is also highly sensitive to *large* sample sizes, where you are more likely to produce false-*negative* results.
- The Mann-Whitney U test performs poorly when there are many tied ranks (e.g., one tie in this dataset). Where possible, including additional digits in your floating-point data can minimize the effect and frequency of tied ranks.
- There's a lack of consensus among statisticians and analysts on many aspects of the Mann-Whitney U test and its usage. For example, there are different recommended approaches for handling tied ranks and the appropriate minimum sample size necessary to draw practical conclusions. Most statistical software and packages choose between approaches and require you to adhere to their choice unless you can write a custom module.
- If you search for the application of the Mann-Whitney U test, you'll also discover the lack of agreement between otherwise reputable resources on basic information about the test. My research found discrepancies in the formula, assumptions, data types, minimum sample sizes, and other information. Be prepared to dig into peer-reviewed research on this test to ensure the information you seek is accurate.
- Unlike the t-statistic, the U statistic does not include negative values indicating the direction of the relationship. You must compare the U values or medians between groups to determine which has significantly higher ranks.

Figure 5.7 shows the steps to calculating the Mann-Whitney U statistic to compare daily temperatures between New York City and Boston.

When reporting the results of a Mann-Whitney U test (or any non-parametric test that uses a rank-sum method), I strongly recommend presenting your stakeholders with *median* values between groups rather than *mean* values (discussed extensively in chapter 4). Rank-sum values, by definition, will align with which group has a higher median but will *not* reliably agree with the interpretation of mean values. Including both or only the mean may create confusion or inaccurate interpretations of your results.

COMPARISONS WITHIN TWO GROUPS

The Wilcoxon signed-rank test is a non-parametric test for *repeated-measures comparisons* between two groups. It's designed to be used in place of a within-subjects t-test when the assumption of normality cannot be met.

Similar to the Mann-Whitney U test, the Wilcoxon signed-rank test uses the rank of each data point to calculate its test statistic. Since this is a repeated-measures test, it ranks the difference in values between each *pair* of data (e.g., a participant score before and after treatment). The W-statistic is generated by taking the rank of the

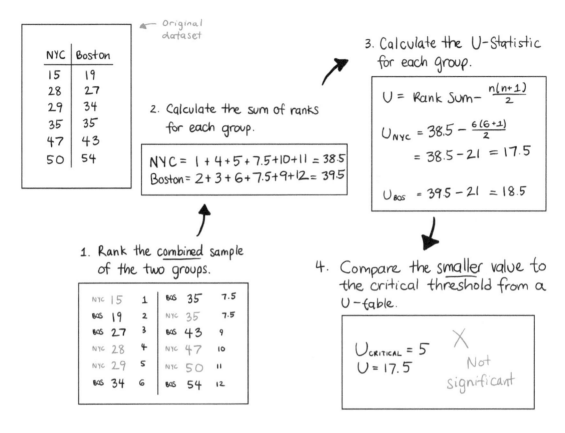

Figure 5.7 Steps to calculating the Mann-Whitney *U* test statistic

absolute value of differences between pairs and then attaching the sign of the original difference value to the rank. The resulting set of rank values combines negative and positive values, grouped by sign and added together for the *sum-of-ranks* calculation. The lower *W*-value between the sum of positive ranks (difference values in the *positive* direction) and negative ranks (difference values in the *negative* direction) is selected as the test statistic and compared to a critical value. Wilcoxon's *W*-statistic is calculated in figure 5.8 on a dataset of test scores before and after a study session.

The Wilcoxon signed-rank test shares many advantages and limitations with the Mann-Whitney *U* test. The test can be used with continuous and ordinal data and does not require you to have normally distributed data. However, it *does* require that two assumptions be met to ensure the accuracy of results:

- The differences between pairs of observations should be *symmetrical* (e.g., not skewed) around the median. This is tested by visually observing the distribution of differences and checking the skewness and kurtosis values.

Before	After
68	74
72	70
75	84
58	70
81	80
76	85
62	65

← Test scores before and after a study session

2. Rank the absolute value of the difference. Attach the sign of the difference score to "sign" the rank.

Difference	Rank	"Signed" Rank
6	4	4
-2	2	-2
9	6	6
12	7	7
-1	1	-1
8	5	5
3	3	3

4. Compare the _smaller_ W-value to the critical threshold from a W-table.

n	a = 0.05	a = 0.01
6	0	–
7	2	–
8	3	0
9	5	1
10	8	3
11	10	5

1. Calculate the difference between each pair.

Before	After	Difference
68	74	6
72	70	-2
75	84	9
58	70	12
81	80	-1
76	84	8
62	65	3

3. Calculate the positive and negative W-statistic values by taking a sum of ranks with the same sign.

$$W+ = 3+4+5+6+7 = 25$$
$$W- = 1+2 = 3$$

Figure 5.8 Steps for calculating the W-statistic

- Ties in ranks should be eliminated by introducing minor, decimal-value differences at random. A large number of ties in your difference values will reduce the statistical power of your test and increase your likelihood of false-positive results.

In addition to reporting statistical test results, it will likely be valuable to report summary information about medians and proportions to your stakeholders for clarity. A synopsis of your findings might include the following:

- The median score was 8 points higher (76%) after the study session, which was determined to be highly statistically significant.
- Seventy percent of students saw an increase in scores after the study session.

As with any non-parametric test using rank sums and relative positioning, it's important to stress that your statistical tests did *not* evaluate mean scores. In my experience, this is easier to convey if you use clear statements on why you chose your summary metrics and depict visualizations such as boxplots. This can help to focus your readers on the relative position of your data points in their distribution rather than having them looking for an average score.

Analyzing non-normal and ordinal data

Let's revisit our case study from chapter 4. As you'll recall, Naomi is a research scientist at a pharmaceutical company analyzing the results of a randomized control trial on a new medication to treat insomnia. She used an independent samples *t*-test to evaluate differences in the experiment and control groups on the primary measure of interest, *hours of sleep*.

In addition to the continuous, normally distributed data that Naomi collected for the sleep study, she has several variables in her dataset that are unsuitable for parametric statistical tests (*t*-test and ANOVA). Each of the following was collected or derived as part of the study:

- In addition to the time spent awake during the sleep cycle, the study captured the *number of sleep interruptions* as a separate measure to identify the number of times a participant woke up. This is captured as discrete count data ranging from 0 to 7, making it an *ordinal* dataset.
- The difference in the number of hours of sleep before the beginning and end of the sleep trial was captured separately for the experiment and control groups and is highly skewed for both.
- Participants' age, which has a bimodal distribution.

Naomi decides to conduct two statistical tests. She chooses a Mann-Whitney *U* test to compare the number of sleep interruptions between the experiment and control groups at the end of the study. She also decides that a separate Wilcoxon signed-rank test for each participant group (experiment and control) is appropriate to compare the number of sleep hours at the trial's beginning and end.

She first calculates the *U* statistic, yielding a highly significant value of 79,635 and a *p*-value of less than .001. She notes that the experiment group has a median of 2 sleep interruptions, and the control group has a median of 3. She is aware that the *U* test is highly sensitive to larger sample sizes and includes a note in her report that she may need further exploration to answer this research question appropriately.

For her second question, Naomi is interested in comparing the hours of sleep before and after the trial for the experiment and control groups. She calculates the *W*-statistic for each of the two tests being conducted separately. She obtains a *W*-statistic for the experiment group of 8,794 and a *p*-value of less than .001. She notes that the experiment group had a median of 7.75 hours of sleep during the final sleep study, compared to 5.86 hours during the first sleep study before receiving the experimental medication.

By comparison, the test comparing hours of sleep for the control group had a *W*-statistic of 54,674 and a *p*-value of 0.64. The group had a median of 5.93 hours of sleep during the final sleep study, compared to 5.83 during the sleep study at the start of the experiment.

She concludes that the experimental drug was highly effective at increasing the median hours of sleep and reducing the number of sleep interruptions compared to the placebo.

COMPARISONS BETWEEN TWO OR MORE GROUPS

There are two common alternatives to the one-way ANOVA used to compare three or more groups. The Kruskal-Wallis test compares the medians of two or more independent samples. Similar to the Mann-Whitney U test, it calculates the sum of ranks between each of the groups and applies a weight to each rank based on the sample size of the group. This test can also compare main and interaction effects with two independent variables, as you would expect to do with a two-way ANOVA.

The Kruskal-Wallis test also does not make assumptions about the underlying shape of your data. The H-statistic of this test provides information on the magnitude of the difference between groups but does not indicate the direction of that difference. The Kruskal-Wallis test can compare as few as two groups in conjunction with or in place of the Mann-Whitney U test. Figure 5.9 shows the steps to calculating the Kruskal-Wallis H-statistic with three groups.

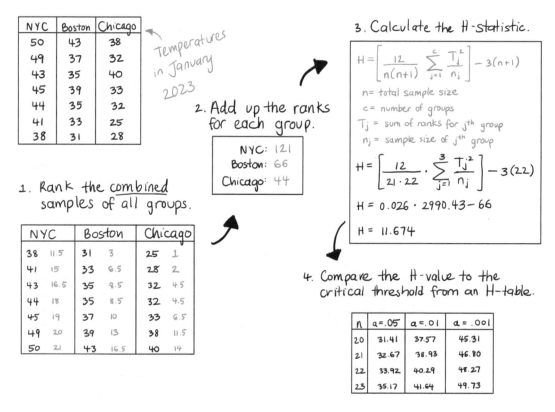

Figure 5.9   Steps for calculating the *H*-statistic with three groups and *n*=21

The Kruskal-Wallis test shares the same applications (non-normal or ordinal data) and limitations (lower power than a one-way ANOVA) as the tests we've discussed. There are some considerations worth noting in your use of this test:

- All tests comparing three or more groups, including the Kruskal-Wallis, require a *post hoc comparison* to determine which of your groups are significantly different from each other. This type of test runs individual two-group comparisons for all combinations while applying a *correction* to adjust the significance level based on the number of comparisons, reducing the risk of false-positive errors. *Dunn's test* is the most commonly used post hoc comparison for the Kruskal-Wallis test, applying a similar correction to the *Bonferroni test* used in one-way ANOVAs.

- Despite the *H*-statistic's more complex formula than the Mann-Whitney *U* test, their performance is identical when conducted between two groups. The test statistic results will differ, but their distributions are calibrated, so the resulting *p*-values will nearly match between tests. We can demonstrate this in Python using two simulated datasets:

```
import numpy as np                                          ◁──┐ Import the
from scipy.stats import skewnorm, kruskal, mannwhitneyu       │ libraries.

np.random.seed(99)              ◁──│ Set a random seed for reproducible results.

group_a = skewnorm.rvs(a=9, scale=2.2, size=99) + 4.5   ◁──┐ Generate two
group_b = skewnorm.rvs(a=11, scale=1, size=99) + 4.6       │ skewed
                                                            │ distributions.
H = kruskal(group_a, group_b)       ◁──┐ Run a Kruskal-Wallis test
U = mannwhitneyu(group_a, group_b)     │ and Mann-Whitney U test.

print(f"Kruskal-Wallis Test, H={H[0]}, p={H[1]}")    ◁──┐ Print the
print(f"Mann-Whitney U-test, U={U[0]}, p={U[1]}")       │ results.
```

The code produces the following output:

```
Kruskal-Wallis Test, H=16.037, p=0.001
Mann-Whitney U-test, U=6515.0, p=0.001
```

- If you expect to run more than one test to compare a variable number of groups (e.g., comparing student test scores among grades 6, 7, and 8 in two schools using two one-way tests), using a Kruskal-Wallis test for both will make for an easier comparison of test statistics than using a Mann-Whitney *U* test for the second comparison (even though you can do so without jeopardizing the accuracy of your results).

In practice, I have seen both the Mann-Whitney *U* and Kruskal-Wallis tests used for non-parametric comparisons. The leading case in which I've seen a clear preference for a Kruskal-Wallis test is when colleagues expected to run group comparisons programmatically over time. We anticipated variation in the number of groups being compared (between 2 and 3), so running the Kruskal-Wallis test allowed for the automation of the periodic calculations.

COMPARISONS WITHIN THREE OR MORE GROUPS

Finally, let's discuss the *Friedman test* as an alternative to the one-way repeated-measures ANOVA. The Friedman test compares the ranks of three or more related samples and can be used instead of an ANOVA when the assumptions of normality or sphericity are violated.

The *Q*-statistic (also referred to as the X^2/chi-square statistic) is calculated as the *sum of squared ranks*, ranked for each participant, summed, and squared for each group. If you reject the null hypothesis, the Mann-Whitney *U* test can be used as a post hoc test with a *Bonferroni correction* (a calculation to reduce the *p*-value threshold based on the number of group comparisons) to identify where sample differences are present. Figure 5.10 shows the steps to calculating Friedman's *Q*-statistic.

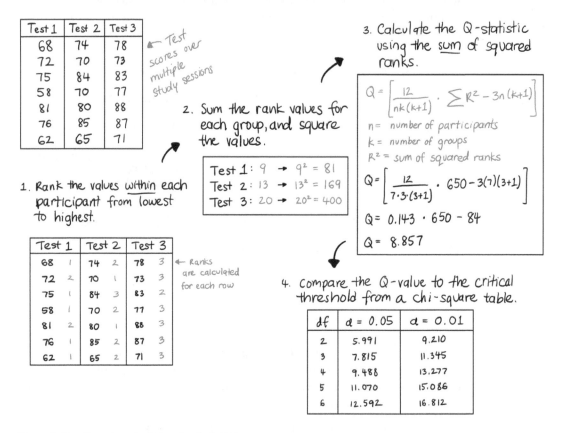

Figure 5.10   Steps to calculating the Q-statistic

The Friedman test uses the same sum-of-ranks approach as all of the non-parametric tests we've covered so far, with some notable exceptions:

- Unlike the Kruskal-Wallis test, the Friedman test *must* compare at least three groups. You can't use it interchangeably with the Mann-Whitney *U* test the way you can with an independent samples comparison.

- The previous tests in this section take an opposite approach to their parametric counterparts in interpreting the test statistic—the test value needs to be *below* the critical threshold to be statistically significant. The Friedman test does *not* take this same approach; instead, the *Q*-statistic takes the same approach as the univariate parametric tests and must be higher than the X^2 critical value to achieve statistical significance.

When your analysis yields a significant result, you will usually need to conduct post hoc tests to identify the significant group differences, as expected with repeated-measures ANOVA. The most common approach is to manually apply the Mann-Whitney *U* test for each pair of groups and apply a Bonferroni correction to the *p*-values to minimize the likelihood of false-positive results.

WHY NOT USE NON-PARAMETRIC TESTS FOR EVERYTHING?

The non-parametric tests we've covered have clear advantages over parametric tests in many cases—they can be used with more data types, they're largely agnostic to the underlying shape of your data, and their calculations are relatively straightforward and available in most statistical software. That's great! So why don't we use them everywhere and toss parametric statistics to the wind?

Non-parametric methods leveraging rank-sum comparisons have some key limitations that can limit their applicability:

- Parametric and non-parametric tests *cannot* be compared one-to-one since parametric tests typically compare means and variances, and non-parametric tests compare medians or ranks between groups.
- Due to non-parametric tests' use of median and rank comparisons, you may have to modify your hypothesis to account for the different types of comparison (the median and rank instead of the mean).
- When your data *does* meet a parametric test's assumptions, a non-parametric test will typically have lower statistical power. This is especially true when working with an extremely large (thousands or above) or very small (dozens or less) dataset. While there are upper limits to the sample size you can use with a parametric test, you're more likely to generate false-positive results with a large *n* when using a non-parametric approach.
- While the non-parametric tests we covered are available in Python packages such as `scipy` and `statsmodels`, many of their post hoc tests are not. You may have to use additional packages such as `scikit-posthocs` or do some manual work to conduct multiple comparisons depending on your comparison of choice. The following code shows an example post hoc comparison:

```
import numpy as np                        Import the
from scipy import stats as st             libraries.
import scikit_posthocs as sp

                                          Set a random seed for
np.random.seed(99)                        reproducible results.
```

```
group_a = st.skewnorm.rvs(a=9, scale=2.2, size=99) + 4.6
group_b = st.skewnorm.rvs(a=11, scale=1.5, size=99) + 4.6
group_c = st.skewnorm.rvs(a=9.1, scale=2.0, size=99) + 4.6

data = [group_a, group_b, group_c]
H = st.kruskal(group_a, group_b)
post_hoc = sp.posthoc_dunn(data, p_adjust="bonferroni")

print(f"Kruskal-Wallis Test, H={H[0]}, p={H[1]}")
print(post_hoc)
```

Generate three non-normal series of data.

Perform a Kruskal-Wallis test and a Dunn test as a post hoc.

Print the results.

The code produces the following output:

```
Kruskal-Wallis Test, H=3.328, p=0.068
          1          2          3
1  1.000000   0.230991   0.494148
2  0.230991   1.000000   1.000000
3  0.494148   1.000000   1.000000
```

Where possible, applying *both* a parametric and non-parametric statistical test is an excellent strategy for validating your results and counterbalancing the limitations of each. Having two statistical tests with convergent results provides strong evidence supporting your hypothesis. When your tests *diverge*, you have an opportunity to tease apart whether your group's means or medians/ranks differ. Table 5.1 provides some ways in which you can explain divergent results to your stakeholders.

Table 5.1   Divergent test results aren't necessarily bad—they can teach a lot about your data.

Result	Suggested interpretations	Stakeholder communications
Parametric and non-parametric tests are significant.	Results are highly likely to reflect *true positive* differences between the actual *and* relative position of values between groups.	"Students in Classroom A had higher average *and* higher ranked test scores than Classroom B."
Only parametric tests are significant.	The sample size may be too small to detect group differences with a non-parametric test. Parametric test results may reflect *false-positive* errors. Assumptions of the parametric test may not be met.	"Students in Classroom A had significantly higher average scores than Classroom B. However, the two classes appear similar in rank, indicating that the average differences can be attributed to a small number of high performers."
Only non-parametric tests are significant.	The assumptions of the parametric test may not be met. The non-parametric test results may reflect *false-positive* errors. The dataset may contain extreme outliers.	"Classroom A had higher scores relative to Classroom B." "Average scores did not differ between classrooms; however, Classroom A ranked higher than Classroom B."

The robust and widely known parametric methods we covered are far from the only non-parametric methods available for analyzing data. Statisticians continually propose new methods and publish them in statistical journals. Many offer advantages when working with specific data types or answering questions that don't quite fit into the paradigm we've covered. If you frequently answer atypical questions with quantitative data, I strongly recommend keeping yourself up to date with this type of statistical research.

RECAP

Your ability to apply parametric and non-parametric tests as appropriate will significantly bolster your career and capacity to deliver high-quality and accurate results. While they're not often taught in introductory statistics coursework (and, truthfully, are often left out of intermediate and advanced coursework), these tests are proven alternatives to the *t*-tests and ANOVAs we're familiar with.

Keep the following in mind to choose the right approach (parametric or non-parametric) and individual test to most effectively compare your data across groups:

- Non-parametric tests are an appropriate choice when your data doesn't meet the assumptions of normality and equal variances that are required for parametric group comparisons.
- The tests we covered have been shown in studies to be slightly less sensitive than parametric tests, which means they may have lower statistical power to detect differences between groups [4].
- Each test can be used with continuous *and* ordinal data, making quantitative analysis possible on more data types than parametric tests.
- Non-parametric tests are *not* a silver bullet. As discussed in chapter 4, you may have difficulty accurately detecting group differences with a small or very large sample size.
- When communicating results to stakeholders, you may need to calibrate expectations about *which* measure of central tendency is being compared (*not* the mean).

5.2.2 *Exercises*

The following code generates three non-normal distributions. Let's assume that each distribution represents a group's performance on an assessment, and we are looking to determine which of the three groups (distributions) has the highest scores:

```
import numpy as np                    ⊲┐  Import the
from scipy import stats as st          │  libraries.

np.random.seed(99)                     ┌  Set a random seed for
                                      ⊲┘  reproducible results.

x_a = np.random.normal(loc=47, scale=4, size=55)   ⊲┐  Generate three non-normal
x_b = np.random.normal(loc=53, scale=4, size=65)    │  distributions for comparison.
X1 = np.concatenate([x_a, x_b])
X2 = st.skewnorm.rvs(83, size=120) + 51
X3 = np.random.exponential(scale=10, size=79) + 44
```

Run the code in the Python environment of your choice (terminal, Jupyter Notebook, etc.). You must have `numpy` and `scipy` installed for this step, and you'll need `matplotlib` for the remainder of the exercises:

1 Create a histogram of X1, X2, and X3 to visualize each data series. How would you describe the shape of each distribution?

2 Try transforming X1, X2, and X3 into a normal distribution. Which can and which cannot be successfully transformed?

3 Based on the possible transformations, can you run a between-subjects ANOVA?

4 Run the following code to conduct a Kruskal-Wallis test. The code assumes you have already imported the libraries in question 1. How can you interpret the results?

```
H = st.kruskal(X1, X2, X3)
print(H)
```

5 Double the sample size values in the `size` parameter for x_a, x_b, X2, and X3. How do your results change?

6 Which group has the highest score? What is the best measure to report based on the comparison type in the Kruskal-Wallis test?

7 Research the available documentation on the `scikit-posthocs` library. What post hoc tests are available in this library for the Kruskal-Wallis test? Try implementing at least two different tests and compare the output. How do the *p*-values differ between these tests?

5.2.3 Comparing categorical data

Based on your research question, there will be situations where your data doesn't allow you to compare an ordinal or continuous measure by groups. If your independent and dependent variables are categorical, you will likely need to use a chi-square test for comparisons.

The *chi-square test* is a non-parametric statistical test used to identify differences between categorical variables by comparing frequencies between each category (e.g., those shown in figure 5.11). This is one of the few non-parametric tests included in

	customer_id	sign_up_date	state	subscription_tier
0	28465	2021-09-09 18:40:27.789150	Florida	Enterprise
1	31656	2022-01-09 07:42:27.789150	California	Team
2	33206	2020-10-15 21:01:27.789150	California	Individual
3	36624	2019-07-08 10:37:27.789150	Florida	Individual
4	12498	2020-06-10 18:06:27.789150	California	Free
5	57147	2021-01-10 12:02:27.789150	New York	Enterprise

subscription_tier state	Enterprise	Free	Individual	Team	Total
California	301	300	308	303	1212
Colorado	299	335	289	325	1248
Florida	295	318	340	361	1314
New York	296	315	313	302	1226
Total	1191	1268	1250	1291	5000

Figure 5.11 Comparisons of two categorical variables can be presented as a contingency table, pivoting the results into summarized rows and columns you can easily view.

introductory statistics curricula in undergraduate and graduate courses. In my experience, it's often taught toward the end of the semester with limited focus on the methodology and how it differs from previous tests.

A chi-square test compares *observed* to *expected frequencies* (how the null hypothesis is conceptualized) between categories, assuming no differences between categories. It can be used as a one-way test (one variable) or a two-way test (a comparison between two variables).

You can use multiple types of chi-square tests to compare one or two samples:

- The *goodness-of-fit test* compares observed frequencies in a single sample against the expected frequencies.
- The *test of independence* compares observed to expected frequencies between *two* categorical variables. The data compared can be presented as counts of observations or proportions of the dataset.
- The *test for trend* determines if there is a trend or pattern in a categorical variable *over time* or across groups.

Chi-square tests aren't often used in many fields of study and work. Analysts may not apply this test for years after completing their statistics coursework. This is not necessarily tied to the applicability of this test—in fact, chi-square tests have many advantages over tests of group comparisons. They can be a helpful tool for deriving insights about where there is *disproportionality* in your data compared to expectations (either static values or relative proportions in your dataset).

Unlike each test we've covered, large sample sizes don't negatively affect the chi-square test. The test statistic calculation shown in figure 5.12 compares each cell's expected value (count or proportion) in a contingency table to the actual value. As your sample size increases, the test becomes more sensitive and more likely to detect small differences between observed and expected values. Conversely, smaller sample sizes make it more challenging to detect differences, which can lead to fewer significant results.

$$\chi^2 = \sum \frac{(O_i - E_i)^2}{E_i}$$

χ^2 = chi squared
O_i = observed value
E_i = expected value

$$E_i = \frac{\text{Row Total} \cdot \text{Column Total}}{\text{Total Sample Size}}$$

Figure 5.12 Breakdown of the equation for the X^2 (chi-square) test

APPLYING THE CHI-SQUARE TEST

Suppose we are analysts on a product analytics team at a SaaS company that offers a subscription service to customers. We recently concluded an A/B/C test on three versions of a new recommendation engine, and we're interested in seeing whether any of the versions significantly affected user engagement.

To test this hypothesis, we can use a chi-square test of independence to compare the frequencies of users who engaged with each version of the recommendation engine and the control group to see if there are any differences by country. We'll start by comparing the observed number of users from each of the four countries' user bases in the experiment (United States, Canada, England, France) broken out by experiment group. This ensures that we have appropriately stratified our sample before analysis (see figure 5.13).

country	Canada	England	France	United States	Total
recommender					
A	415	443	441	434	1733
B	395	385	365	392	1537
C	467	444	421	398	1730
Total	1277	1272	1227	1224	5000

Figure 5.13   Count of users who engaged with the feature, broken out by country and experiment group

From figure 5.13, it's unclear whether any country disproportionately represents any of the experimental groups. A chi-square test for *independence* can be conducted to validate that the sample is appropriately stratified:

```
import pandas as pd                          Import the pandas and stats         Import the
import scipy.stats as st                     libraries from scipy.               recommender group
                                                                                 assignments crosstab.
assignments = pd.read_csv("assignments.csv", index_col="recommender")

chi_sq = st.chi2_contingency(assignments)          Conduct the chi-square test.

print(f"Chi-square value: {chi_sq[0].round(3)}")          Print the results.
print(f"p-value: {chi_sq[1].round(3)}")
print(f"Expected Frequencies:\n {chi_sq[3].round(2)}")
```

The chi-square test results and expected frequencies follow:

```
Chi-square value: 6.73
p-value: 0.875
Expected Frequencies:
[[ 442.61  440.88  425.28  424.24 1733.  ]
 [ 392.55  391.01  377.18  376.26 1537.  ]
 [ 441.84  440.11  424.54  423.5  1730.  ]
 [1277.    1272.    1227.    1224.    5000.  ]]
```

The chi-square test shows no significant difference in the number of users assigned to each experiment group. The low chi-square value and corresponding *p*-value are far from significant, leaving little room for ambiguity.

Next, we'll create two tables for our chi-square test: a table showing the number of users who *clicked* the recommendations by group, and the number that we *expect* would click by group if there were no differences. The observed values are shown in figure 5.14.

country	Canada	England	France	United States	Total
recommender					
A	117	131	119	80	447
B	82	76	77	105	340
C	113	120	133	143	509
Total	312	327	329	328	1296

Figure 5.14 Summary table of the number of recommendation clicks by group

We can see that 1,296 out of 5,000 users in the experiment clicked on the recommendations. This is a total proportion of 25.96%, which is used to calculate the *expected* click rates per group based on their initial sample size. This resulting summary table will be used as the *expected frequencies* for the chi-square test:

```
expected = assignments * .2596
print(expected)
```

Calculate the expected frequencies based on the total proportion.

Print the expected proportions.

The resulting code output follows:

```
country     Canada   England   France   United States     Total
recommender
A           107.73    115.00   114.48          112.67    449.89
B           102.54     99.95    94.75          101.76    399.01
C           121.23    115.26   109.29          103.32    449.11
Total       331.51    330.21   318.59          317.75   1298.00
```

Then, if we import the crosstab of customers who clicked recommendations by group and country, we can compare it to the expected values, as follows:

```
clicked = pd.read_csv("clicked.csv", index_col="country")

chi_sq = st.chi2_contingency(clicked, expected)
print(f"Chi-square value: {chi_sq[0].round(3)}")
print(f"p-value: {chi_sq[1].round(3)}")
```

Import the crosstab of clicks by country and recommender.

Calculate a chi-square test.

Print the resulting test statistic and p-value.

This is the printed code output:

```
Chi-square value: 22.994
p-value: 0.028
```

In addition to the test statistic and *p*-value, the chi-square test also includes a table of *expected frequencies* if there were no differences in relative group proportions. In most statistical software and packages, you must manually subtract the expected from the observed frequencies to interpret the results. If your deliverable includes presenting these differences to stakeholders, you may want to color code the results with a heat-map for easy interpretation:

```
import seaborn as sns               ◁──┐  Import Seaborn and the
from operator import sub               │  subtraction operator.

diffs = list(map(sub, clicked.values, expected.values))        ◁──────┐
diffs = pd.DataFrame(
    diffs,
    columns=assignments.columns,      Subtract the corresponding values
    index=assignments.index,          between each item in the observed
)                                                  and expected frequencies.
sns.heatmap(          ◁──┐  Convert the differences to a heatmap
    diffs.iloc[:-1, :-1],  │  for a more presentable display.
    cmap="vlag",
    annot=True,
    cbar=False,
)
plt.xlabel("")
plt.ylabel("Recommender Version")
```

Our second chi-square test yielded a statistically significant result, and figure 5.15 allows you to easily identify which countries and experiment versions had the highest and lowest click rates. We've thus used the *same* statistical test to determine if we had an equal number of records in each group, and *then* to determine which countries and recommenders had the highest click rates.

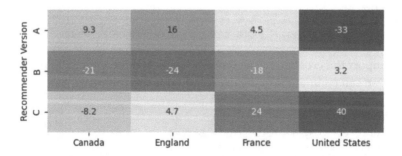

Figure 5.15   Human-readable heatmap of differences between observed and expected click rates

CONSIDERATIONS WHEN RUNNING A CHI-SQUARE TEST

If you choose to use the chi-square test in your work, there are several limitations to keep in mind when evaluating your methods and results:

- Chi-square tests are highly sensitive to small samples and typically require larger quantities of data than tests comparing continuous and ordinal data.

- Use a chi-square test with a test evaluating continuous or ordinal data. You must choose an appropriate sample size far more strategically to minimize false-positive results.

- Chi-square tests require an expected frequency of at least 5 in each cell to produce accurate results. If your categories have uneven distributions, check your expected frequencies to ensure they meet this minimum.

- The chi-square test doesn't include information about where disproportionality exists in your frequency tables. You will likely need to conduct a post hoc test to identify which pairs of groups are responsible for the significant differences. This application is often manual; for example, pairwise comparisons for a chi-square test can be performed in Python using a loop and reconducting 2×2 comparisons for each pair. For simplicity, we'll compare the *overall* performance of experiment groups instead of by country:

```
from itertools import combinations        ◁───  Import the combinations function.

pairs = list(combinations(assignments.iloc[:-1, :-1].index, 2))     ◁───┐
chisq_values = []                                                        Generate pairs of
p_values = []               ┌─ Conduct a chi-square test with a          experiment groups
                            │  correction for each pairwise              and empty lists.
for p in pairs:      ◁──────┘  comparison of experiment groups.
    c = clicked[(clicked.index == p[0]) | (clicked.index == p[1])]
    chi2, pv, dof, exp = st.chi2_contingency(c, correction=True)
    chisq_values.append(chi2)
    p_values.append(pv)
    print(p, ", Chi-square =", chi2.round(3), ", p =", pv.round(3))
```

Print each pair and its corresponding p-value.

These are the resulting chi-square pairs and test statistic data:

```
('A', 'B') , Chi-square = 18.95 , p = 0.001
('A', 'C') , Chi-square = 15.171 , p = 0.004
('B', 'C') , Chi-square = 2.0 , p = 0.736
```

5.2.4   *Recap*

A lot of value in data exists outside of analyzing continuous or ordinal data. Performing high-value categorical analysis is a skill for which many data professionals lack expertise. This is not for lack of value—much of the untapped value in data exists in less-than-perfectly structured fields.

Knowing how to compare proportions of data against other variables or benchmarks can highlight where behaviors differ between segments of users and customers, determine whether a factory produces goods that pass quality inspection at or above a static threshold (a proportion of goods pass), and much more.

5.3   *Responsible interpretation*

Suppose you have just completed a large deliverable for your stakeholders detailing the performance of multiple initiatives. You followed every best practice in designing your questions and enumerating hypotheses and diligently chose your statistical tests. The interpretation of your findings should be relatively straightforward at this point, right?

Well, not exactly. Your efforts have made a difference in how your stakeholders use your recommendations and how much value they will generate from your findings. Given that your work as an analyst involves *inference* and *predictions*, the accuracy of findings is never guaranteed. It's disturbingly easy to intentionally misconstrue results to support preconceived notions, special interests, and biased messaging. When leveraging statistics or machine learning, it's even easier to miss areas of nuance, previous research, or perspectives outside your own. There are countless ways to use statistics poorly and far fewer ways to use them well.

Instead of continuing on this topic (I can rant eternally about responsible, irresponsible, and malicious uses of statistics), I recommend reading *How to Lie with Statistics* [5]. This book was first published in *1954* and remains a timeless source of advice on applying healthy skepticism to the information you digest.

The topics in this section are frequently discussed in statistics curricula (Type 1 and Type 2 errors, confounding variables). However, few classes include strategies and considerations for mitigating and avoiding these errors outside of a highly controlled laboratory environment (and even in those settings, mitigating these errors is often highly subjective). We'll discuss real-world strategies for limiting these errors and using scientific best practices to set your project up for success across areas of study and practice.

5.3.1   *Statistical errors*

Statistical errors refer to discrepancies between the true values of a population compared to the inferences and estimates made based on a sample. The term "error" doesn't inherently mean that you're doing something wrong; we're ultimately using limited information to make educated guesses about events we haven't measured and that may not have happened yet. There's no way to eliminate errors from inferential statistical approaches, but understanding the types and sources of errors is crucial for maximizing the accuracy and reliability of your results.

TYPE 1 ERRORS

A Type 1 (false-positive) error refers to rejecting the null hypothesis when it's actually true. These errors typically occur when a statistical test identifies a significant difference or effect when, in reality, the difference isn't meaningful or isn't present in the broader population.

Some examples include

- A patient receives a positive result on a flu test, even though they are not infected with the influenza virus.
- A person who did not commit a crime is taken to trial and found guilty.

In both examples, the false-positive result has a drastic real-world effect on the individual. The person found guilty may be fined, imprisoned, and experience long-term disruptions to their economic and social status. The patient may be required to take time off of work or may be prescribed ineffective medication. Both of these can stress their finances, family, and other areas of daily life. The consequence of false-positive results in analytics is often far more challenging to pinpoint. Even if you can identify when it occurs, estimating the effect is often more theoretical than tangible.

There is no definitive guide for detecting and eliminating Type 1 errors. In an ideal world, you would either be able to compare the results from your sample to the entire population or have the resources to repeatedly test the same phenomenon and see if somebody can replicate your initial findings with a different sample. However, there *are* conditions in which Type 1 errors are more likely to occur:

- *Tests with an alpha level (significance threshold) at or above 0.05* are likelier to return a Type 1 statistically significant result. A *p*-value of .05 (5% probability of obtaining differences at least as large in future samples) may seem low, but a 5% chance is one out of every 20 based on random variation alone. A *p*-value of .1 (10%) can occur in 1 of 10 tests.

- *Tests with multiple comparisons* are more likely to produce significant results, even when you use a corrected *p*-value. When comparing large numbers of categories or interactions, your chances of finding a significant result increase based on the number of comparisons alone (e.g., figure 5.16). If you use tests such as two-factor ANOVAs, restrict the number of groups you compare as much as

Average Time on Website by Country and Age Cohort

	Age 18-24	Age 25-29	Age 30-34	Age 35-39	Age 40-44	Age 45+
U.S.A.	34.6	46.2	23.9	55.8	32.2	63.9 *
Canada	20.8 *	45.4	18.5	52.3	25.8	41.7
France	59.0	28.1	66.4 **	21.9	39.5	54.7
England	30.8	49.2	24.0	61.4 *	40.9	57.6
Spain	19.0 **	48.2	35.8	64.2 *	22.7	52.8

* $p < .05$ ** $p < .01$

Figure 5.16 I implore you not to run excessive comparisons, even with a sufficiently large sample size.

possible. In my work, I limit my study designs of two-factor ANOVAs to a 2 × 3 design (one variable with two groups and another with three groups).

- Both *small or very large sample sizes* have a higher chance of returning false-positive results. As demonstrated in chapter 2, many test coefficients will eventually cross the statistical significance threshold with a large sample-size increase, even if no actual difference is reflected in the population.

Suppose you suspect your statistically significant results may result from a Type 1 error. What do you do? There are some straightforward steps you can take to limit the occurrence of these errors in your work:

- *Choose appropriate statistical tests*— Everything we've discussed in this and the previous chapter—checking assumptions, transforming data, and choosing a test (or multiple tests) based on the characteristics of your data—is a *huge* step toward mitigating Type 1 errors.

- *Set the alpha level (significance threshold) conservatively*—It is *probably* best not to exceed the most commonly used alpha level of 0.05 in most cases. While interpreting this threshold flexibly is often beneficial, I don't recommend setting higher approximate thresholds (e.g., 0.1). As we've discussed, you may want to set an alpha level below 0.05 (e.g., 0.01) when the stakes of reporting a false-positive result are especially high.

- *Interpret your p-value dynamically*—On the flip side of setting a conservative alpha level, many analyses may benefit from flexible interpretations of the *p*-value. Suppose you are analyzing data on human behavior (e.g., the time a user spent completing a workflow in your app). In that case, you can set a threshold of 0.01 if you believe it is vital to ensure that one version of the workflow design is better. However, you probably *won't* want to throw away both versions of the workflow when your analysis yields a *p*-value of 0.015 if you have reason to believe your results are meaningful (e.g., users who saw version A of the workflow had *consistently* lower times to complete the workflow for the duration of the experiment and across user types). As you grow your expertise in a domain, you will develop confidence in your ability to judge the appropriate thresholds for the phenomena you are analyzing.

- *Replicate your findings*—The most reliable way to validate your findings is to replicate your results with different samples. If you can do so in your work, replication can be performed or estimated in several ways:
  - *Retest your results with a new sample*—Conducting the same assessments and tests with a new sample over time adds significant weight to the validity of your results and recommendations. If you expect to collect new data over time for your analysis, test the next set separately before incorporating them into the larger sample.
  - *Bootstrap your results*—Bootstrapping is a technique for estimating the parameters of your population by taking *smaller samples with replacement* from your entire sample. This flexible approach can be applied to almost all statistical

tests. We won't cover this technique in depth in this book, but it *can* be useful to build more realistic distributions of your data. Let's take a dataset with *n*=500, draw 1,000 samples of *n*=50 with replacement, and run a *t*-test comparing two groups within that sample. We can then *build a distribution of t-statistics* to estimate how often results will be significant. The following code and figure 5.17 show a quick example using the scipy package:

```
import numpy as np                                         Import the
from scipy import stats as st                              libraries.
import matplotlib.pyplot as plt

X1 = np.random.normal(loc=75.5, scale=6.2, size=500)       Generate two normal
X2 = np.random.normal(loc=76.2, scale=6.5, size=500)       distributions for
                                                           independent t-test
def t_stat(X1, X2):                                        comparisons.
    return st.ttest_ind(X1, X2)[0]        Create a function to
                                          return only the t-value
t_values = st.bootstrap(                  from an independent
    (X1, X2),                             samples t-test.
    t_stat,
    n_resamples=1000,                     Calculate bootstrapped t-values
    batch=50,                             with 1000 samples of n=50.
    method="basic",
    vectorized=False,
    random_state=99,
)                                         Calculate the
                                          (negative)
t_crit = -st.t.ppf(q=0.95, df=49)         t-critical value.       Plot the distribution
                                                                  with the critical value
plt.hist(result.bootstrap_distribution, bins=25)          as a vertical line.
plt.axvline(t_crit, color="black", linestyle="dashed")
```

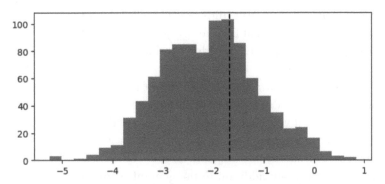

Figure 5.17   The majority (but not all) of bootstrapped samples have *t*-values above the absolute value of the critical threshold.

In addition to putting these recommended guardrails in place, mitigating Type 1 errors requires using your domain experience. As you build expertise in an area, you will become familiar with previous research and the group differences and trends reported in those findings. Over time, that experience will provide a comprehensive perspective on variables that may be missing in an analysis, which we will discuss further in the section on confounding variables.

TYPE 2 ERRORS

A Type 2 (false-negative) error occurs when a test result yields a negative result (e.g., a non-significant *p*-value) when the alternative hypothesis is true in the population. This leads to the conclusion that there are no significant differences between groups or relationships between the variables compared in your analysis.

In practice, Type 1 errors are given more attention than Type 2. However, Type 2 errors can produce just as consequential outcomes in the real world as Type 1. Type 2 errors can look like the following:

- A patient receives a *negative* result on a COVID-19 test, even though they *are* infected with the virus. They do not quarantine or take measures to prevent the spread of the disease and infect several people. One of these people infected becomes critically ill from the disease.
- A person who committed a violent crime is taken to trial and found innocent. The person is released and goes on to commit additional violent crimes.
- A public health study using several million dollars in research grants is conducted over two years. The results come back as negative, even though the treatment did produce a long-term effect on the participants. The potential benefit to the broader population and the value of the research grants are not realized.

Type 2 errors are more likely to occur under conditions you can control for or detect as an analyst. Some causes and factors contributing to Type 2 errors include the following:

- *Small sample sizes*—A true difference can be challenging to detect when your sample size is too small for the test you are using. If you're unsure how many data points to capture, consider conducting an *a priori power analysis*, as discussed in chapter 4.
- *Inappropriate statistical test*—If you do not meet the necessary assumptions of a statistical test, you're far more likely to generate both Type 1 and Type 2 results. Additionally, if you choose the wrong test for the type of study design (e.g., an independent samples *t*-test for a repeated-measures design), you will likely generate inaccurate results that confuse your stakeholders.
- *High variability*—In addition to the general shape of the distribution, parametric statistical tests assume that your data has a standard variance (measured by the distribution's *kurtosis*). A dataset in which both groups have very high variance will likely return either a false-positive or a false-negative result. In these cases, you may want to use a non-parametric test even if the dataset is normally distributed.

CONFOUNDING VARIABLES

Confounding occurs when the effect of one variable on the outcome of interest is mixed up with the effect of another variable that is often not measured as part of the analysis. In other words, a confounding variable is a *covariate* of your model (a factor that varies *with* your independent and dependent variables) that you have not accounted for. This can lead to incorrect or misleading results about the relationship between the variables.

They're exceedingly common, given that the complexity of most analyses we do relate to human phenomena. Consider these examples:

- A researcher finds a relationship between sleep duration and academic performance. However, the study didn't control or account for caffeine consumption related to sleep duration and academic performance.
- An analyst finds a relationship between the geographic location and online product preferences of website users without noting that their median age differs drastically by location.

Controlling for confounding variables is generally accomplished through a combination of strategies in the design of your research and the statistical approaches to your work. Taking these steps early in your analysis process can increase the validity and reliability of your results, saving resources and maximizing value from each analysis you invest time in:

- *Peer-review your initial study design*—This is likely the most important step you can take to mitigate confounding variables. Asking others with domain-specific knowledge if there's anything you might be missing or didn't account for is an underrated and effective step you can take to alleviate blind spots in your research. As with other areas we've covered—*not accounting for every possible variable does not mean you failed as an analyst.* Peer review and collaboration are a necessary part of science and analysis.
- *Build a knowledge base of known covarying factors*—Where possible, performing and circulating analyses that teach your organization about trends and differences in key covarying characteristics can help better structure your questions. If you, your colleagues, and your organization generally know where key types of users and customers differ on behavior, needs, and outcomes, you will have an easier time accounting for confounding variables. We will discuss this at length in chapter 11.
- *Stratify your randomized samples*—If you're conducting experiments with random selection (e.g., A/B tests), checking and stratifying the random sample according to *known* confounding variables can help reduce their influence.
- *Use a statistical model that accounts for covariates*—When using a *t*-test, ANOVA, or non-parametric alternative to these tests, you generally are limited to sampling and randomization methods to account for covariates. Techniques such as regression analysis and ANCOVA (analysis of covariance) allow you to include covariates and *control for them* as part of your model.

5.3.2 P-hacking

The previous section discussed problems and situations that can unknowingly affect the accuracy and quality of your results. They're less often due to the intentional action of the researcher but rather to an omission or a blind spot concerning study design and variable selection. This section covers the steps that you as an analyst can (but should *not*) take, and that amount to direct manipulation of your results.

P-hacking, also known as data fishing, is an approach to data analysis where researchers and analysts manipulate the data and statistical tests to obtain results that reach statistical significance, often leading to results that don't reflect the population. In other words, *p*-hacking involves continually testing multiple hypotheses, designs, statistical tests, outlier removal methods, or transformations until *something* reaches statistical significance (see figure 5.18). This is the analyst's version of "throwing it against the wall until something sticks."

Figure 5.18 *P*-hacking involves testing a dataset indefinitely until something returns a significant value.

P-hacking can take a wide range of forms. Some of these approaches differ if you're in an academic or industry setting, but any of the following are possible. As analysts, it's our responsibility to be diligent in where the following approaches may be present in our work:

- *Conducting large or indefinite permutations of statistical tests until a desired result is achieved*—This does *not* refer to the steps commonly involved in exploring a dataset to report descriptive findings (e.g., "70% of users visit the app once per week or more"). *P*-hacking with statistical tests refers to conducting numerous statistical tests to make inferences about the population (e.g., "changing the layout of the app will cause 10% more users to visit the app at least once per week"). At an alpha level of 0.05, at least 5% of the tests you run will reject the null hypothesis and risk committing Type 1 errors. The probability of any test returning a significant result is *additive* (the more tests you run, the more likely you are to find something). Thus, running two tests increases the likelihood of rejecting the null to 10%, to 15% with three tests, and so on. To mitigate these risks, keep the following top of mind:
  - *Don't change the variables of the analysis*—During exploratory data analysis, exploring relationships between many variables (e.g., all questions in your survey or study) is a sensible choice. If you're preparing a statistical test, changing your variables and altering your hypotheses and interpretations for those new variables can degrade the quality of your work. This is especially true if you work at an organization and have access to many variables at your fingertips—it can be very tempting just to *keep trying new things* until something comes back significant.
  - *Don't change the study design*—Proposing multiple study designs in your analysis plan at the early stages is an excellent way to approach a problem from numerous angles. You're unlikely to approach your work with the same rigor or accuracy if you're trying every permutation possible to achieve statistical significance.
- *Manual removal of data points*—This refers to the selective removal of individual data points in a dataset (usually outliers) to alter the shape of the distribution and achieve a desired result. This is *never* an appropriate approach to your work. *Do not do this.*
- *Manual modification of the sample*—This refers to the revision of the existing sample by any of the following means:
  - *Non-random or random selection of a subsample that achieves the desired result*—As was shown in figure 5.17, bootstrapping of a sample shows how smaller samples of data will vary in their test statistics and *p*-values. There's always a chance that your *p*-value will be significant by chance alone—especially with a small and manually curated sample.
  - *Exclusion of subgroups within the sample*—It's usually worth highlighting key subgroups and segments among your users, customers, or participants. The time to do that is *not* at random to generate a statistically significant result.

P-hacking is usually performed with the intention of publishing and reporting results. Analysts and researchers commonly experience pressure to generate *something* as far as insights to receive grant funding for a lab or organization, for continued employment in academic settings, or to maintain relationships with stakeholders.

As analysts and researchers, I understand that we are often under tremendous pressure to prove our worth and value to an organization. Often, the organization's success relies on the results we are expected to produce.

But *p*-hacking is *never* worth it. The incorrect and misleading conclusions generated through this approach will catch up to you and have tremendous negative consequences on others who rely on your findings.

Summary

- The majority of *parametric statistical* tests were developed a hundred years ago or more for specific types of analysis and have since become the dominant method of choice for most fields of study and work. However, these tests are *not* ubiquitous and are not always the best choice for every analysis.

- *Non-parametric statistical tests* are alternatives to parametric statistical tests that do not make assumptions about the underlying distribution of the data. They can be used with a broader variety of data types than parametric statistical tests (you can use either continuous or ordinal data), providing analysts with a wide range of options.

- There is a wide range of *non-parametric tests* for group comparisons. Each test compares the *ranks* and *relative positions* of the data points in each group rather than making calculations based on the actual values of the data points. These are the most common:

  - The *Mann-Whitney U test* for comparing two independent samples
  - The *Wilcoxon signed-rank test* for two dependent samples
  - The *Kruskal-Wallis test* for two or more independent samples
  - The *Friedman test* for three or more dependent samples

- *Post hoc tests* are statistical comparisons conducted after a test with three or more groups indicates that there are significant differences among group means—they are used to identify which specific groups differ from each other. These tests apply corrections to control the increased risk of false-positives (Type 1 errors) that occur due to multiple comparisons, ensuring the reliability of the results.

- The *chi-square test* is a common test that you can use to compare one or two categorical variables. The test compares the difference between the observed to expected frequencies for each row and column in a *contingency table*.

- A *Type 1 error* occurs when a true null hypothesis is incorrectly rejected, representing a false-positive in hypothesis testing. Conversely, a *Type 2 error* happens when a false null hypothesis is mistakenly accepted as true, resulting in a false-negative.

- Part of being a responsible analyst involves ensuring the integrity of your approaches, even when your stakeholders aren't watching. Choose your design ahead of time, and don't be afraid to report non-significant results for the long-term accuracy of your work and the trust of your stakeholders.

Are you measuring
what you think
you're measuring?

This chapter covers

- The theoretical underpinnings of effective measurement
- Identifying the strengths and limitations of a measurement
- Reliably measuring information about your concept or process
- Ensuring your measures are valid representations of your concept or process

Measurement is central to data analysis, but turning data into something you can quantify is rarely straightforward. The information you need to answer meaningful questions is often hidden in unstructured formats or may not be recorded at all. While some organizations have well-structured systems that make capturing insights relatively simple, most of us contend with messy data or vague, unexplored ideas. Transforming those ideas into actionable insights requires rigor, creativity, and a strong grasp of the methods researchers use to make sense of our complex world.

The process of quantifying information is both an art and a science. Every method has its strengths and limitations, and as an analyst, you'll often have the freedom to decide how best to approach your task. Along the way, you'll need to consider key questions: Are your metrics reliable and consistent? Do they accurately reflect the phenomenon you're studying? Without thoughtful evaluation, even the most carefully collected data can lead to flawed or misleading conclusions.

This chapter will guide you through the foundations of designing meaningful metrics, offering practical advice on how to gather and interpret the right data to address your research questions. We'll explore the theories that shape modern approaches to quantification, strategies for identifying useful information, and techniques for assessing whether your metrics are robust and effective. By honing these skills, you'll set yourself apart as a thoughtful and trusted partner to your stakeholders.

6.1   *A theory of measurement*

Transforming abstract phenomena into something you can observe and quantify is not an easy task. Anyone can develop a survey from scratch and deliver it to an audience of their choosing, but doing so risks capturing inaccurate information or no valuable insights. To measure what you think you're measuring, it's important to apply key principles from *measurement theory* to generate high-quality data.

Measurement theory is a framework for assigning numerical values to abstract concepts, events, or objects. This framework provides analysts with standardized criteria to develop and evaluate their measures. If you are creating a measure of stress, you have decades of recommendations available on how to operationalize stress, develop and administer a questionnaire, appropriately quantify degrees of stress, and analyze the results. Stress is inherently subjective and thus can be challenging to quantify. To ensure your results are *interpretable* using quantitative methods, an accurate reflection of people's experiences, and aligned with other definitions of this concept, you can apply best practices from each component of measurement theory:

- Conceptualize or define the phenomena of interest. This involves enumerating the components of what you're interested in to operationalize the concepts. We covered these steps in chapter 2.
- Develop an appropriate measurement scale, identify appropriate measures among readily available data, and identify proxy measures where direct data capture on your phenomenon is impossible.
- Review and test your measure's limitations to ensure they remain consistent, accurate, and stable over time.

Peer-reviewed papers, textbooks, and other resources on measurement theory typically cover it from the perspective of social sciences and psychological research. Researchers assume that you are primarily developing questionnaires, performance evaluations, and other rating scales designed for participants to self-report behavioral and cognitive processes. However, you can apply most of these steps to develop measures for the various types of data in an organization.

As in previous chapters, we will continue to draw from best practices in the social sciences. If you're tracking user actions on your app, customer sentiment, customer renewals, time to resolve support tickets, or nearly anything we've covered so far, you are measuring a *behavior* or a *cognitive process.* By definition, psychology is the study of those two things. If you've taken a psychology class during your education, this chapter is an excellent place to pause and review the materials from your curriculum and apply the lens of a behavioral scientist in your work.

6.1.1   *Translating ideas into concepts*

As an analyst, much of your job at the early stages of a project involves clearly defining and operationalizing a concept so that you can measure it. If you're starting with a new question that your organization hasn't yet investigated, your first step is determining if you *can* agree on a definition for measurement. Even with agreement, you may find that existing measures familiar to your organization may be limited in their applicability to a new project. As we saw with NPS, just because something has been measured a certain way for a long time or is widely adopted does not necessarily make it the best choice for delivering value.

Conceptualizing an abstract phenomenon or construct involves providing explicit definitions of the components, dimensions, and characteristics of that construct. This step enables you to create a precise understanding between your team and stakeholders to ensure everyone agrees on what is being measured.

You can break down the process of conceptualizing a measure into the following steps:

- *Identify the phenomenon and the rationale for analyzing it.* What are you or your stakeholders interested in learning more about? Why is it important? Why now?
- *Review existing conceptualizations.* Are there ways this concept has been previously defined? You will likely want to gather appropriate context from peer-reviewed literature, industry standards, peer organization practices, and previous work within your organization.
- *Specify key components of your concept.* Often, measuring a concept involves aggregating multiple behaviors, cognitive processes, sentiments, or data sources. You and your stakeholders will likely need to align on compiling available information into a comprehensive strategy for guiding decisions.
- *Align on the definition of your concept.* Once you have a definition, it's essential to ensure it aligns with how stakeholders see the concept. Doing so at this stage will minimize confusion and save you time in the project lifecycle.
- *Identify related concepts.* How does your concept relate to other similar processes? Do you expect to find any relationships or associations as you measure them?
- *Iterate on the definition.* Your first concept definition will likely not be your last. As you gain more information about the limitations of your first iteration, you will want to continually improve in aligning with your stakeholders.

Figure 6.1 depicts a flowchart of the steps to refine a concept, as well as examples you can reference to get started.

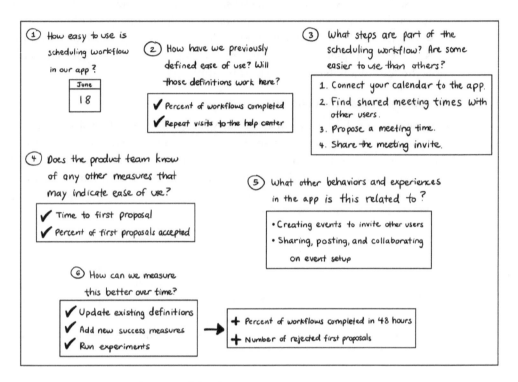

Figure 6.1   Steps to defining and refining the concepts you want to measure

Clear definitions are necessary for using your organization's data and resources appropriately. However, not everything can be neatly measured. Many concepts lack consistent, agreed-upon definitions, making them difficult to quantify (e.g., intelligence, creativity; see figure 6.2). Even with abundant resources, you may not develop a measure that all your stakeholders agree on. Measuring subjective concepts is challenging but necessary to understand complex human processes.

Figure 6.2   Can you measure the "best" in subjective areas like creative art?

Measuring employee experience in human resources

In our case study for this chapter, Arthur is an analyst on the human resources team at a large supply chain company with over 10,000 employees. The company is interested in understanding their employees' engagement in their work, the company culture, and whether engagement can predict retention and attrition.

Arthur meets with his manager to understand the rationale for the project and its value to the company: Is the company aiming to improve its headcount planning for next year? Is it trying to reduce employee turnover across the company or within specific departments?

Arthur's manager tells him the company has seen increased turnover in some departments. They want to use the insights from this project to get ahead of any potential future attrition.

Arthur searches peer-reviewed literature and finds several measurement scales assessing employee engagement and job satisfaction. He works with his team's manager to align on critical components of employee engagement. Together, they decide to investigate the following topics:

- Satisfaction in the current role
- Perception of workload
- Interest in company events
- Satisfaction with salary and benefits
- Productivity in the current role
- Performance in the current role

Arthur hypothesizes that similar concepts, such as motivation in an employee's current role, will be associated with employee engagement. He also hypothesizes that each of the components will correlate with each other.

6.1.2   *Understanding common measurement tools*

Have you ever responded to the sort of question shown in figure 6.3? Perhaps you've seen it on a website or a marketing email from a service you use. The aggregate score calculated with this measure is known as the *net promoter score* (NPS). NPS has been used for 20 years across industries, business sizes, and specializations to gauge *customer satisfaction* and *loyalty* to the business's products and services.

On a scale of 0–10, how likely are you to recommend our business to a friend or colleague?
0   1   2   3   4   5   6   7   8   9   10

Figure 6.3
The net promoter score is used across industries and products.

NPS is calculated using the question's 11-point rating scale from 0 to 10, where 0 means "not at all likely" and 10 means "extremely likely." Scores are categorized into three groups (illustrated in figure 6.4):

- *Promoters*—Customers who respond with a 9 or 10 are classified as *promoters.* These are considered enthusiastic customers who are likely to continue using a business's products or services and refer others to the company.
- *Passives*—Customers who respond with a 7 or 8 are classified as *passives.* These are considered neutral by neither actively promoting nor discouraging others from engaging with the business.
- *Detractors*—The *detractors* category comprises customers believed to be dissatisfied with the business's products or services and, therefore, likely to discourage others from engaging with the business.

On a scale of 0–10, how likely are you to recommend our business to a friend or colleague?

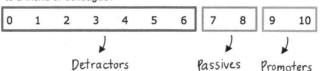

Figure 6.4   NPS responses are categorized into three groups: promoters, passives, and detractors.

The NPS is calculated by subtracting the percentage of detractors from the percentage of promoters, resulting in a standardized score from –100 to 100. The resulting number is used as a *benchmark* against competitors, peers, and unrelated businesses.

How would you rate this approach to measurement? NPS is derived using a straightforward calculation that results in a standardized score. It's simple, easy to understand, and widely adopted. Does that make it a good measure?

Not quite. The NPS is far from perfect, and many businesses and organizations fail to derive value from its measurement. Let's look at some of those limitations:

- *NPS is overly simple, using only one question to infer multiple aspects of customer experience, satisfaction, and loyalty.*
- *The measure assesses a general likelihood to recommend the business or its services with a limited ability to understand the reasons for the score provided.* Customers may be dissatisfied with the product, customer service, or a specific feature.
- *NPS interprets its 11-point scale as a universal standard, but people don't treat numerical scales equally, as we will discuss in this chapter.* NPS assumes that all customers likely to recommend the business will respond with a score of 9 or 10.
- *The approach to categorization makes the score susceptible to minor fluctuations.* If a few customers answer with an 8 instead of a 9, they are not included in the score, even though the difference in numerical answers may not represent a material difference.
- *NPS focuses only on customers who respond to the survey and ignores the response rate and characteristics of customers who refuse to answer.*

- *Although it's standardized, you cannot compare NPS one-to-one across businesses with different customer bases.* Not every business can be recommended or referred to a "friend or colleague" in the same way.

- *Overemphasis on NPS can lead to long-term neglect of other customer satisfaction indicators.* This tunnel vision can have detrimental effects on the performance of the business.

Ideally, NPS should be used as *one possible measure* of customer satisfaction among many; if you cannot do this, it's better not to use it.

6.2 *Choosing a data collection method*

Once you and your stakeholders align on how to break down the concepts, it's time to translate them into measurable indicators for your analysis. Your goal at this stage is to develop clear *observable, measurable* indicators of your concept to use in your work. This process of operationalization (discussed in chapter 2) enables you to decide on the best method for *collecting* the data you need.

There are numerous ways to categorize data collection methods. If you completed statistics or research methods coursework, you might be familiar with the distinction between *direct measures* (e.g., a person's height) and *indirect measures* (e.g., historical archives). This distinction categorizes data *based on the actions of the researcher*, i.e., whether the researcher measured and recorded the data *directly* as opposed to using previously existing information.

6.2.1 *Types of measures*

Instead of categorizing data based on how the researcher collected it, we will be focusing on how the user or participant *provided* the measure of interest.

- *Self-report measures*, such as questionnaires, interviews, and feedback forms provide information that users or participants directly input. Surveys are the most common self-report measure, ranging from a single question (e.g., the NPS question) to lengthy, comprehensive assessments of multiple concepts. Any data recorded *directly* by your users (e.g., in-app feedback form, user preferences, and settings) is included in this category.

- *Behavioral measures* refer to data collected via *direct observation or measurement.* For example, a person's height is directly measured using a standardized instrument (a measuring tape). An increasing volume of primary data is available in many organizations; sales records in a database, fitness data on your phone, and job applications are all direct measures of *behavior.*

Table 6.1 lists examples of common self-report and behavioral data that you may encounter in your work.

In practical scenarios, most organizations possess a blend of self-reported and behavioral data, with preferences for one type or the other depending on the team involved. For instance, tech companies typically have detailed behavioral data reflecting user interactions with their software. Consequently, their product and analytics teams depend heavily on such data for strategic decision-making. However, the same organizations' marketing and user research teams might lean more toward customer surveys, interviews, and focus groups for insights.

As an analyst, your vantage point provides a more comprehensive understanding of the data spectrum within an organization compared to stakeholders, who are focused on specific domains. This unique position allows you to act as a consultant, advising stakeholders on the most suitable measurement approach to address a question. As discussed in previous chapters, your approach will be influenced by the question, the organization's available data, and the most efficient measurement method considering your resources.

Table 6.1   Examples of self-report and behavioral data you may encounter at a software company

Self-report data	Behavioral data
Employee satisfaction survey	User interaction logs (e.g., clicks, page views)
User feedback survey on software features	Time logs of employees on project management software
Self-assessments of productivity	Reports of software bugs or problems
User surveys on software ease of use	Version control history
User biographies in the software	Helpdesk ticket data

SELF-REPORT MEASURES

When you recommend a measurement approach to stakeholders, it's valuable to enter the conversation with an understanding of the pros and cons of each approach. Self-report measures offer several key advantages:

- *They're easy to administer and start from scratch*—Self-report measures can be quickly developed and administered to participants. They also make it far easier to gather insights if no data about the phenomenon you are measuring exists.
- *You can assess detailed, personal experiences*—Self-report measures allow you to ask participants about their thoughts, feelings, and experiences about a phenomenon that is difficult or impossible to assess using behavioral measures.
- *They're flexible*—Self-report measures are adaptable to the needs of an organization and analytics team. They can be gathered online, in person, and at various milestones relevant to your organization.

Self-report measures also have several *disadvantages* that are important to share with your stakeholders:

- *Self-selection bias*—By definition, participants can choose whether or not they want to participate in your study. There may be characteristics of participants who *do* and *don't* participate that are relevant to your topic of interest. For example, if you're conducting a survey about stress and time management, you'll probably get lower response rates from potential participants with less free time!

- *Measurement bias*—Minor changes to survey measurements can drastically affect the responses you receive. If you ask the same question with slight variations in wording, response scales (e.g., a scale from 1 to 5 versus 1 to 9), and the descriptors used on the scale (e.g., "Strongly Disagree" to "Strongly Agree") can result in wildly varying response patterns.
- *Indirect measurement*—Self-report measures are limited because you cannot directly measure the phenomenon of interest. When surveying people, you are limited to assessing people's *perceptions* of a phenomenon.

Section 6.1.2 introduces the NPS question as an illustration of a self-report measure. When employing this tool, researchers must thoughtfully weigh the inherent pros and cons of this measure and how it's used. Table 6.2 reviews some of the most important of these considerations.

Table 6.2 Advantages and disadvantages of the self-reported NPS question

Advantages	Disadvantages
Data is easily stored in a spreadsheet.	Answers on the 11-point scale will differ between respondents independent of their sentiment based on immeasurable personal factors.
Assesses personal beliefs about the likelihood of recommending a product or service.	Changes to the question's wording (e.g., company name, company type, part of a business's offering) may drastically affect results.
Quickly asked online using a survey tool or in person as a quick survey. Often built into marketing and email campaign software.	Measures respondents' *perception* of their likelihood to refer, not their *actual* referral behaviors.

While they offer simplicity, flexibility, and the ability to access personal experiences, self-report measures are susceptible to numerous forms of bias outside your control (in figure 6.5, a survey participant may give a completely different response to a survey

Figure 6.5   The quality of data from self-report measures depends on numerous factors outside the control of the researcher or analyst.

question in a retail setting after getting caught in a thunderstorm). When recommending a measurement approach, it's crucial to carefully weigh these factors and consider the specific needs and goals of the stakeholders involved.

BEHAVIORAL MEASURES

By circumventing the need to ask users or participants to report on the phenomenon of interest, *behavioral measures* offer an opportunity to bypass the limitations of self-report measures. Overall, they provide the following advantages:

- *Direct, objective measurement*—A behavioral measure involves directly recording when a phenomenon or action occurred. The participant or user of interest isn't *asked* about the occurrence, eliminating the bias associated with self-reporting.

- *Precisely timed*—Behavioral measures make it easier to associate a precise time with the occurrence of an event. For example, a researcher can directly record a timestamp if they are observing a participant, or a timestamp can be recorded in a database when a user clicks a button.

- *Comprehensive measurement*—Behavioral measures can be combined with other behavioral or self-report data about the same user or participant. For example, a set of predefined behaviors a researcher can observe or multiple user activities can be recorded in a database and synthesized into a picture of their use of your app.

Each advantage of behavioral measures enhances the value of the data and insights you can provide. So why don't we abandon self-report measures entirely? Not every research team or organization can capture behavioral measures for *every* topic they're interested in. Even for those who do, they come with several distinct disadvantages:

- *Intrusiveness*—Many behavioral measures capture information about users and participants through direct observation. A researcher may observe participants to identify specific behaviors (e.g., shoppers in a mall), or a cookie might be installed on a user's browser to track their clicks and page views. This can often occur without the consent of the person being observed.

- *Resource-intensive*—Most behavioral measures require more resources to capture data than self-report measures do. A self-report survey can be developed using a free tool, distributed online, or via an advertisement, and have data captured in a spreadsheet. Physical observation requires the time and labor of a research team. Observing behaviors via online tracking often requires significant software, compute, storage, and labor costs.

- *Legal and ethical concerns*—Many businesses and organizations are subject to regulations associated with the collection and retention of data. If you are working with legally confidential data (e.g., protected health information or PHI), your organization may be required to have strict controls around its use that may limit the types of analyses you can perform. Further, ethical implications may be associated with the data you collect and potential information you can conclude about people via behavioral observation. We will discuss this in more depth in chapter 8.

Table 6.3 reviews the pros and cons of self-report and behavioral measures that you should consider when you're choosing a data collection method.

Table 6.3   Pros and cons of self-report vs. behavioral measures

Self-report measures	Behavioral measures
✓ Easy to administer	✓ Direct, precise measurement
✓ Flexible questions and responses	✓ Easily combined with other data sources
✗ Prone to multiple forms of bias	✗ Concerns about ethics and intrusiveness
✗ Indirect measurement of a concept	✗ Resource intensive to set up data capture

To create an equivalent behavioral measure of the NPS question, a researcher must *directly* assess how often users refer friends or colleagues to the business. This quickly becomes complicated—do you count the number of referrals received? How do you count how often they make verbal recommendations to others that don't lead to new business? How do you tell if they make recommendations to competitors instead?

Short of invasive surveillance of your customers, you're unlikely to get a good read on this phenomenon as a direct measure of behavior. This data type may be more accurate and precise, but it's not always feasible for what you need. An analyst's job involves balancing the choice of measures based on the best use of resources available to their team and organization.

> ### Employee satisfaction: From concept to measure
>
> Arthur begins the project's next phase by identifying available measures at the organization to assess the components of employee engagement they decided to focus on. He evaluates whether these measures are direct observations of employee actions or employees' subjective evaluations of their experiences:
>
> - *Satisfaction in the current role*—Arthur discovers that the company conducts annual employee satisfaction surveys. He reviews the survey items and finds questions related to job satisfaction that can be used as self-report measures for this analysis component.
> - *Perception of workload*—The company has data on employees' work hours and workload through project management software. Arthur identifies this data as a behavioral measure. Additionally, he finds self-report measures in the employee satisfaction survey that ask about workload perceptions.
> - *Interest in company events*—Arthur learns that the company maintains attendance records for company-sponsored events. He decides to use this attendance data as a behavioral measure for this component.
> - *Satisfaction with salary and benefits*—The employee satisfaction survey includes questions related to satisfaction with compensation and benefits, providing Arthur with self-report measures for this component.

(continued)

- *Productivity in the current role*—Arthur finds that the company has data on employee productivity, such as key performance indicators (KPIs) and project completion rates. These metrics serve as behavioral measures for the productivity component.
- *Performance in the current role*—The company's performance management system tracks employee performance through regular evaluations and ratings. Arthur recognizes that while this data is not self-reported by the employee, it's subject to the biases of a self-report measure, since the employee's manager reports it.

Arthur determines that each self-report measure associated with the annual employee satisfaction survey is readily available via a survey tool where he can download the dataset as a CSV. Each behavioral measure is housed in a different system and requires additional effort to extract and combine the data with self-report measures.

6.2.2 Constructing self-report measures

What's the difference between the measurement scales in figure 6.6 when used in a survey?

1	2	3	4	5
Strongly Disagree	Somewhat Disagree	Neutral	Somewhat Agree	Strongly Agree

Strongly Disagree	Somewhat Disagree	Neutral	Somewhat Agree	Strongly Agree

1	2	3	4	5
Strongly Disagree	Disagree	Neither Agree nor Disagree	Agree	Strongly Agree

Figure 6.6   Varying methods of presenting the same response format

Slight variations in wording, response formats, and rating scales (such as those shown in figure 6.6) can substantially affect the responses you receive on a self-report measurement. In the social sciences, researchers will often directly tweak, manipulate, and test rating scales and response formats to get as close as possible to a read on an abstract concept. These small changes and tests are crucial to minimizing error and deriving value from self-report data.

WORDING THE QUESTION

As an analyst, your efforts to *intentionally* craft well-structured, unbiased, and precise questions will enable you to minimize ambiguities, response biases, and other potential problems that may compromise the quality of your data. This attention to detail in self-report measurement design will ultimately lead to more accurate and reliable findings, enabling you to make well-informed decisions and effectively address the research objectives or practical challenges.

Figure 6.7 shows several different ways that survey questions can be worded. Each one of them uses a different structure, and the same people might provide different answers based on how it's presented. Consider the following problems to *avoid* when wording your question or evaluating an existing measure (example questions are included for reference):

- Respondents may provide inaccurate responses if a question is *ambiguous*.
    - Less effective: Do you like our software?
    - More effective: What aspects of our software do you find most helpful in your day-to-day work?

- *Leading language* in a question subtly suggests the "desired" answer or contains assumptions about the respondents. Avoid this.
    - Less effective: Wouldn't you agree that our software saves time and effort?
    - More effective: To what extent do you agree that our software saves you time and effort?

- *Double-barreled statements* are questions about two distinct concepts that make it difficult for respondents and users to provide an accurate, comprehensive answer to both parts.
    - Less effective: Do you agree that the software's user interface is intuitive and the customer support team is helpful?
    - More effective: Two distinct questions asking, "How intuitive would you rate our software?" and "How helpful is our support team?" with the ability to respond to each separately.

- *Negatively framed questions* are a leading format that can introduce bias in your results. A positively or negatively worded question assessing the same concept will elicit different responses.
    - Less effective: How often do you hate using our software?
    - More effective: How often do you have trouble using our software?

- In addition to leading and negatively framed questions, *emotionally charged or judgmental language* will heavily bias responses to your questions. Use neutral and objective language wherever possible.

- Less effective: How do you feel about the excessive number of notifications you receive in our software?
- More effective: What is your opinion on the number of notifications you receive from our software?

- *Colloquial speech, specialized language, or technical terminology* may lead to confusion and incorrect responses. Use clear, everyday language that you are confident will be easily understood by your target respondents or users.

  - Less effective: To what degree have our software's API integration capabilities affected your workflow?
  - More effective: How does the ability to connect our software with other tools affect your workflow?

- Very often, *the order of your questions* can influence the quality of your answers. If you expect one question to prime your respondents in a specific way, carefully consider the order or randomization you use in your measures.

  - Less effective: Do you believe our software's latest feature has improved its usability? How often do you use the new feature in our software?
  - More effective: How often do you use the new feature in our software? Do you believe our software's latest feature has improved its usability?

How would you rate the ease of navigation of our software?

Our software is user friendly and easy to navigate, isn't it?

How easy is it to navigate, find help, and complete workflows in our software?

How challenging would you say it is to navigate our software?

How often would you say it's challenging to navigate our software?

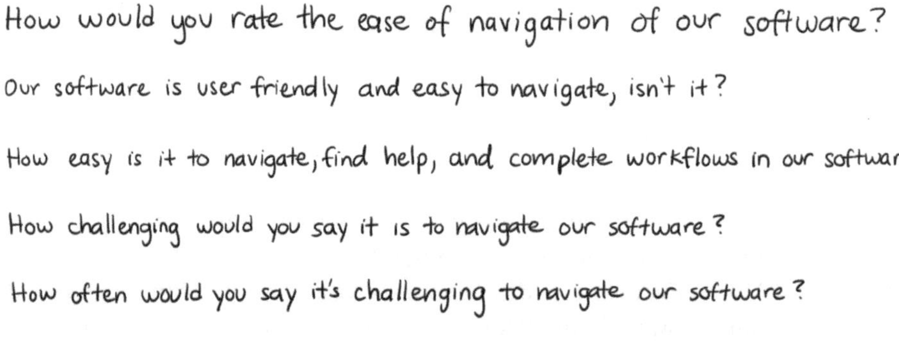

Figure 6.7   How do you think the wording of these questions might affect the responses you receive?

Appropriate wording of questions can take a significant time investment in your work as an analyst. However, you rarely need to start from scratch when measuring new concepts. The field of *psychometrics* has decades of research into applying innovations in measurement theory to develop measures for behavioral and cognitive processes. Many of the concepts we analyze in our work are closely related to human behavior and cognition, which enables us to make use of a wide range of available peer-reviewed resources in our work:

- Countless tested and validated questionnaires are available in peer-reviewed papers on Google Scholar or specialized databases. Each was designed to assess a behavioral or cognitive process and can be strategically modified for specific use cases.
- Academic resources (peer-reviewed papers, books) that include research on wording questions in self-report measures can be used to make decisions about creating measures from scratch or modifying existing ones. If a large portion of your work in analytics involves developing self-report measures, I strongly recommend taking the time to familiarize yourself with this research.
- Existing research on operationalizing your concept of interest and assessing it as a self-report measure can help guide you, your team, and your stakeholders in developing these measures. This type of research can help build institutional knowledge of your organization's domain, which we will discuss in chapter 12.

USING THE RIGHT RESPONSE SCALE

Designing self-report measures includes selecting an appropriate format for your response scale. Most questions only use specific response types (e.g., open-ended questions typically use free-text responses). Still, there's a tremendous amount of flexibility in how you set up those formats. Unsurprisingly, just like with wording your question, small and subtle changes can lead to shifts in the responses you receive.

Let's first break down common types of response formats in self-report measures. Each of these is available to you in most survey tools, such as Google Forms:

- *Free-text boxes* allow respondents to answer open-ended questions in their own words. These can yield valuable *qualitative* data but may be more challenging to analyze. The text box size can also affect the length of the responses you receive.
- *Single-response questions* allow respondents to select only one answer from a dropdown or scale. These typically use Likert scales (e.g., a 5-point scale from "Strongly Disagree" to "Strongly Agree").
- *Multiple-response questions* allow respondents to select more than one answer from a list. Limited or unlimited choices may be allowed to the respondent from a set of *categorical* options.
- *Ranking questions* ask respondents to rank items in order of preference. These questions focus on *relative* rather than *absolute* preferences or priorities assessed with single-response Likert scales.
- *Sliding scales and other interactive response formats* can allow for more nuance in responses (e.g., a sliding scale from 0 to 100 instead of a 0 to 10 point scale). It's essential to use these cautiously and only in cases where you are confident that the additional granularity in the response is meaningful to participants.

The NPS question is presented to potential respondents with an 11-point *single-response* Likert scale. It's often followed up with a free-text box asking respondents to provide additional context on why they responded the way they did to the question.

These two pieces of information are commonly used in organizations to create and track the NPS as a metric over time while also breaking down qualitative responses to infer some of the positive and negative aspects of the business or service assessed.

Most surveys use single-response Likert scales to gather self-reported information from respondents. Initially developed in the 1930s, a *Likert scale* consists of a statement or question followed by an *ordinal range of response options* representing the degree to which you agree or feel strongly about the question. Likert scales often contain an odd number of response options with a midpoint allowing for a neutral response. The most common Likert scales use 5, 7, or 9 points and contain response statements like those shown in figure 6.7.

Likert scales are widely used in surveys due to their flexibility in question and statement types, ease of understanding by respondents, and the ability to compare responses across multiple questions and concepts measured. Given their widespread use, benchmarking against other datasets using the same measures and scales is often straightforward. You can see, for example, whether respondents in different states feel the same way about a candidate running for political office or have differing opinions.

Despite being a universally used response format in surveys, details on how to use them best and why are rarely included in developing these measures (surprise, surprise!). Like with question-wording, extensive research is available on the effect of small changes on response formats. Strategically choosing between the available response formats in survey software can help minimize errors in your responses and give you a better estimate of the concepts you're measuring. The following criteria should be applied to *all* Likert scales:

- A *balanced Likert scale* provides an equal number of positive and negative response options. Unbalanced scales that favor positive or negative choices will invariably skew responses in that direction.
- Not everyone has an opinion or feeling on a topic of interest. Likert scales with a *"neutral" midpoint* (e.g., "Neither Agree nor Disagree") or an *opt-out response option* (e.g., "Unsure/Don't Know") are less likely to receive arbitrary responses.
- The *number of response options* affects the granularity and distribution of responses. Including too few options may limit respondents' abilities to convey their feelings, and too many options can lead to confusion, choice paralysis, and arbitrary selection of values. You can ask most questions with 5 to 7 response items.

Let's return to the NPS question to see how it performs with these criteria. At face value, the NPS question *does* have a balanced Likert scale. The scale ranges from 0 to 10, with an *implied* range from least to most likely. While the range appears balanced, it's not interpreted in a balanced way for reporting and metrics calculations. Only the top two scale points (9 and 10) are considered *promoters*, and the next two (7 and 8) are considered *neutral* points. Most of the scale (0 to 6) is interpreted as *negative*. The scale is also quite long, with 11 points from least to most likely. Given this granularity, it's challenging to prove whether a person responding with a 9 is more likely to promote your business or organization than someone who responds with an 8 on the scale.

Once you've developed a balanced scale with a strategically chosen number of items and the most suitable option for a midpoint or neutral item, it's time to fine-tune the scale for your use case. Small changes in formatting and presentation, as shown in figure 6.8, can influence how respondents interpret and complete your measures. When developing measures, there are a few formatting decisions to consider:

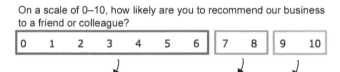

On a scale of 0–10, how likely are you to recommend our business to a friend or colleague?

| 0 | 1 | 2 | 3 | 4 | 5 | 6 | 7 | 8 | 9 | 10 |

Detractors   Passives   Promoters

X Interpretation of Likert scale is imbalanced
X Midpoint available, but evaluated as negative
X Scale has 11 points, which may create confusion

Figure 6.8 Assessment of the NPS question on the appropriate Likert scale criteria

- *Labeling*—Labeling your scales involves selecting between the presence of verbal (e.g., "Strongly Agree") labels and numeric labels (e.g., 1 through 5) for each point on the scale. A scale is typically presented in one of the following ways:
  - *Fully labeled*—A fully labeled scale includes a verbal descriptor that clearly explains the meaning behind each numeric point. This creates clarity on the meaning of each point, which may improve the consistency and accuracy of your responses. It may also enhance the *accessibility* of your survey to respondents. However, a long survey with many fully labeled questions can increase fatigue associated with responding to each question.
  - *Partially labeled*—A partially labeled scale usually includes verbal descriptors for the end and mid-points. This approach can visually simplify your scale and create less cognitive load than a fully labeled scale. However, participants may interpret the unlabeled scale items differently (e.g., "Slightly Agree" versus "Agree" versus "Somewhat Agree"), which may reduce the consistency of your responses.
  - *Fully labeled without numerical points*—A fully labeled scale can hide the numerical points associated with each verbal descriptor. This approach allows you to focus on the meaning of each point and remove any pre-existing cognitive associations that respondents may have with numerical values.
- *Response order*—The order in which verbal descriptors are displayed (e.g., "Strongly Disagree" to "Strongly Agree" versus "Strongly Agree" to "Strongly Disagree") can affect the responses you receive. It's generally recommended

that you keep a *consistent* order of response options for the entirety of a survey. If you see responses that are heavily skewed in one direction, you can *counterbalance* the survey in one of two ways:

– Present half of the participants with a scale with response options ordered from positive to negative while presenting the other half with a scale from negative to positive.

– Include multiple questions that assess the same or similar concepts, and strategically vary the wording between positive and negative.

Self-report measurement development is not an exact science—there are multiple variations of questions and scales that you can use to collect data about your target population. As an analyst, you can recommend strategically developing questions and scales to increase the quality of your organization's data over time. Consider selectively testing and iterating on your approaches to asking questions and setting up response scales where possible.

Choosing self-report measures

Arthur's next step is to evaluate the quality of the available self-report measures and measurement scales. He considers the clarity of the questions and the response scales used to determine whether they should be included in his analysis.

He examines each measure in more detail:

- *Satisfaction in the current role*—The satisfaction survey uses a 5-point Likert scale with fully labeled options, ranging from "Very Dissatisfied" to "Very Satisfied." Arthur considers this measure high quality due to its straightforward, easily understandable labels and balanced scale.

- *Perception of workload*—The employee satisfaction survey contains questions related to workload perceptions, using a 9-point Likert scale with partially labeled options from "Light" to "Manageable" to "Overwhelmed." While this scale offers more granularity, the partially labeled options may lead to some ambiguity in interpretation, potentially reducing the quality of the measure. He also notes that the scale ranges from positive to negative items, which requires him to interpret the numeric scale in the opposite direction of the satisfaction questions.

- *Interest in company events*—The company-sponsored event attendance records serve as a behavioral measure. Arthur creates a binary response scale representing attendance (1 = Attended, 0 = Did not attend). This straightforward scale is of high quality and is easy to interpret.

- *Satisfaction with salary and benefits*—The employee satisfaction survey includes questions about satisfaction with compensation and benefits, using a 4-point Likert scale with numeric-only labels. This scale may be more ambiguous and challenging for some respondents to interpret, potentially reducing the quality of the measure.

- *Productivity in the current role*—Arthur notes that the data for this measure is behavioral and skips evaluating any of the available measures as part of this step.

- *Performance in the current role*—The company's performance-management system uses a rating scale of 1 to 5, with 1 representing poor performance and 5 representing exceptional performance. While this measure is not self-reported, it could be subject to biases similar to self-report measures because the employee's manager reports it. As such, the quality of this measure might be affected by the presence of biases, such as leniency, central tendency, or halo effect.

Arthur decides to include each of the available measures in the analysis, noting which ones are the highest quality as he prepares to compute descriptive statistics for the project. He also notes areas where he believes each measure can be improved and plans to include these in the limitations and recommendations section of the final report he will create.

6.2.3 *Interpreting available data*

As an analyst, you'll often have a combination of self-report data and data available from a source, such as a software application in a data warehouse. Much of this data can be used to track and understand behaviors and can be combined with self-report measures for a comprehensive picture of your users or participants. While it's readily available for querying and reporting, this type of data can come with unique challenges and limitations that must be addressed to track behavior accurately. We'll discuss some steps for evaluating the quality of the available data and its viability for measuring behaviors of interest.

DATA COLLECTION PRACTICES

The information available in your organization's data warehouse is likely synthesized from various sources. If you work at a software company, you probably have vast amounts of data about the users who access your software. You may also have data from third-party applications used by different teams (e.g., HR software, support ticket software) that gets combined into one place that you can query, join, and manipulate in your analyses and reporting.

When examining the available data in a warehouse, learning how data is collected and surfaced for analytics will help determine if it can be used to measure a specific behavior. Ask yourself and your colleagues the following questions to determine the viability of a data source for your needs:

- *What is the source of the data?* Is the data collected from the primary source of information about your organization (e.g., sales transactions on the company website, records from a software application), from a third-party application used by your organization, or both? Often, the data you have querying access to is a highly curated version of the underlying data, so it's valuable to understand what information comes from where.
- *How often is the data refreshed?* Is it updated once per hour, per day, or less frequently? A daily or hourly refresh rate will usually suffice to create self-service

analytics tools and insights for your stakeholders. Set expectations with your stakeholders on how often new information is available.

- *Does the data capture objects or actions?* A record in a database can mean many things. Does it correspond to an object (e.g., a show available on an online streaming service) or to an action (e.g., a user "clicked" the description of the show)? Objects can sometimes be used as proxies for behavioral data but may have limited insight into the nuanced actions that led to the creation of that record.

- *Is there a way to track changes?* Many times, records in a database are edited in place but there is no ability to determine what changes were made and when (e.g., a sales transaction record deletes returned items from the purchase history). This can create challenges when tracking information over time.

- *What do the timestamps mean?* Tables in a database will almost always have a timestamp associated with a record. The timestamp can record when an action occurred, an object was created, or the record was uploaded into the data warehouse. Since time is a crucial dimension for most measurements, make sure it means what you think it does.

GRANULARITY AND AGGREGATION

Behavioral data can be measured at different levels of granularity (e.g., individual users, a group of users, or an organization). For example, figure 6.9 captures information at the *grain* of a patient *and* a visit to the doctor's office. If you work at an organization that serves both business or organizational customers and their users (e.g., a doctor's office and patients), this can introduce a level of hierarchy that affects anything you measure. The individual *and* their organization predict the behaviors you capture. This requires additional strategic decisions about how to create an effective measurement. Overall, asking yourself the following questions will help you determine the level of aggregation (or *grain*) of the data that is appropriate for measurement and metrics (more on that in chapter 7):

- *What* grain *does this behavior need to be measured at?* The unit of measurement is generally derived from an understanding of what matters and what you're trying to change. Is it a web page? Is it a series of web pages creating a flow to check out your cart and make a purchase? Is it the user's continued visits to your site? Is it how many users at a company tend to visit your app? The grain you choose determines the level of aggregation and any hierarchical relationships you need to consider in your analyses or models (more on that in chapter 9).

- *Is the data pre-aggregated?* You may encounter data that has already been pre-aggregated (e.g., a data warehouse view that's grouped by hour, as in figure 6.10, a third-party API that gives you a count of records per hour). Information may be lost at the level of aggregation, and it's sometimes necessary to disaggregate the data to derive value.

	visit_id	patient_id	doctor_id	date	time	visit_reason
0	1038	2654	5	2023-05-01	10:00	Annual check-up
1	1039	2114	8	2023-05-03	14:30	Sore throat
2	1040	2025	4	2023-05-05	11:45	Allergy consultation
3	1041	2759	6	2023-05-06	09:15	Flu symptoms
4	1042	2281	7	2023-05-08	16:20	Routine vaccination

Figure 6.9   Each row in this dataset represents a record of a visit to a doctor's office.

	hour	event_id	user_id	browser	page	total_views
0	2023-04-25 06:00:00	9666349	254311	Chrome	Clothing	2
1	2023-05-01 14:00:00	6701590	710429	Chrome	Checkout Cart	3
2	2023-05-01 23:00:00	5451450	650559	Firefox	Blog	2
3	2023-05-03 00:00:00	20957045	75027	Firefox	Blog	1
4	2023-05-08 00:00:00	20792402	52518	Chrome	Accessories	2

Figure 6.10   Each row in this dataset contains information about visitors and the pages they viewed. What level of aggregation exists in this dataset?

DATA QUALITY

Organizations invest varying amounts of time and resources to ensure the quality and accuracy of data in a warehouse. The state and structure of your data warehouse will differ by the industry you are in, the size of your workplace, and how important accurate data is to the performance of the business or organization. Software companies tend to invest in software that their teams need to use data, since there's high potential value associated with data-informed and machine learning features. A small nonprofit may simply not have the capacity to develop the infrastructure necessary for a functioning data warehouse, regardless of the potential value of their data.

The questions you should ask about data quality will differ heavily based on the type of business organization you work with. You may not need to ask them for every dataset and project, but you will want to answer these questions *at least once* early in your role and before starting a task. You will avoid many inaccurate findings and misinterpretations if you do!

- *What steps are taken, if any, to handle duplicate, missing, or otherwise inaccurate data?*
  The ingestion of data into a warehouse is rarely error-proof. You may encounter duplicate records or missing or bad data in your reports if your organization

doesn't regularly perform data quality checks. If you don't have visibility into this work, check with the team that maintains the warehouse (e.g., data engineering) to learn more.

- *If you are capturing data using third-party tracking, is there anything that can limit the accuracy and completeness of the dataset?* Many organizations use third-party software to track behaviors online on their website or application (e.g., page views, clicks). Some options for third-party tracking do not work under certain conditions, such as when a user has an ad blocker enabled. This can create problems with missing data, *not at random,* and limit your ability to accurately report information at the grain of the user.

- *What kind of tables are you accessing?* Are you directly querying data ingested into the warehouse, or are there highly curated analytics tables that combine data sources for ease of use? If your organization has an analytics engineering function that develops and maintains analytics models, you may have automated checks to resolve common data quality problems. Figure 6.11 shows an example of data quality problems that you might search for in a data warehouse using a SQL query.

Check for Duplicate Records:

```
SELECT username, COUNT(user_id) AS n_records
FROM users
GROUP BY username
HAVING COUNT(user_id) > 1;
```

username	n_records
jd_9705	2
data_analyst01	3

Check for Bad Dates:

```
SELECT username, signup_date
FROM users
WHERE
    signup_date > CURRENT_DATE;
```

username	signup_date
python_user8	2025-10-01
coffee_and_data	2024-12-31

Figure 6.11   A few simple queries can help determine if there are problems with the quality of your data.

Inspecting the available data

Arthur's next step is to evaluate the quality, granularity, and data collection process of the available behavioral measure: productivity in the current role.

Arthur examines the data available in the company's data warehouse to assess productivity, and he identifies several potential indicators:

- Number of tasks completed
- Project completion times
- Adherence to deadlines

Arthur recognizes that these indicators may not fully capture the complexity of productivity across different roles and departments within the company. Some tasks may require more time and effort, making it difficult to directly compare productivity levels based on the number of completed tasks.

Arthur speaks with the IT department and managers responsible for tracking this data to understand the data collection process better. He learns that while most departments have well-established productivity monitoring and reporting processes, some use inconsistent and subjective criteria. He proceeds cautiously using these measures and prepares to exclude them entirely from the analysis if appropriate.

6.2.4   *Exercises*

You are a human resources analyst at a company developing a workplace wellness program to reduce burnout and improve employee retention and productivity. You have been assigned a project to identify or develop self-report and behavioral measures to evaluate the program's effect:

1   Go to scholar.google.com and search for "employee well-being questionnaire." Filter your results to papers published after 2019. Are there any papers about developing or validating a scale on employee well-being? If you access the full text, you will usually find the newly developed questionnaire in an appendix at the end of the document.

2   Develop or select a question from one of the available surveys you discovered on the following topics:
   - Stress levels related to your work environment
   - Perceptions of support they receive from supervisors for their well-being
   - Overall satisfaction with the workplace

   What type of response scale would you use and why? What potential biases or limitations may be associated with different response formats? Suggest ways to minimize their effect on the quality of your results.

3   Identify potential behavioral measures to track employee engagement and workplace stress. You can assume that multiple data sources are available in a data warehouse on employee hours, project completion times, meeting deadlines, and more. What characteristics would the data need to have for you to accurately use it for measuring engagement?

4   Propose a hypothesis about which behavioral measure(s) might be correlated with the effect of the workplace wellness program.

5   How will you integrate the self-report and behavioral measures? What information would you need to connect these data sources?

6.3   *Reliability and validity*

Regarding measurement, *reliability* and *validity* are the essential foundation of all conclusions you draw from your data. These two concepts ensure the accuracy and integrity of any analysis you perform. Most strategies for developing reliable and valid measures were designed with self-report measurements in mind, but many of the same steps can be applied when working with behavioral measures. We will cover approaches for working with both types of data.

6.3.1 *Reliability*

Reliability refers to a measurement's ability to assess a concept, behavior, or process consistently and repeatably over time and across different respondents or users. A measure must be reliable for stakeholders to trust the numbers they are seeing and the conclusions drawn from its data.

We will discuss several types of reliability: test-retest reliability, inter-rater reliability, and internal consistency. Each type should be evaluated as appropriate for a measure to be deemed reliable.

TEST-RETEST RELIABILITY

Test-retest reliability refers to how *consistent* a measure is over time. A measure is consistent if the same individuals produce similar results on the measurement when tested and retested over time, assuming your concept of interest has not changed. The following are examples of test-retest reliability:

- A participant in a study on clinical depression provides responses to measurement scales that correlate with each other over time, assuming they have not experienced changes in their symptoms.
- A software user responds to the NPS question with similar scores over time, assuming that the business or service offered has not substantially changed.

Test-retest reliability is vital for data intended to be measured over time, such as data for a business metric or forecasting model. If you're interested in how something has changed and will continue to change, you *must* be confident in the quality of the underlying numbers.

Test-retest reliability can be performed using the following steps:

1 Collect or select the initial dataset on your measure being tested.
2 Choose an appropriate time interval for collecting or selecting your subsequent datasets. This will vary based on what you are measuring and the resources you have available.
3 Collect data for one or more intervals after the initial measurement. To compare measures effectively in most statistical software, you may want to structure your data in a *wide* format, with one row per user or participant and one column per time interval measurement.
4 Compare correlations between scores for each time interval. This is typically done using Spearman's or Pearson's correlation value. The stronger these scores correlate, the higher your test-retest reliability.

Test-retest reliability applies to self-report and behavioral measures about a construct you expect to be stable over time. If the data *consistently* measures a *stable* process about a user over time, using these steps is valuable before reporting on a measure for metrics or experimentation. Figure 6.12 shows a correlation matrix determining whether participants' responses to a happiness and stress measure are correlated over three time periods.

For example, a product analytics team is interested in developing a measure of user engagement on an app. The team starts by measuring the average time spent on the app per user session. To test this measure, the team calculates the weekly average time spent on the app per user. They then select three *non-consecutive weeks* to compare the initial week's data and run Pearson's correlations on each user's time spent on the app. Pearson's correlation values should be pretty high if this is a *stable measure* (e.g., if users are consistent in the amount of time they spend on the app). If they weren't as high as expected, the team could explore further potential sources of error, such as changes in user behavior, app functionality, or data aggregation methods. This type of investigation will build *a lot* of internal knowledge about the user base.

	Happiness at T1	Stress at T1	Happiness at T2	Stress at T2	Happiness at T3	Stress at T3
Happiness at T1	1.00	-0.60	0.72	-0.65	0.58	-0.52
Stress at T1	-0.60	1.00	-0.45	0.68	-0.50	0.72
Happiness at T2	0.72	-0.45	1.00	-0.72	0.68	-0.63
Stress at T2	-0.65	0.68	-0.72	1.00	-0.75	0.80
Happiness at T3	0.58	-0.50	0.68	-0.75	1.00	-0.72
Stress at T3	-0.52	0.72	-0.63	0.80	-0.72	1.00

Figure 6.12 Test-retest reliability correlations are expected to be quite high across time periods (e.g., T1, T2, T3), often with an *r* value above 0.7.

INTER-RATER RELIABILITY

Inter-rater reliability measures the agreement between two or more people evaluating the same dataset. It's typically used when performing analysis tasks that require subjective judgments, ratings, or classifications (e.g., assessing qualitative data or making recommendations based on a large project). High inter-rater reliability means that your raters made *consistent* judgments, indicating the reliability of the criteria used to review the data.

Inter-rater reliability is typically conducted using the following steps:

1 Develop an objective rubric or criteria for raters to follow when evaluating data. This may include categories, a rating scale, or other measures.

2 Have the raters conduct independent evaluations of the data without discussing or sharing input. This will allow them to focus on the evaluation without biasing each other's responses.

3 Calculate the inter-rater reliability using one or more similarity indicators (e.g., the percentage of cases with the same rating, a Pearson's correlation, or a Cohen's kappa.

4 Iterate on the evaluation criteria and processes to improve alignment between raters and the evaluation quality over time.

Figure 6.13 shows an example of how a qualitative measure may be quantified and compared for reliability between multiple raters.

NPS Comment:
"I have had issues with setting up my account and doing basic tasks. The support team helps when I have a question but it doesn't solve the main problem."

Rater # 1	Rater # 2	Rater # 3
Product (negative)	Initial setup (negative)	Product (neutral)
Service (positive)	Service (neutral)	Initial setup (negative)
		Service (negative)

Figure 6.13   Inter-rater reliability involves evaluating how much individuals agree on the topics covered in qualitative data. In this example, all three raters identify "service" as a topic, and there is some variation in the other topics they include. As such, the inter-rater reliability for "product" and "initial setup" will be lower than for "service".

When done at scale and over long periods of time, measures of inter-rater reliability demonstrate a strong and consistent understanding of the qualitative data you are capturing. If a complex evaluation is part of your role or your organization's success, a system of inter-rater reliability evaluation can be set up to continually improve these processes.

INTERNAL CONSISTENCY

Internal consistency evaluates the extent to which a collection of measurements effectively captures data about the same core concept or process. In most analytics projects, you'll likely need to work with multiple measures or develop composite measures to assess complex processes related to your users or participants. For instance, a depression questionnaire typically comprises various questions addressing different symptoms. The participant's responses are then combined to generate a score that reflects the presence of depression. In such cases, it's crucial to take a moment to ensure that the multiple measures you're using are *reliably* measuring the same process before combining them into a single, cohesive measure.

Internal consistency can be evaluated using the following steps:

1 Identify all variables and indicators you hypothesize measure the same underlying concept or process.

2 Calculate correlations between each indicator for each user or participant. You can use any appropriate correlation coefficient for your data (e.g., Pearson's correlation for continuous data, Spearman's rank correlation for ordinal data). Consistent variables should have high correlation coefficients. Variables *unrelated to* the rest should likely be considered a separate process and excluded from any composite measures.

3 Use a statistical method for assessing internal consistency. One of the most common methods is *Cronbach's alpha*, which calculates the average inter-item covariance (unstandardized correlation) between all variables and returns a coefficient from 0 to 1 (see figure 6.14). Cronbach's alpha is not readily available in the Python packages we have covered thus far (e.g., `statsmodels`, `scipy`). Instead, it can be imported using the pingouin library, which has a range of statistical functions that return comprehensive information for common tests and has functions not available elsewhere.

$$a = \frac{k \cdot \bar{c}}{\bar{v} + (k-1) \cdot \bar{c}}$$

k = number of items
$\bar{c}$ = average covariances between items
$\bar{v}$ = average variance of each item

Figure 6.14 Steps for calculating Cronbach's alpha

4 Refine the variables that you include in your composite measure. You may need to remove some or consider adding others related to your concept or process.

To calculate Cronbach's alpha in Python, you can use the pingouin library's `cronbach_alpha` function. We'll use the `weather.csv` data from previous chapters to demonstrate how this calculation is performed. First, we'll create a correlation matrix to view the standardized relationships between each variable:

```
import pandas as pd                ◁──┐ Import the
import numpy as np                     │ libraries.

weather = pd.read_csv("weather.csv")              ◁──┘ Import the weather
                                                        data as a dataframe.
weather_corr = weather.select_dtypes(include="number").corr()   ◁───
print(weather_corr)
```

Calculate correlations between
the numeric variables.

The code produces the following output:

```
              high_temp  low_temp  humidity  wind_speed  precip
high_temp         1.00      0.96      0.15       -0.23     -0.04
low_temp          0.96      1.00      0.18       -0.26     -0.03
humidity          0.15      0.18      1.00        0.03      0.23
wind_speed       -0.23     -0.26      0.03        1.00      0.21
precip           -0.04     -0.03      0.23        0.21      1.00
```

We can see that the temperature variables are strongly correlated with each other and moderately negatively correlated with the wind speed. Next, we will use the pingouin library to calculate the Cronbach's alpha associated with the internal consistency of all items in the dataset:

```
import pingouin as pg          ◁──┤ Import the pingouin library.

cr_alpha = pg.cronbach_alpha(data=weather.drop('day', axis=1))   ◁──┐ Calculate
print(cr_alpha)      ◁──┐ Print the value and its 95%              │ Cronbach's
                        │ confidence interval.                      │ alpha.
```

The preceding code produces the following Cronbach's alpha and confidence interval:

```
(0.5446867046720659, array([0.501, 0.586]))
```

The function returns an alpha value of 0.545, which suggests a relatively low internal consistency. In general, peer-reviewed research suggests the following approximate guidelines for how to interpret the strength of an alpha value:

- *0 to 0.69*—Low internal consistency
- *0.7 to 0.79*—Moderate internal consistency
- *0.8 to 0.89*—Good internal consistency
- *0.9 to 0.95*—Excellent internal consistency
- *0.95 or above*—Suggests there may be redundancy among your variables, and you can potentially remove some without reducing the quality of your measure

The guidelines for interpreting the strength of internal consistency are not exact. They were set as approximate guidelines primarily on the strengths of self-report measures collected as quantitative surveys. While these recommended thresholds haven't been directly tested with behavioral measures, they *are* based on correlation coefficients, frequently used with both data types.

RECAP

Reliable measures are central to ensuring that your deliverables as an analyst continue to bring value to your stakeholders long after you complete them. If you can confidently say that your measures are consistent, stable, and have a meaning agreed upon between professionals, you're well equipped to create self-service and reproducible results. This is key to developing effective metrics, which we will discuss in the next chapter.

6.3.2 *Validity*

Once you're confident that your measures are reliable, it's essential to step back and ask yourself the question in this chapter's title—*are you measuring what you think you're measuring?*

Validity is the extent to which a measurement accurately captures the intended concept or process. A valid measure should be a true, comprehensive representation of what you are analyzing. Establishing the validity of your measurement is crucial to deriving meaningful, trustworthy results for your stakeholders to use in their decisions.

Researchers and analysts use several common types of validity as criteria for the quality of their measurements, including face validity, construct validity, and criterion validity. In most cases, assessing measures for these types of validity are straightforward and can be incorporated into your background research and preparation for your analysis.

CONTENT OR FACE VALIDITY

Content or *face validity* refers to the degree to which your measures sufficiently capture all facets of the concept or process you are measuring. It's primarily assessed through a qualitative evaluation of the underlying theoretical concepts, expert judgments, and existing evidence supporting the definition of the concept. When assessing face validity, reviewing your definitions with subject matter experts is essential. These experts are most often your stakeholders, or colleagues in your field, who work directly with the process you are measuring. Assessing face validity is an *ongoing process* that requires you to keep up to date on new theories and evidence in the domain of study or practice you are working in.

For example, if you want to assess employee job satisfaction, you will first need to *conceptualize* job satisfaction and identify all relevant facets of this concept. You may review peer-reviewed literature in organizational psychology and identify several factors typically included in questionnaires (e.g., satisfaction with work tasks, work environment, manager, colleagues, and compensation for the role). From there, you can use existing peer-reviewed measures or develop your own to assess each of these factors.

CONSTRUCT VALIDITY

Construct validity refers to the extent to which your measurement accurately assesses the theoretical construct it's intended to. It reflects the degree to which the observed patterns in your data align with the relationships you expect based on the underlying theory. Assessing construct validity involves examining two subtypes of this criteria:

- *Convergent validity* refers to the degree to which a measure is related to *other* measures that are theoretically associated with the same construct. This is typically assessed by evaluating the strength of correlations between concepts or behaviors that are theoretically related.
- *Discriminant validity* refers to the degree to which a measure is *not* related to other measures that are theoretically unassociated with the construct. You can also assess this type of validity using correlations; you will generally expect that the strength of the relationship should be *less* than convergent measures.

For example, if you are assessing the construct validity of the NPS question, you will likely want to determine if responses to the question correlate with referral behaviors and if you can track them at your organization. If scores on the question *positively* correlate with referral rates, you can use it as a *valid* measure of the likelihood of referring others to your business or organization.

CRITERION VALIDITY

Criterion validity refers to the degree to which a measure is associated with an external criterion, such as a well-established measure of the existing concept or an outcome of interest. This form of validity is also typically assessed by looking at correlations between the measure of interest and the *criterion* used to assess it.

Criterion validity can be assessed in two ways, depending on your analytics project:

- *Concurrent validity* assesses the relationship between a measure and its criterion simultaneously. Both measures can be administered at the same time (self-report measures) or evaluated at the same or similar time periods (behavioral measures).
- *Predictive validity* assesses the relationship between a measure at a time period *before assessing* its criterion. Analysts may collect data on the criterion measure at a subsequent point or select an appropriate time window, after which they expect a predictive relationship to be present in the data.

For example, suppose you want to assess the relationship between a new financial metric and the company's financial performance. In that case, you will likely want to see if it's an appropriate *predictor* of existing financial metrics. You can compare the data on the new financial metric in the current fiscal quarter to a performance metric such as net income or profit in the *following* fiscal quarter. A valid financial metric should correlate strongly with the company's financial performance.

Determining the validity of employee satisfaction measures

Arthur's final step before conducting his analysis is to assess the reliability and validity of each measure to ensure the insights on the workplace wellness program are accurate and meaningful. He uses the following steps to evaluate each measure:

- *Satisfaction in the current role*—Arthur examines the internal consistency of the survey using Cronbach's alpha, yielding a value of 0.72. He also assesses the content validity of the survey by researching existing definitions and measures and determines that the survey used is comprehensive.
- *Perception of workload*—Arthur yields a Cronbach's alpha of 0.68 for the questions assessing this concept. He assesses content validity by researching existing measures and definitions of perceptions of one's workload.
- *Interest in company events*—Arthur does not assess the internal consistency of this single-item measure. He primarily focuses on the question's wording to ensure it's a clear and objective measure of employee interest in events.

- *Satisfaction with salary and benefits*—Arthur yields a Cronbach's alpha of 0.34 with all of the variables used. He reviews existing research and measures of the concept, concluding that the questions measuring this concept do not all capture the same process.
- *Productivity in the current role*—Since this is a behavioral measure with concerns about reliability, Arthur takes the time to assess the test-retest reliability of the measure across multiple time periods. He discovers that the correlations between time periods are quite high and relatively stable.
- *Performance in the current role*—Arthur assesses inter-rater reliability by comparing performance ratings between managers, supervisors, and directors where available.

By systematically assessing the reliability and validity of each measure, Arthur has ensured that the data collected is of high quality. He will establish confidence in each measure and enable the organization to use the findings and each measure as metrics over time.

6.3.3 *Exercises*

You have shared the proposed self-report questionnaires and behavioral measures to assess employee well-being with your team lead. The surveys have been administered to employees at the company, and you have approximately 600 responses for analysis. You are asked to validate that the measures used were appropriate for measuring each concept of interest in this project:

1. What steps will you take to assess the reliability of each set of measures? As a refresher, we have measures on the following topics:
   - Stress levels related to your work environment
   - Perceptions of support they receive from supervisors for their well-being
   - Overall satisfaction with the workplace
2. What forms of validity are most appropriate for assessing the preceding measures?
3. How will you assess the validity of the behavioral measures that you selected? How do those steps differ from the self-report measures?

Summary

- *Self-report measures* are collected directly from individuals, usually through questionnaires or surveys. These measures capture information about perceptions, attitudes, beliefs, or experiences. In analytics, self-report measures provide valuable insights into subjective experiences and allow for assessing factors that may not otherwise be observable.
- Designing accurate self-report measures (e.g., *questionnaires*) requires *careful wording of questions* and assessment items. Leading language, double-barreled

statements, and negative wording can all reduce the quality of responses you receive.

- There are many ways to structure the *response format* to questions (e.g., *Likert scales*) that can affect your results. A scale should be *balanced*, and have a moderate number of response items (usually 5 or 7) to maximize the quality of responses.

- *Behavioral measures* are records of behaviors or actions captured by direct observation or recorded in a data warehouse as an interaction within an application or tool. These measures can offer direct insights into user and participant experiences without the bias associated with self-report measures.

- *Reliability* refers to the consistency, stability, and repeatability of a measurement. A reliable measure is expected to produce similar results under consistent conditions. Ensuring reliability in analytics is essential to produce accurate and trustworthy results that can inform decision-making and support evidence-based practices.

- Analysts typically assess three common forms of reliability: *test-retest reliability*, which is an assessment of consistency in measurement responses over time; *inter-rater reliability*, which is a measure of consistency between raters for qualitative evaluations; and *internal consistency*, which is an assessment of the degree to which different variables measure the same underlying construct.

- *Validity* refers to the degree to which a measure accurately assesses the concept or process it's designed to measure. Ensuring that your measures are valid is critical to building confidence in your stakeholders that your results are meaningful, accurate, and reflective of the true phenomenon you are investigating.

- Three forms of validity are essential to assess as part of your measurement: *content or face validity*, which is an assessment of how comprehensively your measure captures the concept or phenomenon of interest; *construct validity*, which is an assessment of whether you are measuring your intended theoretical construct; and *criterion validity*, which assesses whether your measure is associated with other measures of similar constructs.

The art of metrics:
Tracking performance for
organizational success

7

This chapter covers

- Understanding the value of metrics for an organization
- Identifying measures of success to use as metrics
- Designing SMART metrics for effective tracking and decision-making
- Identifying and mitigating common pitfalls and errors when creating metrics
- Powerfully communicating progress and insights to stakeholders

When watching or reading the news, you'll regularly see charts tracking information over time. You may be familiar with many of them—stock market performance, the Air Quality Index (AQI), unemployment rate—and you likely understand what it means when the numbers increase or decrease. These metrics enable you to understand the world and how it changes.

Metrics are *standardized quantitative measures* that track processes, outcomes, or activities over time. These invaluable tools allow us to understand immediate and long-term changes that influence nearly every facet of our lives.

This chapter will cover the skills you need to create similarly clear, actionable, and effective metrics (without a century of work!). You will learn how to identify valuable processes to monitor, translate the process into a metric, avoid common pitfalls in metric calculations, and share them effectively with stakeholders. The metrics you design will enable your organization to understand the effect of their actions, make strategic decisions, and understand the complex processes that influence the organization.

7.1   *The role of metrics in decision-making*

Metrics are shown to nearly *everyone*, regardless of their experience with data. For example, the *unemployment rate* is a widely recognized economic indicator across many countries, defined as the *percentage of the labor force not currently employed and actively looking for a job*. The US Bureau of Labor Statistics calculates the unemployment rate every month, reporting it to the public as an indicator of the job market's health (see figure 7.1). People use this metric to make critical life decisions, such as seeking new employment or buying a house. The full concept of *unemployment*, however, is captured as one of multiple indicators providing useful information on the state of the job market at any given time.

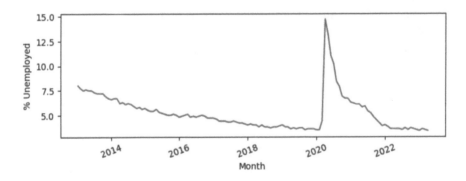

Figure 7.1   The official unemployment rate reported monthly from 2013 to 2023

To provide a comprehensive picture of unemployment in the United States, the Bureau of Labor Statistics (BLS) publishes *six metrics* each month. The official unemployment rate is known as U-3, which includes *all* people in the workforce who are unemployed, looking for work, and available for work. The other five measures include subsets of the population not counted in U-3 (e.g., U-4 includes *discouraged* workers not actively looking for work because they believe no jobs are available). Each measure provides a specific insight, and all six are necessary to understand workforce participation. The BLS unemployment metrics have existed in some form for nearly a century. Decades of research allowed for refining the calculation and data collection into the six indicators shown in figure 7.2.

	U – 1	U – 2	U – 3	U – 4	U – 5	U – 6
Long-term unemployed	✓		✓	✓	✓	✓
Recently unemployed		✓	✓	✓	✓	✓
Finished temporary employment		✓	✓	✓	✓	✓
Discouraged/no longer searching				✓	✓	✓
Marginally attached/ sometimes searching					✓	✓
Underemployed						✓

Figure 7.2 Each unemployment metric includes different types of unemployed or underemployed workers.

Metrics can provide a concrete way of evaluating performance and trends over time and are essential tools in decision-making, strategic planning, and goal-setting. They're often visualized as a line or bar graph, where the *y*-axis captures an aggregated measure and the *x*-axis captures the measure over time, as in figure 7.3.

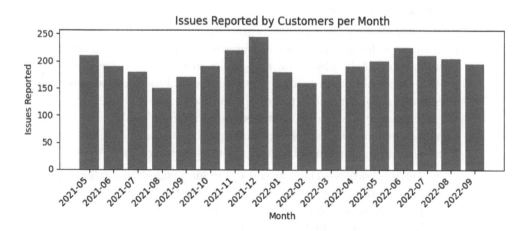

Figure 7.3 Metrics are usually depicted as an aggregate measure over time.

Every organization can benefit from metrics to understand the effect of its actions and decisions on performance. When an organization invests time in developing, tracking, and surfacing metrics to stakeholders, they have a competitive advantage in their strategic decision-making. In this section, we will cover three tiers of metrics that organizations can track:

- *Performance metrics* provide critical feedback on the state of the organization. These are core metrics tracked across many types of organizations, and they ultimately tell you whether or not the organization is succeeding.
- *Organizational strategy metrics* provide information on the effect of specific actions taken within the organization. These allow teams to dive one level deeper than performance metrics and understand actions that correlate with or predict performance.
- *Accountability metrics* hold individuals and teams responsible for producing results. These often overlap with performance metrics but are designed to make the daily work, processes, and successes of individual teams clear and transparent to the organization.

An organization that understands its performance with metrics is generally positioned for better long-term outcomes. Setting appropriate metrics requires an investment in developing an in-depth understanding of the data. An organization that *doesn't* invest in measurement and metric development can easily hit a wall and struggle to achieve its long-term goals.

By taking the proper steps, organizations at any size or stage of growth can learn to guide their strategy with appropriate metrics. The key is selecting measures that align with their goals and offer actionable insights. When they're well implemented, these metrics enable the organization to confidently navigate the complex decision-making landscape.

7.1.1 Tracking performance

An organization should typically begin using metrics to track measures that clearly indicate its performance. These measures most often correspond directly to the organization's key goals, objectives, and ability to continue succeeding (e.g., revenue, profit). Once these foundational metrics are established, the organization can delve deeper into secondary indicators of operational success.

At smaller or newer organizations, your role as an analyst may entail developing organizational metrics from the ground up. The majority of organizations will benefit from establishing performance metrics in the following order:

- *Financial metrics*—These are critical to understanding the financial health of an organization. Most businesses will track and monitor revenue (e.g., figure 7.4), profit margins, and customer acquisition costs (CAC). For-profit companies have well-established sets of financial metrics based on the type of business (e.g., business-to-consumer, or B2C) and method of collecting revenue (e.g., monthly subscriptions) [1]. Non-profit and government organizations will also track inbound funding and revenue as appropriate. However, they often need to customize these calculations to represent how they receive funds. These metrics are *vital* to investors, board members, and shareholders with a vested interest in the organization's financial performance.

- *Operational metrics*—These gauge the efficiency of an organization's operational processes. These can include measures such as production volume, downtime on an app, or the acceptance rates of offers extended for employment. Operational metrics are more granular than many financial metrics and are often calculated as ratios of products or services per employee, or as time to complete an activity. These metrics are necessary for teams to identify areas of inefficiency and bottlenecks, allowing them to improve productivity and reduce costs associated with day-to-day tasks.

- *Customer metrics*—These focus on customers' experiences and interactions with the organization. Examples include customer satisfaction scores (CSAT), churn rates, and lifetime value (LTV). These metrics provide insight into how well an organization meets the needs and expectations of its customers. They often guide organizational strategy, which will be discussed in the next section.

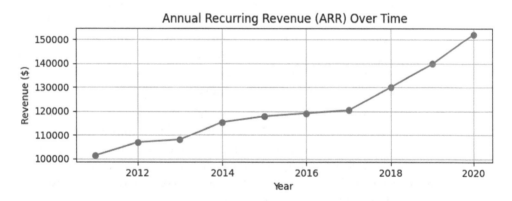

Figure 7.4 Annual recurring revenue (ARR) or monthly recurring revenue (MRR) is a standard financial metric among businesses with subscription-based models.

7.1.2 Informing organizational strategy

Once performance metrics are established, organizations can delve deeper into specific areas of operations and factors that correlate with the success of each performance metric. These might include employee productivity, process efficiency, and customer behavior measures. Understanding this next level of metrics and their relationships to organizational performance enables you to create a data-informed organizational strategy.

Performance metrics don't usually tell you the reason for the value you are seeing. If your organization's revenue decreases in a month, you and your stakeholders can hypothesize any potential causes for the change. *Organizational strategy* metrics enable you to tease apart the factors contributing to performance and take actions to benefit the organization.

Several types of metrics can inform organizational strategy and potentially correlate with performance metrics. In most cases, they can be broken into the following categories:

- *Customer metrics*—These track the behaviors, experiences, and sentiments of your organization's customers. Understanding their needs and experiences with your organization provides you with the information you need to retain and grow your customer base. Some examples of customer metrics include engagement or activity rates, referral rates, and customer effort. Each of these metrics can inform how your organization engages with these customers.
- *Product metrics*—These are used in organizations that offer a *product* or *service*, and they allow you to understand the behaviors and usage of your product or service, and they can inform your product development strategy. Examples of product metrics include usage rates, feature adoption rates, and time to complete workflows.
- *Market metrics*—These enable you to understand the ecosystem in which your organization operates. These metrics usually comprise data gathered outside your organization, such as the many supply, demand, and price metrics provided by the US Bureau of Labor Statistics or similar government organizations around the globe. This data can inform decisions about selling to new customers, adjusting pricing strategies, or investing in advertising.

Identifying appropriate strategy metrics to drive success can require a significant time investment. As an analyst, you must form hypotheses, explore relationships with performance metrics, and recommend which ones to track. It's also important to regularly *evaluate* and *refine* organizational metrics, whose relevance to the overall performance may change over time. You can expect to iterate and revise strategy metrics more often than performance metrics.

Where possible, establishing a causal link between your strategy and performance metrics can significantly enhance decision-making at your organization. Identifying *causality* means identifying whether changes in strategic initiatives directly lead to changes in performance. Demonstrating causality can be complex—there are entire books on methods of causal inference that you can reference if you are considering building expertise in this topic:

- *Causal Inference: The Mixtape* by Scott Cunningham [2] covers numerous sophisticated approaches to establishing causality when working with complex datasets. The book includes examples in R and employs economic data in many of its examples.

- *Causality* by Judea Pearl [3] covers a breadth of approaches to causal inference used in academic and non-academic fields.

If you are constrained in your ability to use sophisticated statistical methods, even simple approaches can provide valuable insights:

- Comparing performance metrics *before and after* an action or change captured in your strategy metrics (e.g., performing a regression analysis using your strategy metrics as predictors and performance metrics as your outcome and visualizing their trends, as shown in figure 7.5).
- Comparing performance metrics *between groups* that were and were not affected by the action or change (e.g., adding group indicators as predictors in your regression model and performing a *t*-test or ANOVA).

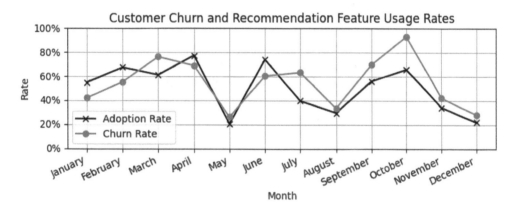

Figure 7.5   Visually representing strong relationships between strategy and performance metrics can help your stakeholders understand long-term trends and whether the relationship strengthens or weakens over time.

Regression models provide additional rigor to your analysis, but remember that correlation does *not* imply causation. A breadth of factors influences organizational performance; as an analyst, you will continually try to understand the relationships you *haven't* yet measured. Over time, you will build a comprehensive picture of the processes and measures that make up the landscape of your organization.

7.1.3   *Promoting accountability*

Metrics are often used to measure the performance of individuals and teams in their roles to enable the organization's success. These *accountability metrics,* often called key performance indicators (KPIs), provide a tangible way to set expectations at multiple levels and measure progress toward goals and responsibilities. Organizations often use these metrics to guide performance reviews, promotion decisions, bonus pay, and team development strategies.

For individuals and teams, these metrics are typically tied to the timely and accurate completion of tasks and projects. For example, a customer support team may track the percentage of customer ticket inquiries resolved in under 24 hours. The team's manager likely looks at the overall metric value for the team, followed by a breakdown by sales representative to understand each person's performance. The information shows which team members meet targets, and which might need additional support, coaching, or reassignment of work.

Accountability metrics at an organization can look like the following, broken down by team:

- *Percentage of sales quota attained* per sales development representative on a sales team, measured quarterly—shown in figure 7.6
- *Average time to fill open roles* per recruiter on a talent acquisition team, measured month over month
- *Time to resolve bugs* (work representing errors or problems on a site or app) on a software engineering team, measured each quarter
- *Number of qualified leads* (inbound customers likely to purchase your product or services) generated through marketing campaigns, measured every six months

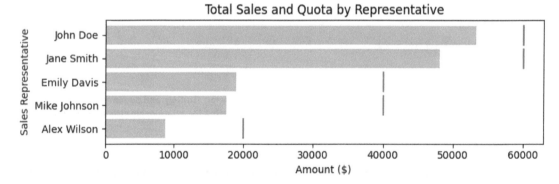

Figure 7.6   A graph showing the sales representative performance compared to their quotas, based on their seniority at the organization

At organizations, accountability metrics are part of larger strategic goals, such as achieving certain profit margins, reducing overhead costs, or improving customer experience. These metrics align different teams' efforts toward the same purpose and can help ensure the organization remains focused on its strategic objectives.

Similar to organizational strategy metrics, accountability metrics should be revisited regularly to ensure they align appropriately with overall performance metrics. As the organization grows and changes, the metrics that teams are held to should evolve to represent their most important work. Ultimately, a thoughtful approach to measuring work for accountability can drive performance and encourage a culture of transparency and continuous improvement.

7.1.4   Exercises

You are an analyst starting a new role supporting a company's marketing department. Your team has some existing dashboards and documentation about the metrics in table 7.1, which are currently being tracked or were previously considered essential to the company:

Table 7.1   Company metrics in presentations and dashboards

Metrics in presentations	Metrics in dashboards
Number of website visitors	Average time on page (measured in minutes)
Number of leads generated	Customer lifetime value (LTV)
Number of webinar attendees	Customer acquisition cost (CAC)
Cost per lead	Revenue growth (% increase in revenue)
Email open rate (% of emails opened by customers)	Conversion rate (% of leads that become customers)
Return on advertising spend	Social media engagement rate (number of views, shares, and clicks per post)
Spam rate (% of emails marked as spam by the customer)	On-time launch rate of campaigns

1 From the list of metrics in table 7.1, identify which might belong to the three metric categories we discussed: *performance, operational,* and *accountability* metrics. Metrics can belong to more than one category.
2 For metrics most appropriate as operational or accountability metrics, which ones might need to be measured separately for individual teams instead of for the entire marketing organization?
3 Propose a hypothesis for which operational metrics might affect overall performance metrics. How would you test this?

7.2   *The key principles of metric design*

Designing metrics is a crucial skill set for an analyst. It requires a deep understanding of your organization's goals and objectives and a comprehensive knowledge of the processes and activities you are measuring. Across nearly any organization, you can apply the foundational principles of metric design to choose appropriate and actionable targets to monitor and use for success. We will delve into the SMART framework for metric design, ensuring you can connect more granular metrics to organizational goals and set appropriate targets to provide the context for evaluating success.

7.2.1   Using the SMART framework

The SMART framework for metric design is a powerful and widely used approach for creating measurable objectives at an organization. SMART (specific, measurable, achievable, relevant, and time-bound) is an acronym that encompasses key characteristics necessary for effective performance tracking. By adhering to this framework, an analyst can develop well-defined and highly effective metrics for the organization to drive performance and guide decision-making.

SPECIFIC

A metric should clearly and concisely represent a *specific* aspect of your organization's performance or objective. You should avoid vague and ambiguous language in your definitions to ensure all stakeholders understand what you are measuring. The metric should specify what needs to be accomplished, what success looks like, and what the expected results are. Table 7.2 shows the difference between a concept and the specific language used in a metric.

Table 7.2   Many metrics are colloquially discussed as concepts and thus require stakeholder collaboration to create specific operational definitions.

High-level concept	Specific metric
The engineering team is productive	Percentage of tasks completed on time
Customers are supported in their needs	Percentage of customer problems and questions resolved on the first contact (first call resolution, or FCR)
Creating an easy-to-use application	Median time to complete the setup flow for new users

For example, if your stakeholders ask you to measure "customer satisfaction," you will need to work with them to specify the *operational definition* of this concept. The metric you choose should be a *reliable* and *valid* (see chapters 2 and 6) quantitative measure agreed upon by teams who intend to use it for strategic decisions. Using customer self-report data, your specific metric could be the "percentage of customers reporting that they were 'Satisfied' or 'Highly Satisfied' with their experience." This precise operational definition will speed up the alignment process with your stakeholders.

MEASURABLE

A metric needs to be quantifiable and capable of being *measured* objectively. Once you and your stakeholders agree on a quantitative and objective measure, your role as an analyst includes ensuring that your organization reliably and accurately captures the data over time. In practice, this requires collaborating with multiple teams to ensure your data can meet the following criteria:

- *The data is captured at regular intervals.* For example, if you're using questions from a customer satisfaction survey measured once per quarter, you should expect a similar number of responses to be recorded during each time period.

- *The organization is committed to continued investment in collecting the data.* Metrics are captured over medium to long periods of time (e.g., monthly over one or more years). Thus, your organization will need to collect data for a minimum agreed-upon time period (e.g., two years) without changes to the underlying data or collection frequency.
- *The data has consistent, defined units of measurement that can be relied upon to aggregate the data.* For example, the formats of the response scales for the customer satisfaction survey should remain consistent. Additionally, the tables in the data warehouse containing responses should only change when necessary and with sufficient warning, allowing you to modify queries and dashboards.
- *The data is high-quality and accurate.* You and your stakeholders should be able to trust that the values are correct representations of the information collected. If there is poor-quality data (e.g., wrong data types, invalid, or duplicate records—see figure 7.7), appropriate steps should be in place to correct for problems that would affect your metric values.

	ticket_id	customer_id	category	priority	status	created_date
0	1527	cid_901	General	Low	Open	2023-06-10
1	1643	cid_986	General	Low	Closed	2023-05-17
2	3390	cid_569	General	High	Open	1023-01-01
3	4389	cid_754	Billing	Low	Resolved	2023-05-28
4	4389	cid_886	Product Inquiry	High	Open	2023-06-07

Figure 7.7 **This dataset contains duplicate primary keys (`ticket_id`) and a bad date value that can degrade the quality of any metrics created.**

ACHIEVABLE

Your organization's goals using metrics should be *attainable,* given the available resources. Organizational performance and accountability metrics can be highly motivating *if* teams believe they can be achieved. An overly ambitious or unattainable target can be frustrating and demoralizing, leading to burnout and lower performance for employees and teams. On the contrary, setting goals that are too easy is unlikely to create meaningful improvement.

Setting achievable and realistic goals requires balance and continuous iteration. You and your stakeholders may easily see that a "100% customer retention rate" metric is unrealistic. However, figuring out an appropriate target requires more understanding of your customers and their needs. If you don't have a concrete understanding of the actions that will contribute to your churn rate, you are unlikely to influence it.

In general, the following information is necessary to set appropriate, achievable targets:

- An understanding of long-term trends in your proposed metric over long periods of time (ideally, at least two years so you can compare seasonal changes).
- Benchmark comparisons of your proposed metric for organizations with similar characteristics (e.g., the same industry, size, geography, and type of service). These benchmarks are valuable in understanding the range of feasible targets for your metric of interest. Figure 7.8 shows an example of how a metric and benchmark might be visualized within an organization.
- An understanding of factors that correlate with or predict your proposed metric. If you wish to set targets for improving a metric's value, your organization needs to understand what strategic actions will enable them to achieve those targets.
- Information about key factors outside of your control that affect your organization, its key metrics, and targets you set. For example, production targets at a clothing manufacturer will typically be lowered when there are shortages of necessary materials.

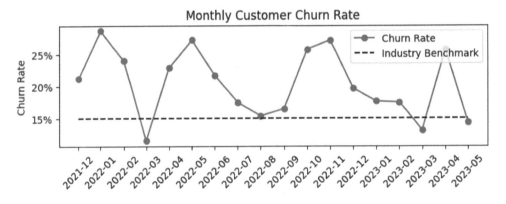

Figure 7.8   This chart shows a company's customer churn rate compared to an industry benchmark. Here, churn tends to be higher than the benchmark, which suggests there may be room for improvement in the customer retention rate.

We will discuss strategies for establishing baselines and identifying the benchmarks necessary to set achievable goals in section 7.2.2.

RELEVANT

Coss-functional investment is required to develop metrics, communicate them, and use them to continuously monitor progress. For an organization to derive value from this effort, a metric should align with the organization's strategic goals and priorities. It should directly relate to the area measured and provide meaningful insights that contribute to decision-making and performance for the organization.

Organizations can easily determine the relevance of their *performance metrics*. These metrics are tied to the bottom line (e.g., finances, efficiency, and customers). Identifying the most relevant *strategy* and *accountability* metrics requires additional analysis to understand the relationship between these metrics and overall performance outcomes.

For example, an engineering team is interested in understanding its effectiveness in supporting the organization's goals. Leadership proposes looking at the *total lines of code* written by every engineer each quarter to measure productivity. While this is easily measurable, and the team can set targets against it, those targets are unlikely to produce meaningful outcomes for the organization. Lines of code written do *not* directly measure the software's performance, usability, or user value and don't provide actionable insights for product development. Instead, the engineering team will likely benefit from focusing on metrics that capture well-defined indicators of success for their users.

The examples in table 7.3 show that a measure can be specific, measurable, achievable, and still *irrelevant* to the organization's goals. Often, irrelevant metrics are chosen due to their convenience, availability, and perceived association with the actions taken by individuals and teams. This can lead to months of wasted effort trying to achieve goals that do not create the desired effect on the organization. Be cautious to ensure that a metric meets *all* the criteria of the SMART framework we have covered thus far before moving to the final step!

Table 7.3   Be prepared to investigate the relevance of your metrics and ensure they are tied to the success of your team and organization.

Domain	Not relevant	Relevant
Engineering	Number of lines of code	Defects per line of code
Product	Number of features developed	Customer retention rate
Marketing	Number of social media followers	Customer acquisition cost (CAC)
Finance	Employee absence rate	Gross profit margin

TIME-BOUND

A metric should have a *defined period of time* for its measurement and goal-setting. A metric should be linked to a specific timeframe, such as daily, weekly, monthly, or quarterly. This allows teams and organizations to monitor and compare metrics to determine progress. Establishing clear time periods for metric targets (e.g., results reported at the end of the quarter) creates a sense of urgency. It helps teams prioritize work and allocate resources based on progress toward the goal.

Setting time-bound metrics requires understanding the timespan in which the underlying behavior changes. As an analyst, you should expect to account for a range of factors related to the time series data of your metric:

- *The time it takes to complete the behavior or process affects the time period you should choose for your metric.* If you are creating a metric for the time to complete a workflow that takes an average of two months, you will likely need to aggregate the data by quarter instead of weekly or monthly to see meaningful changes.

- *The expected length for initiatives intended to influence metric targets should be considered when choosing the time period.* If you are running an A/B test with an expected duration of two weeks, a quarterly metric may not be at the appropriate granularity to represent any real effects of the test.
- *Many processes have seasonal variation that creates recurring daily, weekly, or monthly fluctuations.* You must consider an aggregation period that removes the seasonality to set actionable targets.
- *In addition to seasonal patterns, metrics vary in stability across different periods.* If you want to set targets that you can reliably achieve, you will need to find a time period that mitigates instability without eliminating variability. This can be seen clearly in figure 7.8, where the customer churn rate has a lot of random variation, making it difficult to set goals for an individual month.

While many problems can be mitigated using a larger time period (e.g., monthly instead of weekly), doing so can obscure the effects of actions taken to affect the metric. An initiative that starts in the third month of a quarter will have minimal effect on that quarter's metric, and it may take the entire *next* quarter to see results. The best time period to choose will depend on the process, your organization's needs, and the shape of the data. Table 7.4 provides some examples of appropriate time periods for different metrics.

Table 7.4   Recommended considerations when choosing a time period for metric aggregation

Time period	Visible seasonality	When to use	When to avoid
Daily	Weekly, monthly	Short-term tracking, processes needing a quick response	Long-term tracking
Weekly	Quarterly, yearly	Short- to medium-term tracking where daily data contains too much noise	Long-term tracking, short-term tracking where daily fluctuations are meaningful
Monthly	Yearly, multi-year	Medium- to long-term tracking and forecasting	Short-term tracking and multi-year tracking (3+ years)
Quarterly	Multi-year	Long-term tracking and forecasting	Short-term tracking

Creating SMART metrics at a software company

In this chapter's case study, Alex is a sales analyst at a high-growth SaaS (software as a service) company. The sales team is looking to expand its base of potential customers but has struggled to determine which marketing efforts are most effective. Alex is tasked with researching and proposing a metric to address this problem, and he decides to apply the SMART framework to evaluate potential metrics.

- *Specific*—Alex recognizes that the sales team needs a metric that reflects the effect of marketing efforts on the sales team's processes, specifically. Thus, he decides to focus on whether sales leads are *qualified* (likely to purchase the software). He proposes a "Percentage of Leads Qualified for Sales" metric.
- *Measurable*—Alex determines that the Percentage of Leads Qualified for Sales metric can be quantified by tracking the number of leads originating from each marketing source that the sales team validates as high quality (Qualified Sales Leads). This is available using the organization's system for recording lead source data.
- *Achievable*—Alex proposes implementing the new metric using existing processes for tracking leads. The only change required would be to ensure that the sales team tracks the factors in the system that determine whether a lead is *qualified*. He notes that the team can easily be trained, but the data is manually entered and may need to be monitored for quality.
- *Relevant*—Alex is confident that the proposed metric directly addresses the sales team's challenge of determining the effectiveness of marketing efforts. It can provide insights into where the best leads are coming from, enabling more targeted and effective marketing.
- *Time-bound*—Alex proposes tracking the metric monthly for three months to gather enough data for the initial analysis. He knows all of the company's sales metrics are evaluated monthly or quarterly and that too few sales are made every week for a more granular time period to be valuable. After the initial period, he proposes evaluating the metric's effectiveness with the marketing team and making any necessary adjustments.

RECAP

Designing effective metrics requires strategic consideration of your organization's goals, performance, and the meaning of success. Applying a clear and concise framework like SMART ensures that the metrics you choose align with those goals and are quantifiable, attainable, and meaningful in the long term. Overall, the SMART framework offers a clear structure for the research and development of metrics, which can otherwise be ambiguous and challenging.

7.2.2 Establishing baselines and targets

Creating SMART metrics at an organization requires a lot of background information to set goals and take action to achieve them. After identifying a metric, it's necessary to establish the *current baseline state* to understand performance levels before any changes or interventions are made. This serves as the starting point for strategic decision-making. Determining appropriate baseline values for your metrics involves thoroughly analyzing historical data, peer-reviewed research, and industry standards where available.

The analysis in creating metrics baselines creates structure and clarity for your performance improvement efforts. It allows your stakeholders to build a shared understanding of previous trends, user behavior, and external processes related to your organization's goals. From this data-informed perspective, teams can more easily align on what's possible to achieve and with what effort.

ANALYZE HISTORICAL DATA

Once you have proposed a *specific* and *measurable* metric, an analyst's role is to comprehensively explore historical data on the underlying measure. This allows you to build subject matter expertise in the behavior being represented and recommend strategic approaches to move the needle on the metric. The resulting insights can help determine if your targets are *achievable*, as well as what *time aggregation* is most appropriate and will continue to remain useful in the long term.

Analyzing historical data for a proposed metric requires examining the data from *many* different perspectives. It involves investigating the shape, trends, anomalies, segments, time-series data, and correlations with other known measures and metrics. No two analyses are identical since your findings will lead you toward more granular investigations. At a minimum, I recommend considering the following questions when examining historical metric data:

- *What is the shape of the data?* To visualize the distribution, look at the data using a histogram or boxplot. Is the data skewed, normally distributed, or neither? How concentrated is the data around the median (also known as *kurtosis*)? These characteristics will tell you what's common and possible regarding metric values.
- *Are there outliers in the data?* If so, in which direction? Are they extreme enough to skew the mean of your dataset aggregated for a given time period? Atypical records in your distribution tell you about subsets of users or customers that may be falling through the cracks or that are superusers of your product or service.
- *Are there differences between segments?* Consider how your organization divides its customers and users (e.g., company size, geographic region, age group). How your organization is already partitioning its user base is a great starting point for investigating differences in new metrics. Try comparing measures of central tendency and overlapping distributions between each segment to understand where meaningful differences exist and whether they support existing hypotheses about those segments.
- *How does the data change over time?* Metric values are unlikely to stay constant over the long periods over which they grew and evolved. Try partitioning your data into years or other meaningful time periods. Do you notice any new trends?
- *How do metric values change over a customer or user's tenure with your organization?* What trends do you see if you start calculating data from when a person joins your application, purchases a product or service, or engages with your organization? For example, do new customers have lower scores on your metric than loyal, tenured customers? Are there clear trends in the first 7, 30, 60, or 90 days when someone is a customer with you?
- *Are metric scores correlated with any of the following?*
  - Time of year (month number, week number), indicating seasonality

– Length of time as a customer, indicating growth or decline by tenure with your organization
– User activity metrics (e.g., number of weekly active days), indicating a relationship with one or more other activity and usage behaviors

Let's import a customer activity dataset to see how we can examine a metric with these steps. Each dataset row has the number of days out of the month that the customer logged in. We also have information on each customer's region as a potential segment:

```
import pandas as pd
import matplotlib.pyplot as plt          Import the pandas and
import seaborn as sns                    seaborn libraries.

logins = pd.read_csv("customer_logins.csv")        Read the customer
logins["month"] = pd.to_datetime(logins["month"], format="%Y-%m-%d")   activity metric dataset.
print(logins.head())     Print the first five
                         rows of the dataset.      Convert the month column to
                                                   a datetime for later use.
```

This is the resulting output:

```
   customer_id       region      month  login_days
0           93       Europe  2020-01-01          21
1          346       Europe  2020-01-01          12
2          404         Asia  2020-01-01          22
3          347  North America  2020-01-01         15
4          403         Asia  2020-01-01          30
```

We can start exploring patterns in the metric data by generating a new column representing the *percentage* of days in a month that a customer has logged in, standardizing for the slight variation in days per month. We can then generate a histogram of the percentage values recorded *per customer per month*:

```
                                  Calculate the number of        Calculate the
                                  days in each month.        percentage of active
                                                                days in a month.
logins["n_days"] = logins["month"].dt.days_in_month
logins["login_days_pct"] = logins["login_days"]/logins["n_days"]

sns.histplot(x=logins["login_days_pct"], bins=32)       Create a histogram
plt.title("Distribution of the % of Days Active Per Month")   of percentage
plt.xlabel("% of Days Active")                          values.
plt.ylabel("# of Records")
```

The histogram in figure 7.9 shows that most customers are active between 25% and 75% of the days in the month. There are potentially two or more modes in this wide distribution. Very few customers have months when their activity is above 80% or below 20%.

Let's create a chart of the *count* of active days broken out by the region segment provided in the dataset to provide a more nuanced view compared to the original histogram:

```
sns.histplot(x=logins["login_days"], hue=logins["region"], bins=31)
```

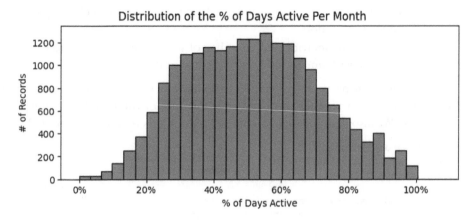

Figure 7.9 A histogram of the percent of active days in a month shows a possible bimodal distribution

We can see in figure 7.10 that breaking out the metric values by segment adds *a lot* of additional nuance. There are distinct underlying distributions for each region. Customers in Asia seem to have the highest median percentage of active days, followed by North America. Customers in South America tend to be the least active. As part of the research into establishing baselines, this finding suggests that the metric should have *separate targets and tracking* for each region.

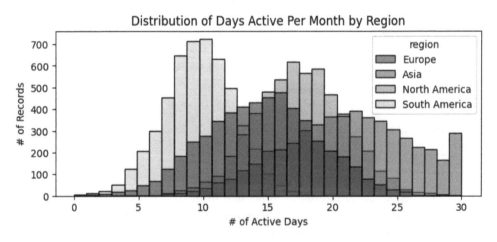

Figure 7.10 Histograms of active days broken out by region segment to better understand the data

Next, we can explore the time series data broken out by the region segment. We'll start by looking at values over the month across all three years in the dataset:

```
avg_logins = (                    ⟵┐ Calculate the average
                                      │ monthly logins by region.
    logins.groupby(["month", "region"])["login_days_pct"].mean().reset_index()
)

sns.lineplot(x="month",          ⟵┐ Plot the average monthly
y="login_days_pct",                │ logins over time.
hue= "region",
data=avg_logins)
plt.xlabel("Month")
plt.ylabel("Avg. % Days Active")
plt.title("Average % of Monthly Active Days Over Time")
```

The data in figure 7.11 shows apparent differences between regions that remain stable over the three years in this dataset. There is some random fluctuation but no discernable trend from one month to another. We cannot say there's evidence of any increase or decrease that has occurred throughout the timespan measured.

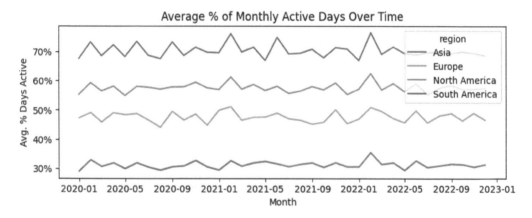

Figure 7.11   Average percentage of monthly active days, aggregated by month across three years

Next, let's investigate potential seasonal trends by aggregating the data monthly and yearly. In order to make the chart easier to interpret, we will also convert the month numbers to names:

```
logins["month_num"] = logins["month"].dt.month     ⟵┐ Save the month and
logins["year"] = logins["month"].dt.year             │ year as new columns.

avg_logins_m = (                                   ⟵┐
    logins.groupby(["year",                          │ Calculate the average
    "month_num"])["login_days_pct"].mean().reset_index()  │ logins by month
)                                                    │ number and year.

                                  ⟵┐ Plot the average logins by
                                    │ month names and year.
sns.lineplot(
    x="month_num",
```

```
        y="login_days_pct",
        hue="year",
        data=avg_logins_m
)
plt.xticks(rotation=45)
plt.title("Average % of Monthly Active by Month and Year")
```

Figure 7.12 shows potential seasonality, where the percentage of active days was slightly higher in February compared to other months. However, the difference is marginal and only noticeable given the small *y*-axis range (50%–58%). The trend should be verified with product, marketing, and customer teams to determine if the increased activity aligns with any known reason (e.g., an annual promotion).

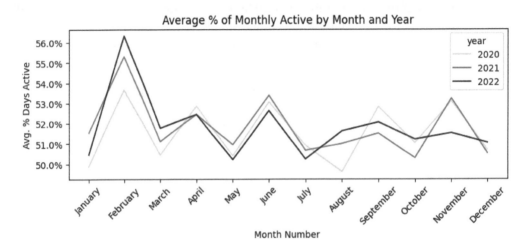

Figure 7.12   **Monthly active days are shown by year and month name to investigate potential seasonality.**

At the organization this dataset is collected from, the next step is to explore potential relationships with existing metrics. Performance metrics such as contract size, add-on purchases, and contract renewal rates should be compared to customer activity rates. Moderate to strong correlations can be the basis for hypotheses about the downstream effect of efforts to increase the new metric.

Correlational relationships can be used to develop hypotheses about *how* to move the needle on customer activity rate goals and what targets might be reasonable. However, correlations with other processes shouldn't be used to establish the *relevance* of a metric. In fact, a metric with extremely high correlations (e.g., 0.8+) is likely redundant and won't add new information to the organization's strategy.

The foundational understanding of historical metrics patterns helps stakeholders use and set goals more effectively. With a standard approach to exploration like the one we just covered, you will enable better, more strategic approaches to understanding the metric and user behavior, and ensuring it meets the SMART criteria.

IDENTIFY APPROPRIATE BENCHMARKS

Benchmarks are reference points used to compare against your metric values. *Benchmarking* refers to the process of comparing your metrics to the reference points you identified. Since a benchmark represents a performance target that has been previously achieved, using these data points serves as a highly effective anchor point when setting your organization's own goals.

Many sources of data can be used as benchmarks to contextualize your metric values:

- *Industry benchmark data* provides an organization with the average performance data for its industry. These benchmarks are available for metrics commonly captured within that industry (e.g., win rates for sales deals, salary ranges for a job your organization is hiring for). This data tends to be collected by industry associations or third-party firms that provide or sell the information at a premium.
- *Peer-reviewed benchmark data* is valuable for organizations in industries that have extensive ongoing research in academia. This type of data is available in academic journals. For example, a healthcare technology company can compare the accuracy of a new device it's developing to diagnostic timelines and accuracy in a database such as PubMed.
- *Governments, NGOs, and non-profits* collect vast data made available for public consumption. If you find value in benchmarking against social and economic indicators, there's a high likelihood you will have information available in your geographic location. Most of these data sources are collected by surveys designed to be population-level estimates of a phenomenon. For example, the unemployment rate metric we reviewed at the beginning of this chapter is updated monthly, along with dozens of other indicators available on the US Bureau of Labor Statistics website (e.g., footwear spending shown in figure 7.13). Measures such as job postings, public health information, population attitudes, public company quarterly earnings, and more are freely available to you and your organization as benchmarks. These high-value data sources can help you understand the broader system in which your organization operates.

Figure 7.13 A footwear company's annual sales compared to a benchmark of estimated footwear spending from the Bureau of Labor Statistics (BLS) Consumer Expenditure Survey

Your organization will benefit from multiple sources of benchmark data for strategic goal-setting. Suppose you can segment and filter benchmark data to better represent your organization's characteristics (e.g., their industry and company size) or their user or customer base (e.g., ages, geographic locations). In that case, your targets will be far more realistic and achievable.

SET REALISTIC TARGETS

Once a baseline is established, the next step is to set targets. A *target* is the desired future state or performance level of a metric that you set, representing an improvement in a process or experience. Targets should be ambitious *and* realistic and must align with the organization's strategic goals.

Organizations complete an in-depth analysis of historical data and benchmark metrics to set informed targets and to understand the landscape in which they operate. This helps ensure that targets are *achievable* and *meaningful* in driving growth and improvement. Consider the following questions when proposing targets to help determine their appropriateness for the teams who will be held to account for their success:

- How confident are teams and stakeholders on what actions to take to drive change? Are there known factors that correlate with or predict change in the metric?
- Is there evidence that the metric is movable? Is the metric stable, or does it fluctuate randomly despite efforts to drive growth?
- Do teams and stakeholders have the capacity to drive growth and improvement at the levels they're targeting? Will they be able to improve the *quality* of their operations, or are they simply expected to take on an additional *quantity* of work?
- Will the targets set motivate the teams to achieve them, or will they reduce morale and degrade their performance capacity if they cannot reach their goals?

For example, figure 7.14 shows a company's goal of adding net new customers that becomes increasingly out of reach over time.

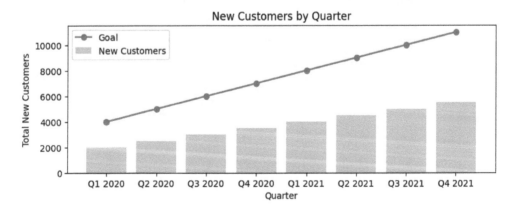

Figure 7.14   A target of achieving two times the quarterly new customer registrations per quarter is unlikely to be successful or to motivate the teams responsible for these goals.

Your analytics team will likely not be setting targets for the *entire* organization, but your expertise on the data will enable you to make informed recommendations on these goals. If the opportunity exists, *it's valuable to advocate for an analytics team member to participate in strategic planning conversations* to inform the goals being set for the organization, teams, and individual employees.

ITERATE

Setting targets is not a one-time task. Organizations and their landscapes constantly evolve, requiring that they revisit and adjust metrics and targets accordingly. This iterative approach keeps metrics relevant and ensures they provide valuable insights and strategic direction.

Targets for improvement should rarely stay static from one time period to the next. For example, a goal of decreasing customer churn by five percent each quarter cannot continue until churn is reduced to nothing. Customers will leave, new customers will join, and users will change their behaviors. It's unrealistic to assume that improvement in a single process will continue indefinitely—you and your stakeholders will be disappointed, and your organization will spend valuable resources on a task with diminishing returns. As part of iterating, shifting focus between relevant processes over time is beneficial. This balanced approach ensures the organization operates with the latest and most pertinent information.

When setting targets, it's worth reminding stakeholders that growth trajectories cannot continue indefinitely (see figure 7.15). Determining *when* your improvement rate will slow is challenging, but knowing it will eventually happen is necessary.

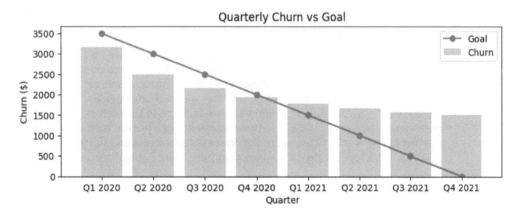

Figure 7.15   Improvement trajectories cannot be linear forever. Within four quarters, a static goal for reducing customer churn quarter over quarter has diminishing returns and eventually becomes unfeasible.

For example, large tech companies like Facebook and Netflix have millions or billions of users. Their metrics will likely include targets intended to drive the growth of their user base and its engagement. Given the scale of these companies, their total user base is, quite literally, limited by the size of the human population with access to the internet. Beyond those levels, they are forced to expand into new industries or accept the limits of their business potential.

Setting up calculations for a metric

Alex's next step is to conduct an exploratory analysis of historical data for the new proposed Percentage of Leads Qualified for Sales metric. This involves reviewing the company's sales data history to understand patterns and trends in the types of leads considered "qualified," how the definition has shifted, and how many leads meet each criterion.

Alex begins by exploring the distribution of the metric using a histogram. He discovers that the metric's distribution has a strong right skew, indicating that very few leads have high scores compared to most leads, whose scores are quite low. When measured over time and grouped by quarter, the percentage of qualified leads fluctuates, but there is no apparent increase or decrease across three years.

Next, Alex breaks out the distribution into three segments relevant to the company: industry, company size, and geographic region. He discovers that the percentage of qualified leads varies widely by industry, with the highest scores seen among technology companies. This suggests that the company is well-positioned to market its product to the technology industry.

Finally, Alex explores the strength of correlations with the Percentage of Leads Qualified for Sales metric and existing sales metrics, such as the win rate (% of leads won) and the average deal size (dollar value of a contract). He discovers a moderate positive correlation between the new metric, close rate, and average deal size. This suggests that leads with a higher score are more likely to convert to sales and that those contracts will be of higher value. This encourages Alex to further recommend the new metric as a potential predictor of sales success.

Alex creates a report with each of the visualizations he created as part of his exploration and an interpretation of each step of the exploration. He presents the findings to the rest of the team. Based on the analysis of historical data and benchmarks for the technology industry's performance, the sales team decides to set a goal of increasing the overall sales qualified lead percentage to the same levels seen among technology companies. Achieving this target will likely involve an increased focus on the technology sector when searching for new sales leads and doing a more in-depth analysis of factors in other industries that have them categorized as qualified leads.

7.2.3 *Exercises*

Now that you've identified the marketing team's performance, organizational, and accountability metrics, let's use them to develop a SMART metric. We will create and validate one or more metrics to represent the broad objective of measuring "website engagement." Assume that you can access website analytics data, including information on page views, session durations, click event data (e.g., for buttons on a page), and summary data about engagement with social media posts:

1 Refine the objective of measuring "website engagement" to be more specific. What are some possible *specific* definitions that will indicate engagement with the website? Based on the available data, are there any pros, cons, or conflicting definitions?

2 Propose one or more ways to measure this objective. Is it already available in the list of metrics and datasets? Is any additional data necessary to collect for your specific definition to be *measurable?*

3 Consider what an improvement would look like for your proposed metric. What would be both meaningful and *achievable?*

4 How can you document where this metric is *relevant* to your organization? How is this important to your team's current goals? What do you hypothesize will be the effect of setting goals for this metric?

5 Propose a specific timeline for achieving this goal. What advantages and disadvantages might exist if your metric is *time-bound* by week, month, or quarter?

6 After assessing each of these criteria, document your SMART metric: What is the name of the metric and its goal that you can communicate to your stakeholders and the broader organization?

7.3 Avoiding metric pitfalls

Not all metrics, or their visual representations, are created equal. While metrics at an organization can guide decision-making and demonstrate progress toward goals, they can also mislead, confuse, and misrepresent reality if not appropriately constructed or displayed. In this section, we'll discuss common mistakes in calculating and presenting metrics that can mask underlying trends, distort findings, and confuse you and your stakeholders. In addition to meeting the SMART criteria, it's necessary to ensure your metric avoids each pitfall in order to provide an accurate direction to your stakeholders.

7.3.1 Representation

A SMART metric can be interpreted and understood differently depending on how it's calculated and presented to end users. While some representations (e.g., mean versus median, bar graph versus line graph) are suitable given the data's shape, some common ways of displaying metrics should always be avoided. It's all too easy for analysts to fall into the trap of using inappropriate representations that can distort your results and detract from the strategic purpose of the metric.

CUMULATIVE VALUES

Metrics that track a count or sum of values over time can be represented as an *incremental* or a *cumulative* calculation. An *incremental metric* includes only new values for a period (e.g., net new monthly sales). This metric type can be directly compared from one time period to another to understand how processes change over time. Incremental metrics are beneficial because they depict fluctuations from one time period to the next, alerting organizations to changes in performance that should inform and motivate actions.

A *cumulative metric* calculates all current and previous values for a given time period. Instead of capturing values for a particular period, a cumulative view of the data shows the total up to that point. While this can be useful for showing total progress over time, cumulative metrics can hide fluctuations or trends that should otherwise motivate strategic choices at the organization (see table 7.5).

Table 7.5   Examples of cumulative metrics and more appropriate incremental alternatives

Cumulative metric	Incremental metric
Total customers by month	Percent change in total customers by month
All-time revenue	Revenue vs. expenses by month

Cumulative metrics document the state of an organization at various points in time. For instance, organizations need to adopt a cumulative view of the data to track the growth of their total recurring revenue and customer base over time. This is illustrated in figure 7.16, where the cumulative total of users each month reflects the user base's current state and overall growth trajectory. To fully understand these trends, the cumulative metric needs to be accompanied by an incremental version of the same metric. We can see that although the user base is growing, the growth *rate* is shrinking. This nuance is harder to discern from the cumulative chart alone.

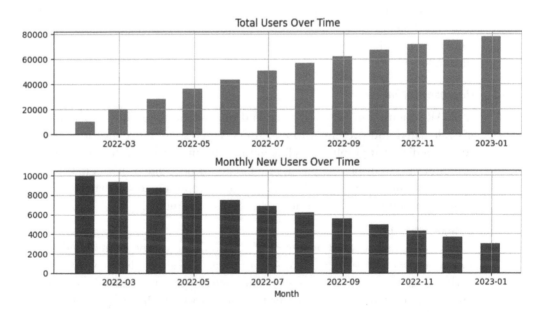

Figure 7.16   A cumulative user count shows the overall growth but may disguise a decrease in growth rate.

When unaccompanied by an incremental calculation, an otherwise SMART metric calculated as a cumulative value can fall into the trap of being a *vanity metric* for an organization. Vanity metrics are data points that look good on paper and are easy to celebrate, but that usually *don't* contribute to actionable insights. A chart with a continually increasing value (e.g., cumulative user base) can be easily celebrated but does *not* inform goals, actions, and strategies.

Ultimately, cumulative metrics are rarely as valuable as analysts and stakeholders believe. They can mistakenly portray areas for concern at an organization in a positive light and often mask subtle trends or shifts in your data. Make sure you accompany cumulative metrics with an *incremental* calculation to ensure your stakeholders know the actual status of goals.

GRANULARITY

Metric development often includes choosing an appropriate *grain* for your data *before* making aggregate calculations. *Granularity* refers to the level of detail available in each row. Like the tradeoffs you make with measures of central tendency (see chapters 4–5), choosing the grain can highlight or minimize different characteristics of the data you present to stakeholders, affecting your decisions.

Organizations differ *widely* in granularity considerations based on their customers, business model, and purpose. The following are some common examples you may encounter in a project:

- In B2B (business-to-business), data is usually collected on *customers* (other businesses) and the *users* of each customer. An analyst must determine whether it's appropriate to calculate a metric at the grain of the user or aggregated at the level of the customer.
- Most organizations collect *geographic information* about their customers and users. Geographic data can be easily aggregated at a variety of grains (e.g., zip code, city, state, country) and types of regions (urban versus rural).
- *Product categories* at companies tend to have multiple levels of specificity and intersecting classifications for tracking and analysis. For example, the database of inventory at a retail company will classify departments by age groups (e.g., children's clothing versus adults) by gender (men versus women) and by type of clothing item (shirt, pants, etc.).

The choice of granularity is ultimately a balancing act. Higher granularity (e.g., zip code instead of state) can offer detailed insights, limiting your ability to identify broader trends. In contrast, lower granularity can obscure trends and hide meaningful subsets of data. As part of your metric explorations, segment your data at various levels of granularity to determine an appropriate *grain* to recommend to your stakeholders.

Let's walk through an example of the exploration and decision process for choosing whether to aggregate data at the user or customer level at a B2B company. The company has several hundred customers across various industries and company sizes.

A sample of the `customers` table in their database is shown in figure 7.17. If the company wants to create and monitor a simple *user activity* metric, it can start by creating an aggregate query that results in the table in figure 7.18.

	id	created_date	status	contract_amount	subscription_type	industry	company_size	referral
0	012	2023-02-17	Churned	13614.88	Pro	Tech	Large	No
1	013	2023-04-18	Active	14798.01	Pro	Tech	Large	Yes
2	014	2023-01-24	Inactive	14781.55	Basic	Finance	Small	Yes
3	015	2023-03-18	Churned	11471.28	Basic	Education	Medium	No
4	016	2023-04-07	Churned	18448.20	Pro	Healthcare	Large	Yes

Figure 7.17   Sample data showing information about customers at a B2B company

	month	total_users	active_users	pct_active_users
0	2022-08	47077	24800	52.679652
1	2022-09	47054	21504	45.700684
2	2022-10	47060	25568	54.330642
3	2022-11	47035	24700	52.514085
4	2022-12	47040	22185	47.161990
5	2023-01	47042	27391	58.226691
6	2023-02	47060	21809	46.342966

Figure 7.18   Example of a monthly active user rate aggregated across all users

Each company in the current `customers` table ranges from 10 to 10,000 employees, shown in the categorical `company_size` column (`Small`=10–99, `Medium`=100–999, `Large`=1,000+). If we take an overall sum for the metric, we are weighting the metric calculation toward the larger customers. Because they have more users, their activity rates will significantly affect the metric more.

To account for the differences in company size, we can *partially aggregate* the data at the company level, generating a user activity score *per company per month.* This intermediary dataset can be aggregated *again* per month overall, effectively removing the weight favoring large companies.

In figure 7.19, each customer is treated as an equal entity in the partially aggregated dataset metric. Assuming the company's strategy is to engage the entire customer base, a metric for average percent of active users by month will provide more accurate and actionable insights on progress toward goals.

	customer_id	month	n_users	n_active_users	pct_active
0	012	2022-08	697	599	0.859397
1	012	2022-09	692	70	0.101156
2	012	2022-10	695	472	0.679137
3	012	2022-11	695	600	0.863309
4	012	2022-12	695	396	0.569784

Figure 7.19 Partially aggregated user activity data by customer and month

COMPOSITE METRICS

A *composite metric*, or an *index*, combines two or more metrics into a single, standard-ized score for reporting to users or stakeholders. These are frequently used when measuring complex processes and reporting on individual metrics might create diffi-culty deriving actionable insights. Theoretically, combining multiple metrics allows an accessible heuristic understanding of the underlying processes being measured.

Indexes are commonly used to report economic and social information, such as the gross domestic product (GDP) provided quarterly by the US Bureau of Economic Analysis. Due to its simplicity and wide use, the percentage change in GDP is comfort-ably reported to general audiences. A shared understanding of the metric is expected; a percentage increase is considered positive, and a decrease is considered negative (see figure 7.20).

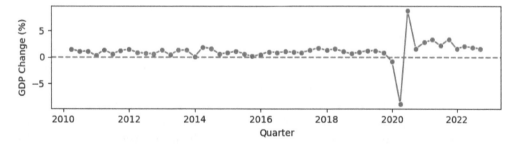

Figure 7.20 The GDP is reported as a dollar value and a percentage value showing relative change from the previous quarter.

Indexes like GDP require extensive research to combine the metrics appropriately. Individual items are expected to vary together, representing the same underlying pro-cess. The reliability indicators we covered in chapter 5 (e.g., inter-item reliability) can be used to identify similar measures that can be used to build a composite scale. How-ever, indexes tend to have serious limitations in the accuracy and actionability of the numbers they provide:

- For each item you add to an index, you reduce the *variability in scores* over time and between entities (e.g., customers, countries). By attempting to simplify the calculation of multiple metrics, you will likely obfuscate valuable trends that you'd otherwise notice in the individual metrics a score is comprised of.

- Including or excluding individual metrics in an index is ultimately an *arbitrary* decision you and your stakeholders have to make. By designing and using an index, especially for internal tracking, you are committing your time to continually iterating on the index based on new findings, processes, or services offered at the organization.

- Depicting a *balance* of competing processes can be challenging. You can create and report on counter-metrics (more on those later in this chapter), but they're unlikely to carry the same perceived importance as the actual index.

Each of these limitations is true for the GDP calculation, which calculates the value of all goods and services produced within a specific period. It's considered a critical indicator of economic health. Still, it *excludes* information such as wealth distribution, the depreciating value of goods produced, or goods and services provided in the black market. Each of these potentially affects the health of the economy and the quality of life of individuals and communities represented in the GDP calculation. In theory, any of these *can* be included in the calculation. However, no single index will provide an entire picture of the economy and still be responsive to change.

Unless your organization has vast resources to dedicate to the research necessary to develop an appropriate, data-informed index, I strongly recommend avoiding creating them. Indexes and composite metrics sound appealing to stakeholders due to their perceived simplicity and ability to represent the concept or process you are measuring heuristically. Still, they often detract from the ability to make data-informed decisions.

COUNTER METRICS

When tracking a comprehensive range of important processes in an organization, you will discover that many appear to be in conflict with each other. For example, a software company may have the following two goals: improving the speed in which new features are launched in the application, and reducing the number of bugs reported in the application by customers. These are examples of *counter metrics* or *guardrail metrics*, which serve as checks and balances and help uncover potential negative consequences from singularly focusing on a goal.

Counter metrics are identified in the *context* of a new metric being designed. They're often existing metrics in the organization that are often monitored for other goals. Identifying appropriate counter metrics is a qualitative process involving critical consideration of your new metric and its behavior or process. Ask your stakeholders questions: What could go wrong if we focus only on this metric? Where might we be sacrificing quality in pursuit of quantity? What processes are potentially in opposition to this metric and still important?

Consider the following examples:

- A customer support team has a metric tracking the number of tickets resolved in under 24 hours. As a counter metric, the team also reports on customer satisfaction scores to ensure they aren't sacrificing the quality of support in pursuit of quantity.

- A software engineering team tracks the number of new features shipped, which is considered one measure of team productivity. As a counter metric, the team also tracks the number of new bugs introduced to ensure that the quality of their code isn't sacrificed to increase productivity.
- A non-profit focusing on education tracks the college attendance rates of high school students participating in their programs. As a counter metric, they monitor college completion and student employment rates in their field of study. Although the non-profit does not have programs that directly affect these processes, they consider it essential to monitor students over the long term to ensure their success.

When preparing your metric deliverables (dashboards, reports, presentations), it's strongly recommended that you incorporate a visualization of the chosen counter metric into that deliverable, explaining the counter metric and its rationale (see figure 7.21). Additionally, counter metrics should always be evaluated alongside any metrics or measures for experiments, A/B tests, or evaluations. Adding a section to a dashboard to visualize all counter metrics with an explanation of *why* they were chosen will empower you and your stakeholders to iterate on them over time and keep track of the complete picture of your goals.

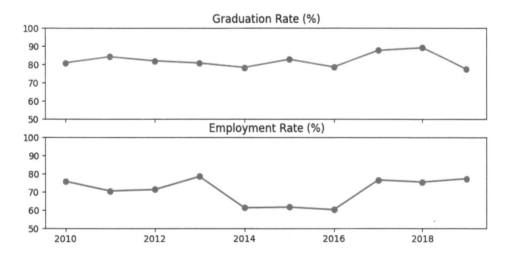

Figure 7.21   A simple visualization of the non-profit's graduation rate and an employment counter metric

7.3.2   *Visualization*

At its core, a metric is a tool for telling a valuable story to your stakeholder, and how you visually depict it is a *massive* part of that narrative. A well-chosen visualization can speak for itself, highlighting trends that would otherwise take paragraphs to explain. However, poor representation of a metric can easily undo all the work you have done to ensure your metrics are interpretable and actionable.

Ultimately, the topics covered in this section apply to data visualization and storytelling. We will focus primarily on the representation of metrics as *time series data* (data presented over time, usually with the time variable as the *x*-axis). However, any type of visualization that isn't time-bound can still benefit from these considerations.

PICKING THE WRONG CHART

Inappropriate chart selection is *very* common. If you pay attention to news segments reporting survey results, studies, or other data, you will notice that the graphs chosen are not always the best choice for the data. Not all charts are appropriate for metrics, and many chart selection decisions can negatively affect your ability to interpret the data:

- A chart can easily *oversimplify* the trends you want to depict with your metric. A single bar or line graph may be helpful for an *overall* picture of your metric across the organization (e.g., figures 7.8 and 7.16), but be prepared for different departments and teams to want a more granular view of the metric (e.g., by region, industry, etc.).
- Conversely, a chart can easily *overcomplicate* a trend if too much information is included or if it's not a visualization that your stakeholders are familiar with. If

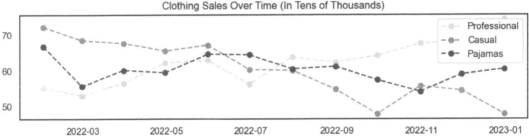

Figure 7.22   Line graphs are typically easier to interpret when visualizing trends between groups over time.

you plan to break out your metric by segments, I strongly recommend using a line graph instead of a bar graph (see figure 7.22). A grouped or stacked bar graph shown over time can be challenging to interpret, compared to following the growth trajectory of a set of lines, provided they are unique in color or representation.

- It's easy to pick the *wrong chart* when developing a dashboard or a report to track metrics over time. Many chart types available in business intelligence tools are tempting, especially when looking to showcase your work. However, if you expect that you'll have to explain the chart's contents to your executives, then it's probably worth using a simpler visualization in deliverables. The type of analysis you perform should motivate your chart selection—not the other way around.

Usually, a grouped bar or line graph is the best choice for appropriately visualizing a metric. Depending on the calculation, you can easily group or stack data, and most of your stakeholders can interpret the graphs without aid. Avoiding more complex charts will minimize the follow-up necessary for you and your team.

DISTORTING THE AXES

Another common visualization pitfall is the misuse of the *y*-axis. The *y*-axis represents the *scale* of your metric, which shows your stakeholders the size of fluctuations over time. It's incredibly easy to distort the meaning of change from one time period to another by manipulating the *y*-axis (see figure 7.23).

There are several key ways in which *y*-axis adjustments can distort metrics:

- *Truncating the y-axis*, or trimming the upper and lower limits, can exaggerate variations in the data. This can make trends appear more influential than in reality, potentially motivating decisions based on only minor differences. This is important to monitor, *even when it's not done intentionally*, as data visualization tools use the range of the dataset to set the *y*-axis limits. If the full range of values extends beyond the minimum and maximum, you must set the limits manually.

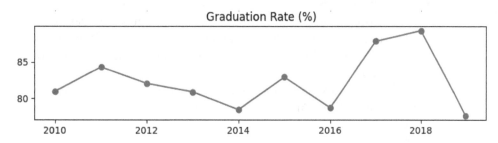

Figure 7.23 This figure shows the same data as figure 7.21, but with the default *y*-axis limits set using `matplotlib` based on the minimum and maximum values in the dataset. These defaults exaggerate the perception of fluctuation in the data.

- *Extending the y-axis* beyond the actual range of values can diminish the ability to perceive trends or fluctuations. Many metrics with an actual minimum and maximum (e.g., percentage values) will only ever return values for a limited subset of that entire range. The graduation rate metric in figures 7.21 and 7.23 can theoretically range from 0% to 100% (see figure 7.24), but a decade's annual data shows no values below 75%. If the upper and lower bounds of the y-axis are set at 0% and 100%, respectively, your stakeholders are unlikely to see fluctuations that may *actually* be meaningful and important to discover. In figure 7.21, the axis is set between 50% and 100%, which depicts the scope of fluctuations without over- or under-representing changes over time.

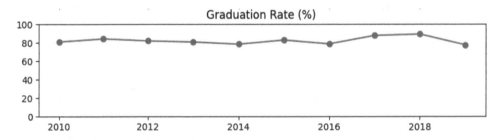

Figure 7.24   The same graduation rate metric appears to have little to no fluctuations when the y-axis limits are extended to 0% and 100%.

- *Using a dual y-axis* can be useful in some contexts, such as showing the relationship between two metrics on the same scale over time. More often than not, a dual y-axis will confuse your stakeholders and require far more time and effort to interpret than if you set up two separate charts. Your stakeholders will assume that the two metrics are on the same scale (e.g., inches, dollars, or percentage points) and may misinterpret the strength of correlations based on visual observation of fluctuations.
- *Nonlinear and logarithmic scales* are often used to visualize data fluctuating over several orders of magnitude (e.g., population growth). Data presented on a logarithmic scale gives the appearance of being linear. While this can make it easier to depict the full range of values, logarithmic scales easily distort the perception of the variation that occurs. These should be used *sparingly* (only when it's impossible to interpret a linear scale), and they should be accompanied with clear interpretations of the scale for your stakeholders (see figure 7.25).

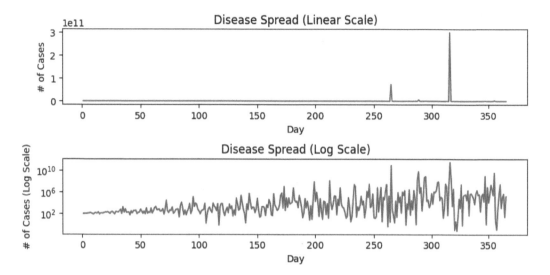

Figure 7.25   Logarithmic scales can help visualize metrics with exponential fluctuations in the data, but they should be used with caution.

Identifying the best counter metrics

As he wraps up the development of the Percentage of Leads Qualified for Sales metric, Alex discovers several steps he needs to take to ensure the usability and effectiveness for his team.

Initially, Alex considers showing a cumulative view of the metric to highlight the company's overall growth of qualified leads. However, he realizes that the cumulative view masks a *seasonal* fluctuation, where more leads generated in the summer months are considered qualified. He decides to share the cumulative qualified leads as a single value to celebrate the team's work and an incremental view of the metric for each time period.

Next, Alex explores the best possible visualizations to show differences in qualified sales leads from month to month. He uses a line graph because it allows him to easily visualize changes broken out by different segments valuable to the team (e.g., region, industry).

Beyond these final considerations, Alex knows the team could lose sight of other valuable processes if they focus solely on this new metric. To balance the indicator, he proposes a monthly counter metric to report with Percentage of Leads Qualified for Sales. The first is the *Lead Response Time*, which tracks the time it takes to contact a potential lead after being identified. This ensures that the team doesn't solely pursue qualified leads at the cost of their prompt response time for *all* leads.

Alex's diligent approach is clear in his presentation to the team, motivating them to adopt the new metric and counter metric to track the success of their efforts.

7.3.3   *Exercises*

Let's continue with the SMART metric you designed in the previous section:

1 Conduct an online search of "website engagement metrics." What types of results do you get?

2 Conduct background research to understand other definitions of website engagement. Are there articles about how to measure this? How do they compare to your metric?

3 Identify some characteristics of metric examples you discovered in your search. Are they measured by day, week, or month? Are there any notable trends or benchmarks you can find that might be valuable to reference?

4 Are there potential counter metrics you should consider for your SMART metric?

Using the Python environment of your choice (terminal, Jupyter Notebook, etc.), import the `website_engagement.csv` dataset. The following columns are available for analysis:

- `website_engagement`—Measured as a percentage of users active each week.
- `session_duration`—The average duration of a website visit session in minutes.
- `bounce_rate`—The percentage of visitors who navigate away from the site after viewing only one page.
- `email_subscribers`—The cumulative total of email subscribers. There is an incremental version of the column, `new_email_subscribers`.
- `social_media_followers`—The cumulative total of social media followers. There is an incremental version of the column, `new_social_media_followers`.
- `avg_page_views_per_visit`—The average number of pages viewed per user session.
- `total_items_purchased`—The total items purchased by users in the given week.
- `total_sales`—The total dollar value of all sales in the given week.

You must have `numpy`, `matplotlib`, and `pandas` installed to complete the following activity:

1 Establish a thorough set of baseline information for website engagement. What trends (e.g., seasonal, distribution shape, longitudinal changes) exist in the website engagement metric that stakeholders should be aware of?

2 Are there relationships with other metrics valuable to note to stakeholders?

3 Identify one or more potential counter metrics in the dataset. How can focusing solely on website engagement negatively affect other business areas?

4 Create one or more visualizations for stakeholders to monitor `website_engagement`. Include information on any benchmarks they should be aware of, and watch the chosen counter metrics appropriately alongside the metric.

5 Using your baseline information, benchmarks, and valuable information you have gathered in this process, propose the first *achievable* goal for your stakeholders. How much should they strive to increase website engagement?

Summary

- *Metrics* are standardized quantitative measures tracked over time. They're frequently used to track progress, outcomes, and activities related to the organization's and its teams' performance.
- Metrics inform decision-making at multiple levels. *Performance metrics* are the broadest category an organization uses to understand its progress toward goals. Some examples include revenue, lifetime value of customers, and operational efficiency.
- *Organizational strategy metrics* track specific components of an organization's performance, such as product behaviors, customer sentiment, and market performance. Metrics in this category help different teams at an organization understand the landscape they operate in and make appropriate data-informed decisions.
- *Accountability metrics* determine the effectiveness and productivity of individuals and teams. These metrics hold individuals *accountable* and guide performance reviews, bonuses, or training.
- The *SMART framework* is an essential guide for defining effective metrics. To ensure your organization can monitor and make strategic data-informed decisions, each metric at your organization should be *specific* (clearly defined), *measurable* (quantifiable), *achievable* (realistic and within reach), *relevant* (aligned with the organization's goals), and *time-bound* (aggregated at an appropriate timeframe).
- Understanding how to set goals for a metric involves gathering multiple sources of information to establish a *baseline* or a foundational understanding of the metric and its trends. These sources include
  - *Internal, historical data* at the organization explored between segments, over time, and in relation to other business metrics
  - *Benchmarks, or comparison metrics*, often gathered from public sources such as government, industry surveys, or peer-reviewed literature
  - *Initial targets*, which allow you to test your ability to drive change in your metric and achieve goals
- How you *represent* your metric is as important as how you define it. There are many *pitfalls* in calculating and setting up a metric that can diminish the value an organization gains. These are some examples:
  - *Cumulative metrics* can create an illusion of continuous improvement despite declining performance. *Incremental views* of metrics are almost always a more appropriate way to provide a clear picture of trends in performance.

- The *granularity*, or level of detail, in your dataset can significantly affect the interpretability and accountability of a metric. Metrics measured and grouped at a low grain (e.g., geography grouped by country) can obscure critical details, while a highly granular metric (e.g., zip code) can confuse your stakeholders with too much detail. Choosing an appropriate *grain* is a balancing act that requires understanding baseline information.

- A *composite metric* combines two or more metrics to measure complex concepts. These tend to be challenging to interpret and act on, and they may obscure competing trends among the individual metrics. Limit efforts to develop these as much as possible.

- *Counter metrics* safeguard against the potential adverse effects of focusing on only one performance indicator. Each metric should include counter metrics to ensure your organization takes a balanced approach to strategic goal-setting.

- *Visual representation* is critical in communicating information about a metric and its performance. The *wrong chart type* can confuse your stakeholders and draw attention away from trends and differences. *Distorting the axes* on your charts can create the impression that there is a large trend where there is none, and vice versa. Your chart type and axes should be carefully selected and set to display your metric.

Part 3

The analyst's toolbox

The skills we covered in the previous two parts will equip you to handle much of the work you encounter as an analyst. Being able to deliver insightful reports, dashboards, and actionable recommendations will position you as an effective contributor to your organization. But as your career progresses, you'll likely face more complex challenges—problems that require you to think outside the box and step up as both an expert and a leader. That's where the next level of skills comes into play, those beyond the day-to-day responsibilities of an analyst. Since we're striving for mastery, we definitely won't stop now!

This section covers five essential areas that will help you expand your expertise and tackle the evolving demands of modern analytics. First, we'll explore the ethical and legal dimensions of working with sensitive data. Whether it's medical records, financial information, or personal data, understanding practices for responsible analysis is critical to your success.

Next, we'll dive into statistical modeling—a vital tool for making sense of complex data and predicting future outcomes. Whether you're recommending individual actions or generating live predictions for your users, statistical modeling will help you generate valuable insights for your organization.

In the third topic, we'll explore the integration of external data sources. You'll learn how to enrich your analyses by incorporating data from APIs, web scraping, and publicly available datasets. These skills will enable you to extend the reach of your analysis, providing a more comprehensive view of the problems you aim to solve.

Fourth, we'll cover the importance of well-structured data and the tools that enable you to manage your data effectively. We'll cover the strategies for *structuring* data for analysis that are integral to the emerging field of analytics engineering.

Finally, we'll look at the modern ecosystem of tools and technologies you can use for analysis, reporting, and self-service analytics, along with the growing role of AI in analytics.

Navigating sensitive and protected data

8

This chapter covers

- The legal and regulatory landscape of sensitive data analysis
- Identifying and handling key types of protected information
- Applying techniques for anonymization to protect individuals in your datasets
- Analyzing sensitive data in a responsible and ethical manner

Let's talk about ethics. Whether intentional or not, data practitioners can produce unintended consequences for their users and the general population. A set of guidelines, ethical principles, and an understanding of the legal landscape will provide a framework for minimizing the likelihood of causing harm with your work and deliverables.

You may be thinking, "What harm could I possibly cause in my work? I work with spreadsheets, codes, and numbers. I write reports on operational metrics to improve my company's efficiency. How is my work potentially harmful to people?"

Hear me out—there *are* countless tasks and specializations where your work will have few to no implications outside of the daily operational functioning of your organization. Many roles (e.g., financial analysis, operational analysis) and tasks narrow in scope can be multiple degrees removed from the organization's relationship to its end users and target population. However, I invite you to consider that many more areas of your work can affect and influence people in ways you may not know.

Let's look at an example. In 2014, Amazon began developing a machine learning model to review job applicants' resumes and rank their qualifications to reduce time spent on the hiring process. The model was trained using a dataset of resumes received by the company over the previous decade. The training set showed an obvious bias toward male candidates, reflecting the overwhelming male pool of candidates in the tech industry. Thus, the model actively penalized women: attendees of women's colleges and candidates who mentioned anything about "women" systematically received lower scores than those who didn't.

After several attempts to remove the underlying gender bias, Amazon abandoned the project. Due to their inability to control for all possible biases that could occur, the model couldn't be trusted to produce accurate and reliable rankings of candidate qualifications. Amazon ultimately discovered one of the problems with data analysis and data science—the quality and fairness of your output is only as good and unbiased as your input. Recruiters and hiring managers vary in their evaluation of candidate qualifications, and different companies, departments, and teams vary in the qualifications they prioritize in a candidate. In short, there *is* no singular measure of candidate quality.

Decisions made based on data or aided by data have tremendous implications for people's lives. Someone may be rejected from a job, evicted from an apartment, denied a loan, or identified as a suspect in crime—all of which can have lifelong effects on their quality of life. This is true regardless of the complexity of the data or model used—a report you generate, a neural network, or a single bar graph are powerful tools that should be created, interpreted, and disseminated cautiously.

This chapter will cover the tools and knowledge you need to understand the scope of ethical considerations in an analyst's role. We'll review the history of legal precedent that guides research and analysis globally and the recent laws in data privacy and machine learning. You will learn practical steps you can take to protect your data, anonymize it, and responsibly use sensitive information in your analysis.

8.1 Consent in research

Discussions of ethics in science have existed for centuries, roughly coinciding with the Scientific Revolution, which started in the 16th century. With rapid scientific advancement came questions about setting standards for scientific practice [1]. Several key questions were raised that affected how we view science today:

- *How should research subjects be treated?* Scientists needed to develop guidelines for which investigative practices are permissible and which should be avoided at all costs. For example, vivisection (live dissection of animals) sparked debates about the ethical treatment of animals.

- *Who benefits from scientific knowledge and advancements?* Not everyone in society receives the benefits from science equally. Medical advancements and technology often take far longer to be available to those who need them in lower socio-economic classes. Scientists had to reckon with their role and responsibility in making their discoveries (e.g., a cure to a disease) widely accessible.
- *How can scientists be proactive about the misuse of knowledge?* Science and technology can easily have negative, unforeseen consequences. Scientists continue to wrestle with the steps that need to be put in place to mitigate harm and with their degree of responsibility when there are unintended use cases for findings.

Figure 8.1 shows that scientific discoveries can lead to benefits for society or large-scale harm.

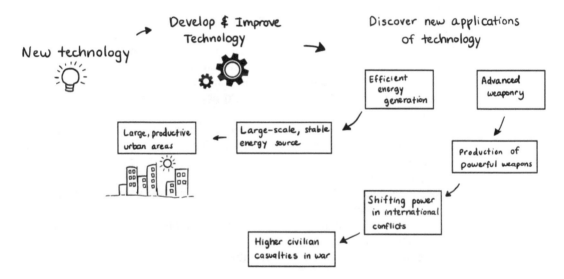

Figure 8.1 The outcomes of scientific discovery can lead society down a path of advancement or collective harm.

As analysts, we operate as the scientists of our organizations. We design and conduct experiments, collect data, and attempt to contribute to the organization's knowledge, which enables it to progress toward its strategic goals. Many of our findings *can* affect our organization's stakeholders, users, and the broader society.

8.1.1 A brief history lesson

As part of the Nuremberg Trials held from 1945 to 1949, the "Doctors' Trials" dealt with war crimes related to medical experimentation conducted in Nazi Germany. The twenty-three doctors on trial were accused of conducting unethical and often deadly medical experiments on inmates in concentration camps. Many of the experiments lacked any scientific purpose and resulted in extreme suffering for people who had no opportunity to consent. Out of the trials, a series of ethical principles known as the Nuremberg Code was developed, and it continues to guide scientific research to this day.

The *Nuremberg Code* is a set of ten principles governing research involving *human subjects* (people). The code actively guides scientific practice, even as methods and tools evolve.

Ten principles of code

The ten principles of the code can be summarized as follows:

1 The person involved in the research should be able to give voluntary consent. They should be provided with sufficient information to understand the research being done so that they can make an informed decision about whether or not to participate.

2 The purpose of the research should be to generate valuable results for the good of society.

3 Experiments should be designed carefully and have a strong justification for human research. Before conducting research with humans, animal studies should be performed in a laboratory where appropriate (e.g., mouse studies).

4 Research conducted should actively avoid physical or psychological harm to participants.

5 It should not be performed if an experiment or research study is expected to cause severe harm (e.g., death or disabling injury).

6 The expected risks from a study or experiment should never outweigh the expected benefits and importance to society.

7 Researchers should adequately plan study procedures to mitigate any possible risk of harm to participants.

8 Experiments should only be conducted by researchers and scientists with appropriate qualifications in the field.

9 Participants should have the right to withdraw their participation in a study or experiment.

10 Researchers should be prepared to end an experiment if continuing may cause harm to the participants.

Outside academic and clinical settings, *participants* generally refers to your organization's users, customers, or target population. Their satisfaction and positive experience are necessary for the organization to meet its goals, succeed, and grow. Much of the work we do as analysts can amount to a large-scale *field study* (conducted outside of a laboratory in a natural setting), which makes ethical guidelines, such as the Nuremberg Code, essential to reference in our decisions. These are a few examples of its application:

- A nonprofit is preparing to launch a new youth after-school program for its target population. Families are provided detailed information about the program's activities, time commitment, and expected outcomes to inform their participation decisions.

- An analytics team at a financial institution carefully reviews results from statistical tests comparing loan repayment rates. If they discover differences in repayment rates by demographic groups or locations, they make sure to thoroughly investigate other factors (e.g., an economic downturn or natural disaster) in their model that are known to correlate with individual characteristics among their user base. This diligence ensures that people are not systematically excluded from loan opportunities in the future.

- A product analytics team collects tracking data about user visits to, and page views of, their website. Each record includes metadata about the user, including their location and IP address, which can easily be used to identify individual users. To protect privacy, the team masks this personally identifiable information in their data warehouse.

While the Nuremberg Code was developed in the context of medical experimentation, its principles resonate powerfully in our data-driven work. Just as the principles in the Code emphasize dignity, autonomy, and well-being, data analysts have a responsibility to uphold privacy, agency, and the rights and needs of those whose data we analyze.

8.1.2 Informed consent

At the beginning of most surveys, respondents are provided with summary information about what they can expect from their participation. These summaries usually include information about the survey length, the topics covered, and contact information for the research team. Some vary in the length and depth of information provided, but all are designed to give you the information you need to inform your decision to participate. In research settings, these are known as *informed consent documents.*

INFORMED CONSENT DOCUMENTS

Informed consent documents in research are formal written agreements providing potential participants with the information they need to consent to participate in a study. This document's primary purpose is to protect participants by ensuring they have all the relevant information they need about the research, its potential risks and benefits (more on that in the next section), and their rights as participants.

Informed consent documents typically follow a standardized format, highlighting several key points that apply to most academic and non-academic research projects. This format is intended to give researchers the structure they need to ensure all critical information is shared with participants.

To create an informed consent document, you should include the following components:

- *Title and objectives*—Begin the document by stating the name and objectives of the research project. The reason for pursuing this project should be apparent and easily understood by anyone reading the document.

- *Description of the project*—Provide a summary of the research project. Include precise details on all steps participants will take and the expected duration of their participation in the project. To respect their time, be realistic about the expected time commitment and steps involved. Do not leave out key details or underestimate the time here!

- *Potential risks*—Explain any potential risks, comforts, or side effects that participants may experience from participating in the project. These should include risks to physical, emotional, and psychological well-being, regardless of how long any discomfort or negative effects are expected to last. Be considerate of any sensitive topics you may be covering.

- *Potential benefits*—Explain any potential benefits that participants may receive from the research project, as well as potential benefits to others (e.g., society, the user base) that may be gained as a result of the research. As part of potential benefits, offering participants an opportunity to receive a copy of the project's results is often valuable.

- *Alternative procedures*—Where applicable, inform participants about any available alternative procedures, treatments, or interventions that can be advantageous to them and potentially pursued in lieu of your research project. This is primarily relevant in clinical and nonprofit settings that provide a service to participants as part of the project.

- *Confidentiality*—Describe the measures your team, institution, or organization takes to keep their information secure. Be clear with participants about what personal information you will collect and store and any steps you will take to maintain their anonymity in your analysis. This should include details about your organization's data anonymization, storage, and security practices.

- *Compensation*—Include details on any compensation participants will receive for their involvement. This can be monetary, store credit, or otherwise, as appropriate to your organization.

- *Voluntary participation and withdrawal*—Ensure that participants know completing the research study is voluntary and that they can withdraw from the research at any time without penalty.

In addition to including each of these sections, informed consent documentation should be well-tailored, readable, and *easily accessible* to the participants you are researching. It should be delivered *before* the research starts, and participants should have clear and reasonable options to opt out of participation without negative consequences. If the informed consent documentation is hidden in a lengthy and complicated agreement outlining the terms of service of using your product or software, participants will be unlikely to understand what they are agreeing to.

OBTAINING CONSENT

In practice, many research projects outside clinical settings require only a summary to set expectations with your participants appropriately. What matters is the effort and intention you put into this process: be clear, stick to the procedures you outline, and honor your commitments to maintain the privacy and confidentiality of your participants. Your clear and honest communication goes a *long* way in establishing and maintaining the reputation of your team and organization. An example of an informed consent document that aims to meet these standards is shown in figure 8.2.

User Experience Feedback on the Application Redesign

Summary
Thank you for agreeing to participate in our survey. The goal of this project is to gather insights about the ease of use, look and feel, and areas of improvement for the application redesign that was recently launched. You will be asked to complete a survey containing 8 questions about each area of the application that was redesigned. The survey should take approximately 15–20 minutes to complete.

Risks and Benefits
By participating in this survey, you are providing valuable feedback that will influence future iterations of the application design. We don't anticipate any risks associated with participating, but you are free to skip any questions that you are uncomfortable with or unable to answer. Your participation is voluntary, and you may also exit the survey at any time.

Confidentiality
Your responses are anonymous unless you opt to provide your contact information at the end of the survey for follow-up or participation in other research. The results of this survey will be stored securely in our data warehouse and only accessed by the product analytics team. Only aggregated data without identifying information will be used in internal presentations and reports.

Contact
If you have questions or concerns related to the survey, please contact Alex Johnson, the lead analyst on this project, at alex.johnson@company.com.

If you agree to participate, please click "Next" to begin the survey.

Figure 8.2   An informed consent document for a survey conducted by a product analytics team

Ideally, an informed consent process should be used where your users, stakeholders, or other target audiences are asked to participate in research. Consider the following example: a marketing analytics team is researching trends in awareness, opinions, and experiences with recent advancements in artificial intelligence. The team hypothesizes that the responses they receive will vary widely, from excitement about its potential to fears about job loss and academic integrity. They know some participants may have had increased stress or changes associated with their employment, which can be tied to this topic. Given that they expect an emotionally charged set of responses, the team ensures that their informed consent document includes the following:

- A clear description of the types of questions participants will be asked, such as their fears, concerns, and hopes about recent advancements in artificial intelligence.

- A statement of risks and benefits outlining the potential discomfort or stress participants may experience when discussing their experiences with artificial intelligence.
- A few sentences explaining the estimated amount of time they will have available to complete all of the survey questions.

As you can see, developing an appropriate informed consent document is a process of exercising *consideration and respect for your participants.* They may not leave your study with any lasting physical or emotional harm, but taking the time to understand their point of view and experiences goes a long way toward obtaining honest and high-quality results.

Next, consider the following example that outlines how the technology we use affects the research we conduct and the data collected: a product research team is conducting customer interviews to test the usability of a new feature. The interviews will be conducted and recorded over a video call. Several dozen customers were emailed, asking them to participate, and each was given access to an informed consent document detailing the following:

- The procedures for interacting with a sample application of the new features and answering questions while exploring its capabilities.
- The tools used to conduct the video call, how they will be recorded, and the security measures that will be used to safely store the video recordings. If participants are uncomfortable being recorded, they are provided with an option to have the researcher take notes, with an understanding that the session will take 15 minutes longer.
- The expected duration of the session (45 minutes), which is *strictly adhered to* by the team. Any unanswered or follow-up questions would require a separate consent process and scheduling at a later date.

While the informed consent practices we've covered were developed in clinical and academic settings, they easily apply to research using new and emerging technologies. Your participants may be uncomfortable with their information being captured or stored by a third party, and their concerns should be treated as valid! In the preceding example, the third-party service being used may be a competitor to their company, may use their audio, video, or images to train machine learning models, or may suffer a data breach that puts sensitive information about them at risk. If participants have concerns, *respect them* and consider alternatives to capturing information that protects their privacy (we will discuss this in depth throughout the chapter).

Finally, consider the following example of the procedures put in place to protect program participants: a nonprofit that aims to help youth in the foster care system is developing a new program for adolescents that aims to assist with job placement, financial literacy, and obtaining scholarships for higher education. The research team develops an informed consent document that outlines the expected procedures for the adolescent participants to read through before agreeing to participate. The document includes the following:

- Language tailored to the age and education level of the prospective participants (adolescents ages 15–19). All technical terminology was replaced with clear, accessible descriptions.

- Detailed information about the steps that would be taken to protect the personal information of participants. The nonprofit research team consulted with previous program participants to understand their concerns about their status as a foster youth being disclosed to teachers, potential employers, and colleges without their consent or potentially being revealed at a later date in adulthood. Per those concerns, all participants were given anonymized IDs in their database, and all identifying information was disconnected from the research program data. These steps were communicated to new prospective participants.

- A list of all the research questions that would be asked as part of the study, enumerating the potential benefits to the participants. Previous program participants had told the research team that they were often sought out to participate in studies with little to no benefit.

Each of these examples shows how obtaining informed consent is more than just filling in the blanks on a structured document; it's a necessary step for understanding the needs, concerns, and perspectives of anyone whose data you collect. Even if you are working with people's data that has already been collected (e.g., data about your users in a warehouse), it's essential to start by asking yourself, "would these users consent to this project if we asked them?" This is an important question regarding data collection in the current legal landscape, which we'll discuss in the next section.

8.1.3   Exercises

You are a health data analyst at a large biotechnology company producing wearable devices that monitor vital signs (e.g., heart rate) and physical activity (steps, workouts, etc.). The company has recently embarked on a project to design features that detect early signs of disease using data collected from the wearable devices.

This project's first study will investigate potential predictors of hypertension (high blood pressure) and heart disease. The potential predictors are primarily activity data and user characteristics already collected by the company. The study will involve recruiting several hundred users who were diagnosed with hypertension or heart disease during the time they have been using the wearable device. Your team will be collecting detailed information about the diagnosis for the study:

1 Propose a written informed consent protocol to be shared with users interested in participating in the study:
   - What potential risks might users incur by participating in this study? Is there any potential for harm that you or your users need to know?
   - What benefits to participating users and society might you share in this document?

2 Consider that your team will collect sensitive information about participating users' health statuses. What steps might your company need to put in place to

protect users from the risks associated with that information being disclosed? Write down your answer and consider it as you read the following sections of this chapter.

3 Suppose a user participating in the study requests to withdraw their consent to have their data included in your analysis. What should you do? What might you and your team need to put in place to honor that request?

8.2 The current legal landscape

Massive amounts of data are collected and are readily available on the internet. This data can often be purchased or otherwise obtained by individuals and organizations that we may not even be aware of—and for purposes we may not consent to. In the United States, research within a clinical or academic setting that works with human subjects must comply with a strict set of federal guidelines [2]. By comparison, data collection and storage practices outside of these settings aren't consistently regulated.

Many parts of the world are grappling with potential legislation to protect people's privacy and their ability to *consent* to data collection and usage to enable privacy in the era of big data. This landscape is changing *rapidly*; everything discussed in the following section reflects current and upcoming legislation as of early 2025.

8.2.1 Data protection regulations

Data protection regulations are sets of laws designed to protect the rights of individuals to have their data securely stored, processed, handled, and deleted when requested. Organizations are expected to adhere to obligations set forth in regulations that are often similar to those in clinical and academic research.

Individual laws vary by region, as we will discuss in this section. Many current regulations cover the following topics:

- *Definitions of personal and sensitive data*—Each set of regulations specifies what constitutes personal data. This typically includes any information that can be used to identify an individual, such as their name, address, phone number, email, and IP address.
- *Expectations for handling data*—Organizations must follow guidelines for storing, processing, and using personal and sensitive data. These include explicitly limiting access to personal data, retaining data only as long as necessary, and limiting the data collected for a specific purpose.
- *Establishing the rights of individuals*—Data protection regulations enumerate individual rights concerning the collection and use of their personal data. These rights include being informed about how their data is collected and used, the right to have their data deleted, and the right to deny consent to its use in a specific manner.

Many organizations, especially those that operate out of multiple locations, fall under these emerging laws and are expected to determine appropriate practices for complying with these laws. In larger companies and organizations, analytics teams will likely partner with IT, security, and legal teams to enact practices that comply with these laws. In smaller organizations, you and your team may have more responsibility in ensuring that the people whose data you collect can exercise their rights under these laws. We'll discuss some of the most influential regulations today and how they can affect the work of an analyst.

GDPR

The General Data Protection Regulation (GDPR) in the European Union governs the collection, retention, and use of personal data, and individual rights related to how that data is used [3]. The regulation went into effect in May of 2018, becoming the first comprehensive set of laws of its kind. It's become a model for subsequent laws adopted in a dozen countries, including a direct replica adopted in the United Kingdom in 2022.

If your organization collects data from offices, clients, or users in the European Union, you're likely required to comply with the GDPR. The specific responsibility of your team will vary, but analysts can expect that the GDPR will affect their work in one or more of the following ways:

- *Minimizing data collection*—When starting a project, you may need to document the questions you're asking and the specific fields of data you need to answer those questions. This documentation will ensure you communicate the project's requirements and *only* collect that information without asking for extraneous personal information about your users or participants.

- *Anonymizing data*—To protect the privacy of your users, customers, or target population, your organization may need to mask all personal data queried or used for analysis (e.g., replacing full names with random strings of letters). This may require you to take extra steps (e.g., requesting access from your IT and security teams) to access personal information like email addresses, phone numbers, or locations for a specific project.

- *Retaining or deleting data*—Your organization may have a *data retention policy* requiring that all data is anonymized or deleted after a set period (e.g., one year). This might limit how long you have to complete an analysis project after data is collected or how far back in time you can access records with personal information.

- *Securely accessing data*—To minimize the likelihood of data breaches, you may be required to adhere to policies at your organization guiding how you can access and share data. For example, you may not be permitted to download personal data onto your local machine or share it over email. It's strongly recommended that you review your organization's policies and available training on data security.

- *Contributing subject matter expertise*—As your organization seeks to remain compliant with evolving legislation, you and your team may be asked to collaborate with IT, security, and legal functions at your company to understand better the data you collect and use. Reviewing the key pieces of legislation that we'll discuss in the following sections will enable you to streamline the process of complying with these laws. You'll also build valuable expertise in data regulations, benefiting your long-term career.

The interpretation, enforcement, and application of the GDPR and similar laws are evolving worldwide. Analysts can expect to share the responsibility for complying with these laws and protecting the personal information of the users whose data you collect.

CCPA

As of early 2025, no single federal law in the United States governs data protection across sectors. As you'll see shortly, data governed by specific sector laws (e.g., protected health information governed by HIPAA) require compliance with national laws. Data protection regulations are primarily being passed at the state level.

The California Consumer Privacy Act (CCPA) took effect in January 2020, defining rights to data privacy for California residents [4]. It bears many similarities to the GDPR—the definitions of personal information and established rights to privacy are nearly identical. However, there are some notable differences in how the law was defined that may affect organizations operating in the state:

- The CCPA applies to data collected about people who are *legal residents of California.* By comparison, the GPDR applies more broadly to anyone in the EU regardless of their citizenship status. In practice, this may mean that fewer residents of California can exercise their right to have data modified, deleted, or restricted in use.
- While the GDPR applies to *any* business or entity that processes data about EU residents, the CCPA only applies to a subset of for-profit businesses that meet one or more of the following criteria:
  - $25 million or more in annual gross revenue
  - Buys, sells, receives, or shares personal data from at least 100,000 consumers or households
  - Makes 50% or more of its annual gross revenue from selling consumers' personal information
- The CCPA includes individuals and *households* in its definition of personal data. This might consist of data fields connecting multiple individuals to the same family (e.g., a unique family ID for an address).

In general, if your organization complies with the GDPR, it can easily comply with the CCPA. The CCPA is considered less restrictive than the GDPR. Still, you and your organization should be aware that this law is actively being modified (an amendment was passed later in 2020, adding additional privacy restrictions).

Calculating organizational metrics

A business analytics team at a multinational company is creating a dashboard to track new metrics. The company has offices in the United States, EU, Canada, and Great Britain. Many of their customers are in the same regions, so their data and information is regulated under the GDPR and CCPA.

The team is looking to calculate three new metrics calculated *monthly*:

- Percentage growth in users
- Count of users by region
- Percentage of active users

Calculating these metrics is easy—each is a count or proportion aggregated by month and measured over time using a line or bar graph. However, the team is aware of some new steps taken to comply with the GDPR and CCPA that may affect the accuracy of their calculations:

- Twelve months after users in the EU are deactivated, all identifying information about them is deleted (e.g., name, email address, specific location), leaving only `null` values for those fields in the `users` table. In addition, their records in the `user_activities` table are deleted entirely. This means the percentage of active users metric will *not* be accurate for EU users before the most recent rolling twelve-month period.
- If a user in the EU or a resident of California requests it, the company has to delete all information about them, including their anonymized record, in the `users` table. This is in accordance with the "right to be forgotten." This means that all metrics will be inaccurate for EU and United States users; this will be especially noticeable for the count of users by region metric, which will be artificially lower than their actual values.

The business analytics team reaches out to the company's data engineering team. They recommend capturing a *snapshot* of the anonymized and aggregated data from the previous day in new, special tables in the data warehouse. The tables can then be used to create the dashboard tracking each of the three new metrics.

The "Calculating organizational metrics" case study is a common example of how analytics, data science, and data engineering teams have had to adjust their practices in recent years to maintain their users' privacy in accordance with new laws. Later in this chapter, we'll cover strategies for striking this balance, including capturing anonymized and aggregated data.

SECTOR-SPECIFIC LAWS

While the GDPR and CCPA apply to a broad range of organizations, many sectors have their own regulations due to the nature of the data they handle. The mishandling of data in health, financial, education, and other fields can have specific implications for individuals whose data is breached or sold without consent. Here are some examples of sectors and laws that govern how organizations can store, access, and use people's data:

- The *healthcare* industry in the United States is governed by the Health Insurance Portability and Accountability Act (HIPAA), which strictly regulates protected health information (PHI) collected by healthcare providers, health insurance companies, and more [5]. This data is considered *strictly* confidential and often requires the person's explicit consent to share, access, or use for specific purposes.
- In *education*, the Family Educational Rights and Privacy Act (FERPA) [6] provides students and parents the right to access and correct student records. It restricts the sharing and use of personally identifiable information unless the student or parent consents.
- In *financial services*, several laws govern the privacy and security of financial information in the United States. For example, the Gramm-Leach-Bliley Act (GLBA) requires financial institutions to explain their data-sharing practices to customers and provides them with the right to opt out [7].

Figure 8.3 illustrates three laws that govern data in specific industries. We'll discuss best practices for handling protected information (e.g., personally identifiable information and protected health information) later in this chapter.

Figure 8.3   Many types of sensitive information are governed by sector-specific laws, both in the US, as in the examples shown here, and around the world.

8.2.2   *Bias in automated systems*

An *algorithm* is a sequence of computations used to process data, perform calculations, or solve a problem. In your work, this may be as simple as developing a set of repeated steps to clean a dataset, summarize it, and generate charts. *Artificial intelligence* is an advanced field that seeks to engineer systems that perform complex tasks typically requiring human intelligence to complete. These AI systems use complex algorithms and large datasets to identify underlying patterns in our data and attempt to replicate decisions based on those patterns continuing to exist in new data.

Algorithms of any complexity (e.g., a set of predefined rules or a neural network) can be used to create automated systems that perform tasks or make decisions that would otherwise need to be done by humans. An increasing number of these systems are designed to assist in our day-to-day work, automating mundane and repetitive tasks and increasing our overall efficiency.

Given an automated system's use of objective rules or large datasets, we can usually rely on them to make better, more accurate decisions than humans . . . right? Not necessarily! The example of Amazon's machine learning hiring system from this chapter's introduction is one of many algorithms shown to produce *biased outcomes* [8]. A simple rules-based algorithm can often have unintended consequences if the system's designers are unaware of how the rules are applied to people. Similarly, machine learning algorithms used in AI systems are trained on patterns in the underlying datasets. Human biases are an ever-present pattern in our data for these purposes.

Let's take a look at an example: a data science and analytics team at a large consumer goods company is looking to automate the categorization process for support tickets. Every day, the customer support team receives hundreds of support tickets on various topics that are manually triaged and categorized before a team member is assigned to each ticket.

Tickets have two categories assigned: a priority level (Low, Medium, and High) and a ticket type (Product Problems, Delivery, Billing, Inquiries, and Suggestions). The customer support team then uses this information to determine how to prioritize tickets in the queue and how quickly each problem needs to be resolved.

The team decides to build two prototypes to test the accuracy of automatically categorizing tickets—a rules-based model and a supervised classification model. They use key insights from an analysis performed by the business intelligence team to inform their approach:

- Most Product Problem, Delivery, and Billing tickets are labeled High priority, most Inquiries are labeled Medium priority, and Suggestions are labeled Low priority.
- An estimated 60% of tickets can be categorized by searching for one of 20 keywords in the text. However, the accuracy of this approach was not thoroughly tested.
- The volume of Delivery and Billing tickets is highly correlated with the number of sales, being more common during the holiday season from November to December (monthly seasonality). Inquiries and Suggestions are more commonly submitted on weekends (daily seasonality).

The team sets out to answer the following questions:

- What percentage of tickets can they accurately categorize with the 20 keywords? How far can they increase the list to 30, 40, or 50 keywords?
- Is a set of rules (e.g., keywords and explicit characteristics) sufficient to categorize most tickets, thereby reducing the volume of work for the support team?
- Does machine learning (the proposed classification model) add value to the project? Is it more accurate than rules, or does it enable the team to perform less manual work?

As figure 8.4 illustrates, rules-based models and more complex algorithms such as neural networks can be used to solve the same problems. Whether or not analysts use machine learning, they often participate in developing algorithms to perform calculations, automate tasks, and streamline the efforts of their stakeholders.

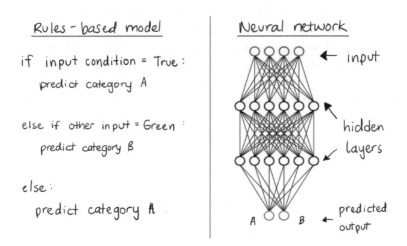

Figure 8.4   An automated system for categorizing data can employ anything from simple rules to sophisticated machine learning algorithms.

Automated systems, regardless of complexity, are frequently used to make decisions about people (e.g., users, customers, and the general population). In the preceding seemingly innocuous example, the information provided by customers is used to *rank* the urgency of their request and *categorize* the submission. It's quite straightforward and can save a lot of time for the support team. However, there may still be unintended long-term consequences on customers depending on their submissions. Let's look at a few possible scenarios that the team may need to consider in the long term.

With the addition of 30 more keywords, the rules-based algorithm classifies 80% of tickets into one of the five categories (Product Problems, Delivery, Billing, Inquiry, and Suggestion), while the remaining 20% are categorized as Other. Those 20% still need to be manually triaged by the support team, which often adds up to five days before a team member is assigned to resolve the problem. After several months of manual triage, the support team discovers the following:

- The 20% of tickets classified as Other appear to disproportionately represent new customers with problems with their first-ever purchase. There are several hypotheses as to why; regardless, the team is aware that this can negatively affect the perceptions and loyalty of new customers.

- Two-thirds of the Other tickets are from customers based in non-English-speaking countries. The entire support team and ticketing process is in English, potentially creating a barrier for international customers.

The data science and analytics team also trains a machine learning model to classify tickets into categories and urgency levels using inputs such as trends highlighted in the business intelligence team's analysis (e.g., week, month). The model they create is depicted in figure 8.5. At first glance, the model performs better than the rules-based approach. With further investigation, the team identifies the following phenomenon:

- The model's accuracy isn't consistent throughout the calendar year. Specifically, Delivery and Billing inquiries are more likely to be misclassified as Product Problems and ranked as Medium urgency during November and December. This can drastically reduce the quality of service received during the most profitable time of year.
- Similar to the rules-based approach, the model has lower accuracy among new customers and those in non-English-speaking countries.

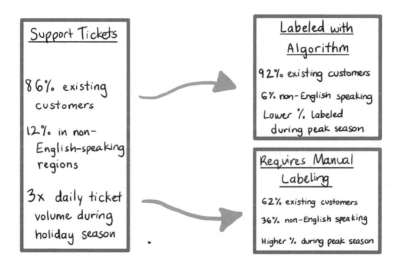

Figure 8.5 The categorization system developed by the data science and analytics team can streamline the work of the customer support team. Still, it may have an unanticipated negative effect on certain groups of customers.

This example scenario has potential benefits for the stakeholder team, reducing repetitive manual work and freeing up resources to focus on other high-value tasks. However, the benefit that may be passed to customers is *not* even, and it can even reduce the quality of service that certain subgroups receive (e.g., new customers, international customers). This is an example of two forms of *bias* in an automated system—*disproportionate accuracy rates* and *disproportionate outcomes*.

BIAS IN HIGH-STAKES DECISIONS

Take the example we just covered and replace the following:

- Substitute *automating job candidate qualification ranking and categorization* for *support ticket classification*
- Substitute *candidates applying for a job* for *customers*
- Substitute *open jobs* for *support tickets*
- Substitute *candidate quality level* (e.g., not qualified, somewhat qualified, highly qualified) for *ticket urgency*
- Substitute *candidate outcome* (interview, reject) for *ticket category*

Suddenly, the effect of inaccuracies in an automated system is not so harmless. We know human decisions are biased, and developing a model based on previous human decisions only codifies that bias. The problem with many automated systems is that they're sold as unbiased tools to aid or perform decision-making. Models attempting to replace human decisions often make selections that disproportionately favor certain subgroups while producing less accurate results for these or other groups.

Ranking certain groups of candidates as less qualified than others isn't a meaningless side effect of automation; it's potentially affecting the income, career trajectories, net worth, and other long-term outcomes for real people. It doesn't matter if you're using a set of rules or a deep learning model—the potential for harm remains.

Analysts can have a lot of power throughout our careers. When stakeholders take action based on our recommendations, we can shape an organization's strategy and the people it serves. If we don't thoroughly audit our work, we risk downstream effects that we cannot otherwise anticipate.

AUDITING AUTOMATED SYSTEMS IN HUMAN RESOURCES FOR BIAS

In July 2023, a new law regulating automated systems in employment decisions took effect in New York City. Specifically, any company that uses AI or any other automated decision tool in hiring and promotion decisions must disclose the tool's use to candidates and employees, as well as participate in annual third-party audits evaluating the tools for bias [9]. These laws apply to businesses with employees or job candidates in New York City and may cover a wide variety of systems integrated into HR processes. Some examples of the tools this may apply to include the following [10]:

- Third-party software that an HR team pays to rank the hundreds of candidates who apply to each job on their website using a machine learning algorithm.
- A complex set of rules developed internally that uses keyword matching to identify candidates whose skills match a given job.
- A vendor that generates a quality score for candidates and automatically rejects anyone below a certain threshold.

Bias in these automated systems is defined as differences in the scoring and selection of candidates by protected classes (e.g., race, ethnicity, sex, and intersecting groups). As an analyst, you would want to ask, "Is there any difference in the predicted ranking, rating, or selection rate for a job/promotion by race, ethnicity, sex, or any combination of the above?" The New York City government website provides specific metrics to calculate as part of the audit, ensuring standardized estimates of bias across different companies.

WHAT'S NEXT

Mandated audits and regulation of automated systems are new areas of legislation. Given that this law is the first of its kind, there will likely be iterations on the provisions and enforcement of the law in the coming years. It will also likely serve as a model for other laws being considered inside and outside of the United States.

As an analyst, you have an opportunity to build real expertise in an emerging field by monitoring the changing landscape in regulation related to data collection, usage, and the effect of automated decisions. To keep your knowledge up to date, I suggest taking one or more of the following steps to synthesize information:

- Subscribe to data analytics and data science newsletters, many of which can be discovered with a quick Google search. Try looking at sources of information on Medium and Kaggle if you're unsure where to start.
- Set up alerts with news outlets that discuss technology (e.g., Tech Crunch, Forbes, Wall Street Journal, etc.) on topics related to data, AI, and machine learning ethics and regulations.
- Set up alerts on Google Scholar for similar keywords as for news outlets—analytics, data science, AI, and machine learning ethics and regulations. These sources will be far more in-depth and technical than news outlets, and you'll often learn of key topics before they reach general-audience news sources.

8.2.3 Exercises

The study conducted in your previous exercise has been a huge success! You and your team have discovered clear predictors of several common diseases that are all easily available from the activity data you collect. As such, your company will be launching a new AI-driven feature that alerts users to potential health problems.

1. To maximize the study's benefit to society, your company is partnering with clinical researchers to publish their findings. Your team plans to anonymize all user data before sharing it with external research partners. Which GDPR principle is the company adhering to with their research partnership?
   - Data minimization
   - Integrity and confidentiality
   - Accuracy
   - Transparency

2. Your company recently had a surge of new users in California. As such, what data policies will they need to have in place to comply with the CCPA?

3. Six months after launch, your team discovers that the AI-driven feature is less accurate in predicting health problems for users over 65. What are the legal and ethical implications of the bias present in this algorithm?

8.3 *Analyzing sensitive data*

Now that you have a comprehensive understanding of the ethical foundations of research, data analysis, and experimentation, as well as knowledge of an emerging legal field, let's discuss some pragmatic skills you can use to work with sensitive data effectively and ethically.

Sensitive data refers to information about individuals or organizations that can have negative consequences if shared without consent or authorization. This type of data typically requires elevated security practices to protect against misuse and comply with regulations. There are many categories of sensitive data, including the following:

- *Personally identifiable information* (PII) can be used to identify a specific individual or sensitive characteristics about them. This category includes social security numbers, phone numbers, email addresses, and demographic characteristics.
- *Protected health information* (PHI) includes all health status, medical history, or medical payment information that can be tied back to an individual.
- *Financial information* includes information about an individual's financial status, bank accounts, credit card numbers, and financial transactions.
- *Authentication data* includes usernames, passwords, and any other login credentials. Breaches of authentication data can easily lead to leaking all other forms of sensitive data.

Throughout this section, we will use examples of PII and PHI, given their prevalence in the work of an analyst. The best practices in data security, anonymizing data, and putting guardrails in place can apply to any form of sensitive data where there is a risk of identifying a person based on available information.

8.3.1 *Data minimization*

Perhaps the easiest way to handle protected information is to *not* handle it at all—in many situations, this is the best-recommended approach to your work. Before determining the best approach to managing protected information, it's valuable to determine if you need it at all. As a rule of thumb (shown in figure 8.6), it's usually worth treating protected information as inherently risky to use.

Figure 8.6   When all else fails, treat protected information as radioactive.

Data minimization (as covered in section 8.2.1) is the practice of limiting the collection, storage, and use of personal data to only what is directly relevant for a specific purpose. In essence, this practice encourages you to think strategically about the purpose of any information you collect and to only store it for as long as needed.

There are several aspects to practicing data minimization as an analyst:

- *Limit the data you collect to only what is necessary*—Research and analysis have a long-standing tradition of collecting as much information as possible about users and participants "just in case" it might yield a statistically significant result when nothing else does. If you cannot justify the reason for collecting a piece of information, don't.
- *Limit the length of time for which you store data*—Many organizations collect data about their users, customers, and population for seemingly indefinite periods of time. However, due to its lack of relevance, most analyses don't end up using data from more than a few years prior to the current date. Work with your team to set a data retention policy and delete, scrub, or limit access to data after a certain amount of time has passed.
- *Limit access to raw data as much as possible*—This is a data minimization principle that analysts often have a lot of opportunity to enact. Where possible, do not share raw data with stakeholders that don't otherwise have permission to view it (e.g., in your data warehouse). Do not share sensitive data over insecure channels (e.g., a CSV of customer data attached to an email). Instead, use secure file-sharing methods at your organization (e.g., Google Drive, Proton).

Let's look at an example: the analytics team at a large e-commerce company is currently rearchitecting its strategy for collecting and analyzing website user behavior. Previously, the data warehouse had available details about every user who visited their website—first name, last name, phone number, IP address, and specific location. Their security team recently flagged their data collection and retention practices as a risk for expanding into Europe and complying with the GDPR.

To better protect information about their users, the team recommends the following strategy:

- Replace all personal information (e.g., name, email, phone number) with an anonymized user ID from the data warehouse.
- Remove the specific location fields (latitude and longitude) and replace them with more general location information (city, state, country).
- Set a retention policy for all website user behavior data: granular data (e.g., one row per user per visit) would only be available for the previous 12 months. After this point, the data was aggregated to a count of visits by user, page, and day, and it was saved in a new table.
- Restrict access to the granular website user behavior data to only approved analytics team members who have completed security policies training.

These intentional steps enabled the analytics team to effectively comply with the GDPR and mitigate the risk of data security breaches that might otherwise put customer data at risk.

Often, out of habit, we collect sensitive information in excess of what is necessary. Participants are used to filling out surveys asking for their age, race, gender, location, and more, so they rarely balk at these questions. However, having this information freely available and indefinitely stored at your organization can produce long-term risk for data breaches and compliance problems, generating the mistrust of your users. Minimizing the data you collect, retrieve, and include in your final analyses can help you avoid many situations where you must take extra measures to protect personal information.

8.3.2   Anonymizing and pseudonymizing data

Now that you've eliminated every case where you don't need protected data, we can skip this section, right? If only that were the case! While avoiding using protected information is preferable, there are some legitimate scenarios where access to that information is vital for completing your work effectively. In these situations, having the skills necessary to process that information safely and to anonymize it where possible is valuable.

> **When is using protected information necessary?**
>
> A data analyst may need to use protected information in one of the following scenarios:
>
> - Conducting an analysis of health outcomes using protected health information (PHI) to understand patient diagnoses, treatment efficacies, and quality of care.
> - Developing tailored and personalized marketing strategies often includes using a combination of user demographic characteristics and behaviors to understand what products, goods, and services they might be interested in purchasing.
> - When combining data across multiple third-party sources, sometimes the only unique key available is a name or email address to connect information.

In cases where using protected information is unavoidable, countless tools and techniques are available for masking that information in your analysis. The first technique, *anonymization*, refers to the explicit removal of personal information so that an individual cannot be identified. Data that is *fully* and *irreversibly* anonymized is no longer considered personal data, meaning it falls outside the scope of current data protection regulations.

Pseudonymization refers to the deidentification of data using pseudonyms, fake identifiers, or other information that limits (but does not prevent) the identification of an individual. Pseudonymization is *reversible*—with the correct information, you can tie an anonymized ID back to the protected information about that record stored in a separate table. This approach is preferable when there's a need to anonymize data for analytics but store sensitive and protected information for specific use cases later on. For example, an e-commerce company likely needs to store customer contact, address, and credit card information in a database to enable them to make recurring purchases without re-entering that information with every new transaction. However, the information isn't necessary for analysis, so it won't be made available in the data warehouse for analysis.

Table 8.1 shows examples of how an analyst may anonymize or pseudonymize different types of protected and sensitive information.

Table 8.1 Examples of anonymized and pseudonymized data

Example	Anonymized	Pseudonymized
Medical research	Patients have names, birthdays, and contact information removed from the data warehouse.	Patients have names replaced with pseudonyms and a unique identifier that can be tied to their contact information.
Human resources management	Employees have names, social security numbers, and birthdays masked from view.	Employees have all identifying information stored in a separate table with restricted access.
Customer surveys	Respondents have no identifying information collected.	Respondents can share their emails for future studies, which are only accessible by survey tool admins.

ANONYMIZING PROTECTED INFORMATION IN PYTHON

Often, you can use the same tools and approaches in Python to anonymize or pseudonymize your data. The difference is in whether you save the protected information in a separate table, with the anonymized IDs available to be joined to the datasets used for analysis when necessary.

Let's look at an example of a dataset at an online retailer. The `transactions` table the follows has information about each item purchased by a customer and a wealth of metadata about that customer:

```
import pandas as pd                              ⟵ Import the pandas library.

transactions = pd.read_csv("transactions.csv")   ⟵ Import the transactions
transactions.head()                                  dataset and display
                                                     the first five rows.
```

The dataset shown in figure 8.7 has every piece of information necessary to contact a customer—names, emails, phone numbers, and addresses (note: to protect the privacy of real people, this information has been generated with the faker library in Python). In all likelihood, none of the sensitive and protected fields will be directly necessary for analysis. It may be possible to *derive* valuable information from some fields (e.g., standardized location information from the address), but it's unlikely that we will use the sensitive data directly.

transaction_id	name	email	phone	address	purchased_item	price
t-834207	Keith White	keith.white@example.com	490-356-3466x219	PSC 7000, Box 0663, APO AP 61947	Cool tablet	627
t-194507	Nicole Weaver	nicole.weaver@example.com	(581)642-5743	Unit 3524 Box 6820, DPO AE 31360	Retro mobile phone	584
t-310414	Joseph Perez	joseph.perez@example.com	297.447.3481	50270 Graham Alley, Lake Brittany, NH 15851	Yet another laptop	405
t-947522	Cheryl Salinas	cheryl.salinas@example.com	945.248.4798x675	51407 Jones Drive Suite 478, Wattsstad, CA 53037	Cool tablet	537
t-156647	Monica Foster	monica.foster@example.com	(738)712-8058x1408	81902 Roberts Route Suite 280, Port Andrewmout...	Retro mobile phone	943

Figure 8.7   This table contains numerous fields with protected information about the customer.

Let's drop the name and phone number fields from the dataset outright:

```
transactions.drop(["name", "phone"], axis=1, inplace=True)
transactions.head()
```

Now that our dataset no longer has names and phone numbers (see figure 8.8), let's extract nonprotected standardized geographic information from the `address` field. The `usaddress` Python library offers the ability to extract and normalize addresses in the United States; when working with international addresses, you can use more comprehensive libraries, such as `libpostal`, which can parse addresses worldwide. We'll use this library for the `transactions` dataset, since all of the addresses are in the United States.

transaction_id	email	address	purchased_item	price
t-834207	keith.white@example.com	PSC 7000, Box 0663, APO AP 61947	Cool tablet	627
t-194507	nicole.weaver@example.com	51407 Jones Drive St Box 6820, DPO AE 31360	Retro mobile phone	584
t-310414	joseph.perez@example.com	50270 Graham Alley, Lake Brittany, NH 15851	Yet another laptop	405
t-947522	cheryl.salinas@example.com	51407 Jones Drive Ste 478, Wattsstad, CA 53037	Cool tablet	537
t-156647	monica.foster@example.com	81902 Roberts Route Ste 280, Port Andrewmout...	Retro mobile phone	943

Figure 8.8   When sensitive data isn't necessary for analysis, you can drop the fields from your dataset.

You'll first have to install the `usaddress` library at the command line or in your notebook as follows:

```
pip install usaddress
```

To parse addresses in the entire dataset, we will define a function that extracts your choice's specific standardized geographic information. Keeping data minimalist principles in mind, we'll keep only the city, state, and zip code (assuming we know we will need them for our analysis!). Additional standardized information is available in the dictionary we get from this library (e.g., street address); since it's not needed, we won't keep the dictionary in our final dataset:

```
import usaddress        ⟵┤ Import the usaddress library.

def parse_addresses(address):
    try:
        parsed = usaddress.parse(address)
        parsed_dict = {item[1]: item[0] for item in parsed}
        city = parsed_dict.get("PlaceName", "")
        state = parsed_dict.get("StateName", "")
        zip_code = parsed_dict.get("ZipCode", "")
        return city, state, zip_code
    except:
        return "", "", ""

transactions["city"], transactions["state"], transactions["zip_code"] = zip(
    *transactions["address"].apply(parse_addresses)
)

transactions.head()   ⟵┤ Display the first five rows.
```

Create a function to parse the address column.

Add error handling in case addresses cannot be parsed (a common issue).

Extract individual geographical data points of interest from the parsed dictionary.

If an address cannot be parsed, return an empty string.

Create three new columns with city, state, and zip code by applying the function to the address.

Figure 8.9 now shows the standardized geographical information we want for analysis, excluding the user's full address.

	transaction_id	email	purchased_item	price	city	state	zip_code
0	t-834207	keith.white@example.com	Cool tablet	627	APO	AP	61947
1	t-194507	nicole.weaver@example.com	Retro mobile phone	584	DPO	AE	31360
2	t-310414	joseph.perez@example.com	Yet another laptop	405	Brittany	NH	15851
3	t-947522	cheryl.salinas@example.com	Cool tablet	537	Wattsstad	CA	53037
4	t-156647	monica.foster@example.com	Retro mobile phone	943	Andrewmouth	WV	50204

Figure 8.9 Standardized geographic information is easily extracted from the address column. We can then drop the original versions.

Finally, let's drop the original `address`, `name`, and `phone` columns, effectively *anonymizing* a lot of your users' information. The resulting dataset is more valuable for analysis and less risky to your customers in the event of a data breach:

```
transactions.drop(["address", "name", "phone"], axis=1, inplace=True)
```

In most cases, standardized city and state information will be sufficient to understand widespread geographic trends among your users and customers. In cases where you need more granular neighborhood-level trends, the zip code is an appropriate unit used in the majority of social research. Many publicly available data sources (e.g., the US Census) have comprehensive information about residents of each geographic granularity that you can use to compare to your users.

PSEUDONYMIZING PROTECTED OR SENSITIVE DATA

Next, let's move on to the final column containing PII—the `email` address. This may prove to be more complicated, as email addresses can be a decent option to join data between sources within an organization where another unique identifier doesn't exist. For example, if you need to combine data from your application's database and two separate vendors, it's unlikely they share the same anonymized ID to link records. In cases like this, where the following criteria are met about a sensitive data field, you likely need to *pseudonymize* this field:

- When it's needed in your data warehouse, such as to join data between sources
- When the data itself is not used for analysis (or you can extract non-sensitive components), and it can be hidden from analysts and stakeholders
- When analysts mainly need to identify unique individuals with a primary key, such as a random string of numbers

In such a case, you can *pseudonymize* this field and retain it in a separate, secure table not directly available for analysis. This is often done using a process called *hashing* the data. *Hashing* is a process that transforms your data into a fixed-size value (e.g., 256 bits) using an algorithm known as a *hash function*. The resulting *hash code* (e.g., the codes in figure 8.10) has the following characteristics:

- It's *deterministic*, meaning each unique value has a different hash code, and repeated values will have the same one. Thus, it can be used as an anonymized primary key in place of sensitive data.
- Slight differences in the original data result in very different hash codes—similarity between hash codes is not an indicator of similarity in the underlying data.
- At present, it's impossible to reverse-engineer the original data only from its hash code. However, this may not always be the case, so I strongly recommend keeping up to date on information security best practices.

Hashing values in a pandas dataframe is easily performed using the standard `hashlib` Python library, which contains several hashing algorithms to choose from when anonymizing your data. Let's use SHA-256 (Secure Hash Algorithm 256-bit): this is

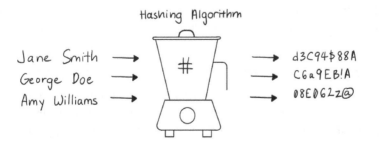

Figure 8.10 Hash functions are like a smoothie blender, taking the original data and scrambling it so you cannot undo it and retrieve your original ingredients.

relatively quick to compute and widely used for encrypting data in a warehouse and sharing and transporting between individuals, organizations, and over networks:

```
import hashlib                    ◁──┤ Import the hashlib library.

                                                      Write a function to hash the
def hash_email(email):                         ◁──┘ email column's values.
    return hashlib.sha256(email.encode()).hexdigest()

transactions["email_hash"] = transactions["email"].apply(hash_email)    ◁──┐

                                                          Apply the function
transactions.head()   ◁──┤ Display the first five rows.    to a new column.
```

Figure 8.11 shows a long alphanumeric code containing the hashed email value.

transaction_id	email	purchased_item	price	city	state	zip_code	email_hash
t-834207	keith.white@example.com	Cool tablet	627	APO	AP	61947	e9a78df1d0bfbcb8def1f0c0...
t-194507	nicole.weaver@example.com	Retro mobile phone	584	DPO	AE	31360	b1fd301be283df2e485c4408...
t-310414	joseph.perez@example.com	Yet another laptop	405	Brittany	NH	15851	702b9181b695c10f21dbcffc...
t-947522	cheryl.salinas@example.com	Cool tablet	537	Wattsstad	CA	53037	299d0bea719deb861a41d56e...
t-156647	monica.foster@example.com	Retro mobile phone	943	Andrewmouth	WV	50204	28776c6cd2896da2240017eb...

Figure 8.11 **The resulting hash is a long sequence of random letters and numbers.**

Finally, let's save the email and email_hash as a separate dataframe and drop the email from the transactions table:

```
                                                          Save the email and its hash
emails = transactions[["email", "email_hash"]]      ◁──┘ in a separate dataframe.
transactions.drop(["email"], axis=1, inplace=True)   ◁──┐
transactions.head()        ◁──┐                           Drop the email column
                                Display the first five    from transactions.
                                rows of transactions.
```

The new emails table in figure 8.12 retains the original PII in a separate location from the transactions data used for analytics.

	transaction_id	purchased_item	price	city	state	zip_code	email_hash
0	t-834207	Cool tablet	627	APO	AP	61947	e9a78df1d0bfbcb8def1f0c0...
1	t-194507	Retro mobile phone	584	DPO	AE	31360	b1fd301be283df2e485c4408...
2	t-310414	Yet another laptop	405	Brittany	NH	15851	702b9181b695c10f21dbcffc...
3	t-947522	Cool tablet	537	Wattsstad	CA	53037	299d0bea719deb861a41d56e...
4	t-156647	Retro mobile phone	943	Andrewmouth	WV	50204	28776c6cd2896da2240017eb...

Figure 8.12 **The final transactions table can identify customers without sensitive or protected data.**

In situations where it's necessary to tie new data sources to your existing data (e.g., a new vendor that only contains the email address as a unique identifier), the following steps can be taken:

1 Join the new data source to the `emails` table.
2 Add the `email_hash` to the new data source.
3 Drop the original `email` column from the new data source, instead using the `email_hash` as a primary key for your users or customers.

Where possible, this is a task that should be done in collaboration with the data engineering or IT team that manages your data warehouse. These teams will typically be able to restrict or permit access to PII, such as the `emails` table, and create highly curated sets of views for analysts to use in their work.

At a smaller organization (e.g., a nonprofit with limited resources), you may not have these teams to collaborate with. If you don't have the resources available to manage sensitive and protected information at scale, you can use the steps in this section to anonymize, pseudonymize, and restrict access to PII as much as possible. Data sources such as the `emails` table can be stored and password-protected in the most secure manner that your organization offers and *only* be accessed when necessary by members of your analytics team.

8.3.3 *Preventing deanonymization*

Believe it or not, the removal of PII is often not enough to prevent the identification of individuals. In 2006, Netflix released a dataset of 100 million movie ratings from 500,000 users as part of a competition to improve their movie recommendation system. The dataset had been stripped of all PII (e.g., names and email addresses) and released publicly to anyone interested in the competition.

A research team from the University of Texas developed a deanonymization algorithm using contextual information about the users from their reviews (e.g., the dates, ratings, and text of the reviews) to cross-reference with publicly available ratings on the movie database IMDb [11]. With the information in the original dataset, they were able to identify startling amounts of personal information—names, contact information, sexual orientation, and more.

This incident is one of many situations where anonymization can be insufficient to protect the privacy of individuals, who can easily be identified based on context. *Contextual information* refers to combinations of non-sensitive data that provide sufficient clues as to an individual's identity. It's often shockingly easy to do so, given the volume of publicly available data available today. Consider the following examples:

- A dataset of payments for a local bus in a small city can be cross-referenced with social media check-ins. Since many commuters keep using the same transit card over time, individual travel patterns can be identified and potentially cross-referenced with social media check-ins.
- Combinations of demographic characteristics like age, gender, race, ethnicity, and zip code can easily be used to narrow down individual identities. A 2000

paper estimated that 87% of the United States population can be uniquely identified using just the zip code, gender, and date of birth [12].

- In 2006, AOL publicly released a dataset of 20 million search queries performed by 657,000 users. While all user information was removed from the dataset, PII was still present in many searches. As such, the *New York Times* was able to easily identify a specific user from search queries alone [13].

Analysts are often responsible for the formatting, structure, and dissemination of data that, while anonymized, can easily be reverse-engineered to determine who a person is. Depending on your specialization, this can occur very frequently, putting your users, customers, or coworkers in a difficult position if they're identified.

Protecting anonymity in employee engagement reports

An HR analytics team at a nonprofit with 1,200 employees has just completed its annual employee engagement survey. Every year, employees are given a 30-question survey about their workload, morale, and perceptions of management. The results are analyzed by the team and compiled into a comprehensive report, showing question scores by department, office, employee tenure, gender, and more.

Given that many questions were of a sensitive nature, the team enacted the following *guardrails* to maintain the anonymity of responses to encourage honest responses:

- The team configured the survey to only collect *anonymous responses*. Nobody would be able to connect a response to an individual employee.
- Individual responses were *never* reported on. Instead of sharing comments, the team synthesized overarching themes and sentiments in the qualitative data. This ensured that an employee couldn't be identified by their writing style or the topics they discussed.
- Since the report often included multiple breakouts (e.g., average satisfaction by department and age), the team set a *minimum aggregation* level of five. If a subgroup had under five employees, the report did not show results.
- For sections of the report where the number of employees was consistently too low, the team avoided displaying multiple breakouts (e.g., average satisfaction only shown by department for small teams).

In addition, the team publicized this list of guardrails to the company to ensure employees felt confident in their anonymity when responding to the survey. This helped increase the response rate from 67% the previous year to 81%, enabling more comprehensive insights into the data.

Guardrails are a set of predefined criteria put in place to ensure the accuracy of your analyses. They're designed to maintain anonymity, protect individuals, and prevent biased or inaccurate interpretations that can result from your work in their absence. Teams will often develop these as a general checklist for their work. A typical set of guardrails might look like the following:

- All datasets must have a minimum sample size chosen in accordance with the statistical test being used.

- All groups, subgroups, and breakouts in reports must have a minimum sample size of five to show aggregate data. Any group with fewer than five individuals should be excluded or combined with another group.

- Reports and other deliverables should not include access to the raw data unless absolutely necessary to prevent deanonymization. If necessary, the data should be shared securely and only with those who need it.

- Any report or deliverable that includes breakdowns and interpretations based on demographic characteristics (e.g., gender, race, ethnicity, age, disability status, veteran status) should be approved by a peer-review process with the team. The peer-review group should discuss the potential for harmful interpretations, inaccurate representations, and perpetuating stereotypes.

- Every step in the analytics lifecycle should be well documented, from data collection to processing and results interpretation. Another team member should be able to reproduce an analysis based on the available documentation alone.

In practice, a chart like the one shown in figure 8.13 would violate these guardrails. The n value label shows the total number of employees in each department and EEOC group. Several subgroups have fewer than five employees represented (and one subgroup has only a single person!). It would be extraordinarily easy to identify which employees these are, creating a difficult situation should they be expressing negative sentiments or concerns about their work.

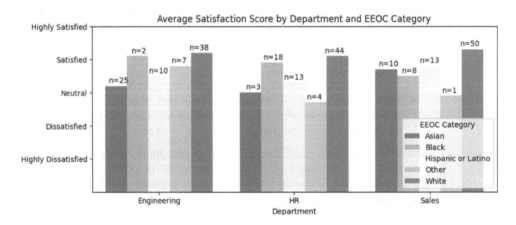

Figure 8.13 An employee engagement survey with multiple breakouts can accidentally deanonymize individuals in groups with few members. For example, the sales department has one EEOC group with *n*=1, making it easy to identify the person and their satisfaction.

An analytics team's efforts to prevent deanonymization will generally have multiple benefits for the quality of work produced. Many inaccurate and harmful interpretations can arise from beliefs that a response belongs to a specific person or that an aggregate value for a small sample size represents their broader group. Remembering when your data is about people and seeking to use their data responsibly will set you and your team up for success in your work.

8.3.4 *Exercises*

Your biotechnology company has seen a surge in users using the new AI-generated alert feature. To ensure the feature produces accurate data over time, users are asked to confirm whether or not they received a diagnosis for the health problem they were alerted to. This data is used to periodically retrain the underlying machine learning model powering the feature:

1 What type of data is being used to train the model powering the AI-generated health alert feature?

2 The company's product team is discussing whether they should erase all unnecessary identifying information about users or replace it with coded references while maintaining a separate list of actual data. What data protection methods are they considering? How would you weigh the pros and cons of each method?

3 Propose a set of guardrails for the analytics team to use when reporting the results of clinical trials. Include at least one guideline on data minimization, anonymization versus pseudonymization practices, and minimum aggregations for reports and peer-reviewed journal submissions.

Summary

- The *Nuremberg Code* was established in the aftermath of harmful experiments in WWII. It set guidelines for ethical human subjects research, emphasizing voluntary consent and the rights of participants.

- The *informed consent process* in research ensures that participants have sufficient information about the purpose, procedures, and potential risks of a research project or study to make informed decisions about participating.

- The *General Data Protection Regulation* (GDPR) in the European Union provides individuals control over how their personal data is stored and used. It requires that companies have guardrails in place to protect the privacy and security of people's data and that they obtain consent to store and use personal data for specific purposes.

- The *California Consumer Privacy Act* (CCPA) is a regulation that offers data protection rights similar to the GDPR, specifically for California residents. It allows consumers to know about and opt out of the use and sale of their personal data.

- Automated decision tools using rules-based or machine learning algorithms can potentially produce biased output that disproportionately affects subgroups of your users, customers, or the general population. New York City recently passed a law requiring these decision tools in hiring to be audited for bias. This is a new category of law in the data world, and it will likely develop quickly in the coming years.

- *Sensitive and protected data analysis* refers to the analysis of personal information governed by law or that may risk producing harm if it were released without consent. This type of analysis requires special care to maintain the privacy and confidentiality of people and organizations.

- *Protected information* is data that, if exposed, could produce harm for the individual:
  - *Personally identifiable information* (PII) refers to individual characteristics such as names, addresses, phone numbers, and social security numbers. This type of information is governed by regulations such as the GDPR and CCPA.
  - *Protected health information* (PHI) refers to medical records, transactions, diagnoses, and any other information that, if breached, could risk disclosing confidential medical conditions.

- *Data minimization* is a key principle in analyzing sensitive data, recommending that you only collect the data you need for a specific project and retain it for as long as necessary. This is intended to reduce the risk of data breaches and misuse of sensitive information.

- *Anonymization* is the process of completely removing PII from your data to prevent the identification of individuals.

- *Pseudonymization,* in contrast, is the process of removing PII from specific datasets and replacing it with a pseudonym or key. The data is then retained elsewhere, in case it's necessary for other purposes.

- Analysts have a responsibility to minimize the likelihood of *deanonymization* of data. Since anonymized datasets can be easily re-associated with individuals, a set of guardrails for your team should be established to protect individuals from unintended consequences associated with re-identification.

The world of
statistical modeling

This chapter covers

- The purpose and application of common classes of statistical models
- Evaluating the information available when fitting a model
- Fitting a statistical model to a dataset and iterating on it to improve performance
- Explaining the results of statistical models and generating predictive deliverables

Three data analysts walk into a bar. The first says, "I bet I can figure out the top five traits that predict whether a person orders beer, wine, or spirits. We can use that model to better plan the inventory." The second retorts, "Well, give me info on the next 100 patrons, and I'll use your model to forecast all their orders in advance." The third smirks, "Why wait? Give me real-time data, and I'll use your model to predict a drink right as they're about to order it. Now, that will really impress the patrons!"

What's the difference between the type of model that each analyst is proposing and the other two? Are all three approaches valuable? Can they all genuinely use the same statistical model to predict the same phenomenon, with a different approach and desired output? And are the analysts *actually* proposing successively better alternatives?

The answer to the first three questions is yes—a small handful of statistical models can be used for a wide variety of purposes and deliverables. The same model can often inform decisions *and* generate predictions in the most appropriate format. None of the preceding examples is inherently *better*—instead, there are different strategic approaches to deriving value from each approach.

In this chapter, we'll cover the different approaches to statistical modeling that allow you to explain and predict phenomena such as people's drink orders in a bar or at a larger scale. You'll learn how to evaluate the performance of a statistical model, fine-tune it, and produce the best deliverables to meet the needs of your stakeholders. We'll cover each step using a single example dataset you may be familiar with from chapter 4 (remember the rat complaints in New York City?), building upon the specific skills you need to create models for different purposes.

9.1 *The many faces of statistical modeling*

> *All models are wrong, but some are useful.*
>
> —George Box, British statistician

Statistical modeling is the process of mathematically representing relationships between one or more independent variables (inputs, or *x*-variables) and one or more dependent variables (outputs, or *y*-variables) in a dataset. Models are developed to describe and quantify your data's underlying structure and patterns. Through statistical modeling, we aim to understand the nature of complex processes that we would otherwise struggle to represent with descriptive (e.g., mean, median), univariate (e.g., *t*-test, ANOVA), and bivariate (e.g., correlation) statistics.

Analysts can use statistical modeling for many purposes, such as the following:

- *Making inferences* about the statistical significance of one or more independent variables and their shared relationship with a dependent variable.
- *Predicting outcomes for future values* that are within the same range as your dataset, but aren't actually part of the original sample used to fit the model.
- Deriving *insights* to enable *data-informed decisions* at your organization. Statistical model results can increase confidence in strategic plans and actions.

A *statistical model* is a mathematical formula (equation) used to represent underlying patterns in your data. The modeling process aims to find a formula that appropriately *fits* or *represents* the relationship between one or more predictors and an outcome, allowing you to make inferences and predictions about the phenomena that the outcome represents. For example, figure 9.1 shows a line fit to a dataset with an equation representing the formula that best explains the relationship between the variables.

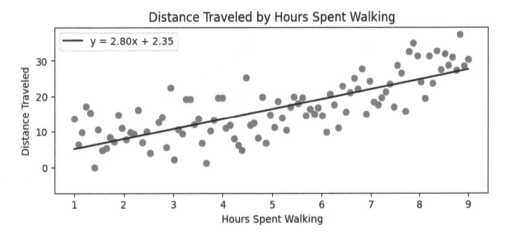

Figure 9.1   A linear regression with two variables (a predictor and outcome) is one of the simplest forms of statistical models to fit to your data.

In most cases, a good-fitting model can *approximate* patterns in your data but will rarely allow you to predict future values with 100% accuracy. The real world is complex, and most of what we measure is intertwined with so many processes that we can never completely figure out what predicts or causes an outcome. A *useful* or *good enough* model represents the general shape and trend of your data.

The typical process of statistical modeling follows these steps:

1　Select an appropriate model for the problem you are attempting to solve (e.g., regression versus classification). We will discuss this in depth later in this section.

2　Select a *formula* (e.g., a line) to fit the data. The line fits the data using an *objective function* to identify the model coefficients (e.g., β_1 and β_2 in linear regression models). We'll discuss objective functions later in this section.

3　Evaluate the model's performance and ability to describe the patterns in the data. Optimize the model by adjusting the formula and model parameters.

In figure 9.2, a *linear* and *polynomial* model are fit to the same dataset and compared. From visual observation, the two variables appear to have a negative exponential relationship—as the height above sea level increases, the atmospheric pressure exponentially decreases. Thus, the polynomial model better represents the relationship between these two variables.

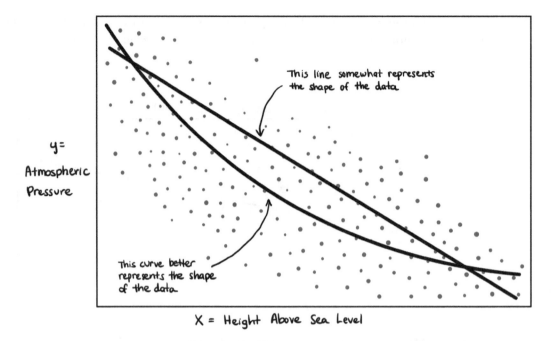

Figure 9.2   **Many mathematical formulas can represent the shape of relationships in your data, such as a linear formula (line) or a polynomial formula (curve).**

9.1.1   *Classes of statistical models*

When looking to make predictions, identify intricate underlying patterns, and estimate future events, analysts have *countless* statistical models to choose from. Many models have variations in their formulas and algorithms to help solve specific problems, which can be an intricate and complex web of options to navigate.

For the purpose of this chapter, we'll group many of the common models into *classes*, organized by the problem they're trying to solve. We'll define a *class* as a group of formulas and algorithms that share common characteristics and that are designed to solve a *specific type of real-world problem.*

For example, *regressors* are a class designed to predict *continuous outcomes* based on one or more input variables. *Linear regression* assumes that a line can represent the relationship between your predictors and outcome; other formulas are available for data that cannot fit a line. While *logistic regression* uses a similar formula to a linear regression, it's used to solve *classification problems*—the model is similar, but it's used to predict a categorical instead of continuous outcome.

The problem you are looking to solve will typically guide your selection of a class of models. Some of these problems may look like the following:

- Predicting the dollar value spent during a store visit based on several properties of the customer, timing, and store location.

- Identifying factors contributing to whether or not a student passes their final exam (a binary, categorical outcome).
- Forecasting the business's sales for the coming nine months, accounting for seasonal changes and economic predictions.

Table 9.1 lists the classes of models we'll discuss in this section. Figure 9.3 shows a map of each class listed, some examples, and their connections.

Table 9.1 Classes of models, their purposes, and examples

Class	Purpose	Example
Regression	Predict outcomes represented with continuous data	Predicting student test scores
Classification	Predict outcomes represented with categorical data	Predict which students will graduate on time
Clustering	Identify underlying patterns and natural "groups" in the data	Find clusters of student performance across classes
Dimension reduction	Identify shared variance among predictors to simplify model input	Find 2 underlying components to represent scores in 12 classes
Survival analysis	Predict the time until an event occurs	Predict the time to withdraw from an intensive graduate curriculum

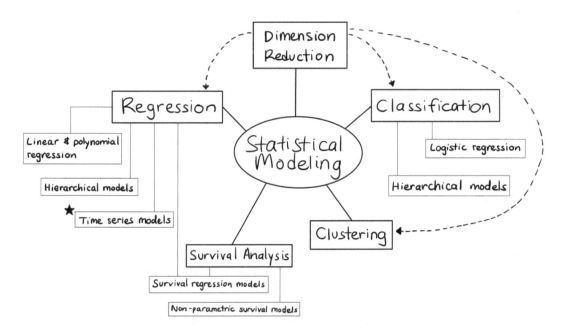

Figure 9.3 A map of common classes of statistical models organized by the problem they solve. Time series models are starred in the diagram because they are a special class of models, as will be discussed shortly.

While most of your problems will likely fall into one of these classes, they are by no means the only approaches in this field. Within your specific domain, you'll probably discover that most of the problems you solve will belong to a limited subset of the available classes of models. The full scope of each class of model and its possible application cannot be covered in a single chapter. Thus, we'll focus on the strategies and approaches that can be applied to most of these categories while only using regression and classification models as examples.

REGRESSION

Regression models are fitted to datasets with a *continuous outcome*. The predictors in the model can be either continuous or categorical. If you're asked questions such as the following, a regression model may be a good choice for producing a deliverable:

- What factors predict the return on investment (ROI) for different marketing channels such as social media, search engines, and email?
- What factors contribute to employee tenure at our company?
- Can we predict the expected lifetime of machinery in a manufacturing company based on its usage, maintenance data, and other potential factors?

Figure 9.2 showed an example with a continuous variable for the outcome (atmospheric pressure), so you would want to fit a model *regressing* the atmospheric pressure (*y*-variable) onto the height above sea level (the predictor or *x*-variable).

CLASSIFICATION

Instead of a continuous outcome, *classification models* attempt to understand underlying patterns in your data that determine which *category* or *discrete outcome* a data point belongs to. A classification model can help you answer questions such as the following:

- Can we predict whether or not a patient has a specific type of cancer using a set of biological, psychological, and social factors?
- Can we use the same factors as the employee tenure regression model question to predict whether or not an employee will resign in the next quarter?
- Can we predict whether a crop will be healthy, at risk, or likely to be diseased based on weather conditions, soil quality, and crop type?

The underlying mathematical approach to regression and classification can be quite similar—predictors can be continuous or categorical, and many formulas can be used for both approaches (e.g., linear regression versus logistic regression, random forest regression versus random forest classifier). Figure 9.4 shows a simple example of how a classification model is fitted to a dataset compared to a regression model—instead of a line, a curve is fit to the model, and a *decision boundary* is estimated as a threshold for where data points are classified into each category.

Often, the questions you receive from stakeholders can be answered by either a regression or classification model. The second example questions in this and the previous section can likely use the same data sources as inputs, and the resulting models will primarily differ in how the outcome variable is structured. Work with your

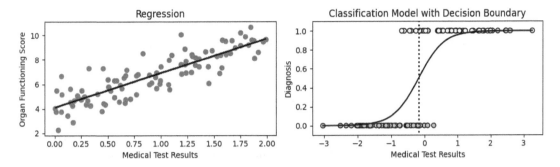

Figure 9.4   Regression and classification models are among the most commonly used in statistics.

stakeholders to determine whether a continuous or categorical outcome better meets their needs.

TIME SERIES

Time series models are a special type of model that uses historical data captured *over time* to predict future values. These models account for factors in previous data (e.g., seasonality, overall trends, recent trends) to provide an estimate for future time periods. For example, businesses often attempt to forecast their revenue over the coming weeks, months, and quarters. Questions that you answer using a time series model often look like the following:

- What is a city's forecasted daily electricity consumption over the next seven days?
- Can we predict weekly sales for a retail store while considering the upcoming holidays?
- Is it possible to predict hospitalizations for a specific disease over the coming season? What factors enable us to predict these values accurately?

Time series models are invaluable in finance, economic forecasting, environmental studies, etc. These models involve unique challenges, where analysts need to account for the unique *components* of the model (e.g., seasonality, trend, and noise). For example, figure 9.5 shows a model with seasonality (patterns recurring over a time period)

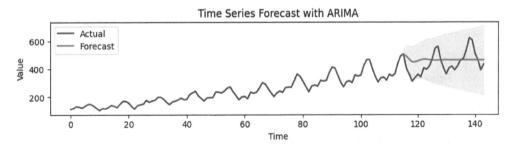

Figure 9.5   Time series models look for patterns in data captured over time to predict future values.

and an *increasing trend.* Each of these needs to be separately accounted for to forecast future values appropriately. Models like ARIMA (autoregressive integrated moving average) and Holt-Winters can identify and adjust for the specific trends you're working with.

SURVIVAL ANALYSIS

Survival analysis models attempt to predict *how much time will pass* until an event occurs. Essentially, these models seek to estimate how long individuals (e.g., a cancer patient in treatment) will *survive* a period of time. This model class partially overlaps with regression; however, powerful nonregression techniques are available for this type of problem. These are commonly used in clinical trials to predict the survival time of patients with serious illnesses. Outside of clinical research, survival analysis models can be used to answer questions such as the following:

- When will a machine in a factory fail?
- How long will a customer remain subscribed to your service?
- What factors contribute to users dropping off the paid subscription sign-up process?

At each time interval, survival curves estimate the probability of survival for the sample used to fit the model. The curve in figure 9.6 appears like a decreasing step, showing that the probability of survival drops after each subsequent time interval for the sample. The drop-off is more pronounced for the control group, suggesting that the treatment is associated with a prolonged probability of survival. The `lifelines` library in Python allows you to easily apply many common formulas for survival analyses, such as the Kaplan-Meier survival curve shown in figure 9.6.

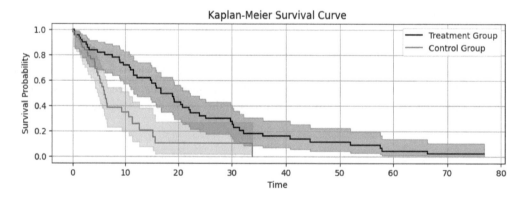

Figure 9.6 Survival analysis models predict the probability of surviving an event after each time period.

HIERARCHICAL MODELS

Hierarchical or *multi-level models* are extensions of regression and classification models that account for situations where your factors have an inherent *hierarchical structure* (e.g., a city within a state within a country). These models look for patterns at the level of the individual you collect data from *and* the nested groups they belong to. Hierarchical models can help you answer questions that otherwise require separate models, such as the following:

- What is the performance of different subcontractors in our company, considering hierarchical relationships between each subcontractor and the primary contracting company?
- What is the expected tenure of new employees hired in each department?
- Can we model student test performance, considering individual student factors, classroom-level factors, and school-level factors that can each affect test scores?

Figure 9.7 shows how a hierarchical model can evaluate testing performance for individual students, their schools, and their US states.

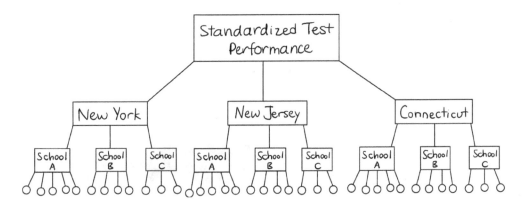

Figure 9.7   Hierarchical models allow you to capture multiple levels of underlying patterns in your data.

Hierarchical models are valuable when studying complex real-world phenomena in the social sciences and related domains. If your work involves understanding people in their day-to-day environments (e.g., nonprofit or public sectors), hierarchical models may be a common choice in peer-reviewed research that you can reference in your work, and they may also be an excellent choice to answer your stakeholders' questions. Many hierarchical models can also be used to better model *sparse* data (data where most values are zero or the sample size is low) with more than one level.

CLUSTERING

Clustering models look to categorize data points into *groups* or *clusters* based on their underlying similarity according to variables you select, where you don't have a designated outcome or *y*-variable. Most clustering algorithms are considered *unsupervised models* in machine learning, dealing with data that has no pre-existing categories. In those cases, it's up to the user to interpret the model's outcome and determine if there is value in the clusters to which each data point was assigned.

Questions answered using a clustering model tend to be more open-ended and may look like one of the following examples:

- Can we use patterns in customer browser behavior, purchase behavior, and feedback to identify distinct *groups* or *segments*? Can these segments help us improve how we meet customer needs?
- Can we group neighborhoods based on median income, school performance, and population density to support urban planning and resource allocation efforts?
- What underlying patterns of customer behavior exist based on the usage pattern of our software? Can we discover underlying groups based on login frequency, number of actions taken in the app, and time spent on the app?

Figure 9.8 depicts a scatterplot of two variables and four clusters assigned using a *k*-means clustering algorithm.

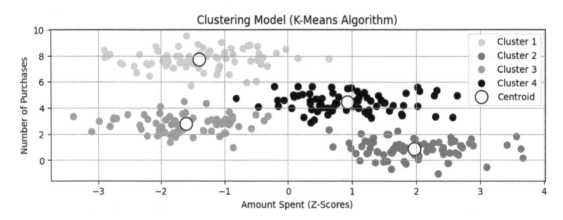

Figure 9.8   Clustering models look for underlying patterns to create categories based on the data.

Clustering models can be a valuable tool for surfacing patterns you didn't know existed. However, these models are *not* magic—there's a lot of manual work necessary to determine if the clusters generated are meaningful, easily differentiable, and able to generate value for your organization. Be prepared to spend *a lot* of time understanding the differences between clusters after you fit the model.

DIMENSION REDUCTION

Dimension reduction models aim to reduce the number of variables in a dataset by creating *composite variables* that represent the majority of the variability present in the data. The new composite *dimensions* correspond to *combinations* of the original set of variables and are then used as inputs in other models to replace those original sets. These techniques are used when you are working with a large number of inputs that would make it challenging to discern meaningful patterns in the data.

For example, the dataset in figure 9.9 has ten columns that we can potentially use for predicting the amount of time until the next purchase or the amount of that purchase. While there's no hard cutoff for the number of predictors in a model, including all ten may put us at risk for overfitting the model and reducing its ability to generate accurate predictions on future data. A dimension reduction model, such as *principal component analysis* (PCA), can potentially represent the variation of these ten inputs in three or four "components."

age	income	avg_spend	visit_freq	last_purchase	n_purchases	loyalty_card	time_in_store	n_returns	feedback_score
56	103763	406	27	17	81	0	102	8	2
69	28680	21	49	1196	98	1	33	0	3
46	104896	616	13	1670	13	0	69	8	2
32	103879	311	33	1624	99	0	131	8	4
60	91295	907	34	325	68	1	140	8	2

Figure 9.9 Dimension reduction models are used when models contain too many inputs to tease out the effect of any individual variable.

For example, the plot in figure 9.10 (known as a *scree plot*) shows the proportion of total variance among the input variables explained by each additional component. A cutoff is selected at the "elbow," a visual point of diminishing returns from each additional component.

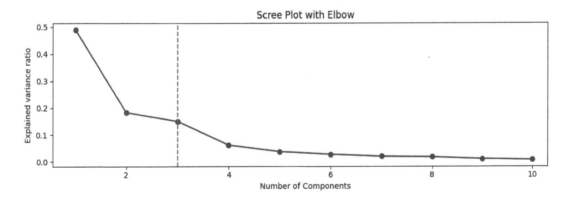

Figure 9.10 Often, a large number of variables can be represented with a fewer number of "components."

9.1.2   *Model output and diagnostics*

Fitting a model in Python, R, or any proprietary software is straightforward. A few lines of code in Python summarize an *ordinary least squares* (OLS) regression model, a common formula for estimating linear patterns in your data.

With this and any model you fit to your dataset, you can calculate several *diagnostics* that inform you about its behavior, fit, and performance. These include coefficients signifying the importance of individual predictors, metrics that evaluate the overall predictive accuracy, and residuals that assess discrepancies between observed and predicted values.

The statsmodels library gives you a detailed summary of a fitted regression model containing nearly every diagnostic you will need to evaluate your model:

```
import statsmodels.api as sm

import pandas as pd
housing_prices = pd.read_csv("housing_prices.csv")
```
Import statsmodels, pandas, and the dataframe.

```
X = housing_prices[["sq_footage", "n_bedrooms"]]
y = housing_prices["price"]
X = sm.add_constant(X)
```
Create an X and y variable for the predictors and outcome, respectively.

Add the y-intercept to the model.

```
model = sm.OLS(y, X).fit()
print(model.summary())
```
Print the model results.

The model summary produced by the code (figure 9.11) contains *a lot* of information. Each value you see contains unique information about the model's performance. Some of the information is unique to regression models, some is useful for interpret-

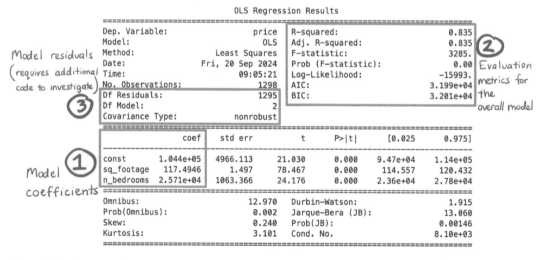

Figure 9.11   A statsmodels summary output for an OLS regression predicting housing prices using the square footage and number of bedrooms.

ing classification models, and some has parallels to other models. We'll focus on the three critical pieces of output shown in the figure:

1   Model coefficients
2   Evaluation metrics
3   Model residuals

As discussed, we will spend most of this chapter focusing on the coefficients, evaluation metrics, and residuals in a regression model. We'll highlight where there are differences between model classes so you can follow up with additional resources specific to these models.

MODEL COEFFICIENTS

A regression model aims to estimate or predict a dependent or *y*-variable using one or more independent or *x*-variables. The model's *equation* allows us to input new data collected about our input variables and estimate the outcome. As we covered in chapter 4, the equation representing a regression model with a *linear formula* is depicted in figure 9.12.

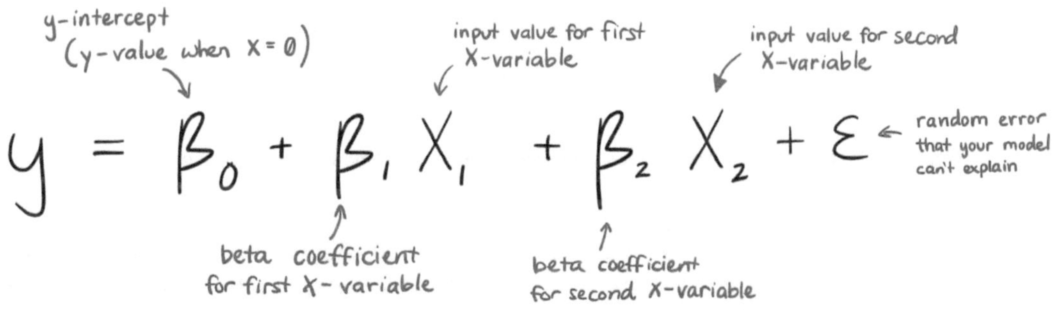

$$y = \beta_0 + \beta_1 X_1 + \beta_2 X_2 + \varepsilon$$

y-intercept (y-value when X = 0)
input value for first X-variable
input value for second X-variable
random error that your model can't explain
beta coefficient for first X-variable
beta coefficient for second X-variable

Figure 9.12   Linear multiple regression equation with two independent variables and an error term

Essentially, the beta values in a regression equation are multiplied by the value of each corresponding independent variable for a row in your dataset, and they're added together with the *y*-intercept, providing you with an estimated *y*-value for that record. From this formula, we can create a real-world example to estimate house prices using the price per square foot and the number of bedrooms.

After fitting a linear multiple regression model, we get a *y*-intercept and a set of coefficients that we can input into the equation. The first set of circled values in figure 9.11 are precisely the ones we need—they only have to be multiplied by 100 to get a final predicted house price in the hundreds of thousands. Figure 9.13 shows the regression equation with the beta coefficients for house prices.

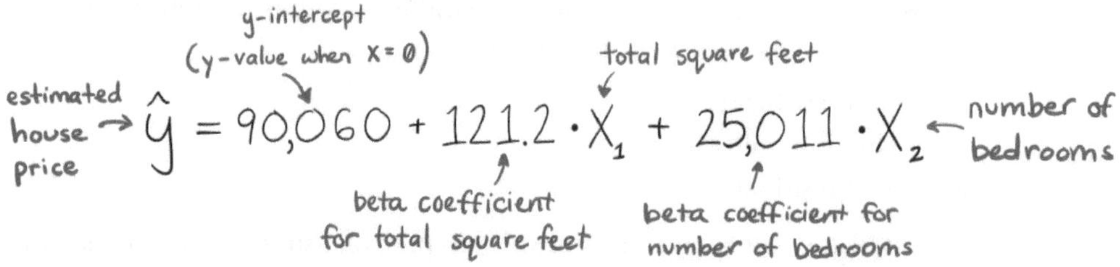

$$\underset{\substack{\text{estimated} \\ \text{house} \\ \text{price}}}{\hat{y}} = \underset{\substack{\text{y-intercept} \\ (\text{y-value when } X=0)}}{90{,}060} + \underset{\substack{\text{beta coefficient} \\ \text{for total square feet}}}{121.2 \cdot X_1} + \underset{\substack{\text{beta coefficient for} \\ \text{number of bedrooms}}}{25{,}011 \cdot X_2} \underset{\substack{\text{number of} \\ \text{bedrooms}}}{\leftarrow}$$

total square feet

Figure 9.13 A linear model estimating the price of a house based on the price per square foot and number of bedrooms. The carat on the y denotes that we are working with an estimate.

From there, when considering a house with 1,500 square feet and three bedrooms, we can input those values into the model to estimate the price the house would sell for in the dataset. This gives us the price estimate in figure 9.14.

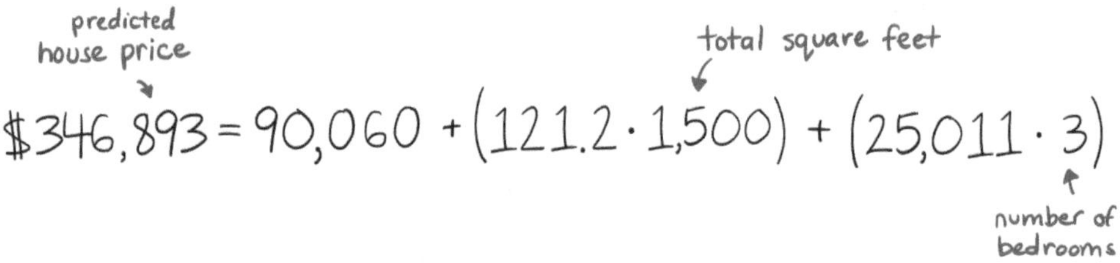

$$\underset{\substack{\text{predicted} \\ \text{house price}}}{\$346{,}893} = 90{,}060 + \underset{\text{total square feet}}{\left(121.2 \cdot 1{,}500\right)} + \underset{\substack{\text{number of} \\ \text{bedrooms}}}{\left(25{,}011 \cdot 3\right)}$$

Figure 9.14 Estimating a house price with new inputs not included in the original sample

If we have input data about houses *not* in the original sample, we can use this equation to estimate the price the house will sell for. These *out-of-sample* predictions are the basis for so much of the value generated with a fitted model. *Predictive modeling*, as it's known, is the process of using statistical models and machine learning algorithms to *predict future outcomes based on historical data.*

Predictive modeling involves a rigorous process of fitting, fine-tuning, and rigorously testing a model to ensure its applicability in the real world. For example, our housing price equation will probably only apply to the geographic region from which its original sample came. An appropriate model will also need to include other inputs (e.g., money spent on renovations, commuting distance to an urban center) so that it doesn't falter when encountering new information not present in the original dataset. We'll cover this more in sections 9.2 and 9.3; what's important to remember now is that the model equation with its coefficients *is* the deliverable for a situation where we want to predict future values.

EVALUATION METRICS

On their own, model coefficients don't tell us about the ability to predict our outcome variable. We have access to a wide range of diagnostics available for this purpose.

These *metrics* are designed to be evaluated together, giving you a comprehensive picture of how well your fitted regression model performs.

Let's unpack the evaluation metrics for the overall model (shown at #2 in figure 9.11). There are two types of metrics shown here—*absolute indicators* that tell you about the performance of the single model you are evaluating and *relative indicators* used to compare between models. The first three are *absolute indicators*, which we can interpret for one model:

- The *R-squared* (R^2) value is the proportion of variance in your output variable explained by all input variables. When presenting the effect of your model to colleagues and stakeholders, R^2 is your go-to number. R^2 values range from 0 to 1, with a larger value indicating that your model explains a greater proportion of the variance in your output variable. For example, in our housing model from figure 9.11, an R^2 of .836 captures about 83.6% of the variation in a house price. This is a *very* strong score, indicating the model has a lot of potential for many possible deliverables.

- The *adjusted R-squared* value modifies the original R^2 score based on the number of predictors in the model. While the R^2 score increases as you add more predictors, the adjusted R^2 value can decrease if those predictors don't sufficiently improve the model's fit. You don't want to add infinitely more predictors, and a more discerning metric like the adjusted R^2 reminds you to be careful when increasing a model's complexity. With only two predictors, the model summary in figure 9.11 shows an adjusted R^2 of identical value to the original score.

- The *F-statistic* is a coefficient from a test of the overall statistical significance of your model (remember this from chapter 4?). The *F*-test in a model assesses whether your predictors *collectively* influence the outcome. The accompanying *p*-value is interpreted the same way as any other statistical test—the probability that the true *F*-statistic is the same or larger than you generated, assuming your null hypothesis is true (e.g., the predictors collectively do not influence the outcome). Figure 9.11 depicts a very high *F*-statistic and a *p*-value less than 0.001, indicating that, collectively, the predictors are highly statistically significant predictors of housing prices.

The other three metrics in this section are *relative metrics* designed to be compared *between* models:

- The *log-likelihood* is an overall indicator of how well your model fits the data. It can range from negative to positive infinity, but the actual value produced for one model cannot be evaluated independently. It calculates the following two indicators: popular choices in predictive modeling and machine learning.

- *Akaike information criterion* (AIC) evaluates the overall *quality* between models, defined as a balance between fit and complexity—the lower the AIC, the better the model. You have many decisions to make as an analyst—transforming variables, adding predictors, and more. Performing each of these actions is a trade-off—you may increase your R^2, but you reduce your ability to make accurate and actionable predictions. AIC helps you balance these trade-offs and understand the effect of various changes to your model.

- *Bayesian information criterion* (BIC), like AIC, is used to evaluate the overall quality of your model. It's interpreted similarly to AIC—the lower the value, the better the model. It does include a heavier penalty for the complexity of your model, so this indicator is a good choice when you need to err on the side of model simplicity. We'll discuss practical situations where AIC and BIC are better choices for model evaluation later in this chapter.

Let's increase the complexity of the model shown in figure 9.11 by adding a third predictor, the *number of floors*. If we fit a linear regression to the data once again and display the summary, the resulting model is shown in figure 9.15.

```
                            OLS Regression Results
==============================================================================
Dep. Variable:                  price   R-squared:                       0.836
Model:                            OLS   Adj. R-squared:                  0.836
Method:                 Least Squares   F-statistic:                     2203.
Date:                Sat, 14 Oct 2023   Prob (F-statistic):               0.00
Time:                        18:13:12   Log-Likelihood:                -9882.1
No. Observations:                1298   AIC:                         1.977e+04
Df Residuals:                    1294   BIC:                         1.979e+04
Df Model:                           3
Covariance Type:            nonrobust
==============================================================================
                 coef    std err          t      P>|t|      [0.025      0.975]
------------------------------------------------------------------------------
const          900.8486     53.029     16.988      0.000     796.816    1004.881
sq_footage       1.2123      0.017     72.438      0.000       1.179       1.245
n_bedrooms     250.1204      9.660     25.892      0.000     231.169     269.072
n_floors        -0.3320     37.225     -0.009      0.993     -73.360      72.696
==============================================================================
```

Figure 9.15 Housing prices summary with an added predictor that introduces complexity to the model.

Each evaluation metric we discussed differs slightly with the addition of a third predictor:

- The R^2 and adjusted scores did not change with the additional predictor. This suggests that the third variable did not enable us to explain more variance in housing prices.
- The *F*-statistic is lower than the original model, though it's still statistically significant.
- Each relative metric is identical to the first model, suggesting we didn't add valuable information to the model with this new variable.

- Further, we can see that the *t*-value and *p*-value for the third predictor (in the bottom square of the output) are *not* statistically significant. Overall, this suggests that the number of floors in the house doesn't add any information not already captured in the original model, and they should probably be dropped. Thus, the best linear model we have fit contains two predictors.

Our example here is overly simple compared to an analyst's steps in the real world. Typically, you can expect to compare multiple models, testing different formulas and combinations of predictors to best represent your outcome variable. These steps are pretty similar across classes of models, but the evaluation metrics differ. Still, your task is to compare absolute and relative models to produce the best output for your deliverable.

RESIDUALS

No model perfectly explains all of the variability in your data. Some examples come close (e.g., an R^2 of .95), but you're far more likely to encounter situations where achieving a high-quality fit is challenging. Understanding the parts of your model you *cannot* explain is as important as what you can.

This is where residuals come into play, spotlighting the gaps between your model's predictions and the actual data. A *residual* is the difference between an observed outcome and the model's predicted value. By sifting through residuals, you can identify patterns or trends indicating quirks in your data that your model may be missing. This is usually done by plotting the *residual* values against the *predicted* values. Continuing with the model used to generate figure 9.11, we can save and plot our residuals as follows:

```
housing_prices["residuals"] = model.resid
housing_prices["predicted_values"] = model.predict()
```

Save the residuals and predicted values as new columns in the dataframe.

```
plt.scatter(
    housing_prices["predicted_values"],
    housing_prices["residuals"]
)
```

Create a scatterplot of the predicted values against the residuals.

```
plt.axhline(y=0, color= "black", linestyle="-")
```

Add a horizontal line at 0 to better display the residuals centered around 0.

Figure 9.16 shows the scatterplot of residuals versus predicted values generated by the code.

Ideally, the residuals should be equally spread out from zero about the *y*-axis, indicating low differences between predicted and actual values. The scatterplot should resemble a cloud across both axes. If any clear shape or trend is visible, you may have a problem with *heteroscedasticity* in your model (a fancy term suggesting that your spread of residuals isn't consistent across your data). For example, if your residuals are positively correlated with your predicted values, your model is less accurate at predicting high or low values.

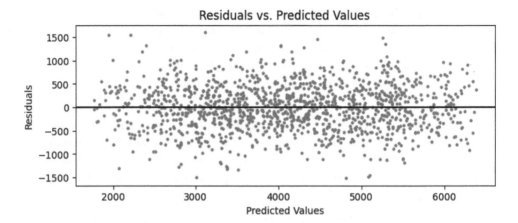

Figure 9.16   Scatterplot of residuals versus the predicted values for each record in the dataset used to fit the regression model

A histogram of residuals can be equally revealing. We expect residuals to be *normally distributed* when working with linear regression models. We can generate a quick histogram of our housing price prediction residuals here:

```
plt.hist(housing_prices["residuals"], bins=30)
```

The residuals for the housing price prediction model with *two* variables (shown in figure 9.17) are normally distributed, indicating *no relationship* with the predicted values. Combined with the high R^2 value, this model seems a good fit for the data! When these criteria *aren't* met, you can take the following steps to diagnose and improve your model:

- Check whether the formula you're using for your data (e.g., linear) is appropriate for the shape of the actual relationship between predictors and outcomes. If the *actual* relationship is nonlinear, you may find that your residuals are not normally distributed.

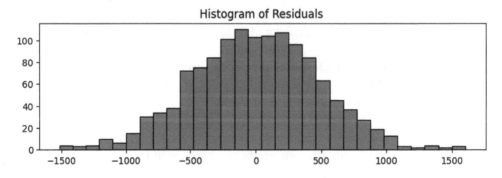

Figure 9.17   Distribution of residuals for the housing prices model

- If you have a small number of extreme outliers in your residual plots that represent erroneous data, you can try removing those records and refitting your model.
- Think about the domain you're working in—are there any predictors or explanatory variables that might be missing from your model? Sometimes, an obvious missing variable can cause residuals to capture patterns they shouldn't, and incorporating additional relevant data can remove those patterns. This is necessary if you plan on making causal inferences from your model.
- If the preceding steps don't work, it might just be that your data isn't a good fit for a linear model. Consider trying more robust techniques such as generalized linear models (GLMs), support vector regression, or random forest regression. You have no shortage of options for trying to model your data.

9.1.3 Exercises

1 A researcher is trying to predict the exact height of people based on their age, weight, and shoe size. What type of statistical model is most appropriate?

2 In survival analysis, what are we typically trying to predict?
   - The amount of time until an event occurs
   - The number of events occurring in a time period
   - The class label of a row in a dataset
   - How many components we can reduce our dataset into

3 A company wants to predict whether a user will click on an advertisement (yes or no) based on their age and the number of times they've viewed it. What type of statistical model is best suited for this problem?

4 Write the general equation for a multiple linear regression model with four predictors. How does it differ from the equation shown in figure 9.12? What problems might arise as you continue adding more predictors?

5 Consider the output of a model fitted to answer question 1. How would you interpret these metrics if the R^2 value is 0.55 and the AIC and BIC are 810 and 920, respectively? What does each suggest about the model's performance and complexity?

6 If the model residuals for question 1 show two extreme positive outliers, what steps can you take to handle these records? You can assume that the rest of the histogram of residuals appears normal, and the scatterplot of residuals and predicted values is otherwise shapeless and randomly distributed.

9.2 The modeling process

An effective predictive modeling strategy starts with (surprise!) a question. Whether you and your stakeholders want to understand factors contributing to churn or predict whether users will complete a paid sign-up workflow, the steps to finding a good-fitting model are often similar. In this section, we'll cover the investigative techniques you can use to fit many predictive models.

First, let's pay attention to the questions we're going to ask in this section—they're more open-ended than questions you might ask when designing a controlled experiment. With experiments, you will typically manipulate one or two variables to test for very specific differences in an outcome. When asking more complex questions in less controlled environments, you can cast a wider net with the number and types of variables you include in your hypothesis and eventual model.

Let's look at an example. Do you remember the rats dataset from chapter 3? Fun stuff, right? In chapter 3, we discovered some noteworthy correlations between the total daily rat sightings reported in New York City and several daily weather parameters. If we're interested in *predicting* the number of daily rat sightings, we might start by asking the following question: "What factors predict the number of daily complaints about rat sightings in New York City?"

As expected, this is a broad question that doesn't yet specify what we expect will predict our outcome. We probably have an outcome in mind—reducing rat complaints—and are open to whatever information will help us reach that desired end state. However, we have a starting point; we discovered several weather parameters with strong correlations to the number of rat sightings, which can potentially predict that variable.

First, let's import the rats dataset, join it to the weather dataset, and display Pearson's correlations. Since we may not have rat sightings *every* day, we'll inner join the rats dataset to the weather dataset and fill in null records with a 0 value in the combined dataframe. The result is shown in figure 9.18:

```
rats = pd.read_csv("rat_sightings.csv")        ⟵┐ Import the rats and
weather = pd.read_csv("weather.csv")             │ weather dataframes.

rats_weather = pd.merge(
    weather,
    rats,
    on="day",                        ┌ Merge the dataframes and
    how="left"                       │ fill in missing values.
).fillna(0)                        ⟵─┘

rats_weather["day"] = pd.to_datetime(
    rats_weather["day"],
    format="%m/%d/%y"                ┌ Convert the day
)                                  ⟵┘ field to a datetime.
                                              ┌ Generate
rats_weather.corr().round(2)               ⟵─┘ correlations.
```

The high and low temperatures strongly correlate with rat sightings, and the wind speed has at least a weak to medium correlation. While we can't claim that the weather *causes* rats to be present in visible parts of the city, we *can* assume that more rat sightings will be reported to the city's hotline on warmer days with less wind.

If we're working with a city agency looking to forecast the number of complaints they will respond to, this is precisely the type of model we can try to build. Each of these weather parameters is available as part of a 7- or 10-day forecast, so a model with a good fit can be an excellent tool for planning purposes.

	high_temp	low_temp	humidity	wind_speed	precip	rat_sightings
high_temp	1.00	0.96	0.17	-0.22	-0.04	0.60
low_temp	0.96	1.00	0.19	-0.25	-0.03	0.61
humidity	0.17	0.19	1.00	0.04	0.23	0.15
wind_speed	-0.22	-0.25	0.04	1.00	0.21	-0.24
precip	-0.04	-0.03	0.23	0.21	1.00	-0.03
rat_sightings	0.60	0.61	0.15	-0.24	-0.03	1.00

Figure 9.18 **Pearson's correlations between daily weather and rat sightings, rounded to two decimal points**

From these variables, we can develop a hypothesis that informs our initial model:

H_0: No discernable factors predict the daily rat sightings in New York City.

H_1: Hotter temperatures and lower wind speeds predict higher daily rat sightings in New York City.

We'll iterate on this hypothesis several times as we discover more about the relationships between predictors and derive additional variables. For now, the strong correlations suggest that linear regression is an excellent place to start.

9.2.1 Exploratory analysis

Exploratory data analysis is woven into every step of our work. Just as you'd explore the underlying trends when conducting a *t*-test or building a dashboard, a detailed exploration is necessary to understand the complex statistical relationships you're attempting to model. Regardless of your model's assumptions (e.g., linearity for linear regression), you'll perform many of the same steps: visually exploring your data, deriving additional variables, and transforming one or more variables to meet those assumptions.

DERIVING ADDITIONAL VARIABLES

The first version of a dataset you synthesize for analysis will rarely enable you to fit a model with value to your organization or business. Most processes easily measured at your organization require some wrangling to get what you need for modeling. This work, also known as *feature engineering* in machine learning, combines your domain knowledge, mathematical insight, and analytical intuition to find the best possible predictors.

Take our rats dataset—this was synthesized using 311 data, which contains billions of detailed records for an incredible range of calls to the city's hotline. Since we want to predict the *volume* of rat sighting complaints at a given point, the data was filtered and aggregated to a count of sightings in a given time period. Since we're assuming that a city agency will use the data to forecast the number of complaints and how much staffing they require to respond in a timely manner, we chose a *daily* frequency to enable that process. If the city agency requires the data at an hourly grain, that can easily be updated.

Next, we gathered daily temperature data from a weather service that provides detailed daily historical data. We're combining this weather dataset with the rats dataset for two reasons—local weather parameters are often great predictors of various phenomena within the same geographic region (*analytical intuition*). Additionally, as a lifelong resident of New York City, I can confirm that rat sightings are far more common in warmer weather (*domain knowledge*).

As a reminder, a sample of the resulting dataset is shown in figure 9.19.

	day	high_temp	low_temp	humidity	wind_speed	precip	rat_sightings
0	2018-01-01	19.0	8.0	67.0	22.0	0.00	15
1	2018-01-02	26.0	14.0	59.0	21.0	0.00	36
2	2018-01-03	30.0	18.0	53.0	16.0	0.00	36
3	2018-01-04	29.0	20.0	92.0	37.0	0.02	14
4	2018-01-05	19.0	11.0	56.0	31.0	6.54	18

Figure 9.19   Preview of the combined rats and weather dataset

In chapter 3, we saw that rat sightings are seasonally dependent, with repeated increases in summer months and decreases in winter months. The daily high temperatures vary with similar patterns, as shown in figure 9.20. The time series plots tell us

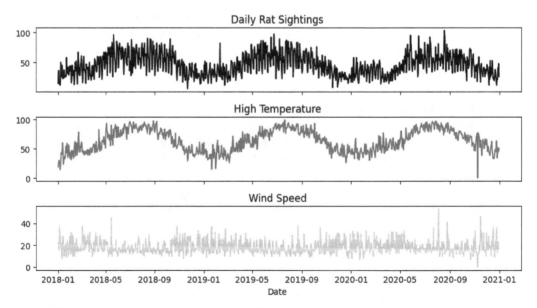

Figure 9.20   Time series plots of our outcome variable and two selected predictors

that daily high temperatures follow the same *yearly seasonal trend* as rat sightings. This isn't the case for humidity, which is still moderately correlated with rat sightings. The low correlation between temperature and wind speed also tells us that these are distinct processes. If they *were* highly correlated, we'd want to pick between the two variables, since they don't capture distinct variations in the outcome.

There's something else worth noting in these graphs—the daily rat sightings seem to have an additional, more frequent seasonal trend that could be worth capturing in our model. Since the data is captured once daily, we might see a weekly or monthly seasonal trend worth capturing in our model. This points us to our yet unexplored variable—the *day* field. You can extract *a lot* of valuable *ordinal data* from dates and timestamps to represent each type of seasonality—day of the week, day of the month, month number, week number, and day number are all easy features to derive and explore when time is an important variable in your model. Let's extract the month number and day of the week as new, separate columns:

Add a column with the day of the week number (from 0 to 6) starting with Monday.

```
rats_weather["dow"] = rats_weather["day"].dt.dayofweek
rats_weather["month_num"] = rats_weather["day"].dt.month
rats_weather.head()
```

Display the first five rows of the dataset.

Add a column with the month number (from 1 through 12) in a calendar year.

The two new columns shown in figure 9.21 have *integers* representing *discrete ordinal* rather than *continuous* data. This means that we cannot reliably run Pearson's correlations on the data and use them in our model directly.

	day	high_temp	low_temp	humidity	wind_speed	precip	rat_sightings	dow	month_num
0	2018-01-01	19.0	8.0	67.0	22.0	0.00	15	0	1
1	2018-01-02	26.0	14.0	59.0	21.0	0.00	36	1	1
2	2018-01-03	30.0	18.0	53.0	16.0	0.00	36	2	1
3	2018-01-04	29.0	20.0	92.0	37.0	0.02	14	3	1
4	2018-01-05	19.0	11.0	56.0	31.0	6.54	18	4	1

Figure 9.21 First few rows showing the new integer columns with the day of the week and month number

Let's instead look at the distributions of rat sightings for each month number and day of the week, respectively:

Create boxplots to visualize the distributions of rat sightings by month number.

```
import seaborn as sns
```

Import the seaborn library.

```
sns.boxplot(data=rats_weather, x="month_num", y="rat_sightings")
```

Unsurprisingly, the median number of daily rat sightings in figure 9.22 shows a seasonal variation that matches the time series graphs in figure 9.20. It's unlikely that the month number provides any new information beyond the daily high temperature, so we can exclude it from the model.

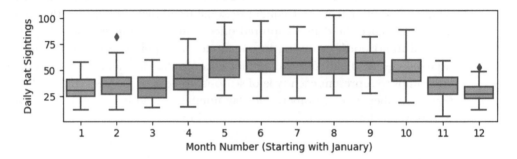

Figure 9.22   Boxplots showing the median and distributions of rat sightings for each month

Next, let's look at the same graph grouped by the day of the week variable:

```
sns.boxplot(data=rats_weather, x="dow", y="rat_sightings")
```

Figure 9.23 suggests that the `dow` (day of the week) column is a promising new variable—fewer rat sightings are reported on weekends compared to weekdays. This also introduces a new type of seasonality into the model (there's no reason to believe that daily temperatures and wind speed vary based on the day of the week), so we're unlikely to risk introducing collinearity into our model. It's also a meaningful variable in a model where we want to generate actionable predictions because we can reliably include it for future days. It also represents an essential *behavioral* component of the process that we haven't yet captured—when residents are most likely to see rats and take action to inform the city.

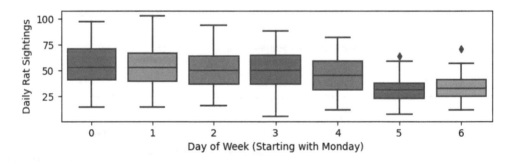

Figure 9.23   Boxplots showing the median and distributions of rat sightings for day of the week

Let's update our hypothesis to include the third variable:

> H$_1$: Hotter temperatures, lower wind speeds, and weekdays predict higher daily rat sightings in New York City.

In order to represent the day of the week, let's *dummy code* the dow column so we can include it in our model. *Dummy coding* is a technique used to represent categorical variables as a set of *binary* (0 or 1) variables indicating the presence (1) or absence (0) of each category. This method allows linear models to incorporate categorical data by treating each category as a separate variable. If we were to dummy code each day of the week, we would create separate *categorical variables* for each day of the week, as in figure 9.24. For each day of the week variable (e.g., "Monday"), the value is equal to 1, indicating that it is "Monday" on the day corresponding to that row.

	Day	Friday	Monday	Saturday	Sunday	Thursday	Tuesday	Wednesday
0	Monday	0	1	0	0	0	0	0
1	Tuesday	0	0	0	0	0	1	0
2	Wednesday	0	0	0	0	0	0	1
3	Thursday	0	0	0	0	1	0	0
4	Friday	1	0	0	0	0	0	0

Figure 9.24 Dummy-coded variables for each day of the week. The final set of variables for a model will often exclude the last category, which is implied when all other categories are absent.

Often, dummy-coded variables exclude the final category (e.g., Sunday), which is implied when all other variables equal 0. However, we know from figure 9.23 that there's little difference in the number of rat sightings between each weekday. We may be able to better represent the variable by creating a simple binary variable indicating whether or not a given day is a weekday. Let's calculate the variable and examine our Pearson's correlations again:

```
rats_weather["weekday"] = (rats_weather["dow"]<5).astype(int)     ⟵┐
rats_weather[                                                        Convert the day
    ["high_temp", "wind_speed", "weekday", "rat_sightings"]          of the week into
].corr().round(2)        ⟵┐ Recalculate correlations with            a binary weekday
                           the new dummy variable.                   column.
```

Figure 9.25 shows a strong correlation between the new binary weekday column and the number of daily rat sightings—as well as *no* correlation with the temperature or wind speed. Therefore, it seems sensible to include it in our model.

There's no hard and fast rule for how much time or effort you should spend deriving additional variables. You'll need to use your best judgment as an analyst for any

	high_temp	wind_speed	weekday	rat_sightings
high_temp	1.00	-0.22	0.01	0.60
wind_speed	-0.22	1.00	0.02	-0.24
weekday	0.01	0.02	1.00	0.47
rat_sightings	0.60	-0.24	0.47	1.00

Figure 9.25 Correlation matrix including the new binary weekday column.

project, estimating the time it takes to derive each new feature, the pros and cons of increasing the model's complexity, and when your model is *good enough* for its intended purpose. We've hit a stopping point for our example in this section—we found a new promising variable, and any other inputs would likely require identifying and combining our rats data with a third set of variables.

EVALUATING ASSUMPTIONS

Since we've chosen to start by fitting a linear model, we'll need to evaluate the assumptions associated with a linear process. Specifically, we'll need to answer the following questions:

- Are the relationships between our predictors and the outcome of interest linear? Do we need to perform a transformation (see chapter 4) to better represent the relationship?
- Are the predictors correlated with *each other*? This is known as *collinearity*, which makes it challenging to isolate the effect of any one predictor and can lead to inaccurate model coefficients and poor-quality predictions.

The seaborn library has a great option known as a *pairplot*, which visually represents a correlation matrix and includes histograms for individual variables on the identity (diagonal). A pairplot can be generated for an entire dataframe, but these tend to be quite large, so let's subset this to the variables we included in our hypothesis:

```
sns.pairplot(
    rats_weather[["high_temp", "wind_speed", "weekday", "rat_sightings"]]
)
```

Figure 9.26 shows some interesting trends we should consider testing further, before fitting a linear model:

- The relationship between wind speed and rat sightings may be *slightly* curvilinear. We won't know until we transform one of the variables, since the scatterplot is densely packed.
- Unlike the other variables in our dataset, the day of the week variable follows a *uniform distribution*. You'll notice it's also a discrete and finite integer rather than a continuous value, which may affect the quality of the model. We'll see if including this variable affects the normality of our residuals later in this section.

- There are no strong relationships between predictors, which aligns with the *r*-values shown in figure 9.18.

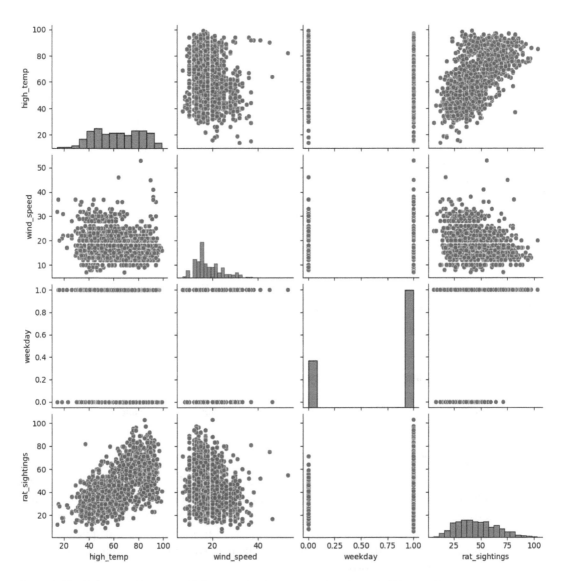

Figure 9.26 Seaborn pairplots are similar to a visual representation of a correlation matrix.

We can quickly test the first consideration to determine whether a transformation may improve our model. It's not immediately clear whether the scatterplot shows a curvilinear relationship in the bottom-left or top-right quadrant, so let's both square and take the square root of wind speed values to see if there's an effect on Pearson's correlation:

```
import numpy as np      ◁——| Import the numpy library.

rats_weather["wind_speed_sq"] = rats_weather["wind_speed"]**2
rats_weather["wind_speed_sqrt"] = np.sqrt(rats_weather["wind_speed"])    ◁——┐

rats_weather[
    ["wind_speed_sq", "wind_speed_sqrt", "wind_speed", "rat_sightings"]
].corr().round(2)      ◁——┐  Compare the Pearson's
                           correlations.
```

Create new columns with the square and square root of the wind speed column.

The correlation values in figure 9.27 are nearly identical—the squared and square root of wind speed are slightly less correlated with rat sightings than the actual value. Even if they were one point higher ($r=0.25$), it would not be different enough to suggest that the relationship isn't linear. Thus, on the whole, we can say that we meet the model's assumptions so far. We will test this again once we fit our model and examine the residuals.

	wind_speed_sq	wind_speed_sqrt	wind_speed	rat_sightings
wind_speed_sq	1.00	0.94	0.98	-0.23
wind_speed_sqrt	0.94	1.00	0.99	-0.23
wind_speed	0.98	0.99	1.00	-0.24
rat_sightings	-0.23	-0.23	-0.24	1.00

Figure 9.27   Pearson's correlation values between the transformed variables and the outcome

9.2.2   Fitting a model

Yes, we've finally made it! It's time to fit and evaluate the model! In practice, you'll probably test the model's fit through exploratory iterations. There are only so many times in this chapter I can show you the same output with minimal variations, but you'll get no judgment from me if you choose to test something out quickly. If you perform your exploratory steps with due diligence, you can select whatever work pattern aids your strategic process.

Let's fit our model with the three predictors we've been working with:

```
X = rats_weather[["high_temp", "wind_speed", "weekday"]]
y = rats_weather["rat_sightings"]      ◁——┐  Create an X and y variable for the
                                            predictors and outcome, respectively.
X = sm.add_constant(X)    ◁——┐  Add a constant to
                               represent the y-intercept.
```

```
model = sm.OLS(y, X).fit()
print(model.summary())
```
◁─┐ **Print the**
  │ **model results.**

EVALUATING OUTPUT

What do you notice about the model output in figure 9.28? At first glance, would you say this is a good-fitting model? How do you know? A first glance at the evaluation metrics we've covered tells us the following:

- The R^2 of the model is 0.588, indicating that we can explain nearly 60% of the variation in the number of rat sighting calls per day. The adjusted R^2 value is only marginally lower, suggesting the complexity of the model isn't being heavily penalized at this point.
- The overall F-statistic is quite large and statistically significant, indicating that our chosen model fits the data well.
- Each predictor has a statistically significant t-value, indicating that each significantly contributes to the variation in daily rat sightings. The relative size and direction of the t-value align with what we saw in the Pearson's correlation matrix in figure 9.18, suggesting that any collinearity present is not affecting the predictions.

```
                            OLS Regression Results
==============================================================================
Dep. Variable:          rat_sightings   R-squared:                       0.588
Model:                            OLS   Adj. R-squared:                  0.587
Method:                 Least Squares   F-statistic:                     519.6
Date:                Wed, 27 Dec 2023   Prob (F-statistic):           1.02e-209
Time:                        21:27:59   Log-Likelihood:                 -4245.3
No. Observations:                1096   AIC:                             8499.
Df Residuals:                    1092   BIC:                             8519.
Df Model:                           3
Covariance Type:            nonrobust
==============================================================================
                 coef    std err          t      P>|t|      [0.025      0.975]
------------------------------------------------------------------------------
const          4.0289      1.949      2.067      0.039      0.205       7.853
high_temp      0.5598      0.020     28.559      0.000      0.521       0.598
wind_speed    -0.3766      0.061     -6.206      0.000     -0.496      -0.258
weekday       18.7393      0.781     24.000      0.000     17.207      20.271
==============================================================================
Omnibus:                       11.688   Durbin-Watson:                   1.337
Prob(Omnibus):                  0.003   Jarque-Bera (JB):               14.968
Skew:                           0.135   Prob(JB):                     0.000562
Kurtosis:                       3.505   Cond. No.                         381.
==============================================================================
```

Figure 9.28 Summary of a linear regression model predicting daily rat sightings.

These initial findings suggest we can reasonably estimate the number of rat sightings per day with these three data points. Next, let's evaluate our residuals by plotting them against the predicted rat sighting values for the model:

```
rats_weather["residuals"] = model.resid
rats_weather["predicted_values"] = model.predict()

plt.scatter(
    rats_weather["predicted_values"],
    rats_weather["residuals"], color="gray", s=5
)
plt.axhline(y=0, color="black", linestyle="-")
```

◁— **Save the residuals and predicted values as new columns in rats_weather.**

◁— **Create a scatterplot of the predicted values against the residuals.**

◁— **Add a horizontal line at 0 to display the residuals centered around 0.**

The residual plot in figure 9.29 isn't as uniform as our example in figure 9.16. The majority of the cloud appears formless, but there's a noticeable gap of values on the far left of the plot—specifically, you can see a few outliers in the top-left and an absence of values in the bottom-left quadrant. Without one or more of these outliers, the cloud of residuals would seem far more "formless" than expected.

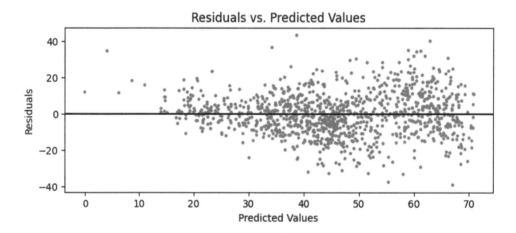

Figure 9.29 Plot of residuals against the predicted rat sighting values

Let's display the records in the dataset with low predicted values:

```
rats_weather[rats_weather["predicted_values"]<10]
```

One problem is immediately evident in figure 9.30—row 1,042 has no weather data! We filled the null weather values with 0 earlier in this chapter, potentially skewing predictions based on illegitimate values. As such, we should *drop this record from our model.*

The remaining records appear to be legitimate outliers, which we can consider handling in several ways. We'll discuss that in the next section as we iterate on our model.

	day	high_temp	wind_speed	rat_sightings	weekday	residuals	predicted_values
5	2018-01-06	14.0	32.0	12	0	12.18	-0.18
6	2018-01-07	18.0	21.0	18	0	11.80	6.20
13	2018-01-14	23.0	22.0	27	0	18.38	8.62
1042	2020-11-08	0.0	0.0	39	0	34.97	4.03

Figure 9.30   Preview of dataset records with low predicted values

ITERATING ON THE MODEL

We've come a long way, but don't forget that this is the first actual model we've fit together and evaluated from end to end. We can make many minor improvements to ensure we're meeting all the necessary assumptions for linear regression and generating the best predictions for our stakeholders.

We identified two steps to take when evaluating our model:

- Handle the missing weather data by removing or replacing it as appropriate.
- Determine if we should perform a transformation on one or more variables to reduce the number of outliers in our residuals.

Let's start by removing the outlier from the dataset and fitting the model again:

```
rats_weather = rats_weather[rats_weather["high_temp"]!=0]
```

When we fit the model a second time, we get the overall model summary in figure 9.31.

```
                          OLS Regression Results
=============================================================================
Dep. Variable:         rat_sightings   R-squared:                    0.591
Model:                           OLS   Adj. R-squared:               0.590
Method:                Least Squares   F-statistic:                  526.6
Date:               Wed, 27 Dec 2023   Prob (F-statistic):        1.66e-211
Time:                       22:01:14   Log-Likelihood:              -4237.3
No. Observations:               1095   AIC:                          8483.
Df Residuals:                   1091   BIC:                          8503.
Df Model:                          3
Covariance Type:           nonrobust
=============================================================================
```

Figure 9.31   Overall regression results for the model with bad data removed

The R^2 has slightly increased by removing *a single* erroneous data point. You'll notice that the AIC and BIC values have also decreased.

Next, let's examine the residual plot in figure 9.32 for any changes. As expected, the most extreme outlier we observed in figure 9.29 is no longer present. However, the change did little to alter the overall shape of the residual plot or remove the extreme outliers on the left side of the plot. You'll recall from figure 9.30 that each of these outliers was present on days where the daily high temperatures were quite low—the weather itself was an outlier on each of these days, which is potentially throwing off the model and leading it to underpredict the number of rat sightings when it's extremely cold.

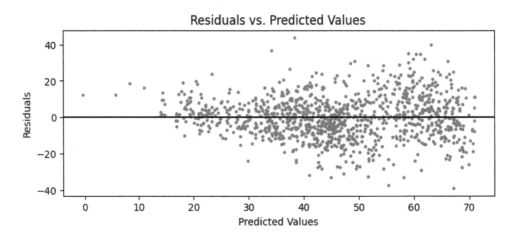

Figure 9.32   Residual plot for an adjusted model, showing the removal of the outlier

We can try to handle this problem by taking a square root of the *y*-variable, in case a curvilinear relationship is present that we could not detect visually. This is done by adjusting the model-fitting code as follows:

```
X = rats_weather[["high_temp", "wind_speed", "weekday"]]
y = np.sqrt(rats_weather["rat_sightings"])          Take the square root of the
X = sm.add_constant(X)                              number of rat sightings as
                                                    the new y-variable.
model = sm.OLS(y, X).fit()        Fit the model again
print(model.summary())            and show the results.
```

This second iteration of our model, shown in figure 9.33, explains up to 60% of the variance in the square root of rat sightings, and the *F*-statistic is much larger. You'll also notice that the AIC and BIC of this model are *far lower* than the first two, indicating that the transformation produces a model that better explains our outcome variable.

```
                         OLS Regression Results
===============================================================================
Dep. Variable:         rat_sightings   R-squared:                      0.604
Model:                           OLS   Adj. R-squared:                 0.603
Method:                Least Squares   F-statistic:                    554.8
Date:               Wed, 27 Dec 2023   Prob (F-statistic):          6.74e-219
Time:                       22:04:56   Log-Likelihood:               -1382.8
No. Observations:               1095   AIC:                            2774.
Df Residuals:                   1091   BIC:                            2794.
Df Model:                          3
Covariance Type:           nonrobust
===============================================================================
```

Figure 9.33   Overall regression results for the model with a transformed *y*-variable

We'll conclude our iterations for this section; this model has served its purpose of demonstrating the model fitting, evaluation, and iteration process. However, determining an appropriate stopping point is ultimately a judgment call you will have to make as an analyst. Eventually, you will reach a point of diminishing returns on model quality, and spending vast amounts of time for little to no added value is easy. As you engage with the process of model iteration and improvement, consider the following questions:

- Do you have a strong justification for any new predictors you want to add? Is something about the process you're measuring missing from your model?
- What do you and your stakeholders achieve by producing a model with an additional 5% accuracy or variance explained? How about 10%? Is it necessary and worth it to derive value?
- Is there a point where the added complexity of additional predictors diminishes the value of your model? If your stakeholders want to take action based on the independent variables you include, how many different processes can they take on simultaneously?

Table 9.2 summarizes some benefits and limitations to keep in mind when fitting a linear regression model to your dataset.

Table 9.2   Key benefits and limitations of using linear regression models

Benefits	Limitations
✓ Ease of identifying potential factors/predictors	✗ Assumptions need to be met: linearity of relationships with outcome, normality of residuals
✓ Ease of interpreting the relationships between factors and the outcome	✗ Factors should not be correlated with each other (colinear), as this can affect the accuracy of the output
✓ Relative ease of explaining relationships to your stakeholders	✗ A large number of factors can diminish the quality and interpretability of your model

9.2.3   *Exercises*

You're an analyst working at a supply chain company. You've been provided with a dataset called production_costs, which contains several variables that may predict the profit margin of a specific item. The dataset includes the following variables:

- production_scale represents the scale in which the product is manufactured; the price per unit often decreases as the scale increases.
- corporate_tax_rate is the functional rate of taxes paid by the company manufacturing the product.
- renewable_materials is a binary variable indicating whether or not renewable materials are being used in manufacturing the product.
- hourly_labor_cost represents the cost per hour of all labor associated with the product's manufacturing.
- product_margin is the final profit margin on the sale price of the product.

In total, there are over 20,000 records in the dataset:

1   Use the provided dataset to fit a model of your choice. Perform the necessary exploration steps for that model, such as calculating Pearson's correlations and examining the shape of relationships. Based on your observations, is a linear regression appropriate for your model?

2   Which variables are you including in your model, and why? Are the relationships that you see appropriate to include in your model, or do you need to transform any variables to best represent the shape of the trend?

3   Once you fit the model, interpret the coefficients. What does each coefficient tell you about the relationship between that predictor and the product price? Are there any relationships that changed from Pearson's correlations?

4   Notice the R^2 and *F*-test results. Do they suggest that it's a good fit for the data? How would you explain the model's fit to someone unfamiliar with statistics?

5   Plot the residuals of your model against the predicted values. Do you see any patterns? What does this imply about your model's assumptions?

6   Perform at least one iteration on your model (e.g., add or remove a predictor, transform a variable). How do the AIC and BIC of your model change with these iterations?

9.3   *The statistical model and its value*

Think back to the joke at the beginning of this chapter. Three analysts are arguing about creating what amounts to a model predicting the same outcome but focusing on a different type of deliverable. Which one is *actually* more valuable?

Truthfully, none of the three options presented are inherently *better* than the rest. Each type of deliverable is valid and valuable when it's the right choice for your stakeholders' needs. You'll generally want to work with your stakeholders as early as possible to determine their needs and the types of follow-up questions you might receive.

Modeling click-through conversions from ads

Anthony is a senior data analyst supporting the marketing team at a large meal plan subscription company. He has a vital role in steering the marketing strategies of the department by providing valuable and timely insights to leadership.

One of the team's marketing managers is looking to understand the probability that each person who clicks an ad will eventually convert into a paying customer. Ads are placed in a wide variety of formats and on different websites, each of which attracts a subset of the target audience. When a person clicks an ad, the marketing team is provided some basic metadata about that person—browser type, location, and internet service provider. They also have information about the individual ad that was clicked and whether that customer then proceeded through the sign-up process that includes a free trial meal kit.

Anthony knows to start this project by narrowing down the question with the marketing manager—specifically, he asks the following questions:

1 What types of ads are run by the company? Are there classes of ads that need to be accounted for as hierarchies in the model?

2 We know that the conversion rate to paying customers is very low (less than 1%), but the conversion to the free trial is about 27%. Does it make sense to create a model that predicts free trial conversion and a separate model predicting free trial to paid conversion?

3 How will the results be used? Does the team want an explanation of the most important factors contributing to conversions, or a live model that predicts the conversion likelihood of each person as they click an ad?

Your stakeholders' responses to questions such as Anthony's will inform what type of deliverable you need to produce—an *explanatory model* that guides future strategy or a set of *predictions* to estimate future events or outcomes.

These are arguably the most important questions to answer in your modeling strategy. Your stakeholders' specific needs determine what models you can use. If you can anticipate how your models will be used, you will likely minimize confusion and follow-up questions. And who knows—you may win a bet like our hypothetical analysts at the beginning of the chapter!

9.3.1 *Explanatory models*

An *explanatory model* seeks to clearly describe the *fit* and *shape* of predictors and their relationships with the outcome variable [1]. By definition, the deliverable of these models includes *explanations* of the strength, direction, and expected effect on the outcome variable if future actions are taken. If you're working with a stakeholder who asks questions such as the following, you may need to fit a model for explanatory purposes:

- What recommendations should be made to patients with diabetes and chronic kidney disease to improve their daily blood sugar levels?
- Which educational programs should the school district focus on to increase test scores?

- Does users' webinar participation lead to an increase in their product usage activity?

Modeling for explanations typically requires you to model your data so that your stakeholders can build an appropriate mental representation of the relationships you're describing. In short, your model has to make sense to them. It has to provide output and recommendations with clear relationships so that they can develop strategic plans based on the findings. This means that your approach will need to meet the following criteria:

- There is a *strong theoretical and logical justification* for including each of your selected predictors in the model. These models are likely to be interpreted causally, so you will need to pair your work with comprehensive domain expertise to ensure you and your stakeholders can draw appropriate conclusions.
- You can *differentiate between input variables* by their importance in predicting the output variable (e.g., with significance testing in linear models or feature importance in tree-based models)
- You can explain the *shape and direction* of the relationship between each predictor and the outcome variable (e.g., time spent on an educational program).

You'll need to use a linear algorithm in most explanatory modeling scenarios to meet these criteria. You can see this in academic research—most peer-reviewed papers use linear and polynomial regression and classification models. The results sections of these papers include tables and a detailed description of the statistical significance of each predictor—including those that did *not* contribute to the actual model.

Returning to our model predicting daily rat sightings in New York City, let's assume you have the following information from a research science team at a city agency:

- The city's hotline deals with most rat sighting complaints in warmer months, and agencies tend to allocate fewer resources in winter for mitigation efforts.
- Rats are primarily nocturnal, with most sightings occurring between sunset and sunrise the following day. Thus, they hypothesize that the *daily low temperature* has more of an effect than the daily high temperature.
- Rat sightings are unlikely to be affected by very light precipitation, but they may be more likely to leave underground burrows when rainfall exceeds 0.1 inches.

Some of this information is unsurprising; the trends in rat complaints shown in figure 9.20 are easy to use for seasonal planning. Other information provided is about the biology and behavior of rats to help us choose or modify the model's predictors. With this knowledge, let's consider the following steps for our explanatory deliverable:

- We already know that the high temperature correlates *slightly* more with rat sightings than the low temperature. We can include a note in our deliverable showing the relationship between each temperature parameter, the outcome, and the relationship, indicating that they essentially represent the same process.
- We can add a new variable that turns the precipitation column into a Boolean (True/False) field, indicating whether or not the rainfall exceeded 0.1 inches.

Let's add this new column and examine the correlations:

```
rats_weather["high_precip"] = (
    rats_weather["precip"] > 0.1
).astype(int)                          ◁─────┐ Create a Boolean column indicating whether
                                             │ precipitation is higher than 0.1 inches.
rats_weather[
    ["high_temp", "wind_speed", "weekday", "high_precip", "rat_sightings"]
].corr()        ◁────┐ Re-examine
                     │ the correlations.
```

The correlations in figure 9.34 between the new high_precip variable has an *r*-value of –0.04, which isn't meaningfully different from the original precip variable (r = –0.03). If we're optimizing a prediction model, we would *not* consider including this in our model. However, we *can* iterate on our model to show the statistical significance of the variable and its effect on the R^2 before removing it. If we rerun the model with the additional predictor, it gives us the summary in figure 9.35.

	high_temp	wind_speed	weekday	high_precip	rat_sightings
high_temp	1.00	-0.23	0.00	-0.03	0.60
wind_speed	-0.23	1.00	0.01	0.27	-0.24
weekday	0.00	0.01	1.00	0.01	0.47
high_precip	-0.03	0.27	0.01	1.00	-0.04
rat_sightings	0.60	-0.24	0.47	-0.04	1.00

Figure 9.34 Correlation matrix including the new column for high versus low precipitation

```
                              OLS Regression Results
========================================================================================
Dep. Variable:            rat_sightings   R-squared:                        0.604
Model:                              OLS   Adj. R-squared:                   0.603
Method:                   Least Squares   F-statistic:                      415.7
Date:                  Wed, 27 Dec 2023   Prob (F-statistic):           1.71e-217
Time:                          22:16:25   Log-Likelihood:                 -1382.8
No. Observations:                  1095   AIC:                              2776.
Df Residuals:                      1090   BIC:                              2801.
Df Model:                             4
Covariance Type:              nonrobust
========================================================================================
                   coef    std err          t      P>|t|      [0.025      0.975]
----------------------------------------------------------------------------------------
const            3.4041      0.146     23.337      0.000       3.118       3.690
high_temp        0.0429      0.001     29.482      0.000       0.040       0.046
wind_speed      -0.0274      0.005     -5.862      0.000      -0.037      -0.018
weekday          1.4292      0.057     24.870      0.000       1.316       1.542
high_precip      0.0069      0.064      0.109      0.913      -0.118       0.132
========================================================================================
Omnibus:                         30.941   Durbin-Watson:                    1.294
Prob(Omnibus):                    0.000   Jarque-Bera (JB):                39.559
Skew:                            -0.317   Prob(JB):                      2.57e-09
Kurtosis:                         3.682   Cond. No.                          388.
========================================================================================
```

Figure 9.35 Regression results with the added high precipitation variable

If you recall, in chapter 2 we discussed the preparation of written deliverables for your stakeholders that follow the format of a peer-reviewed paper. An explanatory model is one type of those papers—your goal is to summarize the steps you took to find a model with significant predictors and *explain* it to stakeholders in a structured and accessible way. Thus, the methods and results sections of your deliverable can follow a structure like that shown in figure 9.36.

Methods

We used a linear regression model due to strong Pearson's correlations between rat sightings and the following variables:

- Daily high temperature
- Daily high wind speed
- Weekday vs weekend, as a binary column

We took the **square root of daily rat sightings** due to a better model fit.

The following variables were excluded:

- **Daily low temperature**: near perfect correlation with the daily high
- **Precipitation**: no correlation with rat sightings

Results

The three variables included were significant predictors of higher numbers of daily rat sightings reported:

- Higher temperatures
- Lower wind speeds
- Weekdays

Overall, we can explain ~60% of the variation in rat sightings reported

	coef	std err	t	P>|t|
const	3.4028	0.145	23.424	0.000
high_temp	0.0429	0.001	29.519	0.000
wind_speed	-0.0272	0.004	-6.067	0.000
weekday	1.4293	0.057	24.884	0.000

Figure 9.36   Slides showing the summary of methods and results that document conclusions about individual input variables.

Since we're presenting our results to a team of research scientists, we're including more technical details directly in the presentation instead of in an appendix. With the results we've yielded, we can provide the following recommendations to the city agency:

- Use the 7- or 10-day temperature and wind speed forecasts to plan for staffing needs in the following week.
- Prepare for additional staffing needs to respond to complaints in warm weather, *including* unseasonably warm months.
- Prepare for additional staffing costs, including overtime, earlier in the week.

9.3.2   *Predictive models*

So far, we've been using the term *predictive model* interchangeably with *explanation*. On some level, an explanatory deliverable still refers to *inferring* or *predicting* the effect of actions taken based on recommendations. You may track changes in your outcome measure and *infer* the effect of any actions you take; however, you are not making *specific* predictions on individual future events that match the shape of your original dataset.

Predictive models seek to estimate your outcome variable based on *individual records* you can capture before the outcome data is available. These granular out-of-sample predictions can be used for any number of planning and decision-making activities. With a high-quality model, you can predict an incredible range of processes for your business or organization. Some examples might include

- Predicting the probability that each customer will churn at their next renewal
- Forecasting the aggregate sales over the coming six months
- Clustering new customers into predefined segments

In most cases, an explanatory model can be augmented to create a predictive deliverable. This requires two steps: adjusting your model's code, and ensuring you meet the criteria necessary to reasonably apply it in the real world. Starting with the criteria, let's ask ourselves the following questions about our model predicting rat sightings:

- Can we reliably collect data about our predictors *far enough in advance* of the outcome for it to bring value to the team?
- Is the model accurate enough in the ways we need it to be (e.g., precision, recall, balanced accuracy) to meet the needs of our stakeholders?
- Do we have the capacity to surface predictions in an appropriate setting for our stakeholders?

For the first question, we can capture the daily forecasted weather parameters included in the model approximately ten days into the future. However, these values are not the same as the actual weather parameters, and they introduce some unknown error to the model. We'd need to thoroughly test this on multiple samples of forecasted data to better understand the effect on prediction accuracy.

For the second question, we will need to work with our stakeholders to determine how we need to optimize the model. Is it worse if we overpredict the number of rat sightings versus underpredicting? Where might inaccuracies cost the agency money if the model gets it wrong?

Finally, we'll need to discuss options for surfacing predictions to our stakeholders. Ideally, we will need to retrieve forecasted temperature parameters from an API and refresh the data once per day. We will input the forecasted daily high temperature, wind speed, and day of the week into the regression equation, providing a list or graph of projected rat sighting complaints for each of the following ten days. Depending on the resources we have, this can be done via a pipeline into a data warehouse, directly in a business intelligence tool, or in a manual tool such as a spreadsheet if no other options are available.

Let's assume for this chapter that we will need to use a spreadsheet to create the deliverable. We can start by adjusting the model fitting and training process as follows:

- Split the `rats_weather` dataset into separate *training* and *testing* sets, using 80% of the data for training and 20% for testing.
- Fit the model on the training data *only*.
- Generate predictions on the testing set.
- Evaluate the accuracy of the predictions on the test set compared to the training set. Comparable accuracy between these datasets tells us that the model makes suitable predictions for data it has never seen before.

We'll use the `scikit-learn` module to split the data into training and testing sets. In addition to data preparation, `scikit-learn` offers a wide array of algorithms for predictive modeling and machine learning. It provides a less comprehensive summary of individual predictors than `statsmodels`, so it's not particularly suitable for explanatory modeling. Since it's specifically designed for predictive modeling, we'll use it instead to retrain our model for prediction:

```
from sklearn.model_selection import train_test_split
from sklearn.metrics import mean_squared_error
from sklearn.linear_model import LinearRegression        ◄── Import the libraries.

X = rats_weather[["high_temp", "wind_speed", "weekday"]]
y = np.sqrt(rats_weather["rat_sightings"])            ◄─┐ Split the data into
                                                        │ its X and y variables.
X_train, X_test, y_train, y_test = train_test_split(
    X, y, test_size=0.2, random_state=99
)                                              ◄─┐ Randomly split the X and y data
                                                 │ into training and testing sets, with
model = LinearRegression()                       │ 80% of the data for training.
model.fit(X_train, y_train)      ◄─┐
                                   │ Fit the linear regression
                                   │ model to the training data.
```

Once we have fitted the model on the training set, we can use it to generate predicted *y*-values for the testing set and compare them to the actual values. A model that's well suited for prediction will perform similarly on data it hasn't seen before.

To evaluate the model, we'll briefly introduce a new evaluation metric—the *root mean squared error* (RMSE). RMSE tells us the square root of the average sum of squares between predicted and actual values. Essentially, this metric is the standard deviation of predictions from the true *y*-values. The RMSE is a popular evaluation metric in regression models, though there are many other options you can consider for each class of model. The `scikit-learn` library documentation provides a thorough overview of the metrics you can choose to understand your model's performance.

Let's evaluate the performance of our rat sightings model on the training and testing sets:

```
from sklearn.metrics import mean_squared_error          ◄─┐ Import the mean squared
                                                          │ error evaluation metric
y_pred_train = model.predict(X_train)
y_pred = model.predict(X_test)                ◄─┐ Generate rat sighting predictions based
                                               │ on the X training and testing set inputs.
r2_train = model.score(X_train, y_train)
r2_test = model.score(X_test, y_test)         ◄─┐ Calculate the R² value for both
                                               │ the training and the testing sets.
rmse_train = np.sqrt(mean_squared_error(y_train, y_pred_train))
rmse_test = np.sqrt(mean_squared_error(y_test, y_pred))    ◄─┐ Calculate the root
                                                            │ mean squared
print(f"Training Set RMSE: {rmse_train}")                   │ error (RMSE) for
print(f"Test Set RMSE: {rmse_test}")                        │ the predictions.
print(f"Training Set R-squared: {r2_train}")
print(f"Test Set R-squared: {r2_test}")
```

The code results in the following output:

```
Training Set RMSE: 0.84
Test Set RMSE: 0.9
Training Set R-squared: 0.61
Test Set R-squared: 0.57
```

If we evaluate the R^2 and RMSE of the training versus testing sets, we can conclude the following:

- Our model explains slightly more variance on the training set than the testing set (61% versus 57%). The difference is not drastic enough to raise concern, but we should rigidly test the model on a new *validation set* of predictions using forecasted weather data and monitor it for further decreases.
- The RMSE of our model is quite low. The values tell us that, on average, predictions in both the training and testing sets are just under 1 rat sighting away from the true value. That's impressive!

If we're confident in our model's predictive validity, we can move on to determining the best deliverable type for our stakeholders. The output of our model can be delivered to our stakeholders as *batch* or *live predictions.*

Batch predictions are generated from a model in large, grouped sets at scheduled intervals. In this approach, data is collected over time and stored in a database or data warehouse and then processed as a set (e.g., for all new records created on a given day). In the absence of access to a data warehouse or data engineering tools, a simple deliverable can be created using nothing more than a spreadsheet. This method of generating predictions is useful when dealing with large volumes of data that *don't require real-time analysis,* such as predicting customer churn, daily sales, or supply chain problems.

Live predictions involve generating predictions instantly as new information becomes available. These real-time predictions are essential where you need to make or influence decisions based on the latest available information. The tools necessary for these predictions vary greatly in complexity—a live prediction user interface can be as simple as a spreadsheet allowing user input (e.g., our model forecasting rat sightings), or it could require complex infrastructure so that products can be recommended as you browse an ecommerce website.

Predicting paid conversions

How might Anthony prepare his predictions in a format that the marketing team can use when planning ad campaigns?

After additional feedback from the marketing manager, Anthony decides to concentrate on building a robust *predictive model* that predicts conversion likelihood from the free trial to the paid tier. He decides that a set of *batch predictions* generated once per hour is appropriate for this purpose, because it will allow the marketing team to send tailored engagement emails based on the likelihood of converting to the paid tier.

(continued)

Anthony takes the following steps to prepare his deliverable:

1 Anthony gathers and preprocesses the data on individuals who signed up for free trials. In addition to the available data, he derives variables such as the time of day and day of the week to determine if temporal factors influence conversion likelihood.

2 Since he is working on a *classification problem*, he leans toward fitting a logistic regression and one or more tree-based models (e.g., random forest). These models are known to perform well on a wide variety of classification problems and offer insight into the most important variables included in the model. He prepares the training and testing sets so he can appropriately evaluate the model's performance on out-of-sample predictions.

3 Anthony chooses metrics such as accuracy, precision, recall, and AUC (area under the curve) to evaluate his model. After several iterations on the model, he achieves an accuracy of 84%, a precision score of 74%, a recall of 65%, and an AUC of 0.76.

4 Anthony works with the data engineering team to bring the model to production, running on an hourly schedule. The data will be available in a new table in the data warehouse that can be joined to the customer ID. Customers who recently signed up or whose information has changed will have new predictions generated with each scheduled run of the model.

5 Anthony reaches out to the product data science team to discuss additional applications for the model, such as in-app prompts to register and receive targeted discounts on the paid signup process. He also prepares a report for the marketing team to help them understand the most important inputs of the model, and what strategic decisions they can make based on the exploratory data analysis.

A predictive deliverable brought to production can often be used by multiple teams across the organization. High-quality batch predictions are *new data* about your users or customers (e.g., a user segment) that can be used to understand them and better aid your strategy. These batch predictions can also be used in *live tools*, affecting the experience of using software even if they're not generated on the spot.

Ultimately, this type of deliverable will often necessitate a supplemental *explanatory model* for your stakeholders, so they can understand the process and findings. At minimum, reporting on correlational relationships or statistically significant findings may aid in their understanding of your process even when you don't use a linear model. You'll also often need to consider how to make batch predictions available in a *live* user experience. It sounds like a lot, but it's all part of the value that can be generated with predictive modeling!

9.3.3 *Exercises*

Continuing the previous exercises, you are asked to create an explanatory and predictive deliverable using the `production_costs` dataset:

1 The finance team is interested in an explanation of the factors that contribute to production costs and profit margins at the company. Perform the following steps to create the deliverable:
   - Explore each variable in the dataset with scatterplots and correlations with the `product_margin` outcome. Perform any necessary transformations to represent nonlinear relationships.
   - Consider the factors that the finance team might hypothesize are significant predictors of profit margins. Are there input variables that align with those hypotheses, even if they're not highly correlated with the outcome? Should they be included in your deliverable? Which ones?
   - Fit a regression model that enables you to report on the direction and strength of the relationship between each predictor and the outcome.
   - Write a summary of the model's findings for the finance team. Explain which factors affect a product's profit margins. Include recommendations on which factors should be examined for further cost-saving opportunities.

2 The product operations team is interested in predicting the potential profit margin for new products. They want an interactive predictive modeling tool where they can adjust the inputs to estimate how the profit margins will change:
   - Develop a model to predict `product_margin`, focusing on accuracy and predictive power. You can try more advanced techniques (e.g., random forests) if you are interested.
   - Experiment with deriving new features that can improve the model's predictive ability.
   - To assess the model's accuracy, examine evaluation metrics like R^2, AIC, BIC, and RMSE.
   - Consider what your deliverable to the product operations team should look like. What would it look like if you only had a spreadsheet tool to create a resource for this stakeholder?

Summary

- There are many *classes of statistical models* available tailored to solving specific types of problems:
  - *Regression models* use one or more predictors to predict a continuous outcome (e.g., price).
  - *Classification models* use one or more predictors to predict a categorical outcome (e.g., purchased or not purchased).
  - *Time series models* use historical data collected over time to forecast values for future time periods.
  - *Survival analysis* is similar to regression modeling, where the outcome variable of interest is whether a participant or data point "survives" past a specific time period. These models are often used in clinical settings to understand the probability of surviving an illness for certain periods of time.

- *Hierarchical models* account for the nested structure of your data, such as when participants belong to one or more hierarchical groups (e.g., a classroom, a school, a district) that may affect your outcome.
- *Clustering models* identify underlying patterns in your data without an outcome variable (*unsupervised learning* in machine learning). These algorithms can help identify groups of individuals or data points that were not discoverable by visual observation alone.
- *Dimension reduction* techniques consolidate large sets of predictor variables into a smaller set of *components*. Each component represents a significant pattern or aspect of variation within the original data, thus simplifying the dataset while retaining its most informative features.

- *Model evaluation metrics* are available for each class of the models, giving us information we can use to diagnose the quality of its fit to the data. When working with regression models, we can use the following metrics to evaluate a model:
  - *R-squared* (R^2) represents the proportion of variance in your outcome variable explained by all of your input variables.
  - *Adjusted R^2* adjusts the original value, penalizing the score for each additional variable you include in your model. This score enables you to balance model quality and complexity.
  - The *F-statistic* tests the overall significance of the model.
  - *The log-likelihood* is one of several *relative* metrics that tell you how well your model fits the data. These can be used to compare the relative quality between multiple model iterations.
  - *AIC* and *BIC* are relative metrics used to evaluate a model's overall quality. Each score penalizes model complexity, enabling you to balance the fit and complexity to select a best-fit model.
  - *Residuals* are the differences between the observed and predicted outcome values that help you understand the parts of your model not explained by your predictors. When residuals show patterns that aren't normally distributed, it hints at problems such as missing transformations or variables.

- *Statistical modeling* systematically involves data preparation, analysis, and iterative refinement. It begins with understanding your problem, gathering and cleaning data, and fitting one or more models to best represent that data:
  - *Exploratory analysis* is a crucial initial step that involves examining data through visualizations and summary statistics to identify patterns and spot anomalies, setting the stage for informed model building.
  - *Feature derivation* or *feature engineering* involves creating new variables from your existing dataset to better represent the underlying processes in your model. This can include transformations (e.g., square root), extracting components of a column (e.g., month number in a date), or creating combinations of multiple variables (e.g., combined profit).

- *Evaluating assumptions* involves verifying the validity of foundational assumptions inherent to your chosen model. This can include checking linearity, normality, homoscedasticity, and the independence of residuals. These steps are necessary to ensure your model's reliability.
- *Models are refined* using absolute and relative indicators to adjust variables, tune parameters, or change the modeling approach.

- *Explanatory* and *predictive models* are two overarching categories of model deliverables that guide your model fitting and optimization strategy:
  - *Explanatory models* showcase the relationships between individual variables and an outcome, emphasizing interpretability and the statistical significance of coefficients. The predictors included in your model are guided by domain knowledge and rigorously evaluate existing theories and hypotheses. Explanatory model deliverables are usually prepared as detailed reports with recommendations for the intended audience or stakeholders.
  - *Predictive models* focus on the accuracy of out-of-sample predictions and generalizability to new data. Predictions can be delivered in many formats, including interactive tools using the model's equation, batch predictions on large datasets, or live predictions that influence actions taken in real time.

Incorporating external data into analyses

10

Think of the datasets we've used in this book. We've worked with several sources of information, often combining some of them into a single resource we can use to answer questions. Most notably,

- We explored a dataset containing the number of reported rat sightings in New York City.
- We tracked historical weather information in New York City and Boston.
- We analyzed customer login and transaction data for various hypothetical companies.

None of these datasets fell out of the sky or were readily available for us to download in the *exact* format necessary to cover each topic in this book. Multiple approaches to retrieving, structuring, and creating these datasets were used to pre-pare them for analysis.

This chapter will delve into common methods used to retrieve data from sources such as APIs, websites, and public databases. We'll explore common formats in which your data can be retrieved, ensuring you can extract the information relevant to your analytical needs. Beyond running Python code associated, we'll be focusing on the mindset an analyst needs to strategically seek out information that enriches the data available at their organization.

10.1 Using APIs

Consider how requests are made in human contexts and in the digital world. We place an order at a restaurant, expecting a server to return with the dish we requested. We enter the URL of a website, expecting it to return the web page associated with that site. We delete an email, and expect to return to an inbox where it's no longer present.

An API (application programming interface) is a set of protocols allowing you to interact with a software application. An interaction is a *request* that provides you with a *response* defined by the protocols of that specific API (see figure 10.1). Every exchange facilitates the display of information from over the internet (e.g., news feeds, sports scores, weather forecasts) in a predefined format—embedded in a website, an application, or sent to your machine as a raw set of records. Once you've retrieved the available information, you can process and transform it to meet your needs for a specific project.

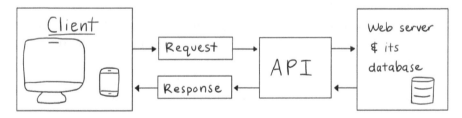

Figure 10.1   APIs allow you to request and return information from a software application.

APIs are an indispensable tool in modern analytics, enabling you to access structured data from the many online services used in an organization. With access to a software application's API, you can retrieve and incorporate up-to-date data from that application into your Python environment or a data warehouse for other analysts. Data from APIs can augment analyses in any subdomain of analytics and can allow for insights that cannot be generated with your organization's data alone. Consider the following examples:

- A marketing agency's analytics team monitors trends in social media and search engine usage, enabling it to shift its product's advertising strategy if new keywords emerge in online posts or a specific type of product declines in popularity.
- A popular job board tracks weekly changes in labor economic data—unemployment, average wages, inflation data—to predict when there will be an increase in users searching their website for a new role.
- A financial firm must monitor the most up-to-date information on the stock market's performance to make accurate, timely investment decisions for its clients.

Each of the data sources in these examples can be accessed on their websites, and for many use cases, this will suffice to access the relevant information. However, when teams have more sophisticated use cases for data (e.g., predictive modeling and analytics), it may be worth using available APIs to incorporate the data into a data deliverable and warehouse.

10.1.1 *Retrieving data: API vs. browser interface*

Let's look at two ways to create a dataset using a web page's interface or an API. In chapter 9, we discussed creating a deliverable for a city government agency that predicts the number of daily rat sightings based on our regression model's inputs, including several weather parameters. This information can be obtained using a 7- or 10-day forecast and input into a tool or interface of our choice.

If we want to access the forecast data directly, we can take the following steps:

1 Search for a source that provides historical weather data. In this case, we'll use data from the National Weather Service website (https://forecast.weather.gov), such as the daily high and low temperatures, wind speed, and total precipitation.
2 Use the website's historical weather search tool to find a month's worth of data at a specific location (New York City).
3 Export or copy and paste the data into a spreadsheet.
4 Repeat the process for each month of historical data you want to include in your dataset.

Repeating the preceding steps becomes cumbersome if we make a deliverable that relies on up-to-date forecast data. Instead, we may want to use the National Weather Service API. This resource provides forecast data for free, so we can write a Python script that quickly refreshes the data for our stakeholders. To do so, we can take the following steps:

1 Review the documentation for the National Weather Service API for weather forecast data (www.weather.gov/documentation/services-web-api).
2 Write a Python script that retrieves weather data from the API for a specific location.
3 Add to the script to structure the data as you need, such as selecting a subset of fields to add as columns to a new pandas dataframe.

4 Incorporate the script into an appropriate tool: a local notebook, a data visualization tool, or a workflow management process managed at your organization.

The Python requests library makes accessing data from various APIs easy. Let's prepare a script for these steps to retrieve the seven-day forecast in New York City:

```
import requests          │ Import the requests
import json            ◄─┘ and JSON libraries.
```

```
url = "https://api.weather.gov/gridpoints/OKX/34,36/forecast"  ◄─┤ Define the URL.
response = requests.get(url)               ◄─┐ Use the requests library to call the
print(response)        ◄─┐ Print the response │ API using the parameters we defined.
                         │ from the API.
```

The `print` statement in the code provides the following output:

```
<Response [200]>
```

HANDLING AND FORMATTING API RESPONSES

What exactly are we looking at in the printed API response? If you search response
code 200, you will see that it means our request to the weather API was successful, and
the `response` variable *should* contain the seven-day forecast data for the New York City
weather station. To display the data returned, we'll need to save it in a JSON format.

JSON is a standard text-based format for displaying data in a human-readable way.
JSON objects often contain nested information that's displayed in Python as a dictionary with sets of key-value pairs, embedded lists, and other subsets of data. Once
you've transformed a request object into JSON, it's relatively easy to view, in order to
determine what information you need to extract into a *tabular* format for analysis.

Let's transform our response variable into a JSON format so we can read the data.
The entire JSON response is very large, so we'll start by printing the keys to determine
which subsets of information we need:

```
forecast = response.json()              ◄─┐ Save the response
print(forecast.keys())   ◄─┐ Print the keys of │ as a JSON format.
                           │ the new JSON object.
```

The code results in the following output:

```
dict_keys(['@context', 'type', 'geometry', 'properties'])
```

As expected, the forecast variable is formatted as a JSON object with key-value pairs
containing subsets of information about the weather. Each API has a unique response
format, requiring you to delve into the response to find your data of interest. The
forecast data is located under the nested `periods` key within `properties`. If we print
the contents of this nested key, we'll return the values associated with the daily and
nightly forecast for the upcoming week:

```
print(forecast["properties"]["periods"])
```

Figure 10.2 shows the printed contents of forecasted information nested inside the JSON retrieved from the weather API:

```
[{'detailedForecast': 'Partly cloudy, with a low around 60. Northeast wind 7 '
                      'to 10 mph.',
  'endTime': '2024-09-22T06:00:00-04:00',
  'icon': 'https://api.weather.gov/icons/land/night/sct?size=medium',
  'isDaytime': False,
  'name': 'Tonight',
  'number': 1,
  'probabilityOfPrecipitation': {'unitCode': 'wmoUnit:percent', 'value': None},
  'shortForecast': 'Partly Cloudy',
  'startTime': '2024-09-21T19:00:00-04:00',
  'temperature': 60,
  'temperatureTrend': '',
  'temperatureUnit': 'F',
  'windDirection': 'NE',
  'windSpeed': '7 to 10 mph'},
```

Figure 10.2   A dictionary nested inside a list containing the first set of forecast data

The nested dictionary key we printed contains a list, each containing *another* nested dictionary with direct key-value pairs of all our weather data. If we want to use the relevant forecast information from chapter 9 (temperature, wind speed) as inputs for future predictions, we will need to extract the data we want into a pandas dataframe. Let's process this data:

```
import pandas as pd       ◁——| Import the pandas library.

forecast_df = pd.DataFrame(forecast["properties"]["periods"])  ◁——┐ Save the forecast
forecast_df[                                                      │ JSON as a pandas
    ["endTime", "isDaytime", "temperature", "windSpeed"]          │ dataframe.
].head()               ◁——┐ Display only the
                           │ columns we need.
```

Figure 10.3 displays the subset of columns we kept in our `forecast_df` dataframe.

	endTime	isDaytime	temperature	windSpeed
0	2024-09-22T06:00:00-04:00	False	60	7 to 10 mph
1	2024-09-22T18:00:00-04:00	True	75	7 to 10 mph
2	2024-09-23T06:00:00-04:00	False	59	10 mph
3	2024-09-23T18:00:00-04:00	True	72	10 mph
4	2024-09-24T06:00:00-04:00	False	60	6 to 10 mph

Figure 10.3   A dataframe containing one row per forecast record from the API response

The forecast data is *nearly* in the format we need as input for our predictive model from chapter 9. As you may recall, the historical weather dataset contained one row per day and included the high and low temperatures as separate columns. The wind speed was also measured as an integer, representing the day's maximum wind speed.

To match this data extract to the existing dataset format, we'll need to update the following:

- Truncate the `endTime` column so that we have one row per day.
- Extract the numerical values in the `windSpeed` column and keep only the highest value. This can be done using *regular expressions* to find a pattern that matches a set of criteria—in this case, we'll search for integers and exclude all other characters.
- Group the dataset by day, taking the maximum and minimum of the `temperature` field for each day and the maximum for the `windSpeed`.

Let's go ahead and transform each column, which is necessary before we can group the data by day and perform mathematical calculations on the available columns. We'll save each category of transformed information as a new column in the dataset:

```
import re                    Import the regular
                            expressions library.          Define a custom function that
                                                          finds all integers and returns
def get_wind_speed(row):                                  the maximum of those values.
    numbers = [int(num) for num in re.findall(r'\d+', row)]
    return max(numbers)

forecast_df["date"] = pd.to_datetime(forecast_df['endTime']).dt.date

forecast_df["wind_speed"] = forecast_df["windSpeed"].apply(       Convert the
    get_wind_speed                                              endTime field to a
)                          Apply the custom function to extract     calendar date.
                           only the highest wind speed integer.

forecast_df[["date", "temperature", "wind_speed"]].head()       Display the first five
                                                                rows of the new data.
```

Figure 10.4 displays the maximum wind speed extracted from the forecast data.

	date	temperature	wind_speed
0	2024-09-22	60	10
1	2024-09-22	75	10
2	2024-09-23	59	10
3	2024-09-23	72	10
4	2024-09-24	60	10

Figure 10.4   Subset of the forecast dataset with the extraneous text information removed.

Finally, we need to group the dataset by date, combining the daily and nightly forecasts into the same row. We'll take the minimum and maximum temperatures to get the daily high and low values while only taking the maximum wind speed, to match the historical data format:

```
daily_forecast = (                          ⟵⎤ Aggregate the forecast
    forecast_df.groupby("date")               ⎦ data by day.
    .agg({
        "temperature": ["min", "max"],
        "wind_speed": "max"})
    .reset_index()
)
                                            ⎤ Rename
daily_forecast.columns = [              ⟵⎦ the columns.
"date", "low_temp", "high_temp", "wind_speed"
]
                                      ⎤ Display the first five rows
daily_forecast.head()            ⟵⎦ of the new dataframe.
```

Figure 10.5 shows the resulting `forecast` dataframe, which now has one record per day.

	date	low_temp	high_temp	wind_speed
0	2024-09-22	60	75	10
1	2024-09-23	59	72	10
2	2024-09-24	60	69	12
3	2024-09-25	61	69	13
4	2024-09-26	63	73	13

Figure 10.5 **Forecast dataset aggregated by day**

Our dataset now matches the formatting we need to use as input for our regression model from chapter 9.

CONSIDERATIONS

Retrieving data from an API varies in complexity from one source to another, and several practices are necessary to ensure you use the available services responsibly. We looked at an example of retrieving a finite number of records from the National Weather Service in a straightforward manner. We retrieved the data in just one step, and most of our work involved shaping the response data to meet our needs.

Using APIs will rarely be this simple. When working with proprietary (paid) sources or public APIs that retrieve larger volumes of data, you'll encounter a number of limitations you need to handle responsibly in order to have continued access to the data:

- *Errors*—Given the high variation in API services and their requirements, you're almost guaranteed to return errors while trying to make a request. The errors returned are almost always HTTP status codes (e.g., 404 for not found, 403 for forbidden, 500 for internal server error). Consider familiarizing yourself with common status codes, and be patient when working to resolve the problems you encounter.

- *Authentication*—Outside of government and academic data sources, most APIs require authentication to ensure data is securely exchanged with authorized users. This is often accomplished by requiring you to generate an *API key* (similar to a password), which is included as a parameter in your request.

- *Rate limiting*—Most APIs will restrict the number of requests you can make in a specific period of time. You're most likely to run into this limit while writing and testing your code (running the same script manually in rapid succession) or if you run into problems when your code is incorporated into a pipeline that runs on a schedule. A good rule of thumb is to use the `sleep` function in Python's built-in time library [1] to pause between requests for at least a few seconds, so as not to make automated requests faster than a person can manually do in a browser. Make sure you thoroughly read the documentation for the API you're using to understand its limits and restrictions, and use that knowledge to plan how often you make requests.

- *Pagination*—APIs that return large volumes of data often limit the amount of data that can be returned in a single request. To get all the data you requested, you may need to make multiple requests through the *pages* of data available. You can implement a `for` loop in your code to call the API as often as required to retrieve and append all the records to a dataset. Just don't forget about rate limiting, and consider adding pauses in your loop if you're at risk of hitting the maximum number of calls.

- *Cost*—While most APIs hosted by government sources are free, most use cases you'll encounter will require a paid subscription to a service or require you to pay a charge per call or result. Read the documentation carefully if you want to use a paid API service—the costs can add up quickly.

Before testing or actively using a new API workflow, make sure you *thoroughly* read the documentation provided before you try making your first request. The public APIs we use in this chapter are provided as free services, so using them responsibly is necessary to ensure they continue to be available to analysts in the future. When working with *proprietary* APIs, accidentally making the wrong request can have financial implications for your organization. Be careful in your work when testing and setting up production API workflows—limit the data you're retrieving, set up appropriate steps to handle errors, and make sure you're processing all of the data you retrieve.

10.1.2 *Determining the value of using an API*

The tasks we just performed—retrieving and processing the weather forecast—were not low effort. If you're starting from scratch with a new API with greater constraints, you may find yourself weighing whether the effort is worth your time. Setting up a pipeline for retrieving data isn't always worth the effort; sometimes, you may find it easier to copy the data you need from a website manually.

Even if you aren't developing these pipelines yourself (e.g., you may hand off the work to a data engineering team), part of your role will be recommending the best data retrieval approach for the organization and your stakeholders. Let's start by reviewing the benefits of gathering your data from an API:

- APIs create a *repeatable process* that minimizes the need for manual work after you initially write the code to gather and process your data.
- Many APIs provide access to *real-time data*, which your organization may need to make fast-paced decisions.
- Retrieving a *large volume of data* from an API is often easier than downloading it manually. Subsequently, processing that data is more manageable in a tool such as Python compared to a spreadsheet. This is especially true if you need your data retrieval process to be repeatable.

Throughout your career, you'll get better at finding opportunities where using an API improves your workflow. In my own work, it took time and many hours of frustration (as in figure 10.6) to be able to confidently identify the best approaches to extracting data. It takes time to learn this!

Figure 10.6   If manually downloading and manipulating data frustrates you and creates additional work, you can streamline the process if an API is available.

With these benefits in mind, consider the following questions as you're creating stakeholder deliverables that might use data from an API:

- Does your organization have an IT or data engineering team that manages an ETL service or vendor? If so, there may be an easy process to automatically run your pipeline on a schedule (e.g., adding new data once per day).
- If your organization *can't* add a new data source to the data warehouse, can you call the API directly in a business intelligence or reporting tool to create your deliverable? What limitations will you run into if you use this approach?

- What would your deliverable look like if you *didn't* retrieve data automatically? Would your stakeholders need to submit manual inputs to get the information they want? Would they use the deliverable if they had to input data manually?
- If you manually retrieve the data, how long would it take to process it? How often would you have to update it? Even if your Python code isn't incorporated into an automatic process, would running your code on your local computer be more manageable than copying it from a website and manually updating it in a spreadsheet?

In most situations where you need regularly updated data that informs organizational decisions, you *can* reduce your team's overhead by gathering your data from an API. As with many other components of your work, answering these questions on your own or in collaboration with the teams that own the data warehouse will help you grow your skillset in anticipating the time involved in a task and the potential return of each approach.

10.1.3 Exercises

A global digital marketing company has recently invested in its data engineering and business analytics teams. You are a business analyst on the team looking for opportunities to add valuable information to the data warehouse to be used across the company for market research. You've compiled the following list of data sources that stakeholders across the company are interested in adding to the warehouse:

- *Stock data* captured hourly for all customers, competitors, and other industry firms of interest that are publicly traded.
- *World countries*, their capital city, most recent annual GDP, two- and three-digit country codes, and several additional methods of categorizing their locations.
- *Page views* on the company's marketing website, including metadata about the visitors' locations, browsers, operating systems, and more.
- *Survey responses* collected from the twice-annual customer feedback review conducted over the past five years. The new data is appended to a spreadsheet.

Your goal is to determine the priority order in which these sources should be added to the data warehouse. Consider the following questions:

1. Which of these datasets is likely to have the highest volume of data?
2. Which of these types of data sources are likely to have an API available to use? Try researching what types of data sources are available about each subject.
3. Which data source will quickly become stale or outdated if not added to the data warehouse, where it would automatically be refreshed once daily?
4. Which data sources can the company use without creating a new pipeline to add the data into the warehouse? Which ones likely *can't* be used effectively without being available in the warehouse?
5. Which datasets will be most actively used across the company if they are available for analysis in the data warehouse and the company's business intelligence tool?

Assume that your data engineering team only has the bandwidth to add one or two of these data sources to the warehouse. Write a list of recommendations for datasets that should be added to the data warehouse by creating a pipeline that calls the API, datasets that can be managed using an API but handled manually, and datasets that you can download manually and access via a CSV file.

10.2 Web scraping

When you think of data, what comes to mind? How would you define it? What *is* and what *isn't* data? In the modern era, data encompasses far more than information neatly stored in a table or easily normalized using an API. So much information is available in an *unstructured format* or a format that isn't available in a predefined data model (e.g., figure 10.7). Many types of information fall into this category, such as the contents of a website, a PDF, or an image of a document. Extracting structured information from one of these sources can provide differentiable value to you and your organization.

```
Employee Feedback:
- Customer A. T. submitted feedback about E1001 on 2023-03-15 rating the serv
ice as 5 stars and commented, 'Outstanding service and smooth installation.'
- Customer S. R. provided feedback about E1002 on 2023-03-16 with a 4-star ra
ting, noting 'Very happy with the service, though minor delays.'
- Customer J. R. praised E1003 's professional team and smooth installation p
rocess on 2023-03-17, giving a 5-star rating.
- Customer C. T. on 2023-03-18 expressed satisfaction with the service by E10
04 but expected quicker customer service, rating it 3 stars.
- Customer M. R. mentioned good service overall from E1005 on 2023-03-19 but
pointed out a lack of communication about installation times, giving a 4-star
rating.
```

Figure 10.7 Unstructured data doesn't have a predefined format and may require extensive processing.

Web scraping is a technique for extracting unstructured or semi-structured data from websites and transforming it into a structured format that can easily be used for analysis. Scraping websites can help you synthesize countless forms of information, such as market insights or social media conversations, into unique curated datasets that can be used for any number of purposes.

There are countless situations where an analyst might want to scrape the web to help augment their workflows:

- Keeping track of *competitors' prices* to develop strategic pricing models. In industries with a large number of goods and rapidly changing prices, up-to-date information is necessary to attract customers. Since this data is unlikely to be available to competitors via an API, scraping the web is often essential to monitor this information systematically.

- *Social media trends, hashtags, and popular topics* can change rapidly. If an organization needs to routinely monitor sentiments, consumer behavior, and perceptions of its brand, scraping social media websites can help fill a gap that's otherwise largely subjective.

- Scraping *financial data* from news websites, stock market portals, and hubs of economic data is often necessary for real-time financial modeling and economic analysis. This type of data also provides the most current information to any company on the financial ecosystem in which they operate.

Evaluating the benefit of web scraping starts with a similar set of questions to using an API. If you need large volumes of data that would be challenging to synthesize manually, but an API *isn't* available, web scraping can help you obtain the information you need.

10.2.1 Scraping the web for data

At its core, web scraping is similar to using an API—you make HTTP requests to a website and receive a response containing information. The primary difference is in the response format—when web scraping, your response contains the HTML content of the web page you requested, and it's *your* responsibility to interpret and extract the information you need.

Let's assume we couldn't access an API to capture the weather forecast. Instead, we might try scraping the forecast page for our location of interest to determine if we can extract and standardize the forecasted parameters we need. We can start by navigating to the National Weather Service's page, which displays forecast data for the New York City weather station (https://mng.bz/Xxel). Once we have the web page we need, we can paste the URL from our browser into our Python environment to extract its data using the requests library. We'll assume that the `requests` and `json` libraries have already been imported from the previous section:

```
lat, lon = 40.7392, -73.9829    ⟵  Create the latitude and
                                    longitude variables for
                                    the New York City
                                    weather station.

url = f"https://forecast.weather.gov/MapClick.php?lat={lat}&lon={lon}"   ⟵  Create the URL for
                                                                            the forecast page
                                                                            using our latitude and
                                                                            longitude variables.
headers = {"User-Agent": "Mona's data exploration"}    ⟵  Add a user agent per
                                                           the weather service's
                                                           API requirements.
response = requests.get(url, headers=headers)    ⟵  Use the requests library
                                                    to call the API using the
print(response)    ⟵  Print the response       parameters we defined.
                      from the API.
```

Our code prints the following output:

```
<Response [200]>
```

If you run the `response.json()` step from the previous section, you'll notice that your code returns an error. This is because you received the entire HTML content of the web page as a response, identical to the content you would discover if you right-clicked and inspected the page. Instead, you can run the following command to retrieve the text content of the response, shown in figure 10.8:

```
print(response.text)
```

```html
<!DOCTYPE html>
<html class="no-js">
    <head>
        <!-- Meta -->
        <meta name="viewport" content="width=device-width">
        <link rel="schema.DC" href="http://purl.org/dc/elements/1.1/" /><title>National Weather Ser
vice</title><meta name="DC.title" content="National Weather Service" /><meta name="DC.description"
content="NOAA National Weather Service National Weather Service" /><meta name="DC.creator" content=
"US Department of Commerce, NOAA, National Weather Service" /><meta name="DC.date.created" scheme="
ISO8601" content="" /><meta name="DC.language" scheme="DCTERMS.RFC1766" content="EN-US" /><meta nam
e="DC.keywords" content="weather, National Weather Service" /><meta name="DC.publisher" content="NO
AA's National Weather Service" /><meta name="DC.contributor" content="National Weather Service" /><
meta name="DC.rights" content="//www.weather.gov/disclaimer.php" /><meta name="rating" content="Gen
eral" /><meta name="robots" content="index,follow" />

        <!-- Icons -->
        <link rel="shortcut icon" href="./images/favicon.ico" type="image/x-icon" />

        <!-- CSS -->
        <link rel="stylesheet" href="css/bootstrap-3.2.0.min.css">
```

Figure 10.8   The first few rows of the HTML content received from our request.

Before we begin processing the response, let's review some concepts of HTML and how to work with it:

- HTML is fundamental to web content and is responsible for the structure and content of web pages. The locations of headers, images, fonts, colors, sizes, and more are all contained in the HTML of a website.
- HTML pages are made up of *elements* represented by the following *tags*:
  - `<p>` for paragraphs
  - `<a>` for links
  - `<div>` for sections of a page

  Similar to what we saw in our JSON data, tags can be nested in a tree-like structure, making for a complex system of information contained within other, higher-level information.
- Tags in a document often include a *class*, which allows the web page to reference a stylesheet containing specific CSS or JavaScript code. A single class can be used across multiple tags and sections, enabling the use of the same design and style code at various points throughout a page.

Knowing that HTML comprises a limited number of categories of information, we can start to see how repeated patterns in the document can be used to extract the information we need. Python's `BeautifulSoup` library is designed precisely for this purpose—to make extracting data from an HTML document exceptionally easy. It parses the content into a `soup` object, allowing you to navigate and search within the tree-like HTML data without knowing the exact position and depth of a tag relative to others. This way, there's less manual digging than in the steps we took to process our JSON-formatted API response.

Let's look at how we can parse the weather forecast document:

```
from bs4 import BeautifulSoup           ←⌐ Import the
                                            BeautifulSoup library.

                                                          ⌐ Create a soup object with
soup = BeautifulSoup(response.text, "html.parser")    ←⌐ the parsed HTML data.
print(soup.prettify())    ←⌐ Print the formatted
                             HTML content.
```

The result is shown in figure 10.9.

```
<!DOCTYPE html>
<html class="no-js">
 <head>
  <!-- Meta -->
  <meta content="width=device-width" name="viewport"/>
  <link href="http://purl.org/dc/elements/1.1/" rel="schema.DC"/>
  <title>
   National Weather Service
  </title>
  <meta content="National Weather Service" name="DC.title">
   <meta content="NOAA National Weather Service National Weather Service" name="DC.description"/>
   <meta content="US Department of Commerce, NOAA, National Weather Service" name="DC.creator"/>
   <meta content="" name="DC.date.created" scheme="ISO8601"/>
   <meta content="EN-US" name="DC.language" scheme="DCTERMS.RFC1766"/>
   <meta content="weather, National Weather Service" name="DC.keywords"/>
   <meta content="NOAA's National Weather Service" name="DC.publisher"/>
   <meta content="National Weather Service" name="DC.contributor"/>
   <meta content="//www.weather.gov/disclaimer.php" name="DC.rights"/>
   <meta content="General" name="rating"/>
   <meta content="index,follow" name="robots"/>
   <!-- Icons -->
   <link href="./images/favicon.ico" rel="shortcut icon" type="image/x-icon"/>
   <!-- CSS -->
   <link href="css/bootstrap-3.2.0.min.css" rel="stylesheet"/>
   <link href="css/bootstrap-theme-3.2.0.min.css" rel="stylesheet"/>
```

Figure 10.9   The first few rows of the "prettified" HTML, which shows the nested document structure.

10.2.2 *Extracting the data we need*

By prettifying the HTML document, we can search for the information we want from this web page. If we search for the terms we saw on the web page (e.g., detailed forecast, high, low, wind speed), we can see that the forecast data is contained in multiple places:

- The temperature data for each day and night is contained in several places, including a `<div>` section with a complete forecast description and a separate paragraph with classes called `temp temp-high` and `temp temp-low`.
- The humidity is available only for the *current* conditions inside a section of the page with the `<div class="pull-left" id="current_conditions_detail">` tag.
- The wind speed is contained in a paragraph describing the forecast as a full sentence.

You can parse the HTML tree using `BeautifulSoup`, displaying only subsets of information that meet your criteria. From there, viewing and processing the information you need in a structured format is far easier. For example, let's retrieve only the contents of the `<div>` section with the forecast descriptions:

```
forecast_items = soup.find_all("div", class_="tombstone-container")        ⟵

for item in forecast_items:      ⟵
    print(item.text)
```

Print the text of each forecast item found inside the section.

Retrieve all HTML content inside the section with the class "tombstone-container".

```
Tonight
Mostly CloudyLow: 31 °F

Tuesday
Mostly CloudyHigh: 37 °F

TuesdayNight
CloudyLow: 33 °F

Wednesday
CloudyHigh: 41 °F
```

Figure 10.10   Cleanly printed text from the selected container

Figure 10.10 shows the resulting text for each forecast item.

This is easy, right? It's also *far cleaner* than the original HTML document we've been working with. The trick is to search the text in each type of tag—sections, links, and paragraphs—to find the format that most readily meets your needs.

Next, we can process the saved text contents to create a structured dataset. If we return to the previous step and run `print(item)` without extracting its text, we'll see two paragraphs we can use to subset our text further—see figure 10.11.

```
<div class="tombstone-container">
<p class="period-name">Tonight<br/><br/></p>
<p><img alt="Tonight: Mostly cloudy, with a low around 31. North wind 6 to 10 mph, with gusts as high
as 21 mph. " class="forecast-icon" src="newimages/medium/nbkn.png" title="Tonight: Mostly cloudy, wit
h a low around 31. North wind 6 to 10 mph, with gusts as high as 21 mph. "/></p><p class="short-des
c">Mostly Cloudy</p><p class="temp temp-low">Low: 31 °F</p></div>
<div class="tombstone-container">
<p class="period-name">Tuesday<br/><br/></p>
<p><img alt="Tuesday: Mostly cloudy, with a high near 37. Northeast wind around 7 mph becoming southe
ast in the afternoon. " class="forecast-icon" src="newimages/medium/bkn.png" title="Tuesday: Mostly c
loudy, with a high near 37. Northeast wind around 7 mph becoming southeast in the afternoon. "/></p><
p class="short-desc">Mostly Cloudy</p><p class="temp temp-high">High: 37 °F</p></div>
```

Figure 10.11   The same printed items, including their HTML tags

The first two items we want (period and temperature) are contained in classes named `"period-name"` and `"short-desc"`. The wind speed is contained inside an image tag with a paragraph description. We can point directly to those tags and exclude everything except the needed information:

```
forecast_data = []

for item in forecast_items:            ←── Create a for loop to process
    period = (                              each forecast record.
        item.find("p", class_="period-name")   ←── Extract the name of the day of the
        .get_text()                                 week, and remove the word "Night".
        .replace("Night", "")
    )
    temp = item.find("p", class_="temp").get_text()   ←── Extract the temperature
                                                           value for the time period.
    wind_text = item.find("img")["alt"]    ←── Extract the sentence that
                                                contains the wind speed.
    forecast_data.append(          ←── Append each processed
        {                              record to a dataset.
            "date": period,
            "temp": temp,
            "wind_speed": wind_text,
        }
    )
                                       ←── Convert the dataset to a dataframe,
forecast_data = pd.DataFrame(forecast_data)     and display the first five rows.
forecast_data.head()
```

In figure 10.12, you can see that the relevant information in the unstructured HTML data is now transformed into a cleaner, more readable dataframe.

	date	temp	wind_speed
0	Tonight	Low: 31 °F	Tonight: Mostly cloudy, with a low around 31. ...
1	Tuesday	High: 37 °F	Tuesday: Mostly cloudy, with a high near 37. N...
2	Tuesday	Low: 33 °F	Tuesday Night: Cloudy, with a low around 33. E...
3	Wednesday	High: 41 °F	Wednesday: Cloudy, with a high near 41. East w...
4	Wednesday	Low: 33 °F	Wednesday Night: Mostly cloudy, with a low aro...

Figure 10.12 Partially structured and transformed forecast data

Finally, we'll want to extract the temperature and wind speed data as integers to perform the same mathematical calculations we did when retrieving the forecast data from an API. There are several ways to approach this; for this example, we will use *regular expressions* to find the patterns in the text we want to keep. *Regular expressions* are a sequence of characters that specify a pattern you want to identify in a text. These powerful tools are used to parse and structure data, enabling you to extract *only* the information you need in various scenarios. Regular expressions are readily available using the native `re` library. Let's look at an example where we will *only* extract the digit values from the `temp` column:

```
import re                    ⎯⎯ Import the
forecast_data["temp"] = [        re library.      Loop through each row of the temp
    int(re.search(r"\d+", t).group()) for t in forecast_data["temp"]    column, returning only the digit
]                                                 values as single integers.
forecast_data.head()    ⎯⎯⎯ Display the first five
                              rows of the dataframe.
```

Figure 10.13 shows that the `temp` column contains only the integer values for the Fahrenheit temperatures on a given day or night.

	date	temp	wind_speed
0	Tonight	31	Tonight: Mostly cloudy, with a low around 31. ...
1	Tuesday	37	Tuesday: Mostly cloudy, with a high near 37. N...
2	Tuesday	33	Tuesday Night: Cloudy, with a low around 33. E...
3	Wednesday	41	Wednesday: Cloudy, with a high near 41. East w...
4	Wednesday	33	Wednesday Night: Mostly cloudy, with a low aro...

Figure 10.13 Dataframe with the temperature integer extracted

Finally, we can extract the wind speed from the lengthy forecast description sentence in the `wind_speed` column. We know we only want the integer associated with the wind speed for a given period, so let's look for patterns in capturing that information.

```
for row in forecast_data["wind_speed"].head():    ⎯⎯ Print the entire text of the first five
    print(row)                                         rows of the wind speed column
```

Figure 10.14 contains the full text about the wind speed contained in each row of our code.

```
Tonight: Mostly cloudy, with a low around 31. North wind 6 to 10 mph, with gusts as high as 21 mph.
Tuesday: Mostly cloudy, with a high near 37. Northeast wind around 7 mph becoming southeast in the afternoon.
Tuesday Night: Cloudy, with a low around 33. East wind around 7 mph.
Wednesday: Cloudy, with a high near 41. East wind 3 to 6 mph.
Wednesday Night: Mostly cloudy, with a low around 33. Light and variable wind becoming southwest around 5 mph
after midnight.
```

Figure 10.14 Full text of the forecast description that contains the wind speed

There are three notable patterns in how wind speed integers are captured in each record:

- The wind speed is captured as either a single integer or a range. When a range is reported, only the upper end of the range lists the unit of measurement (miles per hour, or mph).
- Wind gusts, when present, are recorded *after* the range of values for the sustained wind speed.
- The wind speed values are always reported after the temperature for that time period.

In chapter 9, we used the maximum sustained wind speed as our historical weather data for the linear regression model. As such, we'll want to extract the upper end of the range of sustained wind speed. In each example shown in figure 10.14, this is the *first* integer value followed by mph, indicating that we can extract the digit based on that pattern. Let's start by extracting all values followed by the unit of measurement:

```
forecast_data["wind_speed"] = [
    re.findall(r"\d+ mph", w) for w in forecast_data["wind_speed"]
]
forecast_data.head()
```

Display the first five rows of the dataframe.

Use the re library's findall function to return all integers followed by a space and "mph".

Each row of the wind_speed column in figure 10.15 contains a list of one or more wind speeds.

	date	temp	wind_speed
0	Tonight	31	[10 mph, 21 mph]
1	Tuesday	37	[7 mph]
2	Tuesday	33	[7 mph]
3	Wednesday	41	[6 mph]
4	Wednesday	33	[5 mph]

Figure 10.15 Result of the regular expression pattern matching, formatted as a list

Finally, we only need to select the first item in each row's list, removing the text and leaving only a single integer for wind speed. We'll also group the dataframe by date, creating a low and high temperature column as we did with the API results.

```
forecast_data["wind_speed"] = [
    int(row[0].replace(" mph", "")) if row else None
    for row in forecast_data["wind_speed"]
]

forecast = (
    forecast_data.groupby("date", sort=False)
```

Retrieve only the first list item, remove the text, and convert it to an integer.

Group the dataframe by date and get the low and high temperatures for that 24-hour period.

```
    .agg({"temp": ["min", "max"], "wind_speed": "max"})
    .reset_index()
)                                                         Rename the columns and
                                                          display the first five rows.
forecast.columns = ["date", "low_temp", "high_temp", "wind_speed"]    ◄───┘
forecast.head()
```

	date	low_temp	high_temp	wind_speed
0	Tonight	31	31	10.0
1	Tuesday	33	37	7.0
2	Wednesday	33	41	6.0
3	Thursday	38	48	NaN
4	Friday	29	45	NaN

Figure 10.16   Final result matching the format of the API and our historical weather dataset from chapter 9

Finally, the wind speed column in figure 10.16 contains *only* the first integer from each list.

At last, we have a dataset that matches our historical weather dataset and a Python script that can be run anytime we need to refresh the data! If we *didn't* have access to an API for this data, scraping the National Weather Service's website for forecasted weather might be a viable solution for several deliverable formats you might use (e.g., an interactive report, a pipeline in the data warehouse).

10.2.3 *Determining the value of web scraping*

Parsing and structuring data from an HTML document usually takes more effort than starting with formatted JSON data. As such, you'll also need to evaluate the pros and cons of using this approach for any project. In situations where you don't have access to structured data via an API, web scraping can offer the following benefits for gathering data to augment your analyses:

- Similar to calling an API, web scraping is a *repeatable process*. After writing the code for your pipeline, you only need to rerun it (either manually or as part of an automated workflow) to continue gathering data.
- Web scraping lets you efficiently *synthesize up-to-date information from multiple sources* into a single database. In cases where you or your stakeholders would otherwise need to review each of these sources routinely, this can save a lot of time and effort.
- By scraping websites, you can tap into untold sources of information that would otherwise be challenging to access. With so many more resources available, you'll see opportunities to unlock the potential of any information you encounter.

In addition, there are multiple libraries in Python that you can use for different web-scraping needs. We covered how to use requests and BeautifulSoup, but you can also use libraries such as scrapy (https://scrapy.org) and urllib (https://docs.python .org/3/library/urllib) to perform various web-scraping tasks. If you expect that web scraping will become a significant part of your workflow, take some time to review the documentation for each library and select the one that best meets your needs.

CHALLENGES

While web pages vary from one source to another, extracting information from tags within the page's HTML is essentially the same—find the sections you need, and extract the information. However, web scraping poses additional challenges beyond calling data from an API. When preparing your code, consider the following matters:

- Web pages change regularly—every time a website updates its format, you will need to rewrite your retrieval scripts. As such, your code can be more brittle due to website updates than your API retrieval code is. While you can't prevent errors, you can handle errors in a way that makes it easy to find and correct problems:

  - Set up your code with appropriate error and exception handling [2]. If each chunk of code representing a single task is run inside a `try` statement, you can generate an `except` statement with a message that clearly tells you where your pipeline failed.

  - If possible, set up alerts (messages sent to users when an automated pipeline fails) or audits (reports that regularly check the freshness or accuracy of the data) to notify yourself or your team when your pipeline fails. This way, you can keep track of problems and mitigate them as soon as possible.

- As you can expect with an API, websites can require you to navigate multiple pages of content to find everything you need. If you plan to scrape a website with more than one page, you must format the URL in your request to loop through each subsequent page.

CONSIDERATIONS

While web scraping is generally legal, many websites restrict how or where you can scrape their data and what consequences you'll face if you break the rules. To ensure you don't find yourself in a problematic situation (usually having your IP address blocked on a site), take the following steps when scraping a website:

- Inspect the page to check for code or comments telling you whether you're permitted to scrape the website. Many sites will have warnings at the top of their page telling you if they don't permit scraping. If you disregard these warnings, your IP address can be blocked.

- From the website's home page, check if there's a `robots.txt` file listing the rules for web scrapers (e.g., api.weather.gov/robots.txt). There may be a list of paths you can't scrape if it's present. Ignoring this file can lead to your IP address being blocked.

- Limit the number of calls you make to a website. You're unlikely to overload a server by testing a workflow locally. However, adding pause times between requests is still important, especially if you're looping through pages or retrying after errors.

10.2.4 Exercises

The Web Scraping Sandbox (http://toscrape.com) is a test environment designed for learning web scraping. It contains two sections to scrape—books and famous quotes.

The book scraping site has a thousand books of various genres to scrape, including metadata about each book (e.g., prices, ratings):

1 Visit the main page of Books to Scrape (http://books.toscrape.com/index .html). Navigate to a genre of books that interests you, and examine the page. How many items are there? Are there subsequent pages of items that might not appear in a single API call?

2 Check if there's a `robots.txt` file for the website. If so, what rules does it specify? Are there pages you *aren't* allowed to scrape?

3 Using the `requests` library, request the URL for the book genre of your choice. What do you notice about the results? Does it contain all of the information you saw when viewing the website?

4 Use `BeautifulSoup` to help make the HTML more readable. Find the tags that contain the book titles and other metadata (e.g., publication year, number of editions).

5 Once you've found the tags containing the book titles and metadata, start parsing out the information you believe will be helpful for analysis. Hint: the titles in one type of tag show the complete text and are cut off in others.

6 Compile all the metadata into a dataframe, and convert each column to its appropriate data type (e.g., integers).

7 Imagine that the information from this scraping website belonged to your company's competitor. How could this metadata be used to set prices and promotions? How often might you scrape the site to stay current on this information?

10.3 *Tapping into public data sources*

Finally, let's discuss how to make the most of the vast public data sources available to you. Throughout this book, we've referenced some such sources (e.g., unemployment rates and rat sightings), but we've barely scratched the surface of what's available to use.

As the name suggests, a *public data source* refers to a freely available dataset for public use. These data sources are often maintained by the organizations that make them available, routinely updating them with fresh data that can be used for research, analysis, and decision-making in academic and non-academic settings. Data can come from many sources; some of the most common include the following:

- Government agencies at all levels (e.g., federal, state, and local)
- Non-governmental organizations (NGOs)
- Academic institutions
- Open source platforms

These sources provide a wide range of data topics, including demographic data, economic indicators, scientific research findings, and environmental data. Many offer population-level data (an analyst's dream) or population estimates that can tell you about the ecosystem in which your organization operates.

Assuming the organization you work with doesn't operate in a vacuum (or a fortress, as in figure 10.17), there are many potential benefits to supplementing the data collected internally with public data sources.

Absolutely nothing from the outside world will impact our company or influence our metrics

Figure 10.17 Truthfully, if the places we worked at *did* operate in a vacuum or from within a fortress, that would make an analyst's job *so* much easier.

For many of your projects, public data can offer the following:

- You can introduce new *dimensions* to your dataset, giving you additional inputs that may relate to your organization's performance.
- You can provide *valuable context* to your stakeholders on the social, environmental, and political phenomena that may affect the organization's performance.
- You can cost-effectively obtain large amounts of data (it's free!). Collecting that data on your own would take significant time and resources that most companies, nonprofits, or other organizations couldn't budget for.
- You're saving yourself from having to reinvent the wheel. Even if your organization *did* have the budget to collect data about large swaths of the population, why would you do so? There are great, reliable resources for so many topics that it often doesn't make sense to rely on your data collection capacity.

10.3.1 When did public data become so popular?

The widespread availability of public data is a relatively new phenomenon. In the 1990s, the term *open data* was used to discuss the need for scientific data to be made easily accessible to other research teams who might want to analyze the data further [3]. The idea of freely available scientific findings wasn't new (in fact, it goes back decades), but it was propelled into the mainstream with the rise of *open source software*.

OPEN SOURCE AND OPEN GOVERNMENT DATA

Open source software is any software for which the source code is freely available for users to review and improve (every Python library we've imported in this book is open source). The open data movement sought to create a similar framework for data: information collected about the public (e.g., from governments) should be available as a shared resource for anyone interested in analyzing it. With collective contribution and analysis, it was believed that the quality of analyses and findings would be far higher than if limited to only a small number of individuals.

One of the first memorandums issued by Barack Obama's presidential administration was to commit to public disclosure of government data for use [4]. As such, the federal government's open data portal (https://catalog.data.gov/dataset) was created in mid-2009. In addition to this portal, some US federal agencies continued to share data through their existing tools (e.g., the Census Bureau and the Bureau of Labor Statistics). Many state and city governments also followed this established pattern in the next few years:

- The San Francisco open data portal (https://datasf.org/opendata) was launched in 2009.
- New York City's open data portal (https://opendata.cityofnewyork.us/open-data-law) was established in 2012.
- Chicago's open data portal (https://data.cityofchicago.org) was established in 2012.

These are just a few examples; at least ten states in the United States have state or local open data portals providing information on the range of government services provided to its citizens.

SCIENTIFIC DATA

Despite a long-standing interest in the free availability of data collected for scientific research, sharing datasets is still far from universal. Many fields of study (e.g., public health and medical research) have concerns about disseminating protected health information, and others still have concerns about the risk of deanonymizing sensitive information. Even among less or non-sensitive information, data-sharing practices can vary widely by publication and university. Most peer-reviewed journals don't require researchers to provide their full datasets, and researchers conducting complex follow-up studies (e.g., a meta-analysis) require lengthy outreach to get the data they need.

In the past twenty years, there have been slow shifts in the norms regarding data sharing. Several leaders in the collection of nationally representative datasets publish their data online. An increasing number of peer-reviewed journals require that researchers include the raw data used in the paper. Some organizations compile lists of papers across journals that include their datasets, incentivizing further journals to include the raw data. As of now, data in science is *more* open to the public than in decades past, but there are still further opportunities to participate in open data.

10.3.2 *Types of public data sources*

We've alluded to the many types of public data sources that have arisen from open source and open data initiatives, and we have tapped into such sources for our analyses throughout this book. Let's break down some of the most common types of data available to augment the analyses you'll do for your organization and how to choose the most appropriate source for your needs.

It's important to note that most of the data we've covered thus far is US-centric. This is by no means an indication of what data is available globally; there are tremendous resources available in many regions. I recommend using the examples here as a *starting point* and looking for the data most relevant to you, your world region of interest, and your topic.

GOVERNMENT AND NGOS

Government agencies worldwide publish *lots* of data spanning various sectors and fields. Much of the information is shared in the spirit of transparency, enabling researchers, policy analysts, and businesses to understand the context in which they operate. The specific information you have access to in a given location will vary, but most governments tend to offer some variation of the following:

- *Economic data*—Many governments' labor and finance departments publish data on unemployment, inflation, GDP growth, and national budgets. These agencies publish indicators aggregated over specific periods (e.g., monthly or quarterly). For example, the US Bureau of Labor Statistics regularly publishes granular economic indicators (e.g., inflation of individual goods, unemployment in specific industries).

- *Demographic data*—Demographic data about age, sex, race, ethnicity, income, family composition, and more is published worldwide. For example, the US Census Bureau publishes its census data every ten years, with information available from national aggregates to individual zip codes. Many European Union countries and locales publish their census data via the EU data portal (https://data.europa.eu/en).

- *Public utility data*—Public utility companies and governing bodies often publish data on topics such as energy consumption, power plant energy production, and utilization rates of renewable and non-renewable sources. For example, the UK open data portal (www.data.gov.uk) publishes an annual update to a dataset on energy consumption trends throughout the country.

- *Education data*—Education data is published globally for all age levels, from primary to college and graduate education. You can find data about enrolment rates, school performance, graduation rates, and degrees awarded from numerous countries. For example, Finland is known for having one of the highest-quality primary school systems in the world. If you want to learn more, their open data portal has detailed statistics on many topics (www.stat.fi/org/avoin data/index_en.html).

- *Environmental data*—Federal and local agencies governing environmental regulations often publish data on the indicators they routinely monitor. These indicators can include air quality, water quality, soil quality, and climate change concerns. For example, NASA publishes a trove of data from satellite imagery,

such as floods, droughts, surface temperature, and more (www.earthdata
.nasa.gov/topics).

- *Public health data*—Public health departments and organizations publish data
  on disease outbreaks, population health, and more. This data is essential for
  managing public health crises, improving services, and facilitating health-
  related research. For example, Kenya's National Bureau of Statistics
  (www.knbs.or.ke) publishes information on disabilities prevalent in the country
  and rates of accessing services and accommodations for these disabilities.

Government data sources offer the advantage of being well-maintained, up-to-date,
and representative indicators of the population they're estimating. Most government
agencies hire statisticians and data professionals to ensure the accuracy of the indicators they produce, making this a highly reliable option to augment your work.

ACADEMIC INSTITUTIONS

Research institutes in and outside universities publish scientific findings across all
fields of study. These findings can be peer-reviewed study results with the raw datasets
attached to those studies or datasets *unattached* to a published study. Each of these
offers unique value to your research and analyses.

Let's first look at peer-reviewed research. *Peer-reviewed studies* are considered the
gold standard in the dissemination of scientific knowledge. Before articles are published in academic journals, their contents are reviewed by peers who share the
authors' expertise. This review process *intends* to catch errors and ensure that arguments and conclusions are empirically sound. However, this process is far from perfect, as we'll see shortly.

We've discussed peer-reviewed research in previous chapters and specifically recommended some strategies for keeping informed about the latest developments in
your field (chapters 6 and 8). In addition to the value provided by enhancing your
knowledge base, the findings from research can bolster or even replace the need for
an analysis. This is especially true when synthesizing the data would be a resource-
intensive process. Consider the following scenario:

> *A human resources analyst at a medium-sized software company is tasked with
> helping the leadership team understand employee productivity in key departments.
> Specifically, they're hoping to get a pulse on the speed and quality of deliverables on
> the software engineering teams to propose a plan for accelerating the team's capacity.*
>
> *To start, the analyst and their teammates must identify methods for assessing
> productivity. They propose starting the project by reviewing research in
> organizational psychology for recommended productivity measures, including the
> strengths and limitations of each approach. From there, they can align these findings
> with the data their organization currently collects.*

Does this situation seem like a no-brainer? Exploring peer-reviewed research will usually take a fraction of the time compared to developing a new measure from scratch.
The approaches in the literature have already been vetted, enabling the analytics team

to use peer-reviewed findings instead of conducting their own analysis for part of the project. Essentially, they're taking an opportunity to summarize another study, saving time and preventing their team from reinventing the wheel.

You'll have many opportunities to tap into peer-reviewed resources throughout your career. If you make it a habit to keep tabs on scholarly work in your field and start a new project by seeing what's available, you can hone the strategic direction of your organization *and* save precious resources on your team. The key to searching effectively is knowing what academic fields of study might correspond to the questions you have in industry. Table 10.1 provides a few examples.

Table 10.1 Research terms corresponding to industry terms and subdomains of analytics

Research domain	Search these research fields
Marketing analytics	Market research, consumer behavior
Human resources analytics	Industrial/organizational psychology, personnel psychology, social psychology
Financial analytics	Financial metrics, business performance indicators, econometrics
Product analytics	Cognitive psychology, behavioral psychology
All of analytics	Statistical methods, analysis, machine learning, measurement development

In addition to journal articles, several research institutes in the United States regularly publish raw survey data collected from a sample of the American population. These surveys are routinely collected (e.g., annually) and contain dozens of questions about people's attitudes, opinions, behaviors, and characteristics. Let's review two nationally representative surveys that can be applied to *many* domain areas given the wide range of topics that they cover:

- The General Social Survey (GSS) has been conducted by the University of Chicago for more than fifty years (https://gss.norc.org). Many questions have remained the same over time, allowing for large-scale longitudinal analyses by researchers interested in accessing the data. The survey covers a wide range of topics:
  - Demographic information, including race, ethnicity, gender, family composition, living conditions, socioeconomic status, population density, and access to services
  - Political perspectives, including party affiliations, opinions on high-profile topics, and trust in government institutions
  - Prevalence of physical and psychological wellness concerns, including stress, traumatic events, and substance use
- Monitoring the Future (MTF) is a widespread survey of American youth conducted in parallel with the GSS by the University of Michigan for almost fifty years (www.icpsr.umich.edu/web/NAHDAP/series/35). The survey is

conducted annually with nationally representative samples of students in grades 8, 10, and 12. Many of the questions used in this survey are identical or adapted from the GSS, with some adjustments for age appropriateness and augmentations for concerns specific to youth wellbeing and academic performance (see figure 10.18). Key topics in this survey include the following:

- Demographic information, including all age-appropriate characteristics, is captured in the GSS.
- Political opinions, civic engagement, lifestyle (e.g., figure 10.18), and trust in government institutions.
- Prevalence of concerns related to substance use, peer pressure, mental health, chronic stress, and life at school and home.

```
V3220: How much do you agree or disagree with each statement below?
I would probably be willing to use a bicycle or mass transit (if available)
rather than a car to get to work.

1 = Strongly Disagree
3 = Neither
5 = Strongly Agree
-9 = Missing

 1    587
 2    422
 4    402
 3    384
 5    280
-9     34
Name: V3220, dtype: int64
```

Figure 10.18   Sample question and answers downloaded from the Monitoring the Future survey.

The GSS and MTF surveys can be downloaded on their respective websites in multiple formats (e.g., CSVs), including formats compatible with several proprietary statistical software programs (STATA, SPSS). To make sense of the dozens of coded column names, you will need to download and read the accompanying data dictionary showing the column definitions, data types, available response options, and percentage of respondents who chose each response option when filling out the survey.

Large-scale survey datasets offer the ability to provide insights about subsets of the American population tailored to your organization's needs. Take the following example:

An analyst at a nonprofit that organizes grassroots political campaigns is informed of a new strategy to engage candidates and voters on the West Coast of the United States. Previously, the majority of campaigns had taken place in the Northeast, and the organization is interested in understanding their chances of success in this new geography.

Using the General Social Survey data, the analyst can compare the populations of the Pacific to the two Northeast regions on demographic characteristics, political opinions, and the problems they perceive to be the highest priority for the nation. Using the raw data, the analyst can determine whether there are significant differences in these key areas of importance between the two regions.

Without any direct data collection, the nonprofit can perform a complex analysis of the GSS by comparing only the populations of interest. Many types of organizations (nonprofits, market research, health and wellness) can benefit from getting a pulse on the needs and concerns of the American population. These datasets can unlock those insights for organizations that would otherwise be unable to shoulder the cost of vast data collection.

10.3.3 Accessing public data

Public data repositories are incredibly versatile. Most of the sources we've covered offer multiple methods to access their data, accommodating researchers and analysts with varying technical skills and project requirements. For tasks as simple as charting a metric over time for a quick presentation snapshot, you can probably retrieve your information in a matter of minutes. However, many tasks you encounter will require you to perform a deep dive into the raw data to tailor the information to your organization's needs. Thankfully, most of the public data repositories we've discussed offer comprehensive resources for analyzing custom subsets of the information they share.

THE DATA CATALOG

Most government and academic data repositories include a catalog with each dataset. A *data catalog* documents a dataset's *metadata* (data about the data), giving the information needed to understand what's at your disposal. Data catalogs will often include the following:

- Overall dataset characteristics (codes used for missing values, total sample size, sampling strategies, etc.)
- A list of all variable (column) names and their detailed descriptions
- The full question being asked, if the dataset contains a survey
- Details on the data types (e.g., multiple choice options, integers, Boolean values)
- Any caveats or limitations that can affect result quality (e.g., missing values)

Let's look at the University of Michigan's Monitoring the Future (MTF) data. If you navigate to the most recent survey of grade 12 students (https://mng.bz/5gG4), you will see a Download button with several options, including Documentation Only. This download provides the study's *codebook*—a 1,700-page description of the survey's methodology and available data. You can search the codebook for any topics you are interested in, enabling you to match them to the column names in the dataset. The codebook also provides summary statistics for each question, taking care of part of your exploratory analysis steps.

The MTF's codebook is similar to the other types of documentation we've used throughout this book. It's a tool for understanding a resource, how it was developed, best practices for using it, and tools for getting started with your analysis.

THE DATA PORTAL

Most of the public data repositories we covered in this chapter offer an *interactive web portal*, enabling end users to access their data easily. Most portals have functionality for filtering, aggregating, and visualizing subsets of data directly on the website, reducing the time spent finding the information you need. This is especially helpful when the dataset is large and complex. If you can extract only the five columns you need out of several hundred, your entire data processing pipeline will run in a fraction of the time.

Let's look at the `rat_sightings` dataset we've become familiar with throughout this book. The actual CSV file we've been using has only 5,000 rows, making it easy to open, manipulate, and analyze. However, it's only a subset of the 311 dataset provided in the New York City Open Data portal (https://opendata.cityofnewyork.us). If you search for "311", the first result gives you the entire raw dataset of service requests and complaints from 2010 (https://mng.bz/vKn4). The full table contains 35 million rows, which was unnecessary for developing a statistical model for our specific urban phenomenon. Thus, the dataset was filtered using the data portal's query tool, selecting only records where the `descriptor` field contained the text "rat sighting." Figure 10.19 shows you the interface available on the NYC Open Data portal.

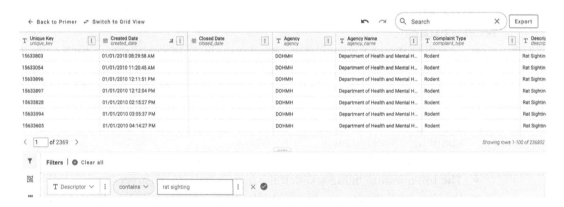

Figure 10.19   The NYC Open Data portal allows you to filter, aggregate, and create simple charts.

The dataset has been reduced to 236,000 records (less than one percent of the original row count). This subset is easily exported to Python, where we can further process it for analysis.

APIs

Data portals can provide all the tools necessary to create your desired dataset when you only need a static file (e.g., a CSV) for a project. This is what I did to create the `rat_sightings` dataset—you'll notice that the most recent date in the file is several months prior to this book's publication. I obtained the data via a direct download; no further updates were needed.

If you're working on a project that requires *regularly refreshed data,* you're in luck—many data repositories provide freely available APIs for custom data access. A data portal is a great way to identify the API parameters you need to subset and preprocess the data for dynamic projects. For example, let's say we need updated daily rat sightings to share with our hypothetical city government stakeholder from chapter 9 so they can regularly assess the accuracy of their predictive model. We could generate an API endpoint directly from the data portal using the Export capability seen on the top right of figure 10.19. The URL generated is quite long, but it's easily modified within your Python code to return *only* the previous day's records of rat sightings:

```
                                        Import the datetime
                                        library functions.
from datetime import datetime, timedelta    ←        Calculate the current date,
                                                     one day, and two days prior
now = datetime.now()                        ←        as inputs for the endpoint.
start = (now - timedelta(days=3)).strftime("%Y-%m-%d")
end = (now - timedelta(days=2)).strftime("%Y-%m-%d")    Construct each portion
                                                        of the endpoint for the
base = "https://data.cityofnewyork.us/resource/erm2-nwe9.json"    NYC Open Data portal.
query = "?$query="                                       ←
select = "SELECT `created_date`, `unique_key` "
where = 'WHERE caseless_eq(`descriptor`, "Rat Sighting") '
dates = f"AND (`created_date` BETWEEN '{start}' :: floating_timestamp AND
     '{end}' :: floating_timestamp) "        ←    Add the date inputs
                                                   to the dates variable.
full_url = base + query + select + where + dates    ←    Construct
                                                         the full URL.
```

The concatenated endpoint URL can now be queried using the `requests` library with precisely the same steps we took in the first section of this chapter:

```
response = requests.get(full_url)    ←    Request 311 rat sightings
print(response.json())    ←               data from Open Data NYC.
                          Print the JSON
                          response.
```

A sample of the JSON response from the 311 dataset is shown in figure 10.20.

```
[{'created_date': '2024-09-19T23:50:34.000', 'unique_key': '62496703'},
 {'created_date': '2024-09-19T23:36:56.000', 'unique_key': '62494046'},
 {'created_date': '2024-09-19T23:33:43.000', 'unique_key': '62495251'},
 {'created_date': '2024-09-19T23:26:01.000', 'unique_key': '62499322'},
 {'created_date': '2024-09-19T23:08:47.000', 'unique_key': '62494031'},
 {'created_date': '2024-09-19T22:21:00.000', 'unique_key': '62497984'},
 {'created_date': '2024-09-19T22:15:36.000', 'unique_key': '62496704'},
 {'created_date': '2024-09-19T22:06:57.000', 'unique_key': '62494032'},
 {'created_date': '2024-09-19T22:02:01.000', 'unique_key': '62499474'},
 {'created_date': '2024-09-19T21:41:30.000', 'unique_key': '62496706'},
 {'created_date': '2024-09-19T21:31:51.000', 'unique_key': '62495254'},
 {'created_date': '2024-09-19T21:01:34.000', 'unique_key': '62499323'},
```

Figure 10.20   A sample of the JSON results from the NYC Open Data 311 dataset endpoint

From there, your data extraction and processing pipeline can be run without the need for manual updates.

10.3.4   Exercises

You are an analytics consultant at a market research firm. You have a new client that sells sustainable clothing and who is looking to add new locations in another US city that best matches the demographic and social characteristics of their current customers in Seattle. The majority of the current customer base tends to have the following features:

- Ages 21 to 50
- At or above the median income for Seattle
- Strong interest in environmental sustainability

Use a public data source to identify opportunities for the client to expand its customer base:

1 Look at the General Social Survey data for 2022 and the US Census data for 2020. Do either of these data sources have information on the preceding characteristics that can help you determine which major US cities have populations with similar characteristics to the target demographic in Seattle?

2 Choose a data source to begin exploring. Use the data explorer tool provided on their website to find the following information about residents in Seattle (or the approximate region of Seattle):
   - The percentage of residents between ages 21 and 50
   - The median income
   - The percentage of residents concerned about environmental sustainability

3 Using the information you gathered, identify two other regions whose characteristics most closely resemble the target demographic of the existing customer base in Seattle. Make a recommendation to the client on where to open a new store location.

4 Determine the best method to help the client monitor this information in the long term. Should you create an automated pipeline to extract and process the data from an API, download it as a CSV file and process it manually, or check the data explorer regularly?

Summary

- *APIs* are a way for two or more computers or services to communicate with each other. They contain a set of protocols that allow you to *request* specific data and information, and to receive a *response* in a specified format. APIs are instrumental for the efficient routine extraction of up-to-date data for analysis.
- The Python requests library makes it easy to retrieve data from an API. With a successful *call*, you'll receive a response object that can be formatted as JSON data.

- The *JSON data* returned by calling an API often requires processing to turn its nested document structure into tabular data that can be read and analyzed with pandas.

- When gathering data from an API, it's essential to ensure you are capturing the information you want. For example, many APIs implement guardrails to limit improper use of their service. These guardrails include requiring authentication with an API key, implementing pagination to limit the number of results per API call, and rate limiting the frequency in which you can make API calls.

- Part of your responsibility as an analyst includes determining the *value* and *viability* of calling data from an API. This includes assessing the time you will save, the available resources for automating the API calls, and the ability to incorporate the data returned into a centralized data warehouse.

- *Web scraping* is a method of extracting unstructured data from a website's HTML, enabling you to transform it into a structured format for analysis.

- Web scraping is performed by extracting information contained within specific tags in the HTML. These tags can be headers, links, paragraphs, sections, etc., that can be selected. From there, you can directly extract information that's easy to process or use regular expressions for complex pattern matching.

- While web scraping enables you to tap into a wide range of resources, it does offer challenges compared to using data from an API:
  - Website content tends to be *dynamic*, making your processing steps far more brittle and prone to breaking when a website changes.
  - Many websites have rules for web scrapers (e.g., pages allowed to be scraped, rate limits). Disregarding these rules can block your IP address on that website.

- *Public data sources* contain information that is freely accessible to the general population, and they are usually maintained by the organization that publishes them.

- Public data is often published by *government agencies* (e.g., the US Department of Labor), international organizations (e.g., the European Union), and *academic institutions* (e.g., the University of Chicago).

- Public data can usually be accessed with an organization's data explorer on their website, downloaded as a CSV, or retrieved from an API.

- Public data can be complex, containing hundreds or thousands of columns. Thus, it's important to review the *data catalog* of all available variables in your dataset.

11

The magic of well-structured data

This chapter covers

- Tools and strategies for storing and processing data
- Approaches to data management at organizations
- Methods of structuring data for analytics
- Developing a strategy for enhancing the value of your data

Think about the data that you've analyzed throughout your education, career, and reading this book—what was the structure of that information? What was contained in each row and column? How much work did it take to transform the data into the shape needed to analyze it? What information was accurate, and what was potentially wrong or missing?

While your answers will vary depending on the data and context, the structure of your data shapes what you can do with it. Well-structured data makes it easy to focus on insights, and poorly structured data takes countless hours of cleaning and reorganization before meaningful work can begin. In most organizations, you aren't bound to the format of the data available, and you can strategically contribute to the data collection, storage, and transformation of information made available for analysis. This chapter will explore the tools and methods that enable you to streamline the generation of valuable insights in your work.

11.1 The analyst's dilemma

Consider the following scenario:

> *A marketing manager submits a request to your analytics team. He asks how long it typically takes subscribers in Europe before they upgrade to the premium tier, and if the higher prices cause them to cancel their contracts sooner. He emphasizes that the request is urgent and must be ready by tomorrow to share with a consulting firm.*

You and your team are frustrated—you remind the marketing manager that your team has a minimum turnaround time of one week for all new requests. He asks if you can "please just quickly get the data for the first part of the question." When you tell him that it will take at least three days to compile the data, he tells you he's struggling to understand why it would take so long to complete a simple request.

 In addition to not knowing your current workload, the marketing stakeholder doesn't have insight into the shape of the data that determines how much work it will take to get an answer. He doesn't know that you'll need to categorize countries into their respective continents or that the query takes more than five minutes to run *each time you edit it* while working on getting the answer!

 Does this situation sound familiar? Have you worked on projects where your stakeholders don't have insight into how long or complex their requests are (such as in figure 11.1)? Do they assume it's as easy as "finding the data," not knowing the work it takes to access, structure, and prepare it to answer their questions?

Figure 11.1 When your colleagues don't understand that data can't be "conjured," it can feel like data analysts are expected to wave a magic wand and generate insights.

If so, you're far from alone. Analysts often spend more time preparing and structuring data than actually doing the analysis—even when using the datasets already available in the data warehouse. The topics covered in the first 10 chapters likely represent a fraction of your day-to-day work compared to the bandwidth necessary to get your data into the right shape. However, if you search for the definition of an analyst, you'll primarily see references to data visualization, statistics, and programming languages. Job posts often ask for skills in deriving insights, guiding decisions, and improving outcomes for a business. They rarely tell you that preparing the data for analysis can take half or more of your time before achieving those goals.

The shape and complexity of data varies significantly from one business to another. A company that creates a fitness tracking watch will have different challenges (e.g., high data volume) than a project management software company (e.g., unstructured text data). The *quantity* of your data is rarely related to its *quality* or ease of use. High-quality data *is* related to the skill set of the data professionals at an organization and the investment in creating a well-structured data warehouse for analysis.

Whether you're a lone analyst or a member of a well-staffed data practice, your skills as an analyst can contribute to making your organization's data more valuable and easier to use (e.g., transforming the data in figure 11.2 into the table shown in figure 11.3, making it available for other analysts to use). When the data tables in the data warehouse are structured with analysis in mind, the entire organization benefits from faster, more accurate insights.

	employee_id	employee_info	category
0	"1"	{"name": "Alice", "months_employed": 14}	Engineering
1	"2"	{"name": "Bob", "months_employed": 8}	Support_1
2	"3"	{"name": "Charlie", "months_employed": 35}	Engineering
3	"4"	{"name": "Diana", "months_employed": 9}	Human Resources
4	"5"	{"name": "Edward", "months_employed": 22}	Support_1

Figure 11.2   **Messy, unstructured, and non-tabular data can be more challenging to analyze.**

	Employee ID	Name	Months Employed	Department
0	1	Alice	14	Engineering
1	2	Bob	8	Support
2	3	Charlie	35	Engineering
3	4	Diana	9	Human Resources
4	5	Edward	22	Support

Figure 11.3   **The same data as in figure 11.2, after it's been cleaned and structured for analysis.**

The more you can extend your comfort zone in working with messy, malformed, inaccurate, and unstructured data, the better you can contribute to turning it into high-quality data for you and your coworkers. Data curated for analysis can be used directly by more people in your organization, which helps to foster a broader data-informed culture.

11.2 Data tools at a glance

Before we develop a strategy for enhancing your organization's data, let's review some foundational terms and concepts related to the data warehouse. Many aspects of data storage, processing, and modeling are implied in the role of an analyst or defined only in context (e.g., tables, schemas, warehouses). Analysts often have access to a curated or otherwise limited subset of the organization's data, making it challenging to fully understand what's under the surface of the information you see. Figure 11.4 shows just how different source data might look from its eventual transformation into resources for analytics.

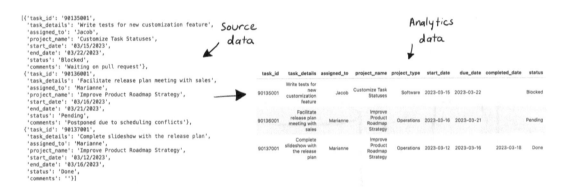

Figure 11.4   When data reaches your doorstep, it often looks nothing like it did at the source.

In the previous chapter, you saw that most data sources require several processing and structuring steps before they are in the right shape for analysis. Now imagine combining dozens or hundreds of data sources into a single data warehouse and designing them so it's easy for the organization to derive value. It's not an easy task! A lot of work goes into making data viable for analysis. Whether or not you're directly involved in your organization's data storage and processing, you have plenty of opportunities to contribute value to the process.

Data infrastructure refers to the data collection, storage, processing, and retrieval systems that power your organization's analysis. This includes every tool and process used to gather data from various sources, synthesize it, and present it to analysts. Depending on your organization, this can involve setting up a shared drive and exporting data once per day, or it can include dozens of tools that handle billions of records every day. The tools at your disposal really depend on what information you work with.

In general, data infrastructure needs tools that perform each of the following tasks:

- Gather information to add to the data warehouse on a regular cadence
- Efficiently store the types of data collected by the organization
- Process and structure data *before* or *after* it's added to the warehouse

Many vendors and open source tools can perform combinations of these tasks, and most organizations use one or more of these options to get the right data in front of analytics teams. We'll explore some options that you may encounter in your role when performing each task.

11.2.1 Data gathering

Organizations keep *a lot* of records. In addition to core information about customers and users, most organizations use third-party software to manage additional business (e.g., advertisements, surveys) and internal processes (e.g., human resources). Smaller businesses often get by using spreadsheets, a shared drive, or a small-scale data warehouse. Larger companies will usually have a centralized data warehouse and many third-party tools. Both will regularly need to *combine data across multiple sources* (as shown in figure 11.5) to analyze it.

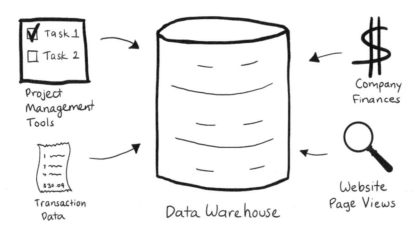

Figure 11.5   Data in a warehouse is combined to create cohesive information about a business process.

Gathering a new data source

Bethany is an analyst at a biotechnology startup who wants to incorporate a new, third-party data source into the data warehouse. She sees it has an API and is prepared to write a custom script to retrieve it. She consults with the data engineering team to determine her options and is presented with the following:

- The business uses a vendor called Fivetran (www.fivetran.com), which offers out-of-the-box connectors for adding a wide variety of data sources [1]. The team recommends searching their documentation to see if a connector is available for the data she is interested in using. If so, she doesn't need to write a script to extract the data—she simply needs to generate an API key and connect it to Fivetran to extract and save the data.
- If Fivetran doesn't have a connector available for her data source, she should prepare a custom data extraction and processing pipeline in Python that will be deployed on the business's workflow management tool, Apache Airflow (https://airflow.apache.org) [2].
- If she *only* intends to use the data source for a limited time, or the data source is relatively static (e.g., census data), she can manually upload the data to a bucket (folder) in AWS s3 (https://aws.amazon.com/s3). From there, the data can be manually added to the warehouse as a static table for her analysis.

Bethany knows that she will need this specific dataset refreshed at least once per week, so she searches the Fivetran documentation to see if they have an available connector for the source she's using. She discovers they don't have a connector, so she works with the data engineering team to prepare a custom workflow for Airflow deployment.

In most organizations, your options for synthesizing data will require varying amounts of effort to connect new information with the data warehouse. The topics we covered in chapter 9 (retrieving data from an API and web scraping) will often come in handy, but in some cases, you can skip them entirely if the organization has the right tools in place!

11.2.2 Data storage

Organizations have several possible combinations of technologies to choose from, each with pros and cons in terms of cost, scalability, and ease of use. Let's look at some of the most common technologies used today.

DATA WAREHOUSES

As referenced throughout this book, a *data warehouse* is a centralized repository for storing, consolidating, and retrieving large volumes of data. Typically, data warehouses are built to handle *related information* (e.g., customers and their transactions) in a relational database that defines keys connecting information between sources. Organizations structure data in relational databases for optimal querying and analysis, enabling teams to use data in their strategic efforts. Data warehouses contain one or more *databases* (a collection of organized data, depicted in figure 11.6), further divided into *schemas* that organize the data by topic or analytical purpose.

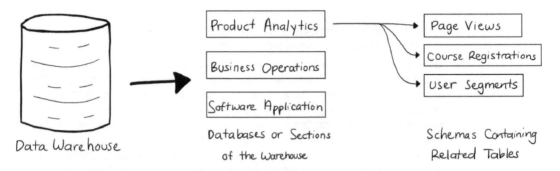

Figure 11.6   **Data warehouses contain sets of information that can be divided into databases and schemas.**

Databases and schemas in a warehouse will often provide organized or layered information for different purposes. Some layers will have data formatted and organized similarly to the source, enabling you to understand where each piece of information comes from. Subsequent layers may be built *on top* of these, combining information from multiple sources into logically organized schemas according to the business's analytical needs. We'll discuss these methods of structuring data in greater depth in section 11.3.

DOCUMENT DATABASES

While relational databases store *structured* information, *document databases* are designed to manage complex *nested* information such as JSON or XML. These databases can contain a range of information within the nested structure in a *schemaless* format, meaning the structure can change over time. Document databases may be used in the following situations:

- A new company is looking to save data in a rapidly evolving format during the early stages of building a cutting-edge IoT device.
- A multimedia company is storing audio and video content with a variety of properties.
- A product allows users to upload documents for employment verification.
- A popular application stores semistructured logs to monitor the app's performance.

Figure 11.7 shows one example of how nested document data may be structured.

Document databases often use NoSQL to query the key-value pairs that make up the data structure [3], requiring analysts to learn a specialized query language to use them effectively. Extra steps are required to transform the nested JSON data into *tabular data* for use, similar to how we transformed the nested web data in chapter 10. Further, due to the dynamic nature of document databases, you will often need to implement *data quality checks* to ensure you're saving the right data in the warehouse. We'll discuss some of these steps (e.g., checking for null records or schema changes) in section 11.3.2.

	userId	document
0	U1001	{'name': 'Ava Patel', 'email': 'ava.patel@example.com', 'age': 29, 'preferences': {'newsletter': True, 'themes': ['science', 'technology']}, 'lastLogin': '2024-02-25T15:30:00Z'}
1	U1002	{'name': 'Liam Johnson', 'email': 'liam.johnson@example.com', 'age': 35, 'preferences': {'newsletter': False, 'themes': ['business', 'finance']}, 'lastLogin': '2024-02-24T10:25:00Z'}
2	U1003	{'name': 'Olivia Brown', 'email': 'olivia.brown@example.com', 'age': 27, 'preferences': {'newsletter': True, 'themes': ['art', 'design']}, 'lastLogin': '2024-02-26T18:45:00Z'}
3	U1004	{'name': 'Ethan Davis', 'email': 'ethan.davis@example.com', 'age': 41, 'preferences': {'newsletter': True, 'themes': ['sports', 'fitness']}, 'lastLogin': '2024-02-23T08:15:00Z'}

Figure 11.7   An example of a document structure in JSON that may exist in a document database.

DATA LAKES

Organizations often set up a *data lake* as the first destination for information saved in the warehouse. *Data lakes*, depicted in figure 11.8, are a centralized place to store a mix of structured and unstructured data *before* curating it in the warehouse for analysis. Data lakes are well-suited to *wide data* (lots of tables and sources) and *big data* (a high volume of records), making them suitable for a wide range of needs.

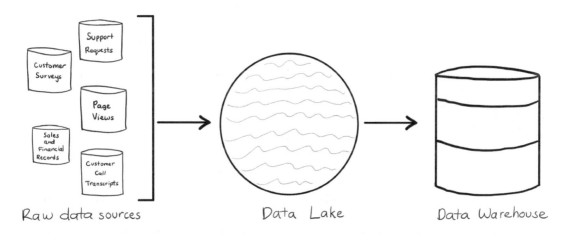

Figure 11.8   Data lakes are the first landing point for the data that organizations synthesize for analysis.

Similar to document databases, data lakes don't require you to predefine a schema before storing the data. This means that data is stored in its *source format*, which is often messy and contains inaccuracies that require cleaning and transformation before you can use it. Getting the information into a clean, structured, and accurate table will require additional work before it's ready for use.

11.2.3 *Data processing*

Data processing includes any operations necessary to convert raw data into a usable format for analytical purposes at *any* stage in the pipeline. This includes steps taken to process information *before* and *after* data is saved in a warehouse.

ETL vs. ELT

In chapter 10, we discussed how ETL (extract, transform, load) processes are used to retrieve and transform data *before* making it available for analysis. But it isn't the *only* method available—in fact, data lakes with cheap storage make it easy to use *ELT* (extract, load, transform; shown in figure 11.9) processes, saving the data transformation steps for after the data has already been stored.

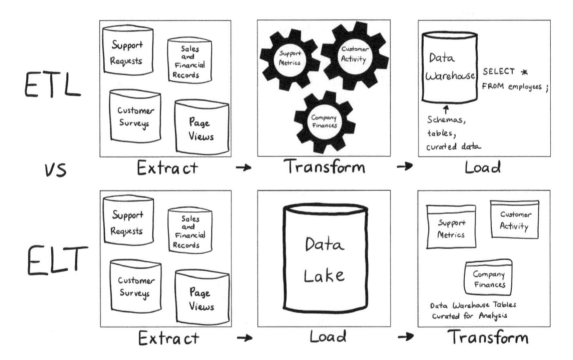

Figure 11.9 ETL and ELT processes transform the data at different steps, leading to structured data in the warehouse.

The choice between ETL and ELT will vary between organizations, their available technology, and the needs of an individual project. In general, ETL offers advantages in the following situations:

- If the data being ingested requires *multiple complex processing steps*, ETL tools will save time and processing power by keeping these steps out of the warehouse. The web scraping examples we covered in chapter 10 would be far more complex to achieve using SQL in the warehouse than with the Python library we used.

- If you know that a data source will only be used in one static format (e.g., the weather forecast data), ETLs allow you to surface data in the warehouse with little to no additional processing before it can be used.
- If the data you're ingesting contains personally identifiable information (PII), protected health information (PHI), or other sensitive information, you may be taking steps to anonymize and pseudonymize that data before surfacing it for analysis (see chapter 8). If you want to avoid saving that information *anywhere*, ETLs allow you to scrub the sensitive information before it's loaded into the data lake or data warehouse.

In contrast, ELT is often preferred in situations where the raw data can be used to bring value in multiple ways. These are a few examples:

- A very large dataset is extracted from a vendor with each hourly API call, making it impractical to transform the data in memory before saving it. The saved data is then only processed for individual queries, performing a just-in-time transformation so that it can be used.
- A hedge fund requires that certain stock data be updated in near real-time to monitor the market. Since every second counts, the data is directly ingested with ELT, and little to no transformations are made before it's shown to the team.
- A company ingests course registration data from a third-party learning platform. Several teams use this data to understand how learning resource usage affects their team's processes. Due to the varying needs of each team, it's ingested in its raw format so it can be flexibly queried and analyzed within the company.

With currently available tools, organizations rarely use *only* ETL or ELT to ingest and process data. As an analyst, you'll likely have to choose the most appropriate option for a given data source and how you and your peers will use it. Table 11.1 depicts some common advantages and disadvantages of using ELT in your data pipelines.

Table 11.1   ELT can offer significant advantages in terms of speed and flexibility of use, but it will result in higher volumes of data being stored in your organization's infrastructure.

ELT advantages	ELT disadvantages
Data can be analyzed and represented in numerous ways	Increased data storage costs
Data can be updated and surfaced very quickly	Data quality problems need to be handled in the warehouse
New data sources can easily be added to the warehouse, compared to ETL	There are security risks with saving raw, sensitive information in the warehouse

DISTRIBUTED COMPUTING

In addition to data lakes, many organizations implement *big data frameworks* to handle massive data ingestion and processing. Few organizations capture true "big data," but those that do face unique challenges that affect data professionals across teams:

- Querying data using traditional data warehouses becomes untenable. Simple calculations can take minutes to run, and more complex queries will time out and fail completely.
- Many traditional data warehouses' storage and computing costs struggle to scale with big datasets (billions and trillions of records).
- Large datasets are difficult to retain in memory, making analysis, statistical modeling, and machine learning in a local environment nearly impossible.

Distributed computing frameworks process massive datasets by dividing the work into smaller, more manageable tasks processed *in parallel* across a cluster of computers. Each *node* in a cluster completes a portion of the overall task, combining the subsets of the task into a final product. This *parallel processing* approach (illustrated in figure 11.10) drastically reduces the time required to complete the work, compared to performing it on a single machine. It's also highly fault-tolerant; if one node fails, its assigned task can be rerouted to other nodes to ensure the overarching process is complete.

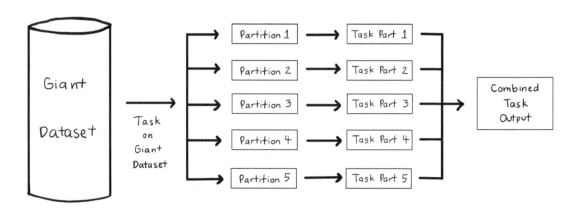

Figure 11.10   Parallel processing divides a data processing task into manageable chunks and recombines it into the final output.

Analysts may interact with distributed computing systems in one or more of the following ways, depending on how the organization operates:

- When *querying data*, you may need to learn the distributed framework's unique dialect of SQL (e.g., Apache Spark uses Spark SQL; https://spark.apache.org/sql). This may include slight syntax differences compared to the dialects of SQL you are familiar with.

- When developing a *statistical or machine learning model*, you may need to familiarize yourself with a new library of tools to wrangle the datasets successfully. For example, if your organization uses Apache Spark, the PySpark API [4] offers data processing and modeling tools that can be used instead of the functions in pandas and `scikit-learn`.
- Processing large datasets can be expensive. Your organization may have practices to limit the size of queries, the number of nodes, or the resources you can use during model development. You may also be asked to participate in cost-monitoring and management steps that aren't as visible in organizations with less data.

When browsing open jobs in analytics, you will notice that organizations with very large datasets typically ask for experience or exposure to big data technology (e.g., Hadoop, Spark). If you expect to work in an industry with vast data collection, familiarizing yourself with this technology will *definitely* pay off in your career.

11.2.4 Exercises

You were recently hired as the lead data analyst for an early-stage renewable energy startup. The company wants to use data to help customers identify optimal renewable energy sources and save on their monthly utility bills. They recently received their first round of funding and are ready to publicly launch their business. The company wants to set up its first data infrastructure tools before this launch.

You are asked to recommend tools and approaches for gathering, saving, and processing data. The company is aware of the following data points they will be collecting as they scale in their first year:

- Daily energy usage statistics from their customers' utility companies
- Page views and clicks on their website
- Advertisement views and clicks
- Customer sign-up information, including at free and paid tiers
- Purchases and installations of renewable energy options (e.g., solar panels)

To develop a comprehensive understanding of the tools that the company can use, read through the documentation available for the following technologies. Write a report for company leadership outlining your infrastructure proposal, including some pros and cons for each option you review:

1. Recommend one or more *data storage solutions* among the following technologies: Snowflake, MongoDB, Redshift, BigQuery, and Azure. Explain the type of solution you chose and your rationale for this decision.
2. Determine which data warehousing options also offer solutions for creating a *data lake*. Do you recommend setting up a data lake at this time? Justify your recommendation, referencing the specific types of data the company collects and your anticipated analytical needs in the next 1–2 years.

11.3 Data management practices

For your data to be accurate, well-structured, and easily used, your organization needs a comprehensive *data management strategy* to appropriately achieve its data curation goals. *Data management* refers to all practices and processes put in place to handle the data used across the organization. This encompasses everything from the tools and infrastructure choices to the structure, quality, security, governance, and accessibility of the data. Each organization requires a unique strategy to handle the quirks of the data, the experience of its data stakeholders, and the needs of its strategic data consumers.

Once you've put the infrastructure in place, you will quickly see that source data is formatted in ways that are *far* from ideal for day-to-day use. Imagine querying the data lake and discovering information with the following properties:

- The `total_amount` column in the `transactions` table is stored as text, requiring you to convert the data into a floating-point value to perform mathematical calculations.
- The `page_views` table, which comes from a third-party event-tracking vendor, has its own unique identifier that doesn't match your application's `user_id`. To get the right key to combine data between the systems, you need to join an intermediary table from the third-party vendor called `tracked_users` that shows both their unique identifier and your application's `user_id`.
- The support team manually adds new tickets to the support software when they receive phone calls, along with extensive details about the customer's problem, which are then populated in the `support_tickets` table. The ticket records often have a lot of errors—inaccurate customer contact information, mislabeled problems, and ticket creation dates in the distant past or future (including one record labeled `2923-02-01`!).

Each of these quirks doesn't seem like a big deal to manage when querying data, but the additional complexity across a data warehouse adds up. The problems need to be incorporated into every query written using a specific dataset. You have to remember to inform your stakeholders about each quirk when they ask you about the data to prevent them from drawing inaccurate conclusions from the data. In all, complexities in a data model limit the number of people within your organization who can query data themselves, as well as slowing down analytics teams in their responsibilities.

If this sounds familiar, once again, you're not alone! Most analysts' domain knowledge about an organization includes its data problems. However, when these problems dominate your work, it's time to look for opportunities to improve the data structure, quality, and availability for everyone's benefit. This section will focus on some of the great tools and resources available to solve these problems, regardless of the infrastructure you have in place.

11.3.1 Data structure

Managing the structure of your data involves taking information from the raw source, cleaning it, and transforming it into sets of information that the organization can use with ease. This involves many steps done in collaboration with data practitioners across the organization, such as joining relevant tables, ensuring relevant join keys are available, and correcting discrepancies between data types.

Structuring data for value

Amir is an analyst at a global tourism company that offers vacation packages, cruises, and guided tours to destinations worldwide. The company knows that weather is one of the most crucial factors affecting revenue, customer experience, and logistics. Instead of having regional managers manually track the weather, Amir plans to use the National Weather Service API to retrieve historical and forecasted weather for every locale where they operate. To integrate this with the data warehouse, he needs to ensure the new information meets the following criteria:

- The weather API uses different naming conventions for some location identifiers (e.g., NYC versus New York City). To ensure all of the company's business locales can easily use this data, Amir recommends saving the `zip_code` used as an input for each API call into the `historical_weather` dataset, ensuring it can be used as a join key with the company's existing data models.

- The ETL used to retrieve the historical weather data updates the `weather_history` table with one new row per zip code every day. Amir has to decide whether to save the entire forecast *every day*, leading to multiple records for each date, or to overwrite the data each day for simplicity. After consulting with the data engineering team, he adds a second field called `date_saved`, enabling him to retain historical records for analysis, such as evaluating the accuracy of forecasts multiple days in the future. He also adds a Boolean field to determine the `most_recent` forecast so operational teams can get the information they need quickly.

- Amir discovers that the date fields he saves with the weather ETL are formatted differently than other data in the warehouse, requiring users to manually convert both fields to a date or a timestamp. He adjusts his ETL script to format date columns as a timestamp and works with the data engineering team to add a `day` field to the tables he will most often join to the weather data sources.

- Amir works with data engineering to directly add weather history and forecast data to the schemas that power the company dashboards. The data in these schemas is aggregated by week (e.g., average temperature, total precipitation) and presented as a time series chart alongside other business metrics. Pre-aggregating the schema data allows the dashboard to refresh the charts in seconds.

Each of these adjustments is designed to ensure data is accurately, quickly, and easily incorporated into every company workflow in which it provides value.

The process of structuring data is largely agnostic of an organization's tools (such as in figure 11.11, where two separate data sources are combined), where effectively combining new data with existing sources involves the following:

- Ensuring that new data sources have a *foreign key* that you can use to join it to other tables in the data warehouse. Whether these are dates, user IDs, or location keys, it's crucial to ensure these are clean, accurate, and available in the same data format as the existing data tables.
- Prejoining datasets together to reduce the number of joins an analyst needs to perform in their work. For example, if a new data source uses customer emails to identify a user, but the rest of your tables use a unique `user_id`, consider creating a data model that joins the tables needed to get the `user_id`.
- Identifying areas where malformed data may occur (e.g., incorrect dates, wrong data types, missing records) and taking steps to address them.
- Determining whether the data source should be available as a new table or set of tables or simply be added to an existing table. In many cases, joining new data to existing information reduces analysis effort as well as the cognitive load associated with understanding the new information.
- Determining if data is available at the correct *grain*. Often, partially aggregated data (e.g., company metrics by week) is easier for stakeholders to interact with directly.

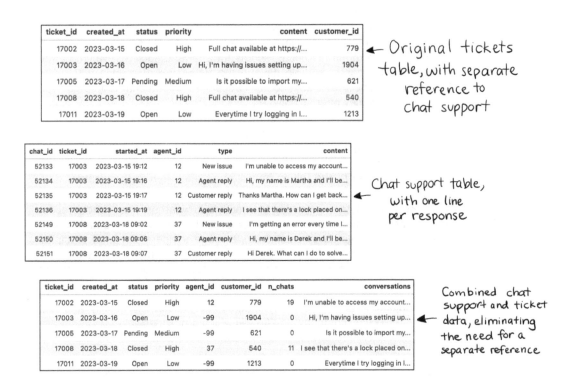

Figure 11.11   Structuring data in a warehouse involves ensuring it can be easily and accurately queried.

In order to take any of these data structuring steps, data professionals will typically define schemas and tables using SQL. These SQL definitions determine the columns, rows, data types, and constraints that shape the data used by the organization. Some new tools, such as dbt (data build tool) [5], enable data practitioners to transform their data management strategies into company-wide collaborative efforts.

With dbt, data teams can easily contribute to the ecosystem of data schemas and tables without having to grapple with the complexities of the warehouse (e.g., complex SQL functions, data manipulation language or DML). Users who are comfortable writing SQL can do any of the following using nearly the same syntax they would if querying data for analysis:

- Create tables that meet the needs of a single team (e.g., metrics for a product team).
- Make data available at different layers of complexity (e.g., source, analytics, metrics) to meet the varying needs of the organization.
- Update and augment core data sources with new information added to the warehouse.

Setting up or editing a dbt table is easy for a wide range of analysts. A model's `.sql` file contains metadata about the table (lines 1–6 in figure 11.12), the SQL query, and Jinja templating syntax (lines 14 and 15) to reference other dbt models or source data in the warehouse. Figure 11.12 shows a relatively simple example of what a model might look like.

```
1  {{
2    config(
3      materialized='incremental',
4      description="Aggregated daily page views per user and URL."
5    )
6  }}
7
8  SELECT
9    u.id AS user_id,
10   DATE(pv.view_timestamp) AS view_date,
11   pv.url_path,
12   usr.first_login,
13   COUNT(*) AS total_views
14 FROM {{ source('data_lake', 'page_views') }} pv
15 JOIN {{ source('data_lake', 'pv_external_users') }} usr
16   ON usr.id = pv.user_id
17 GROUP BY 1, 2, 3, 4
```

Figure 11.12 dbt combines SQL, table metadata, and Jinja templating syntax to define tables.

While dbt has grown rapidly in popularity in the past several years, it's far from the only tool that can be used to structure data. Data warehouses and cloud computing platforms typically offer at least one option for defining tables and views in their suite of tools. Analysts across an organization may vary in their access to these tools, but the principle of defining tables and views is quite similar across the board: use a query language to define and modify the structure of a table, and make it available to a group of users.

11.3.2 Data quality

Data quality is the foundation of a data management strategy. The information you use to drive decisions needs to be *reliable, accurate,* and *usable* for anything else we've discussed to be successful. For some organizations, having accurate data may also be required to comply with the laws in the region where it operates. Data quality typically includes evaluating data for the following components:

- *Accuracy*—Accuracy requires that data actually represents the real-world process it claims to describe. This involves checking for inaccuracies (e.g., a column that shouldn't have negative values) or duplicate data and taking steps to resolve them.
- *Completeness*—This involves ensuring that all required data is present (e.g., no missing values for the `user_id` and `timestamp` in a `page_views` table). Incomplete data may need to be removed, have missing values inferred (e.g., replacing null values with a mean value), or be derived from other sources of information.
- *Consistency*—This requires data to adhere to the rules and constraints defined by the organization. For example, an organization may need to implement checks to ensure that timestamps collected from different data sources are *consistent* in how they represent time zones (e.g., converting to a specific time zone or using the local time).
- *Timeliness*—This involves ensuring that the information at the organization is up-to-date and available when needed (e.g., financial data is available at the close of the month). This may involve checking ETL and ELT workflows to ensure they successfully updated a data source and implementing corrective mechanisms if they fail to do so.

Figure 11.13 depicts a dataset with inaccuracies, incomplete rows, and inconsistent values.

	item_id	product	category	quantity	restock_date	supplier	unit_price
0	1.0	Widget Pro	Electronics	150.0	2923-04-01		200
1	2.0	Gadget Max	Electronics	-10.0	2023-04-02	gadgets@example.com	150
2	3.0	Test Basic	Home Goods	50.0	2023-04-15	test@example.com	75
3	4.0	Widget Pro	Electronics	150.0	2003-04-01	supplier@widgets.com	200
4	5.0	Amazing Gizmo	Gadgets	NaN	2023-04-10	gizmos@example.com	100
5	NaN		Home Goods	30.0	2023-04-05	homegoods@example.com	-45

Figure 11.13 Data without quality checks can be challenging to use and generate insights with.

ETL (EXTRACT, TRANSFORM, LOAD)

Managing data quality is best done proactively by integrating tools and checks into multiple steps throughout the data pipeline before it reaches users. When inaccuracies are identified and resolved *earlier* in the process, you can prevent downstream problems and increase the organization's trust in the information it uses.

Many checks are easily incorporated into the *transformation* step of an ETL workflow to reduce downstream problems with a dataset ingested in the warehouse. We can see this in the `daily_forecast` data retrieved from the National Weather Service API in chapter 10. Figure 11.14 shows a sample of the data.

	date	low_temp	high_temp	humidity	wind_speed
0	2024-01-25	43	53	93	8
1	2024-01-26	44	49	89	7
2	2024-01-27	41	50	86	8
3	2024-01-28	39	42	92	16
4	2024-01-29	31	37	88	17

Figure 11.14   Structured daily forecast data retrieved from the National Weather Service API

If an ETL workflow runs once daily, seven new rows of data will populate a table used as inputs for a statistical model. The predictions generated from this model are used by a hypothetical government organization for planning purposes, so inaccurate data can lead to a poor allocation of resources for the coming week. But how do we determine what to test for and what could go wrong with the workflow?

Using the list of data quality components from the previous page, let's list some of the characteristics our dataset *should* have:

- One row per day
- A humidity value between 0 and 100, since this is a percentage value
- A wind speed value greater than or equal to 0
- No missing values for any of the weather parameters

Knowing these characteristics, let's incorporate some checks into our code to test for each criterion. We can use the capabilities of the `pytest` library to identify each problem:

```
import numpy as np
import pandas as pd
from datetime import datetime, timedelta
import pytest

daily_forecast = pd.read_csv("daily_forecast.csv")

def test_unique_rows():
    list_size = len(daily_forecast["date"].tolist())
    set_size  = len(set(daily_forecast["date"].tolist()))
    assert list_size == set_size, "At least one non-unique date found"
```

Import the numpy, pandas, datetime, and pytest libraries.

Import the seven-day forecast dataframe.

Create a function that asserts whether the criteria are true and prints which criteria are false.

```
def test_humidity_range():
    assert np.all(
        (daily_forecast["humidity"] >= 0)
        & (daily_forecast["humidity"] <= 100)
    ), "Humidity out of range."

def test_wind_speed_positive():
    assert np.all(
        daily_forecast["wind_speed"] >= 0
    ), "Negative wind speed found."

def test_no_missing_values():
    assert (
        not daily_forecast.isnull().values.any()
    ), "Missing values present."

test_unique_rows()          ◁──┐   Run each function for a named
test_humidity_range()           │   dataframe in the current environment.
test_wind_speed_positive()
test_no_missing_values()
                            ┌──   If all tests pass, print a
print("Tests passed.")      ◁──┘   success message.
```

Each of these tests is designed to tell you whether or not your dataset meets a certain set of criteria you defined. You have several options for the actions you want to take when a test *doesn't* pass:

- You can set up alerts that prompt you to edit the data or restart the workflow manually.
- You can set up actions that automatically replace the missing values with appropriate substitutes (e.g., the mean temperature for that month).

How you choose to handle these problems depends on the data you're capturing and your organization's best practices for capturing data.

ELT (EXTRACT, LOAD, TRANSFORM)

Since ELTs often save raw, complex datasets directly in the warehouse, data practitioners will rarely have the chance to catch and resolve problems *before* the data is stored. As such, multiple steps may be necessary to correct the problems before the data reaches analysts and their stakeholders.

If you're aware of specific problems with a data source and know how to solve them, you can often do so in the table definition itself. For example, let's say you discovered some bad date records in the source data used to create the dbt model shown in figure 11.12. You can easily add a WHERE clause statement filtering out dates in the future before you start capturing data. Additionally, if you need to exclude certain types of records (e.g., user_id values that don't match the application), you can add an inner join to the application's users table, effectively excluding any irrelevant values. An updated dbt model is shown in figure 11.15.

```
 1  {{
 2    config(
 3      materialized='incremental',
 4      description="Aggregated daily page views per user and URL."
 5    )
 6  }}
 7
 8  SELECT
 9    u.id AS user_id,
10    DATE(pv.view_timestamp) AS view_date,
11    pv.url_path,
12    usr.first_login,
13    COUNT(*) AS total_views
14  FROM {{ source('data_lake', 'page_views') }} pv
15  JOIN {{ source('data_lake', 'pv_external_users') }} usr
16    ON usr.id = pv.user_id
17  JOIN {{ ref('dim_users') }} u
18    ON u.id = usr.external_id
19  WHERE pv.view_timestamp BETWEEN '2012-01-01' AND current_date
20  GROUP BY 1, 2, 3, 4
```

Figure 11.15   A date filter and inner join to the application's users table can remove several problems that may arise with this data source.

In many instances, you will want to alert your team to inaccuracies in the data that can affect downstream analytics. If something is wrong with a data ingestion pipeline, quietly filtering out records using a WHERE clause can hide the scale of a problem from you and your stakeholders. For example, if the data pipeline captures duplicate user_id records each day, you may not notice until you explore the data and discover row counts that are far higher than expected. Additionally, if the url_path in figure 11.12 produces malformed URLs that don't accurately correspond to the website's available paths for a sizeable proportion of rows, reports and dashboards can produce inaccurate values that lead to wrong conclusions.

To avoid these outcomes and reduce the effect on analysts, tests can be incorporated throughout the data pipeline. Many tests are available out-of-the-box with dbt and can easily be added to your models [6], alerting you to problems that need further investigation. Consider the following examples:

- A customers data model uses the not_null test on the email_address to ensure a value is always present for each row.
- A transactions table uses the unique test on the transaction_id column to alert the financial analytics team if any duplicate records appear, reducing the time it takes to reconcile the financial data for the month.
- In addition to uniqueness, a page_views model uses an accepted_values test to ensure that the url_path column *only* stores one of the twenty-five possible paths a user can navigate on the website.

Investing in data quality enhances the life of everyone in an organization. It reduces the time analysts need to explore and wrangle a dataset, allowing them to focus on creating high-quality insights. It does require a time investment to incorporate these tests into your pipelines, but the benefits far outweigh the costs in almost every situation.

11.3.3 *Using metadata*

Once you're confident in the quality of your data, it's time to ensure your stakeholders can use it. Every data team (data engineering, data science, data analytics, etc.; see figure 11.16) has *downstream stakeholders* that use increasingly curated resources specifically developed with their skills in mind. Over time, organizations will benefit from allowing those stakeholders to *expand* their access to the data to reduce bottlenecks and increase collective data literacy across teams. This doesn't come easily, and it starts with the need for those stakeholders to understand what information is at their disposal.

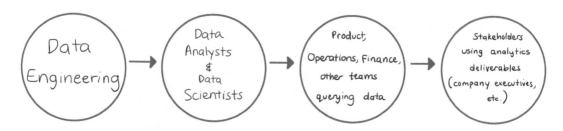

Figure 11.16   Data teams typically have cascading stakeholders that use increasingly curated information.

Data warehouses contain a wealth of *metadata* that offers a great starting point for creating documentation to increase the accessibility of data. *Metadata* is essentially data about your data—in a data warehouse, this refers to its various contents' sources, structure, and formatting. Most data warehouses have an *information schema* available, which you can query just like any other dataset. Information schemas contain records about the available schemas, tables, columns, and properties of each, such as data types, row counts, and primary or foreign key references.

On their own, information schemas are helpful for analysts to understand the data available to them. They aren't necessarily the best resources for the downstream stakeholders, who have more limited analytics experience, or for team members focused on very limited subsets of the data. However, the type of data you see in figure 11.17 can be a great starting point for creating human-readable documentation.

Documentation is a set of written materials designed to explain a system's purpose, structure, and usage. Well-crafted documentation can be shared as a searchable resource with stakeholders interested in finding data or deliverables on their own. Starting with a data warehouse's metadata, which provides the *structure*, you and your

TABLE_NAME	COLUMN_NAME	DATA_TYPE	IS_NULLABLE	COLUMN_DEFAULT	CHARACTER_MAXIMUM_LENGTH
customers	customer_id	INT	NO	None	NaN
customers	first_name	VARCHAR	NO	None	255.0
customers	last_name	VARCHAR	NO	None	255.0
customers	email	VARCHAR	NO	None	255.0
customers	signup_date	DATE	NO	None	NaN
transactions	transaction_id	INT	NO	None	NaN
transactions	customer_id	INT	NO	None	NaN
transactions	amount	DECIMAL	NO	None	NaN
transactions	transaction_date	TIMESTAMP	NO	None	NaN
transactions	product_id	INT	NO	None	NaN

Figure 11.17   Information schemas contain metadata about the information in a data warehouse.

organization can add descriptions of the *purpose* and *usage* of different tables and columns to set up your stakeholders for self-service analytics.

The metadata and descriptions you combine can be collated into a *data catalog* [7] for users to explore and search like a support site. *Data catalogs* are inventories of available data that show how information is connected, how data is built, and who's responsible for maintaining a data source. Having a data catalog allows you to point your stakeholders to a central place for information, reducing the overhead in discovering how to use the data they need.

Data catalogs typically contain several of the following pieces of information:

- Metadata from the information schema used to structure the catalog, allowing users to navigate through sets of schemas and tables to find what they're looking for.
- Descriptions of tables and columns managed by data users across the organization. These are especially valuable for highly curated data models designed for analysis.
- Graphs showing the data lineage of each table, depicting both the upstream tables used to create it and the downstream tables that depend on it for information.
- Example use cases and queries alongside the description of each table.
- The ability to search the catalog for the information needed to answer a question.

Creating an effective source of documentation is a collaborative effort between data teams and their stakeholders.

Creating a product analytics data catalog

Carlos is the head of product analytics at a medium-sized software as a service (SaaS) company that creates productivity software. Given his role, he is aware of many pain points experienced by analysts and product managers trying to use the company's data. Employees often struggle to find what they need to answer simple questions, limiting their ability to use data in their decisions. Carlos has the domain knowledge to point his colleagues in the right direction, but he needs to document that knowledge to serve the department better.

Carlos proposes creating a *data catalog* for the company to use when searching for available data to increase the usage of that data. He reaches out to the data engineering team asking for help in compiling the following resources for a catalog:

- A list of all schemas, tables, columns, and data types in analytics databases
- The underlying source tables (data lineage) used to create each analytics table
- Metadata about which tables are most frequently used for analysis

Next, Carlos reaches out to the marketing and sales operations teams to learn about the data sources they use daily. He discovers that the teams have been using separate, curated schemas containing dozens of valuable columns about users' purchases, behaviors, and survey feedback. He works with the team to grant access to these schemas to the product team, adding them to the data catalog for visibility.

With the foundation in place, Carlos reaches out to the company's data analysts and product managers, encouraging them to add documentation to the data catalog for the tables they use. He tracks the progress on creating documentation, planning an announcement, and launching after 30% of tables have a custom description available. This new documentation source increases the number of unique users querying tables in the catalog.

11.3.4 Exercises

Great news! Your data infrastructure plan at the green energy startup has been approved by company leadership. The company's IT manager and data engineer have supported you in purchasing and implementing the selected tools, the company has begun collecting data from its first customers, and you will be hiring two additional analysts to help the company derive value from its data.

The next task involves developing a robust project plan for data management to accommodate the current data collection and to support the next 1–2 years of growth. The project plan should include answers to the following questions:

1 Propose an approach to structuring the data sources from the activity you completed in the previous section:
   - Read the documentation on dbt projects: https://docs.getdbt.com/docs/build/projects. Can this tool be used with your chosen data storage solution? Why or why not? Are there any tools or capabilities built into your chosen data storage solution?

 – Choose one of the data sources from the previous activity. What tables do you think will be available from the data source? What concerns do you have about whether it's possible to join the data with other sources for analysis?
 – The data table you receive from customers' utility companies is relatively complex—a large, unstructured JSON field contains different information for each utility your company partners with. Which of the options in table 11.2 would you recommend for structuring this data for analysis?

Table 11.2   Options for structuring the utility data

# of tables	Data format
One	The original format of the JSON data is retained and stored in a single column that matches the source data.
Eight	A table is created for each of the eight utility companies, matching the key-value pairs available in the JSON for that utility. All tables are added to the `energy_usage` schema.
One	All fields are extracted, standardized, and combined into a table using a `UNION ALL` statement in the SQL query.

2 Identify data quality problems that might arise with the types of data being collected and with the methods of data collection you recommended for each data source:
 – If any data sources are being collected via an ETL process, propose data quality checks that can be incorporated into the transformation step.
 – Propose a set of data quality checks to perform on tables in the data lake before they're structured for analysis.
 – Recommend tools or scripts that can automate these data quality checks. Are there any pros and cons with each tool?
3 Suggest best practices for using the metadata you capture. Where should you document data source descriptions, the code used to transform the data, and how each table and column should be used? Does dbt have any resources to assist in creating this documentation?

11.4 *Data for analytics*

Well-structured data improves the efficiency of analytics. This is a relatively uncontroversial statement—saving *hours* of repetitive work each week on joining, filtering, and waiting for queries to run gives you more time to focus on deeper insights into your data. But what counts as "well-structured"? How do you know that a source of data creates the value that you and other analysts need?

We've covered several improvements in a standard data management process—correcting mismatches, dealing with missing records, and handling incorrect ones. Many of these problems can be tackled one data source at a time to make routine analytics easier to manage. The *next* step in developing data models for analytics takes time and a sustained collaborative effort to make your data more valuable (the example table in figure 11.18 would require effort to determine the most useful information to include). These strategic efforts aim to deliver cohesive analytics schemas with the most relevant information combined, aggregated, or denormalized into tables grouped by how the organization thinks and operates.

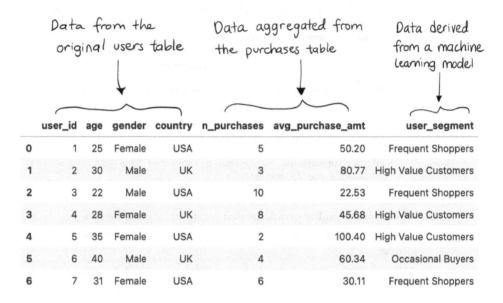

	user_id	age	gender	country	n_purchases	avg_purchase_amt	user_segment
0	1	25	Female	USA	5	50.20	Frequent Shoppers
1	2	30	Male	UK	3	80.77	High Value Customers
2	3	22	Male	USA	10	22.53	Frequent Shoppers
3	4	28	Female	UK	8	45.68	High Value Customers
4	5	35	Female	USA	2	100.40	High Value Customers
5	6	40	Male	UK	4	60.34	Occasional Buyers
6	7	31	Female	USA	6	30.11	Frequent Shoppers

Figure 11.18 Creating tables in analytics schemas involves synthesizing and aggregating multiple sources into one place to reduce time, effort, and inaccuracies when using data.

Organizations vary widely in their management of creating data models for analytics. Some have teams dedicated to these efforts, and others rely on the silent contributions of data analysts taking steps to make their and their stakeholders' lives easier. Even when there are centralized resources for data modeling, analysts are typically involved in the work to ensure that available information meets their needs. As such, learning about the field of analytics engineering and data modeling practices will generally have cascading positive benefits for your organization and its evolving data needs.

11.4.1 *Analytics engineering*

While data modeling strategies go back decades, many implementation practices became challenging with the increased complexity of information being ingested into data warehouses. Data volumes are higher, more data sources are being used, and the structure of the data varies based on its intended use in analytics, statistics, and machine learning. In recent years, the role of the *analytics engineer* emerged to solve many of the evolving problems these teams face.

Analytics engineering sits at the intersection of data engineering and analytics, focusing on delivering data models designed for analysis at the scale necessary to meet the needs of organizations today [8]. To do this, analytics engineers collaborate closely with analysts to understand their routines, tasks, priorities, and pain points. Using a combination of data engineering skills and knowledge of the organization, the profession aims to preprocess, clean, and structure as much data as possible to reduce the repetitive nature of analytics tasks. When their strategy is successful, analysts spend a *fraction* of the time wrangling data and more time analyzing it.

HOW IT WORKS

Data practitioners across an organization can apply analytics engineering workflows to positively affect others who use the data warehouse. Most of the data modeling approaches used in this field are intuitive by design. A wide range of professionals with experience in analytics *or* data engineering can learn them.

Creating data models for analysis

Liam is the first analytics engineer hired at a mid-sized EdTech company looking to improve its use of data across its teams. He has access to all of the tools available on the data engineering team, and he is asked to help identify opportunities to better model and surface data for the analysts across the company.

To build an understanding of the problems he can solve, Liam gathers as much information as possible on the following topics:

- What are the most common questions that stakeholders ask the analysts to answer using data? Are there any ad hoc questions that require repeated or overlapping work?
- Can he determine the most commonly used data warehouse tables using query logs captured by the data engineering team? Are there sets of tables often joined together?
- What does the full landscape of data sources look like? How many sources are available in the data lake? Are there any critical data sources *not* in the data lake that require users to export query results into a different tool?

Once he synthesizes the information from stakeholders, Liam decides to build a *dimension table* about users and their relevant properties. To do so, he follows up with several analysts to understand how the business thinks about its *users*: What properties do stakeholders think about when analyzing data? What information is available, and how is it calculated? Is there information you wish you easily had?

Liam creates a data model using dbt, combining the relevant properties he discovered into a `users` *dimension table*. This table contains over 20 columns about activities, preferences, behaviors, location, etc. It normalizes and cleans several text columns with user information that would otherwise require manual editing each time it's used. Each column was reviewed in collaboration with the company's analysts, who confirmed that having these available would reduce their time writing queries.

> **(continued)**
>
> After deploying the initial model, Liam creates documentation on the design, transformation, underlying sources, and meaning of each new column in the `users` model. He shares the documentation, a process for updating the model, and some sample queries, ensuring that everyone using the data warehouse can benefit from the new table.

Figure 11.19 depicts the work of an analytics engineer—take complex queries necessary to perform analyses, and create accessible data models for an organization.

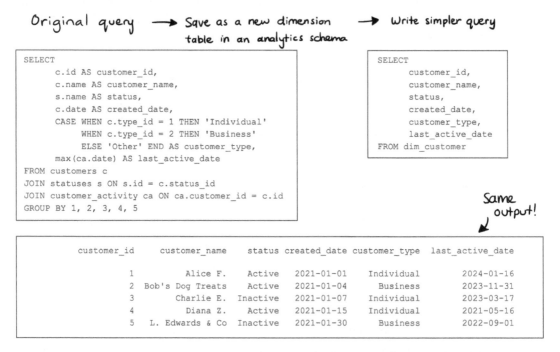

Figure 11.19   Analytics engineering takes the complex queries necessary to handle the nuances of an organization's data and codes them into curated models for analysis.

APPLYING ANALYTICS ENGINEERING PRINCIPLES

When analysts *don't* work with dedicated analytics engineers, they can often expect more data wrangling and cleaning to be involved in their regular tasks. There are many reasons why an organization might not invest in this profession—perhaps their data isn't *quite* complex enough, or their data teams have too few individuals to necessitate hiring a team to own data modeling. Regardless of your team and department structures, you can benefit from applying the principles of analytics engineering to make improvements to your workflow.

Depending on the structure of your organization and the resources available, you have several options available for improving the efficiency of your work and the value of the data available. Consider taking the following steps as they apply to your role:

- If your organization has a data engineering or IT team that manages the data warehouse, reach out to your colleagues on those teams to discuss creating or making specific improvements in analytics *views* or *tables* in schemas that analysts at the company can use. These teams tend to be amenable to such suggestions, since improving the quality of available tables tends to produce less strain on the data warehouse than repeatedly running a complex query in your local environment.

- If your organization uses transformation tools like dbt, consider reaching out to data engineering or IT to enable you and your team to *contribute* to the data warehouse. If you find opportunities to improve your efficiency (e.g., adding a new, useful column to a model), you may be able to make that update without having to wait for another team to perform the work.

- If you cannot contribute to any of the above, you can still enable faster and more efficient analytics at your organization. Many analytics and reporting tools offer the ability to define data sources that others in the organization can use. This way, your colleagues can have access to reliable and trustworthy results for topics that are useful to them but may not belong in the organization's data warehouse directly.

- Across each of these scenarios, *work closely with other analysts at your organization.* When analysts become siloed, there is a high likelihood of duplicating work and creating query definitions for the same concept with different calculations. You can mitigate the risk of differences in measurements through communication and collaboration with everyone using data in their work.

The practices of analytics engineering can be used in nearly any organization. Regardless of the complexity and sophistication of the tools at your disposal, the goals remain the same: create standardized queries that ensure consistency in measurement, try performing common joins and calculations *directly* in models, and work to ensure that data is easy to understand.

11.4.2 *Modeling data in star schemas*

Data is typically captured at the source in a format closely aligned with the single process it measures, and it's saved in formats optimized for efficient storage rather than the needs of analytics teams. This initial format often follows a *normalized structure*, with multiple tables containing unique information about a set of related topics. *Database normalization* is the process of organizing data to minimize duplication (shown in figure 11.20). While normalization is often ideal for the source data structure, it's the opposite of what we usually need when querying data for analysis.

Structuring data for analytics involves the strategic *denormalization* of data, which requires intentionally combining data sources into tables based on a single, cohesive

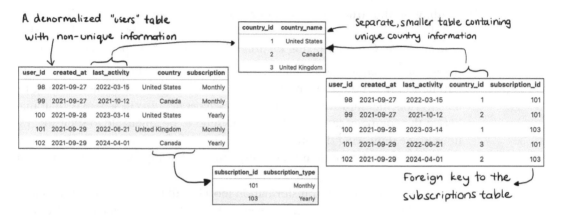

Figure 11.20 As the record of users continues to grow, the subscriptions and countries tables remain small, and the foreign key integers on the normalized table cost less to store than full names.

topic. The resulting data tables are easier to read and interpret than the source data, requiring fewer joins and calculations to perform analyses. Analysts are usually involved in this process, identifying which data sources should be combined based on the queries they frequently write and the resulting information that would derive the most value.

Denormalized tables are grouped into sets known as *star schemas* based on business or organizational logic. *Star schemas* are databases characterized by a central *fact table* connected to at least one *dimension table* [9]. *Fact tables* contain numeric information about a business process or event (e.g., a sales transaction or a page viewed) that's of interest for analysis. *Dimension tables* contain information about the various attributes related to the fact (e.g., customer, user). These attributes often include various aggregated and derived information, such as the n_purchases column in figure 11.18. The resulting schema design, visually depicted as a "star," (as seen in figure 11.21) allows for highly efficient analysis.

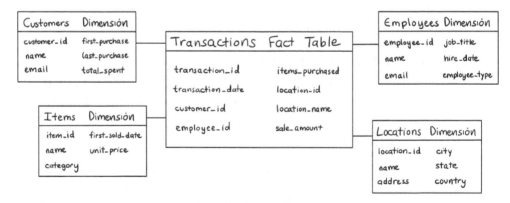

Figure 11.21 Star schemas have fact tables at the center connected to dimensions with related attributes.

Developing an appropriate star schema is more complicated than just reversing the normalization process. It requires in-depth knowledge of the organization, its relevant processes, and its priorities. Analysts across the organization are generally involved in the modeling of the data to ensure it meets all necessary criteria:

- Fact tables represent processes of importance to the organization. Analysts and their stakeholders should understand what the facts (e.g., transactions, page views, clicks) mean in the context of their work.
- Dimension tables contain attributes and properties relevant to analysts and their stakeholders, and they save time for the users of those tables. Each of the aggregated and derived properties of the entity in the dimension should reduce the number of additional table joins needed to perform analyses.
- The contents of fact and dimension tables should be human-readable, with clearly named columns, consistent formatting, and appropriately chosen data types.
- All calculations in fact and dimension tables should be agreed upon between the analysts at the organization as well as their stakeholders. Any differences in measurement or interpretation should be resolved before codifying those measurements in the data warehouse.

As you can see, these steps can't be appropriately performed in isolation or even with one analytics team if others have separate workstreams. Data definitions quickly diverge when teams don't have visibility into each other's work, and those differences can be resolved if each of the organization's analysts is involved in the modeling process.

Creating a product analytics star schema

Carlos, the head of product analytics at a productivity software company, has found the company's new data catalog to be highly successful. Nearly half of the analytics tables have custom descriptions added by the company's analysts, enabling better search and discovery of the information they need.

Through this project, Carlos has uncovered a pain point experienced by analysts on his team. Much of the data used by the product department is more complex than it needs to be. To analyze basic user behavior, the analysts routinely join four or more tables to get the necessary information. Most queries require the same set of filters in the WHERE clause and the *same* CASE statements to correct information in specific columns.

Carlos reaches out to the company's data engineering team to discuss options for improving the usability of product data. They recommend creating a `product_analytics` schema with curated fact and dimension tables that represent the processes of interest to the department. Based on his knowledge of the department's priorities, he recommends creating the following tables:

- A `tasks` fact table showing every time a customer creates, updates, completes, or deletes tasks created on their projects. This will allow analysts to

(continued)

> quickly analyze performance on key metrics, such as the percentage of user tasks completed on time. This is productivity software, so tasks are crucial to success!
>
> - A `page_views` fact table that contains derived columns naming the page associated with each URL path and a column calculating the time spent on the page.
> - A `pages` dimension that contains aggregated information about every page a user can visit on the application, such as the number of views and unique user views in the past 30 days. Carlos expects the aggregate information on this dimension table will allow product managers to answer routine questions within seconds.
> - A `users` dimension table capturing all of the relevant user properties that used to take four table joins to obtain. At Carlos' suggestion, `users` also has several aggregated properties showing the number of logins, last activity date, and the user's segment derived from a machine learning model.
> - A `projects` dimension capturing the properties of the project plans that users create in the application to manage their work. This includes aggregate information from the `tasks` fact table, such as the count of tasks created, completed, incomplete, and overdue.
>
> Carlos is aware that the five tables added to `product_analytics` are the beginning of an ongoing effort to improve product data usability. He and his team present the new schema to the product department and encourage them to submit feedback on additional analytics data models that can be incorporated into the schema over time.

The case study in the "Creating a product analytics star schema" sidebar is an excellent example of how to get started creating a star schema. In most cases, it's most fruitful to first understand the needs and priorities of the business so the result will have immediate value for its intended users. Try starting with the following exercises:

- Enumerate the *actions* your customers or users take that are *necessary for the organization to succeed.* Do they buy products in a store or online? Do they write and share blog posts? Sign up for events? The actions related to the product or service you provide that are measured over time are great candidates for fact tables.
- Review the organization's *key metrics.* What do different teams measure to indicate that their efforts are successful?
- What *entities* essential to the organization are related to the *actions in the fact tables?* Customers and users are common dimensions, which are most useful as *wide* tables with a large number of relevant properties about that entity. Dimension tables are most valuable when they reduce the need to join other tables for information about the entity and contain aggregate information that limits the frequency with which you need to access various fact tables.

When star schemas are created collaboratively with stakeholders, they can improve the performance of every analyst's routine workload. They also enable greater *self-service,* if you have colleagues with limited knowledge of SQL, allowing them access to a star schema with relevant information can also improve their efficiency. If they can answer their questions with simple queries, they won't need to request your team's assistance as often and can be confident in the results they generate.

11.4.3 Exercises

The green energy startup is performing well and growing exponentially, thanks to an influx of customers, a new round of funding, and increased media attention. The data infrastructure and management plan you put in place has enabled the organization to grow and scale with ease—the data lake storage costs are manageable, you can seamlessly add new data sources, and there are comprehensive data quality checks running on all of the business's core data models.

In the time that's passed, your company has also hired five analysts across three other teams that each use the data to support their stakeholders. From talking to these colleagues, you've become aware that the data available for analytics is becoming increasingly complex and challenging to work with. As such, it's time to start developing a strategy for simplifying and restructuring the data for analytics:

1 Review the normalized schema in table 11.3 containing information about the company's core processes. Identify the primary and foreign keys that can be used to join the tables.

Table 11.3 Normalized schema containing available tables collected by the startup

Table name	Description	Columns
customers	Individuals or businesses who have purchased a product or signed up for the utility cost-saving service.	id, first_name, last_name, email, signup_date, customer_type_id, utility_id
customer_types	Type of customer, such as a subscriber to the utility service or purchaser of a product.	id, type
customer_activities	Customer sign-in counts per day.	id, customer_id, day, n_logins, n_activities
addresses	Customer addresses where utilities are being monitored for the utility service. There can be multiple addresses per customer.	id, created_at, customer_id, address, zip_code, country
products	Products sold, such as solar panels and thermostats.	id, created_at, name, type, price
utilities	Utility companies used by customers who signed up for the utility service.	id, name, created_at
utility_readings	Monthly utility usage readings for each customer.	id, month, utility_id, customer_id, usage, cost

2 Which of these tables represents the actions or events related to the business? Propose a design for one or more fact tables based on this normalized schema.

3 Which of these tables represent the entities related to the business? Propose one or more dimension tables to structure that information accordingly.

4 How do the fact and dimension tables connect? Draw a star schema to show the relationships between your proposed dimension and fact tables.

5 How would you collaborate with your stakeholders and other analysts across the company to ensure your proposed schema design meets their needs?

Summary

- The *quality* and *accessibility* of data at an organization enables analysts to quickly and confidently generate insights for their stakeholders.

- An organization's *data infrastructure* consists of the tools and frameworks used to gather data from various sources, combine it into one destination for storage, structure it for its use cases, and retrieve it for analysis.

- A *data warehouse* is a centralized repository for storing, managing, and analyzing structured data from various sources. It's crucial for business intelligence and analytics, providing a coherent, consolidated view of data across an organization to support decision-making.

- *Document databases* offer flexible, *schemaless* storage for data structured in a document format. These databases are ideal for semistructured and nested data (e.g., JSON documents). As such, they're often used for managing content that doesn't neatly fit into a structured tabular format.

- *ETL* (extract, transform, load) refers to the process of extracting data from different sources, transforming it into a structured format, and loading it into a target storage system, such as a data warehouse. This process ensures that the data is clean, consistent, and ready for analysis *before* it's saved in the target system.

- *ELT* (extract, load, transform) is a variation of ETL where the data is extracted, loaded directly into the target system, and then transformed. It uses the computational power of your data warehouse for structuring and transformation, offering a flexible approach when working with data sources used for multiple purposes.

- *Data lakes* are storage repositories designed to hold vast amounts of raw data in structured or unstructured source formats. These raw data sources are then structured, transformed, and surfaced in a data warehouse as needed for analysis.

- *Big data* refers to datasets too large or complex to be handled by traditional data processing strategies. Instead, working with these data sources necessitates using *distributed computing frameworks* to process and analyze them effectively.

- *Distributed computing frameworks* are designed to divide the analysis of large volumes of datasets into chunks of work performed in parallel across *clusters of computers*. These tools are essential for big data analytics workloads.

- *Data management* refers to all the practices and processes in place at an organization to handle the structuring, quality, security, and governance of data, and more. Effective data management strategies ensure that organizations can confidently and appropriately use their data for decision-making.

- *Structuring data* involves organizing and formatting it to make it easily accessible, analyzable, and usable for specific purposes.

- *Data quality* refers to the accuracy, completeness, consistency, and timeliness of data sources used for analysis. High data quality requires data teams to monitor, test, and correct for inaccuracies to ensure it reliably serves its intended purpose.

- *Data testing* is the process of verifying the accuracy of data captured throughout the extraction, load, and transformation pipelines. It involves executing tests against data for problems such as duplicate records, missing values, or other discrepancies and errors, ensuring it meets specified requirements and quality standards.

- *Metadata* is detailed information about the properties of your data—the available schemas, tables, columns, their data types, and more. This information can guide users in discovering the data resources they need and how to use them.

- The field of *analytics engineering* emerged to sit at the intersection of data engineering and analytics, focusing on delivering high-quality data structured for analytics at scale.

- *Star schemas* are sets of tables centered around a fact, or business event, with one or more *dimensions* connected to it that describe the various attributes related to the event. These schemas are designed to align with the organization's key processes.

- *Fact tables* capture numeric information about business events or actions—transactions, clicks, page views, etc. Fact tables are created about the data most relevant to the business or organization for analysis.

- *Dimension tables* capture information about business entities—customers, users, employees, etc. Dimensions contain a range of properties about the entities combined from multiple tables, derived, or aggregated to provide a high-level picture of the entity.

Tools and tech for modern data analytics

This chapter covers

- Key technologies for data-informed decision-making
- An overview of analytics and reporting tooling
- Self-service strategies used in data analysis
- Using artificial intelligence in your work

Data analytics is a constantly evolving field, driven by advancements in technology and a growing demand for data-informed decision-making. The methods we've covered throughout this book (e.g., hypothesis testing, parametric and non-parametric statistics), remain foundational to our work as analysts. However, the tools we use to implement these methods have changed significantly in just the last few years. This makes it necessary to evaluate whether you are delivering value efficiently and effectively.

Keeping up with the current landscape can be overwhelming. It seems like every week there's a new vendor promising to eliminate pain points in your workflow. But what even *are* those pain points? How do you determine *when* to explore new tools to use, *which* tools will solve the problems you are experiencing, and *how* you can use these tools effectively?

This chapter explores several key technologies that are empowering analysts to deliver fast, high-quality insights. We'll look at the last decade's business intelligence and dashboarding platforms and at how notebooks and data apps became popular options for more complex deliverables. You will learn how to keep effective records of your insights to minimize repeat requests, as well as how to develop a self-service strategy that reduces time to value for you and your stakeholders. Finally, we'll cover the emerging role of artificial intelligence in the day-to-day role of an analyst.

12.1 The evolution of data analytics

While completing my bachelor's degree, I worked as a research assistant in a psychology lab that had been operating at the college for decades. The lab's principal investigator had some incredible records spanning his career—*dozens* of boxes of completed surveys and assessments, drafts of journal articles sent for peer review, and large sheets of graph paper used to record study results. The results followed the pattern we're familiar with in analytics—one row per study participant and one column per item assessed during the survey.

The difference, however, was that *everything* had to be calculated by hand, including all summary statistics (e.g., figure 12.1) as well as test statistics. This approach was cumbersome with the sample sizes used in each study (usually less than 200); imagine having to perform these steps manually with datasets that contain tens of thousands or millions of records like we often see today—it would be impossible.

	production_scale	corporate_tax_rate	renewable_materials	hourly_labor_cost	product_margin
count	21288.00	21288.00	21288.00	21288.00	21288.00
mean	5.02	33.33	0.31	50.13	387.19
std	4.94	24.84	0.46	30.48	255.92
min	-13.33	-98.77	0.00	-31.67	-337.89
25%	1.64	17.64	0.00	25.26	209.48
50%	5.06	37.00	0.00	50.14	367.14
75%	8.41	53.18	1.00	75.23	533.61
max	24.68	70.00	1.00	127.33	2034.04

Figure 12.1 Datasets like the `production_costs` CSV file contain tens of thousands of rows. Can you imagine manually entering the data and calculating each of these summary statistics by hand?

The shift from manual to automated analysis has transformed these tasks from manual and labor-intensive efforts to a series of steps that can be completed in seconds.

We (gratefully) no longer need to calculate standard deviations by hand and can perform complex multiple regression models with only a few lines of code. Additionally, direct contact with research and government institutions is no longer necessary to access their data. Many organizations provide vast amounts of information online, leading to the surge of interest in data analysis we've seen in the past few decades—all powered by advancements like those in figure 12.2.

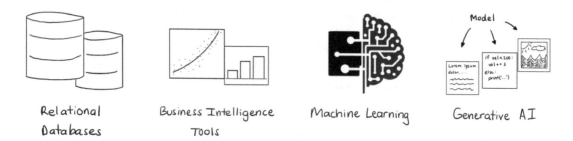

Figure 12.2   Many milestones in the past decades have transformed the field of data analytics.

Each transformation in technology redefines what it means to be a data analyst. When changes happen (and they often happen quickly), new and broader sets of skills are demanded to answer questions more efficiently and at a larger scale. For example, I started writing this book before OpenAI released ChatGPT with GPT 3.5, and my team at work quickly became involved in supporting the company in navigating the ethics and practical use cases for generative AI internally and for our customers. In just the first year since ChatGPT's launch, it seemed like the world of data analytics and data science was becoming unrecognizable.

However daunting the technological shifts may seem, working in a profession at the forefront of innovation offers opportunities to have a meaningful effect globally. By continually learning, developing skills, and embracing new tools, we have the ability to solve bigger problems and shape the future with data. We'll cover some of the most important recent advancements in our field that offer the greatest potential for having an effect in your current and future career goals.

12.2 Analysis and reporting tools

The environment in which you present your deliverables is as crucial as the analysis itself. Even if you uncover valuable patterns in the data, they may go unnoticed if stakeholders can't easily understand or engage with your findings. This lack of clarity can undermine the effect of your work and slow down the decision-making process, leading to more follow-up questions before others can incorporate your findings into an organizational strategy. As a result, the time you could spend discovering new insights is wasted on clarifying or resurfacing existing findings.

With the right analytics and reporting tools, you can easily avoid the pitfalls of repetitive work that many analysts experience. Instead, you can focus on creating deliverables your stakeholders can modify, reuse, and discover at the times most critical to their strategic planning and decision-making.

12.2.1   Types of tools

Data analysts have an array of analytics and reporting tools at their disposal. If you aren't the first analyst working at your organization, you've probably used the tools already in place and familiar to your colleagues. In such situations, you may have opportunities to choose the tools in your local environment or contribute to evaluating new organization-wide tools. We'll explore the ever-growing options available, including some interactive tools that have recently gained popularity.

TRADITIONAL DATA VISUALIZATION

Data visualization tools such as Tableau and Power BI have long been industry standards. These platforms offer drag-and-drop functionality, allowing users to create interactive charts, reports, and dashboards without programming skills. Data visualization tools are designed to scale with organizations, meeting most of your stakeholders' data needs with a well-curated set of charts and tables. However, these tools aren't the right solution for *every* kind of data professional, and they do not replace the need for data analytics professionals.

Data visualization tools offer the following advantages:

- They have relatively intuitive user interfaces, allowing users to create most visualizations with a drag-and-drop workflow.
- You can connect to various data sources, such as data warehouses, some APIs, and spreadsheets, and combine data between these sources.
- You can create sophisticated and presentation-ready dashboards.

However, they're limited in their ability to meet all the needs of analysts and their stakeholders:

- Most aren't designed for the kind of long-form exploratory analyses that are presented to your stakeholders as reports. Projects that typically involve a large amount of exploration can be lost in draft dashboards that are never published.
- Refreshing datasets in published dashboards can take a *very* long time. Many tools have improved their loading speed in recent years, but they're still far from being able to refresh information instantly.
- They're often not built for collaboration, with limited abilities to create reports and dashboards with your colleagues.

Data visualization tools have met a real need in all types of organizations for a long time. Leaders of all kinds understand the concept of a dashboard, making dashboards an excellent choice for presenting information about business and organizational performance. However, there are many other options that you can use to present deliverables to your stakeholders.

INTERACTIVE NOTEBOOKS

What development environment did you use when running the Python code samples in this book? Were you using a Jupyter Notebook (e.g., figure 12.3), Google Colab, or RStudio? If so, you're probably familiar with the individual code and markdown cells that allow you to explore and iterate on an analytics problem. You can do nearly every task we've covered in this book and, when your work is complete, you can render a report with *only* the results you want to deliver to your stakeholders. Best of all, these tools are open source and free to use.

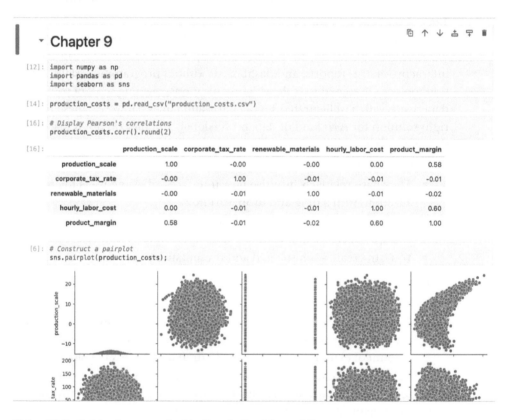

Figure 12.3   Notebooks are nearly ubiquitous in the data analytics space.

In recent years, several *interactive* notebook platforms have gained traction in the data science and analytics worlds. These platforms take the notebook workflow that many analysts are familiar with to the next level. Many offer comprehensive functionality where users can

- Collaborate and pair with coworkers on the same project
- Easily query the data warehouse and combine it with other information, such as data retrieved from an API
- Create reports using the same interactive chart types that make data visualization tools so valuable to organizations
- Keep comprehensive records of previously published deliverables

Together, these tools can streamline the routine data gathering, manipulation, and report setup steps involved in exploratory work. Their native data visualization options enable stakeholders to independently perform simple explorations (known as *self-service*, which we'll cover in section 12.2).

The interactive notebook space is still rapidly evolving, and in a few years, there will likely be popular options that don't yet exist. As of the publication of this book, I can recommend the following interactive notebooks I've used, which offer their product for free to community users:

- Hex (https://hex.tech)
- Deepnote (https://deepnote.com)
- Mode (https://mode.com)

These are far from the only options—again, these are just the tools I suggest based on personal experience. In this section's exercises, you'll discover various interactive notebook solutions and their capabilities.

DATA APPS

If you don't have access to interactive notebooks but still want to create custom tools, *data-powered web applications* are valuable for your work. *Data-powered apps* allow you to develop powerful interactive user interfaces without extensive web development experience. These are useful for creating unique interactive tools requiring complex user input or code that a data visualization tool can't easily implement.

Data-powered apps are also excellent for the *rapid prototyping* of new or niche deliverables. *Rapid prototyping* is a method used in various fields that focuses on creating quick preliminary versions of a product. This approach allows you to iterate on and refine a product with less time spent developing the deliverable upfront. As you seek feedback from stakeholders during the development process, you learn more about what the final product should look like.

If you have experience using R for data analysis, you may be familiar with R Shiny. This tool is the R ecosystem's primary option for creating data-powered apps, enabling users to build interactive apps directly from R scripts. There are several similar options in the Python ecosystem, each of which requires varying programming experience. If you're just getting started in data-powered app creation in Python, I recommend looking at Streamlit.

Streamlit (https://streamlit.io) is an open source framework specifically designed to make data-powered app development easy for data professionals. This tool is relatively new in the Python world, but it has quickly become popular because of its flexibility and ease of use. Streamlit offers several features that make it easy to create and share prototypes, interactive reports, and dashboards:

- The code is easily readable and similar to the packages we've used throughout this book (e.g., pandas and seaborn).
- You can add a variety of input variables (e.g., text boxes, sliders, date filters) to reports that update the dashboard results accordingly.
- You can connect data from multiple sources into one final output, including a data warehouse and APIs.
- Deliverables that are ready to share can be deployed in a variety of ways. If your organization uses Snowflake as a data warehouse, you can create and deploy apps directly in the Snowflake interface. Otherwise, apps can be easily deployed to Streamlit's community cloud.

Figure 12.4 shows an example of a Streamlit app created to forecast the number of daily rat sightings based on weather parameters from the seven-day forecast. The app uses a direct copy of the code we've written in this book: combining the rats and weather datasets, deriving additional variables, fitting a linear regression, and retrieving and processing data from the National Weather Service API. A simple input variable was added to allow users to restrict the number of days they want to be shown. The result is a tool you could quickly share with stakeholders who need to make decisions based on this data.

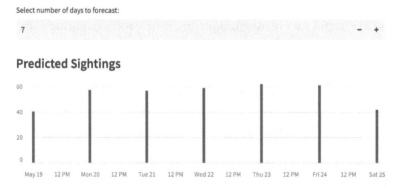

Forecasted Rat Sightings

Select number of days to forecast:

7	− +

Predicted Sightings

Weather Forecast Summary

	low_temp	wind_speed	predictions
2024-05-19 00:00:00	58	9	40.0490
2024-05-20 00:00:00	56	10	57.0581
2024-05-21 00:00:00	56	12	56.4308

Figure 12.4 An interactive data-powered app predicting rat sightings, created using Streamlit.

Data-powered apps like Streamlit and Shiny provide the resources you need to be creative and flexible in providing output to stakeholders. They also give you a high-level introduction to web development without requiring you to learn HTML, CSS, or JavaScript to complete your work.

12.2.2 Libraries of analyses

How often are you asked the same questions by different stakeholders? Changes within an organization—such as shifting project ownership, the arrival of new employees, or updates in priorities—often lead to repeated inquiries (e.g., figure 12.5) from new stakeholders.

In addition to crafting deliverables specifically for one stakeholder, preparing these outputs (presentations, reports, dashboards) for broader use can extend each project's relevance and utility. By making your resources accessible to more colleagues, you can significantly reduce the frequency of repetitive analytics requests for you and your team. This efficiency is achieved through a strategic *knowledge management initiative* within your organization.

Team	Request	Due
Marketing	Hi team! We'd like some help analyzing the performance of our recent email and social media campaigns.	2024-06-15
Sales	Can you provide an analysis of sales trends over the past quarter by product and region? Thanks!	2024-06-10
Finance	Please provide a detailed breakdown of the company's expenses by department for the past fiscal year.	2024-06-18
Support	Is it possible to provide a summary of key issues from customer support tickets over the past month?	2024-06-12
Marketing	We'd like to divide customers by demographics and purchase behavior to identify key customer segments.	2024-06-22
Product	Can you create a dashboard showing the usage of new product features released this quarter? We need it to inform future product development.	2024-06-17
Sales	What are trends in the conversion rates by sales region for the past quarter?	2024-06-14
Product	How successful are email campaigns at driving product adoption?	2024-06-11
Support	Please create a report on the average resolution time for support tickets.	2024-06-13
Finance	We would like to generate a revenue forecast for the next 3 quarters' sales and retention.	2024-06-19

Figure 12.5 How many of these data requests seem like they overlap? Can they be answered by strategically creating and sharing resources with your stakeholders?

KNOWLEDGE MANAGEMENT

Knowledge management refers to the creation, organization, and sharing of information within an organization. For data analysts, this often means turning the insights from your deliverables into more valuable, reusable resources. Whether it's simple summary statistics or complex time series charts, these insights can serve multiple stakeholders over time if they're carefully prepared with long-term usability in mind.

Identifying *which* deliverables should be reused isn't an exact science; it often requires trial and error to pinpoint resources that will provide the most enduring value to the organization. It's helpful to regularly review your outputs to assess *if* and *where* they can be further used.

From reactive to proactive analytics

Amina is part of a business analytics team at the headquarters of a large shipping company. The business analytics team is extensive, with multiple functional units supporting operations, R&D, marketing, sales, customer support, and human resources. Amina collaborates most closely with the sales department, building dashboards to track sales performance and answering occasional questions from potential clients about trends in the business.

In recent months, several new sales leaders have been hired and are being onboarded to their new roles. As such, they have a lot of data questions! Amina has been spending time answering similar or identical questions for each new sales leader, limiting her ability to focus on other tasks.

Amina discusses the increase in requests at the next business analytics team meeting. She discovers that several other analysts have received requests to answer similar questions. Each question is responded to individually by writing a complex query and preparing charts or summary tables for stakeholders. In total, the team is doing *a lot* of duplicate work!

They set up an analytics folder in the company's *New Employee Onboarding* shared drive with reports designed to answer the most common questions, along with a few additional resources about the company that the team believes are important to understand when starting a job. Every two weeks, when a cohort of new employees starts, one of the business analysts delivers a presentation about these resources and shares some general best practices for using data at the company.

The next time you complete a deliverable to answer a stakeholder's questions, ask yourself the following questions:

- Have you addressed this question before for the same or a different stakeholder? How frequently does this topic arise?
- Is the question related to a critical process within the organization? Would disseminating this information more broadly be beneficial?
- What will happen to this information when people leave, or when new employees join the organization? Will the content of the deliverable remain relevant?

If you answered "yes" to any of these questions, designing your deliverable for reuse can be prudent. This approach involves additional effort to format and store the information in an accessible location, but the long-term benefits often outweigh the initial investment.

Table 12.1 covers some example strategies that you can use to update dashboards for stakeholders. Often, just taking these steps can solve problems for you and the teams you support, reducing their need to reach out and submit requests and reducing your workload. Keep the following tips in mind in your work:

- If you're asked to repeatedly provide summary information about a subset of your organization's customers (e.g., the average purchase price for New York

City and Chicago), consider creating a report with standard aggregate metrics for all relevant categories.

- Consider adding filters and groups to reports that allow stakeholders to subset information *themselves*. This is part of a self-service strategy, which we'll discuss in more depth in section 12.2.

Table 12.1 Examples of deliverables updated for increased utility

Original deliverable	Deliverable updated for increased utility
A summary table showing the average contract value for 3 of the 27 industries that customers belong to	A report showing the sum, average, and median contract value, and the total number of customers for each of the 27 industries
A chart showing the number of monthly active users, created to include in a company-wide KPI progress presentation	A dashboard showing the number and percentage of daily active users alongside several other measures of product usage
A dashboard summarizing data about a single customer for the strategic consulting team	A dashboard with a filter enabling the consulting team to run the same report for any customer
A Python notebook created to process a messy dataset	A data pipeline synthesizing the Python code into a series of reusable scripts that can be run on a schedule

CREATING A LIBRARY

The high-utility deliverables you create are best stored where your colleagues can quickly discover them. Organizing these insights into a *library* can help preserve knowledge, increase data literacy at the organization, and save you lots of time. In this context, a *library* is a structured and searchable repository containing records of analytical work. There are many ways to create a library, depending on the tools and capacity of your organization:

- A vendor providing data visualization, interactive notebooks, and the ability to search for specific information in previously saved reports
- A shared drive containing the presentations that analysts have delivered in the past several years
- An open source platform deployed at your organization, such as AirBnB's Knowledge Repository [1]

Having a library available as a first point of contact with data and insights can be rewarding and beneficial. By organizing and surfacing your work, you're *preserving* it and making it easier for the entire organization to find. Just knowing that a wide range of data is readily available can support various teams in their capacity for making data-driven decisions. Further, when your team cannot support all of those colleagues directly, you can often point them to the library to find a large chunk of what they need. There are countless benefits to pursuing this type of effort:

- Your stakeholders' questions can often be partially answered by existing reports and dashboards. Pointing them to these resources can reduce the time it takes to complete follow-up requests and allow those stakeholders to make informed decisions with quicker turnaround times.

- Cross-functional analytics teams using a centralized library can avoid duplicating work or becoming siloed in their efforts. Valuable insights surfaced across teams increases the collective knowledge of the data practice in ways each team likely could not discover independently.
- A library is a *clear* and *tangible* record of the value that analytics provides to the organization. Having this record helps increase your team's efficiency and shows what's possible when data and analytics are invested in.

If you're convinced that setting up a library will benefit your work, the next step is to choose the destination for saving your deliverables. The choice depends mainly on the technology you have access to. Within that, it's sensible to select an option that will provide the greatest ROI while being easy for your team to maintain. Consider the suggestions in table 12.2, based on the most common types of deliverables you create.

Table 12.2 **Examples of deliverables and a library that can effectively store their insights**

Type of deliverable	Library options
Slideshows or other presentations	A shared drive (e.g., Google Drive) that all relevant stakeholders have access to. Onboarding documentation for new employees and analytics team documentation can point employees to the location of these records.
Reports with results from predictive models and other statistical analyses	An interactive notebook tool with "collections" used to organize reports by *topic*—not by team or stakeholder. This way, employees at the company can easily search by product feature or area.
Results from a robust A/B testing program	A record of each test result published in the organization's Knowledge Repository, which contains a summary of the question, hypothesis, and findings. Notifications are sent to employees when new insights are available.
Executive dashboards in a data visualization tool	A folder system in the data visualization tool organized by each dashboard's purpose, e.g., revenue tracking, product usage, and other topics (not organized by the stakeholder or team who created it).
Software applications	An external reference to a code repository (e.g., GitHub), documentation, or live app hosted at a URL accessible to your coworkers.
A combination of the preceding deliverable types	Each library option, clearly documented on the company's intranet, with information on the type of deliverable in each subset of the library.

The library options for each deliverable shown in table 12.2 are proposed for a reason—they're set up in common tools used by the company's analytics teams for the type of deliverable being created. As such, they require effort to name, sort, and share but minimal editing and formatting work. If creating a library involves partially re-creating your deliverables in another location, it's unlikely to be sustainable in the long term.

In most cases, applying the following habits to your library will lead to more successful searches for your colleagues and create minimal additional effort for your team:

- Sort your library by *topic* as it relates to the organization and *not* by the team that created the report. Ownership of business functions changes over time, and it's unlikely that you or your colleagues will take the time to reorganize the library whenever a team changes its priorities.
- Create a *clear* and *readable* naming convention for library deliverables so stakeholders can quickly figure out the topic and type of analysis (e.g., A/B test results, machine learning prototype).
- Ensure your coworkers *know about the library, its purpose, and how to use it.* This can be accomplished through any number of methods—emails, announcements, new employee onboarding, team documentation, and more.
- Communicate regularly with other analysts at the organization! Ensure they're set up to effectively contribute to a library that meets their needs and aligns with their workflows.

Figure 12.6 shows the type of relevant information that may be included in an analytics library.

Title	Labels	Author	Created	Last Updated	Description
Q1 Marketing Campaign Analysis	Marketing, Campaigns	Brandon W.	2024-04-01	2024-05-15	Analysis of Q1 marketing campaigns, including engagement, conversion rates, and ROI.
Employee Turnover Rates by Dept	HR, Turnover	Amina S.	2024-01-15	2024-05-20	Interactive dashboard showing monthly turnover rates segmented by department and location.
Customer Support Ticket Analysis	Support	Brandon W.	2024-02-20	2024-05-12	Summary of key issues and resolutions from customer support tickets over the past month.
Customer Segmentation Report	Marketing, Segmentation	Amina S.	2024-03-25	2024-05-18	Presentation on customer segmentation based on demographics and purchase behavior.
Feature Usage Statistics Q2	Product Adoption	David K.	2024-04-15	2024-05-22	Interactive dashboard showing usage statistics of new product features released in Q2.
Lead Conversion Analysis	Sales, Leads	Amina S.	2024-02-28	2024-05-14	Analysis of lead conversion rates by sales region, with key trends and areas for improvement.
Social Media Engagement Overview	Marketing, Social Media	Amina S.	2024-04-05	2024-05-16	Overview of social media engagement metrics including likes, shares, and comments.
Support Ticket Resolution Times	Support	David K.	2024-02-15	2024-05-11	Dashboard showing average resolution times for support tickets, highlighting trends and outliers.
Quarterly Revenue Forecast	Finance, Revenue	Brandon W.	2024-03-20	2024-05-19	Presentation on revenue forecasts for Q3 based on current trends and historical data.
Product Usage Heatmap	Product Adoption	David K.	2024-03-05	2024-05-13	Interactive heatmap showing the usage intensity of different product features.

Figure 12.6   A library is a searchable reference of analyses with clear labels and naming conventions.

In practice, it *will* take some time to set up a library and populate it with records of your work. You can also expect to put some strategic effort into communicating about its existence and enabling your colleagues to make use of it. Don't get discouraged, however—you will see the payoff if you and your analyst coworkers are bought into the value and can share the work in creating a comprehensive set of library resources.

Your stakeholders will ask more informed questions, your analytics practice will collaborate more effectively, and your knowledge of the organization and its relevant processes will grow.

12.2.3 Exercises

Review Robert Lacok's Data Science Notebooks website (https://datasciencenotebook .org). This site contains an evolving list of open source and commercial notebook tools designed to streamline the work of analytics teams. Choose at least three options on the list and evaluate them based on the following criteria:

1. Does the tool allow you to collaborate with team members on the same analysis? Can you and others edit code in one notebook at the same time?

2. Is the notebook able to create native charts using drag-and-drop functionality, similar to a traditional data visualization tool? Or do you have to use libraries such as `matplotlib`, `seaborn`, and `plotly` to create charts?

3. How does the tool enable you to manage the knowledge you create? Does it have a tool to search for findings by report title, descriptions, keywords, and text descriptions? Is there a library or folder structure where reports can be labeled and categorized for easy discovery?

4. If you were to choose one of these tools to use in your day-to-day work, which would you use? Why? What features would be helpful to you and your team?

If you're interested, create a free account for each tool and try using them to analyze one of the datasets provided in this book.

12.3 Self-service analytics

How many analysts would your organization need to answer every stakeholder question? In most organizations I've seen, analytics teams manage a large backlog of projects they want to pursue, questions they have to answer, and stakeholders they have to turn away for lack of bandwidth. You may benefit from enabling self-service analytics amongst your stakeholders if you have limited resources.

Self-service is a model adopted by many analytics teams—it focuses on enabling nontechnical stakeholders to perform analyses *without* relying on an analyst. This approach involves creating interactive analysis and reporting tools that allow stakeholders to conduct their analyses. As a result, the volume of requests is often reduced, enabling teams to focus on more complex and valuable tasks.

12.3.1 Approaches to self-service

Most self-service efforts in analytics focus on creating deliverables that allow stakeholders to perform *structured explorations* independently. Most of the tools we covered in the previous section offer the ability to create filters and parameters as *inputs* to reports that answer questions about subsets of users or customers in a report. When carefully chosen, these inputs can increase your stakeholders' comfort when working with data directly. Most analysts can benefit from enabling self-service throughout their work by modifying or creating deliverables that meet a set of core needs.

How analytics teams approach self-service

Self-service can be approached in several ways, depending on a team's focus, needs, and stakeholders. Consider the following examples:

- A business intelligence team creates a set of interactive dashboards that cover basic information about every one of the company's core products and processes. The team includes eight filters (e.g., subscription type, customer location) that they recommend stakeholders use to review information most applicable to their needs. When follow-up questions are asked, the business intelligence team looks for opportunities to update the dashboards so that more questions can be answered independently.
- A financial analytics team creates a set of analytics tables using dbt that contain pre-aggregated financial and operational metrics. Many of their colleagues in the finance department have *some* knowledge of SQL (e.g., grouping, aggregation, joins), and the new tables are designed to answer many common questions by only selecting the data. This reduces the number of routine requests, minimizes the risk of error in calculating financial metrics, and makes the department more comfortable writing SQL queries.
- A company with a comprehensive data practice (analytics, data science, and data engineering) chooses a new data visualization and reporting tool to increase the quality and speed of producing its deliverables. They select a tool that can create complex filters based on long lists of user input, partial text matching, and the ability to explore the outputs of machine learning models. The tool enables revenue and sales data scientists to share model prototypes easily, and data analysts can create reports that allow their stakeholders to search the many free-text data fields captured by the organization more efficiently.
- An analytics engineering team delivers training at the company for audiences with varying comfort levels working with data. They teach an introductory course on the company's available data and using SQL, an intermediate course on complex SQL functionality, and an advanced course for data practitioners on contributing to the data platform using tools such as dbt.

Self-service strategies include one or more of the following efforts:

- Adding relevant combinations of filters to dashboards
- Creating interactive reports to explore complex topics
- Creating training materials on interpreting data, using tools (e.g., figure 12.7), and writing SQL
- Automatically updating a spreadsheet with raw or summary data

These strategies can be performed independently or as a cross-functional effort at an organization. Your choice of *which* approaches you use should depend on your stakeholders' ability to adopt the practices you recommend and your team's ability to sustain the training and development of those stakeholders that may be necessary for their success.

Using Data at Our Company

Leverage Existing Reports	Access Data Directly
Tableau (all filterable by customer type and region)	**Tableau**
• KPI tracking • Product usage • Sales and retention	Creator licenses are available to many roles across the company. Ask your manager if this applies to you.
Streamlit	**Snowflake**
• Machine learning prototypes • Research papers • Statistical models	The Snowflake interface has an editor that allows you to create SQL workbooks. Reach out to the data engineering team to get access.

Figure 12.7   Adding information about your data and self-service tools to new employee onboarding documentation can help maximize their visibility.

12.3.2   *Creating a strategy*

Let's look at how you can create a self-service strategy at your organization. This strategic approach is best developed by determining how comfortable your stakeholders are when working with data, and choosing amongst your available tools (or recommending the purchase of a new one) based on their needs and the capacity of your team to offer direct support. We can start by gathering information on these factors to identify areas of opportunity:

- What data requests have you received in the past few months? Note the types of requests you've received for identical or similar information from the same or different stakeholders. These repeated requests can often form your *initial* set of interactive dashboards or reports.
- What are the most common ways your organization tries to understand (or *should* try to understand) its customer or user base to make strategic decisions? Do you compare locations, subscription tiers, company sizes, or other properties? These are often the best *standard filters* and *group comparisons* to include in your dashboards and reports.
- As you develop self-service tools, *ask your stakeholders to test and review them.* Using their feedback, provide additional written guidance within the tool on how to use it and interpret the results.
- Include written documentation in the tool and in separate, relevant locations where your stakeholders can discover it. For example, if you created a set of interactive dashboards for the marketing team, add a page to the department's intranet site with links to the resources and descriptions of how to use them.

- Where appropriate, include external references for stakeholders to learn about relevant topics in data-informed decision-making. For example, there are endless public resources on interpreting charts, descriptive statistics, metrics, statistical test results, and sample sizes, and on writing SQL queries.

Figure 12.8 shows the process of building and improving upon tools (e.g., dashboards) to make them easy for stakeholders to use independently for their day-to-day needs.

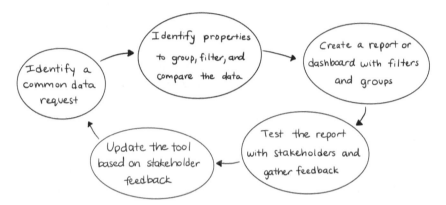

Figure 12.8   Creating self-service tools involves routinely evaluating requests, creating or updating resources, and circulating the updates to your stakeholders.

When successful, a self-service tool is often *highly adopted* by an organization. This means that your intended audience routinely accesses it, gets the data they need, and develops a better understanding of the information being measured. You'll still hear from your stakeholders, and you *should* allot the time and resources to support their questions and implement feedback so these tools are increasingly valuable over time.

12.3.3 Exercises

In this section, you will create a self-service dashboard for stakeholders at an e-commerce company with a social media presence. You will need the following to complete the exercises:

- A data visualization or interactive notebook tool. You can use any of the options we've covered in this chapter. Tableau Public, Hex, Deepnote, Streamlit, and several others have a free tier with the ability to deploy projects to a public cloud offering.
- The `website_engagement.csv` dataset that we analyzed in chapter 7. As a reminder, here are the column definitions for the dataset:
  - `date`—The calendar date for each metric
  - `website_engagement`—The percentage of users active each week
  - `session_duration`—The average duration of a website visit in minutes

- `bounce_rate`—The percentage of visitors who navigate away from the site after viewing only one page
- `email_subscribers`—The cumulative total of email subscribers; there is an incremental version of the column, `new_email_subscribers`
- `social_media_followers`—The cumulative total of social media followers
- `avg_page_views_per_visit`—The average pages viewed per user session
- `total_items_purchased`—The total items purchased by users in the week
- `total_sales`—The total dollar value of all sales in the week

Upload the dataset to your analysis tool and start working on your dashboard by performing the following tasks:

1 Create two to four visualizations to represent the data. Consider using various options, such as single value charts, bar graphs, and line graphs for time series data.
2 Add interactive elements that can be used as filters or grouping variables for the charts. Carefully choose the filtering variables you believe your stakeholders will find the most valuable in their work.
3 Arrange the filters and visualizations on the dashboard to ensure a clear and logical flow for its intended users. Clearly label all elements and sections.
4 Add instructions and descriptions to sections of the dashboard that can guide stakeholders who are new to using your tool.
5 Publish the dashboard to the public cloud available via the tool you choose, and share it with one or more peers for feedback. This is a piece you can add to your portfolio!

12.4   Artificial intelligence

I started writing this book around the time that ChatGPT 3.5 was publicly released. Since then, I've been watching AI become a topic across industries, transforming how we think about generating information and performing a range of tasks. I also found myself leading efforts within my company to identify opportunities to generate value with AI in daily operations and for our customers.

Artificial intelligence (AI) as a concept is not new. The term has been used for decades to refer to the ways that computers can learn and make decisions. Any machine learning, natural language processing, deep learning, or other algorithm that can be used to make decisions based on past data (e.g., figure 12.9) may be considered artificial intelligence.

AI promises to enhance work speed and efficiency and to expand organizations' capacity to make strategic decisions. But does it succeed? We covered some of the limitations of machine learning and statistical modeling in chapters 8 and 9—many apply to artificial intelligence, including more complex generative AI systems such as GPT 3.5. However, understanding and mitigating these limitations poses a unique challenge for analysts, especially since these tools have largely permeated the public

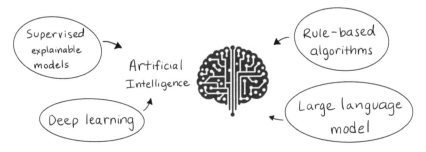

Figure 12.9   Artificial intelligence can incorporate many techniques, and the term is often applied to computer systems that learn from new data and are used in decision-making.

consciousness. AI text generation is being integrated into software products *everywhere*, and we're only beginning to scratch the surface of what it's capable of. Given its important role, we'll conclude this book by discussing how generative AI affects the role of an analyst in helping their organization use AI.

12.4.1 *Generative AI*

Since the public launch of ChatGPT, AI has often become synonymous with *generative AI*. *Generative artificial intelligence* is a subset of AI in which a model *generates content* (data in the form of text, code, images, audio, video, etc.). A model's output is typically based on a user-provided *prompt.*

Many of the models powering generative AI are considered *foundation models*, pretrained on *massive* datasets that enable users to produce general-purpose content for a vast range of use cases. For example, the *large language models* (LLMs) that power GPT 3.5 and GPT 4.0 are designed to generate human-like text output without needing to train the model on a domain-specific problem. Figure 12.10 shows a common example of the output you may receive with a prompt related to data analytics.

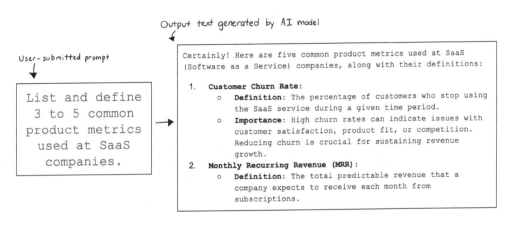

Figure 12.10   Generative AI creates new content based on user-submitted prompts.

Given its general applicability, generative AI is *everywhere*. You can easily find conferences across industries where AI is the primary topic, and there's a high likelihood that your colleagues keep ChatGPT open in a browser tab to use in their work. It's a source of concern and potential risk for many professions, especially in writing and communications. It's also being integrated into software of all kinds as an *assistant* to the company's users.

USING AI IN ANALYSES

As in many professions, generative AI can potentially transform an analyst's day-to-day role. Many common vendors in analytics (e.g., data visualization and interactive reporting tools) are incorporating AI assistants into their interfaces to *assist* in your workflows. Aside from these integrated solutions, tools such as ChatGPT can help in many tasks you've learned to master throughout this book. At present, however, generative AI is far from being able to replace the unique value that analysts provide to organizations.

For example, the best-performing LLMs can easily be used for the following:

- *Writing an initial draft*—You can reduce the time and effort it takes to write an initial content draft. This is sometimes called the *blank page problem*, where an initial cognitive effort is required to create a structured document. Instead of starting from scratch, you can prompt a model to generate, draft, or template sections of a report deliverable.

- *Generating text content*—When generating common forms of content (e.g., cover letters, abstracts, document summaries), LLMs like GPT 4.0 tend to create "B-minus content." These are easier to iterate on, as mentioned in the previous point. In cases where B-minus quality is enough, you may only require minimal edits before the generated content meets your needs. For example, I regularly use ChatGPT to write draft announcements when emailing information to the entire department.

- *Generating code templates*—LLMs specifically trained to write code can drastically reduce the time it takes to develop a prototype statistical analysis, A/B test, or machine learning model. Documentation and examples for most of the libraries we used in this book (e.g., `scikit-learn`, `statsmodels`) are included in many models' training sets, meaning that you can prompt the model to generate code from these libraries for analytics use (we'll walk through an example of this in the next section).

Several well-documented weaknesses can also pose a challenge when incorporating LLMs into your work:

- *LLMs only know what they are trained on*—By definition, models are trained on datasets of *previous information*. LLMs are no different, and their output is typically informed by the generic, publicly available information in its training set. When you prompt the model based on novel situations (e.g., economic conditions not previously encountered), you will likely receive a boilerplate response lacking nuance and strategic value.

- *The context window is limited*—Each LLM has a limited *context window* and *output length,* which restricts the number of tokens (each approximately four characters of text) for both input and output. The gpt-4-turbo has a maximum context window of 128,000 tokens and a response maximum output length of 4,096 tokens.

- *LLMs aren't often updated*—Once released, LLMs aren't frequently updated to include new information. If you prompt ChatGPT 4.0 with questions about world events in the current year (e.g., 2024), you will receive a response informing you about how recently its training set was updated. This affects the model's ability to generate content based on recent information, including code. If you're relying on a Python package that's only compatible with later versions, you may have to troubleshoot differences between package versions when running the code.

- *Generative AIs hallucinate*—Generative AI models of all kinds have been known to hallucinate [2], producing content that's either nonsensical or blatantly inaccurate. These hallucinations are considered inevitable—these models are designed to predict the likely output based on a prompt, and that prediction can be wrong.

The foundation models underlying popular generative AI models represent a significant technological advancement and shouldn't be ignored in your day-to-day work. Despite their limitations, these tools offer the opportunity to increase our overall efficiency. Integrating AI and LLMs into an analyst's workflow can help reduce the effort involved in repetitive and mundane tasks, enabling us to focus on more high-value analyses.

Using generative AI in analyses

Brandon is a senior data analyst at a large utility company. He performs analyses for the customer support teams, including identifying common customer problems, tracking response times, and assessing customer satisfaction. After creating a set of self-service reports to track the department's KPIs, Brandon is looking for opportunities to better understand the customer problems the teams face.

Brandon learns from the customer support team leaders that the department wants to glean better insights from the call transcript, chat, and support ticket text data recorded in the data warehouse for every incoming customer request. The team leaders have seen some of the tools they use incorporate AI text summarization into their interfaces and reach out to Brandon to learn if they can use generative AI to summarize the large volume of text data stored by the company.

With approval from his company's security team, Brandon proceeds to build a generative AI summarization tool that will be shared with end users in an existing KPI report. Using the API for a popular generative AI model, he takes the support text data as input for the model and writes a prompt instructing the model on how to summarize the data.

> **(continued)**
> The resulting output includes a list of the most common problems, key takeaways for team leaders, and recommended focus areas. The summaries drastically reduce the time spent in manual data review, improving the speed and quality of efforts to solve customer problems.

In many cases, AI can help tap into data sources you otherwise wouldn't have the bandwidth to evaluate. The case study in the "Using generative AI in analyses" sidebar shows a use case I've seen in multiple organizations with large amounts of data and limited capacity to understand the processes they represent.

PROMPT ENGINEERING

Prompts are the input users provide to a model that serve as instructions for generating output content. These prompts can range from simple statements to complex directions, guiding the model to produce responses that align with user expectations. Understanding how to craft clear and precise instructions can increase the utility and mitigate some weaknesses of generative AI models.

Prompt engineering is the practice of designing instructions as input to generative AI models that produce the desired output content. This process involves *a lot* of experimentation to find the best phrasing, formatting, and instructions on what to *include* and *exclude* in the output. When successful, the crafted prompt produces more consistent content that enables generative AI to be incorporated reliably into tools and products for end users without spending additional resources training or fine-tuning the model. Prompt engineering is necessary to integrate AI into existing software, create new AI-powered software, and use AI to enhance your analyses.

While crafting a prompt is more of an art than a science, there are some general steps you can follow to generate better output based on the capabilities of the model:

1 *Review the capabilities and performance of the model(s) you will use.* How are scholars and practitioners describing the strengths and weaknesses of that model for your desired task or domain area (e.g., healthcare [3])?

2 *Enumerate the task you want the model to perform.* Include any necessary context on the role or perspective it should take (e.g., a marketing analyst), the profile of the intended audience (e.g., marketing leadership), and the desired format of the output (e.g., a report with clear and understandable descriptions of statistical test results).

3 *Create an initial prompt and review the output.* Identify the characteristics of the output, paying close attention to the length, formatting, technical language, and tailoring to the audience. Note the output components that meet your expectations and those that do not.

4 *Refine the prompt based on your analysis of the output.* Add, update, or remove instructions that didn't contribute to producing your desired output content. As you refine your prompt, test each new prompt *multiple times* to understand

the possible variation in output content. Add or update instructions to increase consistency.

Let's look at an example. If we upload the `website_engagement.csv` data to ChatGPT 4.0 and prompt the model to analyze the data, we can generate a response like the one in table 12.3.

Table 12.3   Initial prompt and LLM response using ChatGPT 4.0

Prompt	Response
Analyze the attached dataset.	The dataset customer_logins.csv contains the following columns: customer_id: An identifier for each customer (integer). region: The geographical region of the customer (string). month: The month of the login data, formatted as YYYY-MM-DD (string). login_days: The number of days in the month the customer logged in (integer). There are a total of 20,844 entries, with no missing values in any of the columns. Let me know what specific analysis or insights you would like to gain from this dataset!

The model produced a generic response to a generic prompt: it listed the name, an inferred description of each column, and a total row count. Let's update the prompt to include more specific instructions on the analysis we want to perform (table 12.4).

Table 12.4   Updated prompt and LLM response using ChatGPT 4.0

Prompt	Response
Provide the mean and median for login_days, and mean login_days values by region.	Here are the statistics for login_days: Mean Login Days (Overall): 15.73 days Median Login Days (Overall): 16.0 days Mean Login Days by Region: Asia: 21.37 days Europe: 14.49 days North America: 17.53 days South America: 9.51 days These metrics highlight how often customers log in per month, both overall and within different regions. If there's more you'd like to explore or another aspect of the data you're interested in, just let me know!

In almost every case, a prompt needs more specific instructions than you might expect. It takes time to iterate on your prompts to discover the appropriate level of specificity needed for a task. If your role includes the need for more sophisticated prompt generation than the tips we've covered, I recommend resources such as the "Awesome GPT Prompt Engineering Guide" on GitHub (https://github.com/ snwfdhmp/awesome-gpt-prompt-engineering).

Prompt engineering is also a useful exercise for breaking down the concepts and heuristics you're familiar with into their building blocks (e.g., specific summary statistics instead of "analysis"). This framing can also help you break down unfamiliar technical concepts and heuristics with your stakeholders.

12.4.2 *Future directions*

As of the end of 2024 (when this chapter was written), many questions remain unanswered about the role AI will play in our day-to-day activities across professions. Enormous resources are being poured into research, so we'll likely continue to see advancements in the coming years [4]. We'll likely continue to see increasing integration of AI in familiar software, high-profile industries (e.g., healthcare and disease diagnosis), and countless aspects of our day-to-day lives. If you're curious about the predictions of expert practitioners, I strongly recommend keeping up with publications both by the scientists involved in developing generative models at big tech companies (e.g., LLaMA at Facebook, Claude at Anthropic, ChatGPT at OpenAI) and by academic research teams with an independent perspective on current and future advancements.

To achieve the potential highlighted by experts in AI, I expect there will be a reckoning with the many concerns that have surfaced in the past few years. AI does have the potential to benefit humanity positively, but it also has the potential to do serious harm. Consider each of the following:

- As we discussed in chapter 8, models trained on datasets of humans and their decisions are likely to identify underlying patterns of bias in the data. This is true for LLMs, which several publications have highlighted are prone to providing biased output in critically important areas (e.g., healthcare [5]).
- Just as generative AI can create useful content with the right prompt, it can easily generate misinformation that can pass as truthful [6]. There are concerns about the risk of misinformation being used to sway voters, affect policy, and more.
- Reports suggest that many professions are at high risk of being augmented or replaced by AI [7], which may result in drastic staffing reductions that affect the overall employment rate. While technological advancements can benefit society, many people are often left struggling to find employment and reskill as their jobs rapidly transform.
- LLMs cost *a lot* of money to train and use. Research suggests that the initial training of models such as GPT 3.5 consumes *vast* energy resources (equivalent to driving hundreds of cars for a year), and just *prompting* a model can cost as much energy as charging a smartphone [8]. These increased energy requirements risk taxing already strained electrical grids in several large cities.

12.4.3 *Final thoughts*

As experts in data analysis and statistics, analysts have real opportunities to contribute to the advancement and future of all things related to data and AI. Not only can you apply and master the skills we've learned, but you can also move us forward into the future of what's possible when analysts have the tools they need to derive insights and steer organizations toward success.

I'll end our journey through the world of analytics and AI with a quote:

The only constant in life is change.

—Heraclitus

Keep learning, growing, embracing change, and driving progress in our work.

12.4.4 Exercises

If you haven't already done so, create an account with OpenAI (https://chatgpt.com), Anthropic (https://claude.ai), or Google DeepMind (https://deepmind.google/technologies/gemini) to access one of their chatbots. You will use the *free tier* of one or more of these tools to evaluate the capacity of generative AI to perform the tasks of an analyst:

1 Upload the `rats_weather.csv` dataset (created in chapter 9 by combining `rat_sightings.csv` and `weather.csv`) to the chatbot.
2 Write a prompt to the chatbot asking it to describe the dataset. Iterate on or engineer the prompt to see how it changes as you refine your instructions.
3 Prompt the chatbot to create a model that predicts the number of daily rat sightings based on one or more variables in the dataset. Ensure it clearly documents the steps taken to create the model and reports the appropriate model performance metrics.
4 Compare the chatbot model's performance to the one we fit to the data in chapter 9. How does it perform in comparison?
5 Prompt the chatbot to return the Python code used to generate the descriptive statistics and predictive model. How does it differ from the code we used in chapter 9?
6 Prompt the chatbot to recommend tools or strategies for a hypothetical city agency to enable them to address rat sightings. Ensure it only uses the input variables in the model to make recommendations.
7 Refine the prompt to exclude any output that doesn't contribute to you and your stakeholders' understanding of the data. Include or update the instructions to adjust the format, language used, or other characteristics that don't align with your expected output.
8 Evaluate the overall performance of the chatbot compared to the analyses we performed together in chapter 9. How effective was the tool at performing the job of an analyst? Where did it succeed and fall short?

Summary

- *Analytics* has evolved in the past few decades from a manual, time-consuming process to automated systems that use vast data sources. This evolution has enabled faster decision-making and deeper insights into complex problems.
- *Data visualization tools* enable you to transform raw data into graphs, charts, and summary tables, making it easier to identify patterns and trends. These tools are essential for simplifying complex information and communicating insights to stakeholders.
- *Notebooks* such as Jupyter and Google Colab provide a versatile environment for programming, visualizing, and documenting analysis workflows. *Interactive notebook solutions* build upon this familiar interface to enable collaboration, interac-

tivity (e.g., filters and parameters on reports), and the ability to store complex reports and insights for the organization.

- *Data-powered web applications* (data apps) allow you to create custom tools for your users to explore and manipulate data in a dynamic way. These tools (e.g., R Shiny, Streamlit) can combine data from multiple sources, present output from statistical and machine learning models, and otherwise share technical information to a lay audience with an intuitive interface.

- *Knowledge management* is the process of intentionally structuring, storing, and surfacing analytical insights within an organization. Effective knowledge management boosts the productivity of the analytics teams and the ability of stakeholders to discover information on their own.

- A *library of analyses* contains records of the reports, dashboards, and other analytical resources that you and your colleagues create. A library is designed to be an accessible, searchable resource through which your stakeholders can discover your work while also being easy for your analyst colleagues to maintain.

- *Self-service analytics* is the practice of setting up tools to enable non-technical stakeholders to explore and analyze data without the direct support of data professionals. These tools are often set up as *interactive reports and dashboards,* allowing users to filter, group, or explore a dataset to meet their needs. This approach helps foster a data-informed culture at the organization by making data more easily accessible and understandable.

- *Artificial intelligence* (AI) is a discipline that seeks to develop machine systems that can perform tasks, solve problems, and make decisions. This is often accomplished by using one or more machine learning, natural language processing, or deep learning models to detect and replicate underlying patterns in datasets containing previous decisions.

- *Generative AI* is a subset of artificial intelligence that creates new *content* (text, code, audio, video, etc.) based on patterns in existing data. Many generative AI models are trained on massive datasets, minimizing the need to train the model to produce reasonable-quality results.

- *Large language models* (LLMs) are a class of models trained on vast amounts of text to enable them to meet needs across multiple use cases. These models are designed to interpret and generate text content that might be written by a human.

- *Prompt engineering* is the practice of crafting input prompts for generative AI models that result in consistent, reliable output for the user. Prompt engineering is an iterative and experimental process that requires updating and testing prompts to optimize for the desired content.

- *The role of AI in analytics is still evolving.* Analysts will often play a role in helping their organizations use AI for internal efficiency, tapping into data sources they haven't previously analyzed, and consulting on how AI is used to improve customer experiences. There are still a lot of unknowns, but it's clear that analysts can be critical drivers of technological advancement for their teams and organizations.

references

Chapter 1

[1] P. Park, "10 A/B testing examples and case studies to inspire your next test," *Unbounce.* https://unbounce.com/a-b-testing/examples

[2] "Data Warehouse," *Gartner.* www.gartner.com/en/information-technology/ glossary/data-warehouse

[3] B. Kelechava, "The SQL Standard—ISO/IEC 9075:2023 (ANSI X3.135)," *The ANSI Blog*, Oct. 5, 2018. http://blog.ansi.org/2018/10/sql-standard-iso-iec -9075-2016-ansi-x3-135/

[4] R Core Team, "The R Project for Statistical Computing," *R-project.org*, 2022. www.r-project.org

[5] D. Johnson, "Spreadsheet workflows in R," *education.rstudio.com*, Aug. 17, 2020. https://education.rstudio.com/blog/2020/08/spreadsheets-using-r

[6] J. Lowndes and A. Horst, *R for Excel Users.* https://jules32.github.io/r-for -excel-users

[7] "Tidyverse." www.tidyverse.org

[8] "Stack Overflow Developer Survey 2022," *Stack Overflow*, 2022. https://survey .stackoverflow.co/2022/#technology-most-popular-technologies

Chapter 5

[1] Sharon Bertsch Mcgrayne, *The Theory that Would Not Die: How Bayes' Rule Cracked the Enigma Code, Hunted Down Russian Submarines, and Emerged Triumphant from Two Centuries of Controversy* (Yale University Press, 2012).

[2] Stephen J. Gould, *The Mismeasure of Man* (Norton, 1981).

[3] J.W. Grice, "Observation Oriented Modeling: Preparing Students for Research in the 21st century," *Comprehensive Psychology*, vol. 3 (Jan. 2014). https://doi.org/10.2466/05.08.IT.3.3

[4] G.Y. Kanyongo, G.P. Brook, L. Kyei-Blankson, and G. Gocmen, "Reliability and Statistical Power: How Measurement Fallibility Affects Power and Required

Sample Sizes for Several Parametric and Nonparametric Statistics," *Journal of Modern Applied Statistical Methods*, vol. 6, no. 1, pp. 81–90 (May 2007). https://doi.org/10.22237/jmasm/1177992480

[5]   D. Huff, *How to Lie with Statistics* (Penguin Books, 1981).

Chapter 7

[1]   T. Stobierski, "13 Financial Performance Measures Managers Should Monitor," *Harvard Business School Online*, May 5, 2020. https://online.hbs.edu/blog/post/financial-performance-measures

[2]   S. Cunningham, *Causal Inference: The Mixtape* (Yale University Press, 2021). www.jstor.org/stable/j.ctv1c29t27

[3]   J. Pearl, *Causality* (Cambridge University Press, 2009).

Chapter 8

[1]   B.E. Rollin, *Science and Ethics* (Cambridge University Press, 2006).

[2]   US Department of Health and Human Services, Office for Human Research Protections, "45 CFR 46," Feb. 16, 2016. www.hhs.gov/ohrp/regulations-and-policy/regulations/45-cfr-46/index.html

[3]   "General Data Protection Regulation (GDPR)," 2018. https://gdpr-info.eu

[4]   State of California Department of Justice, "California Consumer Privacy Act (CCPA)," State of California - Department of Justice - Office of the Attorney General, Mar. 13, 2024. https://oag.ca.gov/privacy/ccpa

[5]   Centers for Disease Control and Prevention, "Health insurance portability and accountability act of 1996 (HIPAA)." www.cdc.gov/phlp/php/resources/health-insurance-portability-and-accountability-act-of-1996-hipaa.html

[6]   US Department Of Education, "FERPA—Protecting Student Privacy." https://studentprivacy.ed.gov/ferpa

[7]   T. Klosowski, "The State of Consumer Data Privacy Laws in the US (And Why It Matters)," *Wirecutter: Reviews for the Real World*, Sep. 6, 2021. https://www.nytimes.com/wirecutter/blog/state-of-privacy-laws-in-us/

[8]   J. Angwin, J. Larson, S. Mattu, and L. Kirchner, "Machine Bias," *ProPublica*, May 23, 2016. www.propublica.org/article/machine-bias-risk-assessments-in-criminal-sentencing

[9]   New York City, Consumer and Worker Protection, "Automated Employment Decision Tools (AEDT)". www.nyc.gov/site/dca/about/automated-employment-decision-tools.page

[10] J. Kestenbaum, "NYC's New AI Bias Law Broadly Impacts Hiring and Requires Audits," *Bloomberg Law*, Jul. 5, 2023. https://news.bloomberglaw.com/us-law-week/nycs-new-ai-bias-law-broadly-impacts-hiring-and-requires-audits

[11] A. Narayanan and V. Shmatikov, "How To Break Anonymity of the Netflix Prize Dataset," *arXiv:cs/0610105*, Nov. 2007. https://arxiv.org/abs/cs/0610105

[12] L. Sweeney, "Simple Demographics Often Identify People Uniquely," *Carnegie Mellon, Data Privacy Working Paper,* Jan. 2000.

[13] M. Barbaro and T. Zeller, Jr., "A Face Is Exposed for AOL Searcher No. 4417749," *The New York Times,* Aug. 9, 2006. www.nytimes.com/2006/08/09/technology/09aol.html

Chapter 9

[1] C. Ismay and A. Kim, "Simple Linear Regression," chapter 5 in *Statistical Inference via Data Science: A ModernDive into R and the Tidyverse,* second edition (Chapman and Hall/CRC, 2024). https://moderndive.com/v2/regression.html

Chapter 10

[1] "`time`—Time access and conversions," *The Python Standard Library.* https://docs.python.org/3/library/time.html#time.sleep

[2] "Errors and Exceptions," *Python Documentation.* https://docs.python.org/3/tutorial/errors.html#handling-exceptions

[3] S. Chignard, "A Brief History of Open Data," *ParisTech Review,* Mar. 29, 2013. www.paristechreview.com/2013/03/29/brief-history-open-data

[4] "Transparency and Open Government," *Whitehouse Presidential Memoranda,* Jan. 21, 2009. https://obamawhitehouse.archives.gov/the-press-office/transparency-and-open-government

Chapter 11

[1] C. Wang, "What is Fivetran?" *Fivetran Blog.* www.fivetran.com/blog/what-is-fivetran

[2] "What is Airflow?" *Apache Airflow.* https://airflow.apache.org/docs/apache-airflow/stable/index.html

[3] MongoDB, "NoSQL Databases Explained," *MongoDB.* www.mongodb.com/nosql-explained

[4] "PySpark 2.4.5 documentation," *spark.apache.org,* Dec. 17, 2024. https://spark.apache.org/docs/latest/api/python/index.html

[5] T. Handy, "What, exactly, is dbt?," *dbt Labs Blog,* Oct. 16, 2017. www.getdbt.com/blog/what-exactly-is-dbt

[6] "About data tests property," *dbt Developer Hub.* https://docs.getdbt.com/reference/resource-properties/data-tests

[7] "Data cataloging," *dbt Developer Hub.* www.getdbt.com/analytics-engineering/transformation/data-catalog

[8] M. Kaminsky, "The Analytics Engineer," *Locally Optimistic,* Jan. 27, 2019. https://locallyoptimistic.com/post/analytics-engineer

[9] "Dimensional Modeling Techniques," *Kimball Group.* www.kimballgroup.com/data-warehouse-business-intelligence-resources/kimball-techniques/dimensional -modeling-techniques

Chapter 12

[1]   N. Ray, C. Sharma, M. Wardrop, and D. Frank, "The Knowledge Repo," *Airbnb Engineering & Data Science.* https://airbnb.io/projects/knowledge-repo

[2]   IBM, "What are AI hallucinations?," *IBM,* Sept. 1, 2023. www.ibm.com/topics/ai-hallucinations

[3]   A. Liu, H. Zhou, Y. Hua, O. Rohanian, L. Clifton, and D. Clifton, "Large Language Models in Healthcare: A Comprehensive Benchmark," *medRxiv,* Apr. 2024.

[4]   M. Heikkilä and W. Douglas Heaven, "What's next for AI in 2024," *MIT Technology Review,* Jan. 4, 2024. https://www.technologyreview.com/2024/01/04/1086046/whats-next-for-ai-in-2024/

[5]   L. Wang et al., "A Systematic Review of ChatGPT and Other Conversational Large Language Models in Healthcare," *medRxiv (Cold Spring Harbor Laboratory),* Apr. 2024. https://doi.org/10.1101/2024.04.26.24306390

[6]   A. Loth and M. Kappes, "Blessing or curse? A survey on the Impact of Generative AI on Fake News," *arXiv,* Apr. 3, 2024. https://arxiv.org/html/2404.03021v1

[7]   P. Gmyrek, J. Berg, and D. Bescond, "Generative AI and jobs: A global analysis of potential effects on job quantity and quality," *ILO,* Aug. 2023. https://doi.org/10.54394/fhem8239

[8]   K. Saenko, "A Computer Scientist Breaks Down Generative AI's Hefty Carbon Footprint," *Scientific American,* May 25, 2023. https://www.scientificamerican.com/article/a-computer-scientist-breaks-down-generative-ais-hefty-carbon-footprint/

index